SCOTTISH CASES
ON CONTRACT

SCOTTISH CASES
ON CONTRACT

BY

ENID A. MARSHALL

M.A., LL.B., Ph.D., Associate R.I.C.S., A.C.I. Arb., F.R.S.A.,
Solicitor

Reader in Business Law
at the University of Stirling

W. GREEN/Sweet & Maxwell

EDINBURGH

1993

First published 1978
Reprinted 1979
Reprinted 1983
Reprinted 1989
2nd edition 1993

ISBN 0 414 01052 3

PRINTED IN GREAT BRITAIN
BY
M & A Thomson Litho Ltd.

PREFACE

THE first edition of this collection of Scottish cases developed out of a typescript collection bearing the same title and used in conjunction with a course of lectures on the law of contract at the University of Stirling.

The book has proved to be of value to the increasing numbers of non-law students who, at Scottish colleges and universities, are required to study, to varying degrees of depth, the Scots law of contract and who seldom have ready access to the reports themselves. Law students have also found the book useful owing to the pressure on library space and the shortage of duplicate sets of reports.

Aiming at a modest size and a modest price necessarily imposes some restraints. In particular, English cases are not included, although many are relevant in this field of study: it will be for the student, with the aid of textbooks, to look up such cases elsewhere – in the appropriate English reports or in one of the several English casebooks. For the same reason, the Notes appearing after the extracts from opinions are not intended to be a "commentary" in any true sense of that word: for the most part they merely provide cross-references to other cases in the book or treat briefly of comparable additional cases.

In addition to selected cases decided since 1978, this second edition has a new appendix consisting of relevant extracts from statutory provisions included in *The Parliament House Book*.

September 1993   ENID A. MARSHALL.

TABLE OF CONTENTS

vii

CHAPTER 3—FORMALITIES FOR CONSTITUTION AND PROOF

CHAPTER 5—INTERPRETATION AND SCOPE

CHAPTER 6—BREACH OF CONTRACT

CHAPTER 7—TERMINATION OF CONTRACT

TABLE OF CASES

(Page numbers in bold type indicate a main entry)

CHAPTER 1

NATURE OF CONTRACT

Unilateral voluntary obligation or promise

Petrie v. Earl of Airlie

(1834) 13 S. 68

In 1831 a meeting was held in Forfarshire to consider the Reform Bill then before Parliament. The Earl of Airlie presided at the meeting. There was a motion disapproving of the Bill, and an amendment approving of it, 24 votes being cast for the motion and 59 for the amendment. The Earl of Airlie was one of the minority.

Shortly afterwards a placard was posted up in several burghs in Forfarshire stating the names of the majority under the heading "Majority in favour of the King, his Government, and his People," and the names of the minority under the heading "Minority against the King, his Government, and his People, and the Bill."

The Earl of Airlie issued a proclamation which stated: "One hundred guineas reward. A most false and scandalous placard, headed 'Reform,' having appeared in several of the burghs of Forfarshire without any printer's name or date being attached to it, ... a reward of one hundred guineas is hereby offered to any person who will give such information as may lead to the detection of the author and printer. The reward will be paid on conviction."

Alexander Petrie, weaver in Arbroath, gave information that his brother, David Petrie, and James Lindsay, printers in Arbroath, were the authors and printers of the placard.

The Earl of Airlie communicated this information to the Lord Advocate and Solicitor-General, who declined to prosecute, since they considered that no indictable offence had been committed. The Lord Advocate advised the Earl that he had himself power to prosecute criminally or to sue for damages in the civil court. The Earl refrained from prosecution.

Alexander Petrie claimed the reward, and the Earl declined to pay on the ground that there had been no conviction.

Held that Petrie was entitled to the reward.

1

LORD COREHOUSE (Ordinary) (at p. 70): "The respondent having obtained from the advocator all that he stipulated for, he is not entitled to evade payment of the price which he offered for it, because it does not answer the purpose which he had in view. If he meant to construe the offer in the sense which he now does, he should have put the advocator on his guard, and not have allowed the disclosure to be made, which he knew, or ought to have known, would never lead to a conviction. He had no right to extract information which would enable him to bring an action of damages for defamation, or at least to expose the parties implicated, and injure their character in public estimation, while he knew, or ought to have known, that the reward which he held out to the informer, and on the faith of which the information was communicated, never could become exigible."

NOTES

1. The Earl's appeal to the Inner House was unsuccessful.

2. The case illustrates the point that a unilateral voluntary obligation, such as a promise to pay a reward, is enforceable.

3. A promise is, however, unenforceable unless communicated to the promisee. *Burr* v. *Commissioners of Bo' ness* (1896) 24 R. 148. At a meeting the Commissioners of a burgh resolved to increase the salary of B., the burgh sanitary inspector, from £10 to £20 per annum.

B. heard of this resolution, but no official intimation of it was made to him.

At a meeting about a month later the Commissioners rescinded the resolution.

Held that B. was not entitled to the increased salary because the resolution had not been intimated to him.

Lord Justice-Clerk (J. H. A. Macdonald) (at p. 151): "The resolution came to his knowledge, but no official intimation of increase of salary was ever given to him. At the next meeting of the Commissioners the resolution was rescinded. I think this was competent, unless anything had been done giving the pursuer a *jus quaesitum* to enforce the increase of his salary. In my opinion nothing was done giving him such a right."

Proof of unilateral voluntary obligation or promise

Smith v. Oliver

1911 S.C. 103

Trustees for a church brought an action against the executor of Mrs O. for payment of the cost of additions to the structure and decoration of their church. They averred that Mrs O. had urged them to make these additions and had undertaken to provide by her will for the cost of them but had not done so.

Held that Mrs O.'s promise could be proved only by her writ, and that there was here merely an oral promise to pay which could not be converted into a bilateral contract by *rei interventus*.

LORD PRESIDENT (DUNEDIN) (at p. 110): "There is in truth no contract at all averred here, but merely a promise to pay. And if that is so, I suppose that it is very well settled law that a gratuitous promise to pay can be proved only by writ.... Now it is quite well settled by a series of cases that a party cannot turn what is, in its nature, a mere promise into a contract, so as to be allowed to prove it by parole, by simply averring that on the faith of the promise certain things were done by him; that is to say, he cannot turn a promise into a contract by *rei interventus*, so to speak. That was conclusively settled by an old case which I think has been held to be law ever since. It is *Millar* v. *Tremamondo* (Mor. 12,395) in 1771....

"That case was followed by the case of *Edmondston* ((1861) 23 D. 995), which, so far as a promise is concerned, is very like the present case. There the promise was to leave money by will, and the consideration upon the other side was that the other person, who was a medical man, should settle in practice in the district. The decision there was to the same effect as in *Millar's* case. These cases settle the law, and settle it quite conclusively. I have no doubt, of course, that it is perfectly possible for one to bind himself in his lifetime to leave something in his will.... But ... I do not think it has ever been suggested that proof of his doing so could be by anything except writ."

NOTE

For the case of *Edmondston*, see p. 68, below.

Gratuitous contract: consideration not required

Morton's Trustees v. The Aged Christian Friend Society of Scotland

(1899) 2 F. 82

M. wrote to a provisional committee which was promoting a charitable society, offering on certain conditions a subscription to the society of £1,000, payable in 10 annual instalments of £100 each. M.'s offer was accepted by the committee, the society was formed, and the conditions of M.'s offer were complied with. M. duly paid the first eight instalments to the society, but died before the two remaining instalments had become payable.

Held that the society was entitled to enforce payment of these two instalments against M.'s representatives.

LORD KINNEAR (at p. 85):"It is a familiar doctrine in the law of Scotland, differing in that respect from the law of England, that an obligation is binding although it may not proceed on a valuable consideration, or may not be expressed in a solemn form, such as a deed under seal. What is necessary is that the promisor should intend to bind himself by an enforceable obligation and should express that intention in clear words. . . .

"Now, these . . . letters appear to me to contain a clear offer which invites acceptance. . . . That offer was accepted. . . .

"The result . . . is, that we have in the letters a definite offer determined by acceptance. I do not know that anything more is required in order to make a contract according to the law of Scotland. The question therefore whether the two remaining sums of £100 each would be enforceable against Mr Morton himself, if he were still alive and declining to pay, is, I think, not a question of difficulty. There is a clear obligation undertaken by him. The only question therefore is whether . . . it may now be enforced against his representatives. It is a general rule that a personal obligation transmits against the personal representatives of the obligor, and although it is perfectly easy to prevent the liability from transmitting by stipulating that the performance shall depend on the survivance of the promisor, there is nothing in Mr Morton's letters to suggest any such limitation of his offer. It is not made on condition of his survivance, but is absolute and binding in all events."

NOTES

1. On the point as to whether M.'s undertaking to the provisional committee could be enforced by the society Lord Kinnear stated (at p. 87): "This was a clear instance of our doctrine of *jus quaesitum tertio*....That is an express stipulation in favour of a third party—that is, the Society—definitely described, and it is in effect an agreement between the two parties to the contract that a stipulation shall be performed with that third party, and the rule in such a case is, that though the person in whose favour the stipulation is made is not a party to the agreement, or at the time assenting to it, he may afterwards adopt the agreement in his favour and sue upon it."

2. In *Wick Harbour Trs.* v. *The Admiralty*, 1921 2 S.L.T. 109 (O.H.), an action for "*ex gratia* payments" which the Admiralty had undertaken to make, Lord Sands (Ordinary) said (at p. 111): "I was referred to the case of *Morton's Trs.* v. *The Aged Christian Friend Society of Scotland* ... as the leading authority as to the law in relation to an obligation to make a payment which is purely voluntary. That is not perhaps an altogether satisfactory authority upon the pure question, as there was an element of *rei interventus*. But I take it to be in accordance with the general principle of our law that if a person voluntarily offers to make a payment which he is under no legal obligation to make, and the offer is accepted, that forms a binding contract."

Intention to create legal relationship

Woods v. The Co-operative Insurance Society Ltd.

1924 S.C. 692

An advertisement in the weekly newspaper *John Bull* invited readers to sign two coupons in order to obtain the benefit of a "free insurance scheme." One of the express conditions of the scheme was that Odham's Press Ltd., the proprietors of *John Bull*, were not to be involved by the scheme in any contractual liability.

W., a reader of *John Bull*, acted in accordance with the advertisement.

A fire occurred in which W.'s household furniture was burned, the loss being assessed at £137 10s.

The Co-operative Insurance Society Ltd., with whom W. had insured his furniture for £150, refused to pay more than one-third of that loss, on the ground that W. was also insured against the same loss under the *John Bull* scheme to the extent of £300.

Held that no contract of insurance had been created by the *John Bull* scheme.

LORD PRESIDENT (CLYDE) (at p. 697): "In this case the pursuer holds a policy with the defenders' Company insuring certain household furniture against the risk of injury or destruction by fire, the insured amount being £150. A fire occurred, and a claim was made; and in answer to that claim the Company founded upon condition 9 of the policy which restricts their liability 'if, at the time of the loss or damage, there should be any other insurance effected by the insured, or by any other person, covering the property.' The contention of the Company (now maintained as a defence to the present action) was that the the pursuer's furniture was covered at the date of the fire by an insurance effected through a newspaper called *John Bull*. The pursuer admits having signed and delivered two coupons forming part of an advertisement in *John Bull* with reference to a 'free insurance scheme,' the conditions of which were set forth in a printed document circulated along with that newspaper. But he denies that any insurance was effected thereby, and he adds that a claim he sent in to the newspaper was not entertained. . . .

". . . It is . . . necessary to examine the defending Company's allegations concerning the insurance said to have been effected with *John Bull*; for, if there is any real difference between the parties, it is as to whether an insurance was effected or not. The substance of those allegations depends on the terms of the advertisement of the 'free insurance scheme,' the coupons, and the printed conditions mentioned above. . . . The advertisement invited the readers of *John Bull* to fill up two coupons in order to obtain the benefits of the scheme. The first coupon, which was to be posted (and which the pursuer did sign and post) to *John Bull*, was to the following effect:—'I have sent an order form to my newsagent for the regular weekly delivery of *John Bull*. Please register me as a regular reader.' The second coupon, which was to be handed to the reader's newsagent (and which the pursuer signed and handed to his newsagent), was a form of order for the delivery of the newspaper until further notice. Along with the newspaper there was also circulated a printed document containing the conditions of the scheme to which the advertisement and coupons referred. It is headed 'Free Insurance Gift,' and is described as a Certificate of Registration of the first of the two kinds of coupons to which I have already referred. According to this document the newspaper announces that it 'will give' certain sums in certain specified events (such as accident, fire, and sickness), and also a number of other forms of insurance benefit. Among the conditions appended there is the following in paragraph (*m*):—'In order to comply with requirements of the law the proprietors of *John Bull* have to announce that while this free insurance scheme does not involve any contractual liability it has the financial backing and support of Odham's Press, Limited, (the Proprietors of *John Bull*) whose issued share capital is over £1,250,000.' How can it be said that an insurance has been effected by participation in a 'free insurance scheme' which involves no contractual liability on the part of anybody, and therefore provides no indemnity? Condition (*m*) makes it perfectly clear that there is no contract, no obligation, no indemnity—in short, no insurance whatever. When condition 9 of the defending Company's policy speaks of an insurance having been effected, it is unmistakeably obvious that a contract of indemnity is meant."

NOTE

Cf. The Clyde Marine Insurance Co. Ltd. v. *Renwick & Co.*, 1924 S.C. 113, which related to the legal effect of "slips" for marine insurance. In the liquidation of the marine insurance company the liquidator was held not to have been entitled to issue policies to slip holders, although the company itself would have been under an honourable obligation to do so.

Lord President (Clyde) (at p. 123): "[The] slip does not constitute a marine policy within the meaning of the Marine Insurance Act 1906. While it undoubtedly reflects a concluded verbal contract of marine insurance made between the Company as insurers and the broker as representing the assured, it is inadmissible in evidence under section 22 of that Act unless and until embodied in a written marine policy. It necessarily follows from this that the slip cannot even be regarded as evidence of a contract to sign and issue such a policy. ... The holders of the slip ... are destitute of any claim enforceable at law against the Company.

"Notwithstanding all this, in the practical conduct of marine insurance business the slip plays a part of the greatest importance. It is by means of the slip that the actual business of the broker and underwriter is done; and, although there is no obligation to pay the premium except against issue of the policy, or to issue the policy except against payment of the premium ..., yet the honourable obligations *hinc inde* between underwriter and broker to carry through the piece of insurance business to which the slip refers are of the highest kind. ...

"... The liquidator had no power to sign or issue policies ... unless in pursuance of his power to carry on the business of the company. The liquidator, however, has not exercised this power to any extent; and it was therefore *ultra vires* of him to convert the slips into enforceable obligations in the shape of marine policies."

Patrimonial interest

Forbes v. Eden

(1867) 5 M. (H.L.) 36; (1865) 4 M. 143

F., minister of the Scotch Episcopal congregation at Burntisland, brought an action against the members of a General Synod of the Episcopal Church in Scotland for reduction of certain canons enacted by the Synod. F. alleged that the canons were in violation of the previous canons in force when he was ordained and were injurious to him as making him liable to be deprived of office if he failed to conform to them.

Held that the action was irrelevant since F. had not made a relevant averment of damage arising out of the violation of a civil right.

LORD CHANCELLOR (CHELMSFORD) (at p. 47): "The case of *McMillan* v. *The General Assembly of the Free Church of Scotland* ((1861) 23 D. 1314) was frequently relied upon in the course of the argument. ... The appellant urged it as a strong authority in his favour, because it was there held that sentences of suspension and deposition pronounced by the General Assembly of the Free Church of Scotland, a voluntary religious association, against one of its ministers, were properly the subject of an action of reduction and damages. ... But it must be observed, that in that case, there were actual sentences of suspension and deposition, from which the loss of the pursuer's emoluments, as minister of the Free Church of Cardross, followed as a consequence.

"The appellant, in this case, has not been disturbed, either in his charge of the congregation at Burntisland, or in his legal position as a minister of the Scotch Episcopal Church. If he had been, though in this latter respect only, I should have considered, with the Lord Justice–Clerk, that 'the possession of a particular status, meaning by that term the capacity to perform certain functions, or to hold certain offices, is a thing which the law will recognise as a patrimonial interest, and that no one can be deprived of its possession by the unauthorised or illegal act of another without having a legal remedy.'

"The appellant not having sustained any injury which can be the subject of cognisance in a civil Court, his appeal might be shortly disposed of upon that ground."

NOTES

1. Contrast *Skerret* v. *Oliver* (1896) 23 R. 468, in which Lord Kincairney (Ordinary) held that a sentence of suspension pronounced against a minister of a congregation of the United Presbyterian Church was of a patrimonial character or of a character equivalent to patrimonial.

Lord Kincairney (at p. 477):"The pursuer maintains ... that even if no legal or enforceable right to a stipend is attached to his office, still his professional status is, apart from its pecuniary advantages, a patrimonial interest of tangible and considerable value, and that loss of it is a patrimonial loss capable of being roughly measured in money. ... I confess that I cannot doubt that the pursuer's view on this matter is correct."

2. In *Murdison* v. *Scottish Football Union* (1896) 23 R. 449 a resolution of a football union suspending a member of a club belonging to the union from playing was held not to involve patrimonial interest.

Lord Kinnear (at p. 466): "If he complains not of the defamation but of the fact that people would not play football with him, that does not appear to me to be a legal wrong or an invasion of any legal right. Nobody has a right which he can enforce at law to compel other people to play a game of football with him. ... Agreements to associate for purposes of recreation, or an agreement to associate for scientific or philanthropical or social or religious purposes, are not agreements which Courts of law can enforce. They are entirely personal. Therefore, in order to establish a civil wrong from the refusal to carry out such an agreement ... it is necessary to see that the pursuer has suffered some practical injury either in his reputation or in his property. No averment of that kind is made."

"Agree" does not necessarily indicate a contract

Macfarlane v. Johnston

(1864) 2 M. 1210

A letter from the C. Co. stated: "We agree to pay you, during February 1859, £100, during March 1859, £100, during April 1859, £100."

Held that this was a promissory note.

LORD JUSTICE-CLERK (INGLIS) (at p. 1213): "The question, therefore, is whether this letter was a promissory note or an agreement? . . .

"It appears to me that the use of the verb 'agree' is of very little consequence; for, when a person agrees to pay a particular sum on a particular day, he grants a promissory note, for the distinction between a promise and an obligation of a different kind does not consist in the use of the word promise. There is a philosophical and practical distinction between a promise and an obligation, which is nowhere better stated than by Lord Stair (i. 10, 3). A promise is a pure and simple expression of the will of the party undertaking the obligation, requiring no acceptance, and still less requiring mutual consent. A promise is distinguished by Lord Stair from a pollicitation or offer which requires acceptance to make it binding, and still more from a paction which, in order to be binding, requires the mutual consent of two parties. It appears to me that when a party, in terms of this letter, agrees to pay £100 during March 1859, and £100 during April 1859, and so on, he is making a promise, and that by the bare act of his will thus expressed he undertakes an obligation to pay, which requires no acceptance, and which is, therefore, not a pollicitation or offer, still less an agreement or paction."

LORD NEAVES (at p. 1214): "The word 'agree' is ambiguous, and, strictly, ought to be confined to pactions; and an agreement, properly speaking, means a paction, a *consensus*, of a plurality of persons *in idem placitum*. But it is also used improperly as a word of unilateral signification; and if it be so used, I see no difference between the expressions 'I agree to pay,' and 'I promise to pay.' I think, therefore, that the words 'I agree to pay' are expressive of a promise."

Presumption against promises in business transactions

Malcolm v. Campbell

(1891) 19 R. 278

A document subscribed by C. before witnesses and delivered by C. to M. stated: "I have agreed to sell my house at corner of High Street, Leven, for one hundred and fifty pounds to M."

Held that the document did not import a promise by C. to sell the house to M. (which would have been effectual without writing on the part of

M.), but imported merely one side of a bilateral contract of sale of heritage, which could have no effect until completed in writing by the other party.

LORD ORDINARY (KINCAIRNEY) (at p. 279): "On the whole, I think that while it may be true that a unilateral promise to convey land is binding on the granter if it imply no obligation on the grantee, yet the cases to which that rule is applicable must rarely occur, and that in this case what is averred by the pursuer is not a promise but a mutual contract, which must bind both parties or neither, and that it is clear that it does not bind the pursuer."

LORD MCLAREN (at p. 281):"Apparently the suggestion is that such a unilateral obligation is an obligation by which one party becomes bound as seller without receiving in return any obligation which he can enforce, the purchaser being entitled to agree to the sale or not as he pleases. . . . It is certainly not a very probable arrangement, or, I think, a very businesslike proceeding . . . , and the presumption must certainly be against such an interpretation of a business matter about which parties are transacting. The view that parties have contemplated a mutual contract of sale is very much more consistent with what is usual in the business of life, and is, in the absence of adverse circumstances, I think, a probable interpretation of the matter, especially when the word agreement is used, as it is in this case. I have no hesitation in coming to the conclusion that the thing which the parties had agreed upon was a sale. Now, if that be so, there not being the conjoint consent of seller and purchaser which the law holds to be necessary to a contract of sale, we have not here a complete expression of that contract in the form which the law requires."

Honourable understanding as distinct from legal obligation

Ritchie v. Cowan & Kinghorn

(1901) 3 F. 1071

R., finding himself unable to pay his creditors C. & W., entered into an arrangement with them to pay 10s. in the £ on his debt to them. The receipt given by C. & W. to R. stated that the amount paid was "in full of" their claim against R., but added "it being, however, understood that the said R. will pay the balance of 10s. per £ whenever he is able to do so."

Held that these additional words constituted merely an honourable understanding, as distinct from a legal obligation enforceable against R.

LORD TRAYNER (at p. 1075): "Looking at the terms of the receipt itself, it does not in my opinion, import an enforceable obligation. It is merely the expression of an honourable intention on the part of the pursuer that when he is in a position to pay the remainder of his debt he will pay it. The defenders may appeal to the pursuer's sense of honour when he is able to pay, but they cannot get any decree to enforce such an appeal from a Court of law."

Contract requires more than one party

Church of Scotland Endowment Committee v. Provident Association of London Ltd.

1914 S.C. 165

S. had entered into a purported contract of ground–annual with himself. *Held* that the contract was ineffectual.

LORD DUNDAS (at p. 171): "It is quite clear that the attempt made by Mr Simpson to create these ground-annuals by means of a so-called contract with himself was ineffectual. A man cannot by any deed constitute a debt by himself to himself, with or without security. The so-called contract . . . is plainly inept and void as an operative instrument."

Sponsiones ludicrae: gaming debt admitted: supervening contract

Robertson v. Balfour

1938 S.C. 207

R. placed two bets with B., a bookmaker, upon two horses "Swift and True" and "Scotch Horse." Both horses won, and R. received from B. £10 to account of his winnings. R. agreed not to insist upon payment of the balance of £33 10s. for a fortnight and also not to disclose the fact that B. had not made full payment timeously.

Held that (1) although the debt was admitted, it was, because of its nature as a gaming debt, unenforceable at law; and (2) the supervening contract, being subsidiary to the original wagering contract, was unenforceable, and that the doctrine that a subsequent contract, made for a new consideration separate from the wagers themselves, validated an action for payment of winnings under the wagers was not part of the law of Scotland.

LORD JUSTICE-CLERK (AITCHISON) (at p. 211): "It is not denied by the pursuer that the transaction between the parties was a wager, and a wager is simply a gaming or gambling contract. Since the end of the seventeenth century it has been, more or less, the accepted doctrine of the law of Scotland, and it is now firmly established, that a gaming contract is null and of no legal effect, and is unenforceable by either party to the contract by any form of action at law. A gaming contract, whether or not it amounts to *pactum illicitum*, is *sponsio ludicra*.

"No better statement of the law can be found than that of Lord Kames in his *Principles of Equity* at page 22, where that celebrated judge said this:—'Neither doth this Court profess to take under its protection every covenant and agreement. Many engagements of various sorts, the fruits of idleness, are too trifling, or too ludicrous, to merit the countenance of law; a court, whether of common law or of equity, cannot preserve its dignity if it descend to such matters. Wagers of all sorts, whether upon horses, cocks, or accidental events, are of this sort. People may amuse themselves, and men of easy fortunes may pass their whole time in that manner, because there is no law against it; but pastime, contrary to its nature, ought not to be converted into a serious matter, by bringing the fruits of it into a court of justice.'...

"While not disputing the general proposition, two points of specialty were argued by the pursuer in the present case:—(*One*) that here the debt was admitted, and therefore that the Court was not being asked to do anything to determine who was the winner of the wager; and (*Second*) that there had been relevantly averred, and therefore there was matter proper for proof, a supervening contract to pay the gambling debt, the consideration being that time should be given by the pursuer to the defender, and that the defender's default should not be disclosed. Both of these pleas, in my opinion, are unsound. As regards the first, it is enough to say that no admission of the debt can alter its true character as a gaming debt. As regards the second, the supervening contract is subsidiary to, and flows from, the original gaming contract, and the original gaming contract being a null contract, and unenforceable in law, a contract to give time to implement its terms partakes, in my judgment, of the same nullity. If subsidiary contracts of this kind have been recognised by the law of England, which, in earlier times, may perhaps have been more favourable to wagering than our own law, they are unknown to the law of Scotland, and it would be wholly contrary to the practice of our Courts in relation to gaming contracts to give any countenance to them now."

LORD MACKAY (at p. 218): "It is said that the Inner House [in *Knight & Co.* v. *Stott* (1892) 19 R. 959] unanimously laid down, first, that horse racing is not illegal; second, that betting is not illegal in the sense of being prohibited or punishable. These are, indeed, the judges' words, and I agree in both. But that does not go very far, because the whole doctrine of *sponsio ludicra*, as borrowed from the civil law by our law, does not proceed upon the act being either 'prohibited' or 'punishable.' The question, as it seems to me, has always been one of disfavour in the whole outlook, which prevents the Court from lending its authority and its modes of execution to the matter. The action was, of course, sustained in *Knight & Co.*, even though it seems to have been *remotely* concerned with bets made on certain horse races at Carlisle. It therefore may be taken as an instance of a small class of apparent exceptions."

LORD WARK (at p. 221): "In my opinion, the law of Scotland has been settled for at least 150 years to the effect that wagering contracts, being *sponsiones ludicrae*, do not afford a ground of action and cannot be enforced in our Courts. This is, in my view, the effect of the decision of this Court, affirmed in the House of Lords, in *Bruce* v. *Ross* [(1788) Mor. 9523 and 3 Pat. 107]. That was an action to enforce a wagering contract with reference to a Parliamentary election. ... I am satisfied ... that the House ... held that the law of Scotland, differing from the law of England and following the principles of the civil law, regarded wagering contracts as *sponsiones ludicrae* and unenforceable at law."

Lord Wark then examined *Wordsworth* v. *Pettigrew* (1799) Mor. 9524, of which he said (at p. 222): "Courts of Justice, it was observed, were instituted to enforce the rights of parties arising from serious transactions, and can pay no regard to *sponsiones ludicrae* as to money gained or lost, in which *melior est conditio possidentis*.

"In my opinion, this principle is wide enough to exclude the present action—which is one to enforce a gaming contract—and it is of no moment that the amount of the debt or the result of the event upon which it was made do not require to be investigated by the Court. Since the case of *Bruce* v. *Ross* no instance is to be found in our books of any case in which a direct action between the parties to a wager has been entertained; although in certain cases the Court has not held itself prevented by the rule of *sponsio ludicra* from adjudicating upon collateral questions of contract or property connected with a wager."

Sponsiones ludicrae: *football pool*

Kelly v. Murphy

1940 S.C. 96

K. brought an action against M., the promoter of a football pool, for £2,497, the balance of the prize money to which K. alleged that he was entitled as winner of the pool.

Held that the action, being simply an action for recovery of a gambling debt, could not be entertained by a court in Scotland.

LORD JUSTICE-CLERK (AITCHISON) (at p. 100): "It was not disputed that an action for recovery of a gaming debt is not maintainable against the party in the gaming contract with whom the bet or wager is made, and it is now settled that it makes no difference to the application of the rule that there does not exist any dispute as to who is the winner of the bet or wager, or as to the amount of his winnings. An admitted gaming debt is irrecoverable by an action at law—*Robertson* v. *Balfour* (1938 S.C. 207). The rule of the common law is that the Court will not lend its aid to enforce a transaction of this nature, not because the transaction is illegal or involves a contravention of the criminal law, for betting *per se* is not illegal, but because it is not every covenant and agreement that the Court will take under its protection, as where the engagement is not of a kind to merit the countenance of law. ... But it was maintained that the rule is subject to an exception where the action is not one brought upon the wagering contract and directed against the loser, but is laid upon a collateral or subsidiary contract of mandate or agency, express or implied, whereby a stakeholder, not being the loser, undertakes to pay to the winner the stakes held by him for behoof of the winner under the gaming contract. ...

"A stakeholder is a person in whose hands money or some other valuable thing has been deposited to abide the issue of an uncertain event. But no money was deposited in the hands of this defender to abide the event. ... I cannot see how this defender can be fitted into the definition of a stakeholder. In any event, it is not every stakeholder against whom an action is maintainable. It depends upon the nature of the contract or engagement upon which the action is laid."

The Lord Justice-Clerk distinguished *Calder* v. *Stevens* (1871) 9 M. 1074, saying (at p. 104): "Where is the analogy between an action for the recovery of a prize brought by the owner of an horse which has won a race and gained the stakes deposited with the clerk of the course, and which in a reasonable case can be regarded as a reward in a contest of skill, and an action brought by a punter to recover his winnings where by a freak of chance he has been successful in a pure gamble into which skill in no intelligible sense can be said to enter? Between these cases I cannot discover any resemblance.

"... *Calder's* case did not lay down that an action is maintainable against a stakeholder for recovery of money won upon a wager. It laid down, I think, a much more limited proposition, namely, that an action may be maintained against a stakeholder for recovery of a prize in a competition involving skill, or prowess, or merit of performance, which is a very different thing. ...

"I have come to think ... that the conception of a sweepstake, or some analogous form of lottery, comes very near to the substance of the defender's pool. ... There is no case in our books in which a successful competitor in a sweepstake or lottery, or any form of gaming transaction, who has won his prize by pure chance, has ever been permitted to make use of our Courts of Justice to recover it.

"... I come without hesitation to the conclusion that this action should not be entertained. Stripped of all refinements it is simply an action for recovery of a gambling debt. I appreciate that there may be a difficulty in saying to what precise legal category the defender's engagement is to be consigned, but that, in my opinion, matters not at all in a case where the frivolous character of the engagement is so transparent that it cannot be pretended that the action is to enforce the rights of parties arising from a serious transaction."

LORD WARK (at p. 116): "The only decision which appears to me to have a direct bearing upon the present question is *Calder* v. *Stevens*. ...

"It is strongly founded upon by the pursuer, who contended that it amounts to a decision that the plea of *sponsio ludicra* is not good in an action against a stakeholder. ... One thing seems clear, namely, that the Court regarded the subject of the action there as a prize lawfully contributed for the purposes of a *certamen de virtute*—a contest of prowess or skill. ... In any event, the reasoning of the judgment seems to me to be inapplicable to the kind of thing which we are here considering, namely, a congeries of wagering contracts in which the element of skill is so largely overborne by the element of chance. I am unable to say that skill is entirely absent from the process of filling up the coupons in the competition. If it were, the pool would be a lottery ... and in that case I have no doubt that an action would be incompetent, on the ground of *sponsio ludicra*. ...

"I have come to the conclusion that *Calder* v. *Stevens* is not in point in the present case. ... The football pool is a modern invention, and it is ... difficult ... to analyse its elements and to say what are the exact legal relations of the many parties to such a scheme. But some things seem to be clear, namely (first) that the defender was not the holder of stakes deposited with him ...; (second) that he undertook to act, in a question with each participant, as the agent of the others, who were undisclosed principals; (third) that the whole scheme was one which was devised, managed and carried through by the defender for the purpose of promoting gaming and wagering. He is not a mere stakeholder. He is carrying on a business which is concerned solely with gaming and wagering; and the moneys sued for are simply the balance of the wagers, under certain deductions agreed between the pursuer and the defender. ... I can see no principle under which the Court should lend its aid to an action against one who is the agent of other unknown wagerers, when action against the wagerers themselves is incompetent."

LORD JAMIESON (at p. 122): "It is not essential ... that a transaction, in order to be a *sponsio ludicra*, should be a *pactum illicitum*. Betting in itself is not illegal, but is illegal only if carried on in certain ways and in certain places, but a betting transaction is a *sponsio ludicra*. But I do not consider that only bets or wagers of a simple nature fall to be regarded as *sponsiones ludicrae*. ... The modern gambler ... may stake his money in a multitude of ways with or without the assistance of mechanical contrivances. In my view, the Court, in deciding whether or not any such transaction is a *sponsio ludicra*, should regard the matter on somewhat broad lines, and from a practical point of view. ... The contract on which the pursuer's case is based was a contract to take part in a gambling transaction, albeit of a complicated nature, and that I regard as a *sponsio ludicra*, an action based on which the Court cannot entertain.

"... It may be that the refusal of the Court to entertain questions arising out of transactions which now engage the attention of a considerable part of the population may open the door to apparent injustice. The rule of law, however, is well settled, and I agree with Lord Robertson in *Wilson* v. *Murphy* (1936 S.L.T. 564 (O.H.)) that, although such transactions may be indulged in by a multitude of people, they remain transactions of no serious business character, and to decide questions arising directly out of them would be lending aid to the enforcement of engagements of a gambling nature."

Sponsiones ludicrae: *sale and purchase of shares*

Shaw v. Caledonian Railway Co.

(1890) 17 R. 466

A certificate of railway stock was deposited with S., a dealer in stocks, by R., a customer, as cover for his transactions. A transfer of the stock, signed by R., was delivered to S. at the same time.

Subsequently, on R.'s failing to pay a debit balance on an account of his transactions, S. sold the stock. R. objected to the registration of the transfer on the ground that it had been granted in security of a gambling debt and was therefore null and void.

Held, upon the evidence, that the contracts were not for payment of differences only, but represented real transactions, both parties being bound to deliver the stocks if required.

LORD SHAND (at p. 475): "I think that the rule or principle to be applied is of this nature—That if it appears clearly that the contracts and dealings between the parties were for differences only, and were not intended in any sense to be real transactions, and were not in fact real transactions, then they must be regarded as gambling transactions, and the Court will not give effect to them. ... But, on the other hand, I think it appears from the authorities, and on sound principle, that if contracts for the sale of stock or shares or of goods, as the case may be, are entered into so as to create mutual obligations upon the parties, on the one hand to give, and on the other to take delivery of shares or stock or of goods, as the case may be; if the obligation is such as can be enforced if either of the parties think fit to do so, then I think we get out of the region of arrangements for mere differences of the nature of betting or gambling. If either one or both parties may, as and when he thinks fit, demand or give delivery of stock, and ask payment of the price under the contract—if that be so as to one of the parties—then I think the transaction has the mark or stamp of a real transaction, and is inconsistent with the notion of a transaction for mere differences."

CHAPTER 2

FORMATION OF CONTRACT

Offer or quotation?

Philp & Co. v. Knoblauch

1907 S.C. 994

K., a merchant in Leith, wrote to P. & Co., oil-millers at Lower Largo: "I am offering today Plate linseed for January/February shipment to Leith, and have pleasure in quoting you 100 tons at 41/3, usual Plate terms. I shall be glad to hear if you are buyers, and await your esteemed reply." The following day P. & Co. telegraphed: "Accept hundred January/February Plate 41/3 Leith, per steamer Leith" and confirmed this by letter. *Held* that (1) K.'s letter was an offer to sell and not merely a quotation of price; and (2) a contract was concluded by P. & Co.'s telegram, although the acceptance did not expressly refer to the condition "usual Plate terms" mentioned in the offer.

LORD ARDWALL (at p. 998): "I think that the letter of 28th December, 1905, contains in the first place a general statement that the defender is selling Plate linseed, and then goes on to make an absolutely definite offer of a specific quantity at a specific price. The defender says, 'I shall be glad to hear if you are buyers.' This does not mean buyers in general, but buyers of the quantity specified at the price quoted, otherwise there would be no meaning in the phrase which follows, 'and await your esteemed reply.' This offer was accepted by telegram, dated 29th December, 1905, sent before the offer was recalled, and the letter and telegram constitute, in my opinion, a concluded contract for the purchase of the linseed in question.

"It was maintained by the defender that there was no concluded contract because the telegram did not fully meet the offer, in respect that it did not refer to 'usual Plate terms'; but with regard to a document so plainly *in re mercatoria* as a telegram, I think the acceptance therein contained, which included a specification of the subject sold, the time of delivery, the quantity and the price, was sufficient, and that it implied an acceptance of the ancillary condition 'usual Plate terms.' "

NOTES

1. The Privy Council's decision in *Harvey* v. *Facey* [1893] A.C. 552 was distinguished on the grounds that the transaction in that case was a sale of heritable property not a transaction *in re mercatoria* and that there was never really an offer.

2. For the second point decided, *cf. Erskine* v. *Glendinning* (p. 32, below).

Undertaking to keep offer open

Littlejohn v. Hadwen

(1882) 20 S.L.R. 5 (O.H.)

H. was the proprietor of the estate of Rielonny in Ross-shire which L. was interested in buying. A letter dated October 21 from B., H.'s solicitor, to L.'s solicitor, offering the estate for sale at £12,000 was signed by B. but written by B.'s clerk. To that letter B. added the following postscript in his own hand: "It is understood that L. has the offer of Rielonny at the above price of £12,000 for ten days from this date." B. initialled the post-script. Acceptance was made on October 28, but meantime on October 26 H. had withdrawn his offer.

Held that the letter of October 21 with its postscript, being neither holograph nor tested, did not constitute a binding offer of the estate to L.

Of the undertaking in the postscript LORD FRASER (Ordinary) said (at p. 7): "According to the law of England, such an offer as this was revocable before acceptance. . . . But the reason for the English rule is not in accordance with the law of Scotland. The English law as to *nudum pactum* is, that an offer being without consideration, is not binding either in law or equity, and therefore a statement that the offer is open until a particular date means merely, that if not accepted on or before that date it will be at an end without further notice of withdrawal."

NOTES

1. Lord Fraser's opinion was approved *obiter* by Viscount Dunedin in *A. & G. Paterson Ltd.* v. *Highland Railway Co.*, 1927 S.C.(H.L.) 32, at p. 38: "Great stress was laid on the distinction between Scottish and English law in respect of the doctrine of consideration. I have on more than one occasion had to deal with this topic, and I do not think I have ever shown any desire to introduce the doctrine of consideration into the law of Scotland. Nay, more, I am prepared to say that the opinion of Lord Ordinary

Fraser, expressed in the now old case of *Littlejohn* v. *Hadwen* in which I was counsel many years ago, is right, *i.e.*, if I offer my property to a certain person at a certain price, and go on to say: 'This offer is to be open up to a certain date,' I cannot withdraw that offer before that date, if the person to whom I made the offer chooses to accept it. It would be different in England, for in the case supposed there would be no consideration for the promise to keep the offer open. But what is the reason of this? It is because the offer as made contained two distinct promises: (1) to sell at a certain price, and (2) to keep the offer open. It seems to me that (2) is completely wanting in the present case. It is just as if a tradesman put up a notice: 'My price for such-and-such goods during November will be so-and-so.' That offer may at any time be converted into a contract by a person tendering the price for the goods, but there is no contract that the tradesman may not change his mind and withdraw his offer."

2. On the requirement for probative writing for the constitution of *obligationes literis*, see *Goldston* v. *Young* (p. 51, below).

3. For an irrevocable offer (contained in a sub-underwriting letter), see *The Premier Briquette Co. Ltd.* v. *Gray*, 1922 S.C. 329.

Offer contained in advertisement

Hunter v. General Accident Fire and Life Assurance Corporation Ltd.

1909 S.C.(H.L.) 30; 1909 S.C. 344

A coupon policy of insurance in a Letts's diary stated that £1,000 would be paid to the executors of any owner of the diary fatally injured in a railway accident provided that the owner had caused his name to be registered at the insurance company's head office and provided that the claim was made within 12 months of the registration.

H. applied for registration on December 25, 1905. He received from the company a letter dated January 3, 1906, with which was enclosed an official acknowledgment dated December 29, 1905.

H. was injured in a railway accident on December 28, 1906, and died the following day. On January 2, 1907, H.'s executrix made a claim under the policy.

The company denied liability on the ground that the date of registration had been December 27, 1905, averring that applications were "registered" by being stamped, dated and filed. It was not definitely proved on what date H.'s application had been so treated.

Held that the burden was on the company to prove the date of registration and that upon a balance of probabilities registration was to be treated as subsequent to the sending of the acknowledgment on January 3, 1906; the claim had therefore been made within 12 months of the registration and the company was liable under the policy.

LORD CHANCELLOR (LOREBURN) (at p. 31): "This singular document has been regarded by all the Judges who have heard this case as an offer by the defenders which can be accepted, and a contract so made, by any person who complies with the conditions. I entirely agree with this view. It is admitted that Hunter did comply with all the conditions necessary to create a contract. He sent on 25th December 1905 the form of application for registration, called the coupon slip, with the necessary remittance. This was an acceptance on his part. . . .

". . . Now, the claim was made on 2nd January 1907, and the defenders have not proved that registration took place before 2nd January 1906, or indeed at what time it did take place.

"It is a matter peculiarly and solely within their knowledge, and the burthen is on them to prove this if they can. So far as the evidence goes, the fact that they did not send their letter of acknowledgment to Hunter till 3rd January 1906, seems to show that the act which constituted registration was not prior to that date."

In the Court of Session, LORD KINNEAR (at p. 353): "In my view there was a valid contract of insurance completed between the Company and the deceased Mr Hunter by his acceptance of the Company's offer to insure. If the offer expressed in the terms of the Company's advertisement had been made directly to Mr Hunter as an individual, and he had accepted it in terms for himself, there could have been no question whatever as to the completion of a valid contract. . . .

". . . It makes no difference, in my opinion, that instead of being addressed directly to an individual it is a general offer made to all persons to whose knowledge it may come, which may be accepted for himself by anyone who receives it.

"It is suggested that this is making a contract by an advertisement, but it is none the worse for being an advertisement if it is a distinct and definite offer unconditionally accepted. The instances of such a contract are familiar. . . . Perhaps the most common example is a contract made by advertisement undertaking to give a definite reward for the performance of certain services. It is held that the offer is accepted by the person who performs the services, and thereupon makes a claim, in respect of his having done so, to the reward in terms of the offer. But the principle is quite clear—that when a general offer addressed to the public is appropriated to himself by a distinct acceptance by one person, then it is to be read in exactly the same way as if it had been addressed to that individual originally.

"There may, of course, be a question—it is always a question of construction merely—whether a public announcement of this kind is in fact an offer, or whether it is a mere advertisement of a desire on the part of the advertiser to do business in a certain way. In the latter case it is not an offer; but if it contains a definite offer undertaking to pay money upon perfectly distinct specified conditions, then it is an offer, and when anyone, into whose hands it has come, accepts the terms and performs the conditions, there is to my mind a perfectly valid contract."

NOTE

Cf. Petrie v. *Earl of Airlie* (p. 1, above), and *Carlill* v. *Carbolic Smoke Ball Co.* [1893] 1 Q.B. 256.

Consensus in idem: *subject-matter must be the same*

Mathieson Gee (Ayrshire) Ltd. v. Quigley

1952 S.C.(H.L.) 38

M. Ltd. wrote to Q.: "We are prepared to supply the necessary mechanical plant for the excavation and removal . . . of the mould at present deposited in your pond."

Q. wrote in answer: "I . . . have pleasure in confirming my verbal acceptance . . . of your offer to remove the silt and deposit from the pond."

Held that no contract had been concluded.

LORD NORMAND (at p. 41): "The first question . . . is whether there was a contract between the parties or whether there was no *consensus in idem.* . . .

"The respondents' letter of 2nd March appears to me to be free from all ambiguity. It is an offer to supply the necessary mechanical plant. . . . The letter of 3rd March is, when it is studied, equally unambiguous and it is a purported acceptance of a contract to remove the silt, a *locatio operis*, a different kind of contract from that in the offer, and with different incidents. . . . No contract existed between the parties. The respondents offered one sort of contract and the appellant accepted another kind of contract. . . .

"I have no doubt that, when the parties to a litigation put forward what they say is a concluded contract and ask the Court to construe it, it is competent for the Court to find that there was in fact no contract and nothing to be construed, and I respectfully agree with the Lord Chancellor Loreburn's opinion on this point, as expressed in *Houldsworth* v. *Gordon Cumming*."

NOTE

For *Houldsworth* v. *Gordon Cumming*, see p. 159, below.

Consensus in idem: *acceptance must be unqualified*

Nelson v. The Assets Co. Ltd.

(1889) 16 R. 898

L., a Glasgow house-factor, wrote to A. Ltd. offering to purchase specified parts of the tenement known as "His Lordship's Larder" for £3,000.

A. Ltd. accepted the offer "for our interest in the property known as 'His Lordship's Larder.' "

On an examination of the titles it became apparent that A. Ltd. had no clear and undisputed title to certain parts specified in L.'s offer.

L. assigned his rights under the offer and acceptance to N., and N. brought an action to have A. Ltd. ordained to implement their part of the alleged contract and to deliver a valid disposition of the subjects.

Held that the missives did not constitute a completed contract.

LORD ORDINARY (KINNEAR) (at p. 900): "The defenders' manager does not accept the offer in the exact terms in which it is made, but accepts it as an offer for 'our interest' in the property described, and that appears to me to introduce into the acceptance a qualification which was not in the offer. It is a qualification which it was very natural to make in the circumstances, because the state of possession was such as to render it not improbable that questions might arise as to the exact import and bearing of the title. It was very natural, therefore, that the defenders should introduce a term into their acceptance which would serve to exclude from the bargain, if the purchaser agreed to it, any part of the property which did not belong to them, or in which they had no interest. I think the words they have used are sufficient for that purpose, and it follows that their letter is not an absolute and unequivocal acceptance which would make the contract complete, but a counter proposal which the maker of the offer was not bound to accept, and which he has not in fact accepted. There is therefore no contract, because it is very clear in law that no contract can be constituted by missive letters, unless the letters contain an absolute and unqualified acceptance on the one part of the exact terms proposed on the other part."

LORD JUSTICE-CLERK (J. H. A. MACDONALD) (at p. 902): "Now, the pursuer asks that this acceptance should be read as if it had run thus: – 'We accept your offer for our interest as described by you,' for unless the acceptance is exactly for the subjects the pursuer offered for, there can be no valid acceptance.

"I am unable to adopt this reading. I read the letter of the company as it has been read by the Lord Ordinary. I think the acceptance was one simply for the defenders' 'interest' in the property, whatever that might be. ... There was no completed sale, the acceptance not corresponding with the offer. Further writing would have been necessary to complete a bargain."

NOTE

Star Fire and Burglary Insurance Co. Ltd. v. *Davidson & Sons Ltd.* (1902) 5 F. 83 illustrates the same point. A trading company had agreed to insure its works against fire. The policy tendered by the insurance company proceeded on the narrative that the insured had agreed to become members of the insurance company. Under the articles of association of the insurance company members were liable to contribute in the event of the company's liquidation. In an action by the insurance company for payment of the premium, the court *assoilzied* the defenders, holding that they had not agreed to become members.

Lord Justice-Clerk (J. H. A. Macdonald) (at p. 86): "The pursuers offered to accept a fire risk for £5,000 over buildings belonging to the defenders, and the defenders intimated through an agent that they were willing to give them the insurance. But on receiving from the pursuers a policy embodying the arrangement, the defenders found that the policy which they had asked for was made out in their favour on condition of their becoming members of the pursuers' company. They were under no obligation to become members of the pursuers' company, and were in my opinion entitled to declare the whole matter to be off. There was here no *consensus in idem placitum*."

Consensus in idem: *"the battle of forms"*

Continental Tyre & Rubber Co. Ltd. v. Trunk Trailer Co. Ltd.

1985 S.C. 163

T. Ltd. ordered a quantity of tyres from C. Ltd., using their printed form of purchase order on which were printed T. Ltd.'s standard conditions of purchase.

C. Ltd. proceeded to supply the tyres in various batches, each batch being accompanied by a delivery note and followed by an invoice. Both the delivery note and the invoice referred to C. Ltd.'s standard conditions of sale.

The standard conditions of sale of the two companies were inconsistent.

A dispute having arisen about the quality of the tyres, C. Ltd. sought to rely on one of their standard conditions.

Held that in the circumstances T. Ltd. had not assented to the incorporation of C. Ltd.'s standard conditions.

LORD PRESIDENT (EMSLIE) (at pp. 166–168): "In this action the pursuers seek to recover from the defenders the unpaid balance of the price of tyres sold to the defenders for use on trailers manufactured by the defenders to be supplied for civilian use in Saudi Arabia. These tyres were ordered by the defenders by a Purchase Order PO 9503, which was in their standard form, dated 3rd May 1979. . . . There was no written acceptance of this order and the pursuers thereafter proceeded to deliver tyres to the defenders in response to their order in a number of consignments. The first batch of tyres was delivered on 25th May 1979. On making delivery of each batch of tyres, using their own transport, we are asked to assume that the pursuers' driver handed to someone at the defenders' premises for signature what is called their standard form of delivery note. Several days—usually about ten days—after delivery of each batch of tyres the pursuers sent to the defenders an invoice relating to that batch of tyres. It was in their standard form. . . .

". . . The point made was that the standard form of delivery note contained in the top left hand corner the legend: 'All offers and sales are subject to the company's current terms and conditions of sale, a copy of which will be supplied on request.'. . .

". . . In my opinion the Lord Ordinary was well-entitled to hold that the contract was complete as soon as the first batch of tyres had been delivered to the defenders in response to their order and that the 'delivery note' fell to be regarded as a mere receipt for the tyres which had been delivered. The legend in the delivery note which has been quoted was, accordingly, for that reason incapable of having the effect of incorporating into the contract, after performance, the pursuers' standard conditions of sale."

NOTE

Contrast *Uniroyal Ltd.* v. *Miller & Co. Ltd.*, 1985 S.L.T. 101, where an acknowledgment of a purchase order was held to be a counter-offer because it quoted revised prices which made it clear that there was no *consensus in idem* until the terms of the counter-offer were accepted.

Consensus in idem: *faulty transmission of offer*

Verdin Brothers v. Robertson

(1871) 10 M. 35

R. despatched from Peterhead this telegram to V. of Liverpool: "Send on immediately fifteen twenty tons salt invoice in my name cash terms."

Through the fault of the telegraph clerks the telegram received by V. stated: "Send on rail immediately fifteen twenty tons salt Morice in morning name cash terms."

V. sent salt by rail to "Morice, Peterhead" and posted invoices to the same address.

The invoices were returned through the dead letter office, and later R. refused to take delivery of the salt on the ground that it was too late for his purpose.

V. brought an action against R. for the price.

Held that no contract had been completed between the parties, and that therefore R. was not liable for the price.

LORD COWAN (at p. 37): "The first question is, whether or not there has been a concluded contract between the parties. ... The correct message was handed in by the defender to the telegraph office, to be transmitted to the pursuer. But a mistake was made by the telegraph officials, which led to the message being delivered to the pursuer in a materially and essentially altered form. Now, can it be said that there was here *consensus in eundem contractum* between the parties in this transaction? Clearly not. The pursuer may have been willing enough to implement the order he received; but then the defender had not sent that order, and had not consented to it."

LORD BENHOLME (at p. 37): "There has been no such *consensus* between the parties as is requisite for the constitution of a contract."

LORD NEAVES (at p. 37): "This is a demand for a price, and the question is, was there a contract of sale. Sale is a consensual contract. Was there here a *consensus*? *Consensus* may be by the parties themselves or by their authorised agents. Here there was an apparent assent to the proposed sale, but no consent, unless the telegraph officers are to be considered as the authorised agents of the sender, to the effect of making him responsible for any blunder which they may commit. That seems to me an inadmissible proposition, and one certainly of a most serious character to the mercantile classes. To hold that a sender communicating through a telegraph clerk is equally bound as if he had sent the message by a clerk of his own is a proposition to which I cannot assent."

Consensus in idem: *counter-offer may cancel original offer*

Wolf and Wolf v. Forfar Potato Co.

1984 S.L.T. 100

F., a Forfar potato merchant, on November 29, 1977, telexed an offer to sell potatoes to W., an international potato merchant. The offer was open for acceptance until 17.00 hours the following day.

By a telex of November 30, W. purported to accept F.'s offer on certain additional conditions. W. heard by telephone that F. would not agree to these additional conditions, and W. then sent a second telex to F., still within the time-limit, purporting to confirm acceptance of F.'s original offer but requesting the additional conditions be given consideration.

F. did not supply the potatoes, and W. sued for damages.

Held that the original offer had fallen and so there was no contract.

LORD JUSTICE-CLERK (WHEATLEY) (at p. 103): "The first argument advanced by defenders' counsel is a simple and straightforward one, and turns on a proposition in law. In my opinion it is well founded. ... Gloag [*on Contract* (2nd ed.)], under reference to *Hunter* v. *Hunters* [(1745) Mor. 9169] and *Hyde* v. *Wrench* [(1840) 3 Beav. 334], says at p. 37: 'An offer falls if it is refused. If the refusal is not peremptory, but combined with a request for better terms, the general construction is that the offer is gone, and that the party to whom it was made, on failure to obtain the terms he requests, cannot fall back on an acceptance of the original offer.' Whether or not the cases referred to by Gloag in themselves vouch that legal proposition, I am satisfied that it is sound. . . . The case for the pursuers rested on the validity of 6/3 [of process] as a timeous acceptance of 6/1. I do not consider that the fact that the original offer had a terminal date within which it could be accepted takes it out of the category to which Gloag refers. According to Gloag, when the counter-offer is made the general construction is that the offer is gone. Once the offer is gone it cannot be accepted. It is not suggested that the counter-offer in 6/2 was accepted by the defenders, and on that short basis it seems to me that the defenders' case must succeed."

LORD ROBERTSON (at p. 105): "The pursuers' final submission was that, regarding 6/2 as not an acceptance of the terms of 6/1, but as putting forward fresh conditions which did not meet 6/1, 6/3 must be regarded as withdrawing the qualifications set out in 6/2 and timeously accepting simpliciter the terms of 6/1, subject to a plea for further consideration of the points raised. As the acceptance was timeously sent before the deadline set in 6/1 the agreement was valid.

"In my opinion this argument cannot be accepted. Once it is conceded that 6/2 was not an unqualified acceptance of 6/1 but constituted a rejection of 6/1 and a new offer, it follows in my opinion that there could only be consensus in idem in a contract if the defenders subsequently at some time, and in some way, accepted the new offer. I do not find any evidence, or indication, that the defenders ever did so accept the new offer set out in 6/2 at any time. . . .

"The pursuers argued that the effect of 6/3 was to withdraw the qualifications, or counter-offer, in 6/2, and to accept simpliciter the offer in 6/1. They were entitled to do so within the time limit set in 6/1.

"In my opinion this argument fails, for two basic reasons, videlicet:

"(1) The wording of the first paragraph in 6/3 indicates clearly, in my opinion, that Mr Wolf at that time understood that the offer in 6/1 had already been accepted; 6/3 was being sent simply to 'confirm that we have accepted your offer.' This accords with the previously expressed view that 6/2 was an acceptance of 6/1 and the telephone conversation had affirmed that an agreement had been reached. The defenders on the other hand did not agree that any such agreement had been reached. If it had been intended that 6/3 should withdraw the counter-offer in 6/2 and accept 6/1 simpliciter it would have been simple to do so in 6/3. I agree entirely with the reasoning of the sheriff to the effect that 6/3 did not constitute a withdrawal of the counter-offer put forward in 6/2, and that no consensus in idem between the parties was reached by the sending of 6/3. Once it is conceded that 6/2 constituted a counter-offer, an acceptance by the defenders to the terms of that counter-offer was necessary to complete a contract. Such an acceptance was never given. Nor did 6/3 indicate that the counter-offer had been withdrawn. As senior counsel for the defenders put it in an apt phrase: '6/3 was only an inaccurate record of an agreement which had never been entered into.'

"(2) It was argued on behalf of the pursuers that as 6/1 gave them a time-limit before which they were entitled to accept the terms set out in 6/1, they were entitled to accept that offer at any time before the time-limit expired: this applied as a rule of law even although in the meantime they had rejected the offer in 6/1 and proposed a new offer. If that were withdrawn later, they were still entitled to accept the original offer in 6/1, which remained in existence until the expiry of the time-limit. This is what they had done in 6/3.

"In my opinion this argument is unsound. If, as is admitted, 6/2 was a refusal of the offer contained in 6/1, and was a new offer (which was never accepted), the legal effect is that the original offer in 6/1 disappeared. The time-limit was part of that offer and with its refusal that condition fell along with all the other conditions of that offer. See Gloag on *Contract* (2nd ed., p. 37). . . .

"In my opinion the sheriff's conclusion that no consensus in idem and no contract was ever reached between the parties was correct."

NOTES

1. Of the two authorities cited by Gloag Lord McDonald said (at p. 106): "The first is *Hunter* v. *Hunters*. I have read the report in this old case with care and have difficulty in finding in it support for such a general proposition as is stated by Gloag. The other is the English case of *Hyde* v. *Wrench*. I read that case as one in which an offer was peremptorily refused and therefore not one which supports Gloag's proposition. It is moreover a case relating to heritable property in England and based upon the Statute of Frauds. Neither case bears much relationship to the present mercantile transaction."

2. This case was followed by Lord Caplan (Ordinary) in *Rutterford Ltd.* v. *Allied Breweries Ltd.*, 1990 S.L.T. 249 (O.H.) (see NOTE 2 to *Errol* v. *Walker*, p. 54, below), but was distinguished in *Findlater* v. *Maan*, 1990 S.C. 150:

On March 25, 1988, an offer was made by F.'s agents for the purchase of heritable property in Glasgow. On March 28, this was accepted by M.'s agents, subject to certain qualifications. On March 29, F.'s agents accepted these qualifications, subject to further qualifications. On March 30, M.'s agents, referring to the offer of March 25 and their qualified acceptance of March 28, intimated a further qualification. On April 6, F.'s agents accepted the terms of that letter, withdrawing the qualifications contained in their own letter of March 29. By a letter received by F.'s agents on April 7, M.'s agents intimated their withdrawal from the missives. F. raised an action of declarator that the parties had entered into a contract.

Held that (1) the letters of March 29 and 30 constituted two co-existing offers; (2) F.'s letter of April 6 was an acceptance of M.'s letter of March 30 and a withdrawal of F.'s own offer of March 29; and therefore (3) a contract had been concluded.

Lord Justice-Clerk (Ross) (at p. 162): "I have reached the clear conclusion that this case can readily be distinguished from *Wolf & Wolf* v. *Forfar Potato Co.* What was critical in that case was that the qualified acceptance constituted a counter-offer; the result of sending the counter-offer was that the original offer had fallen and could not thereafter be accepted. What the pursuers did in the present case by their letter of 6th April 1988 was to accept the terms of the letter of 30th March 1988. They did not purport to accept the original offer, and accordingly the present case is different to *Wolf & Wolf* v. *Forfar Potato Co.* It is true that the letter of 30th March 1988 refers to the letter of 25th March which was the original offer, but it is plain from the terms of the letter of 6th April 1988 that what is being accepted is the letter of 30th March 1988. The letter no doubt incorporated the earlier offer which had been superseded by the qualified acceptance, but there was no question of the pursuers seeking to disregard the intervening correspondence and to go back to the original offer.

"In my opinion, the true approach to be made in the present case is as follows. The letter of 29th March and the letter of 30th March were two offers which existed at the same time, one at the instance of the seller and one at the instance of the purchaser. They were not written under reference to one another and neither of them superseded the other; they both co-existed. In that situation I am of opinion that it was open to the pursuers to accept the offer contained in the letter of 30th March 1988. It was not disputed that that letter fell to be regarded as an offer, and it was an offer which was open for acceptance. The pursuers did accept that offer by their letter of 6th April 1988. Of course, so long as the offer of 29th March 1988 remained in existence there could be no final *consensus in idem*. However, there was no reason why the pursuers should not withdraw the letter of 29th March 1988.

" 'Except in cases where there is an undertaking to hold the offer open for a definite time, it may be withdrawn at any time before acceptance.' (Gloag on *Contract* (2nd edn.) at p. 37.)

"By their letter of 6th April 1988 the pursuers did withdraw the letter of 29th March 1988, and, in my opinion, the consequence was that consensus was reached and a bargain was concluded for the purchase by them of the subjects from the defender. I am not persuaded that the defender required to consent to the withdrawal of the letter of 29th March 1988. I know of no principle of law which would require the consent of the defender to the withdrawal of such a letter. ... The fact was that on 6th April 1988 there were two outstanding offers. Before there could be *consensus in idem* both these offers had to be dealt with. What the pursuers did was to accept one of these offers and withdraw the other. That having been done, there were no longer any matters at issue between the parties and, in my opinion, *consensus in idem* was achieved."

Acceptance need not expressly reiterate all the terms of the offer

Erskine v. Glendinning

(1871) 9 M. 656

G. wrote to E. who was proprietor of the Wilmington corn and flour mills near Dalbeattie as follows: "I hereby offer to take a lease of the Wilmington corn and flour mills, and pigs' houses and boilings, &c., for the period of ten years, entry at Whitsunday first, at the yearly rent of £80 sterling."

E.'s reply stated: "I beg to accept of your offer for my mill, subject to lease drawn out in due form."

Held that (1) a binding contract had been formed although the acceptance did not expressly reiterate all the terms of the offer and (2) the words "subject to lease drawn out in due form" did not import a condition into the acceptance since the landlord was entitled to require his tenant to enter into a formal lease.

LORD PRESIDENT (INGLIS) (at p. 659): "Both parties knew perfectly well the subjects with which they were dealing, and in these circumstances the defender offered to take the mills and pigs' houses and boilings, &c., for ten years from Whitsunday first, at the yearly rent of £80. Now, here are all the essentials of a lease embodied in this offer. There is a sufficient description of the subjects for identification, there is the entry, the endurance of the lease, and the yearly rent; and this is all that is necessary to make a lease. The whole that Mr Erskine had to do was to answer, yes; and if he had done so, or said anything equivalent, the contract would have been complete. Now, what he does say is, 'I accept your offer.' If he had stopped there it would have been all right; but he goes on to say 'for my mill, subject to lease drawn out in due form.' And it is seriously contended, and has been held by the Lord Ordinary, that the use of the word 'mill' shows that the acceptance referred to a different subject-matter from the offer, and that this invalidates the contract. I have no doubt whatever that both parties were referring to exactly the same subjects, and in such cases it is not the words of parties but their understanding that we must look to.

"But it is further contended, that the addition of the words 'subject to lease drawn out in due form,' imports a condition into the acceptance, and that as parties cannot agree about this lease, therefore the contract cannot stand. I cannot agree with this view either. It did not require the offerer to consent to that, or the acceptor to stipulate for it. The landlord was entitled to require that his tenant should enter into a formal lease whenever asked, embodying the terms of their contract. . . .

"The result is that the pursuer is entitled to have it found that a valid contract was entered into by the missives founded on, and that all that was required after that was to have this informal contract put into regular form. I am therefore of opinion that we should find the contract validly constituted, and remit to a conveyancer to draw a lease conform thereto."

NOTES

1. Compare *Philp & Co.* v. *Knoblauch* (p. 19, above), and *Harvey* v. *Smith* (1904) 6 F. 511: S. wrote to H.: "I hereby offer to purchase from you the subjects in Lochgelly used by you as a model lodging-house, together with the fittings and fixtures therein, and the goodwill of the business carried on in the premises, at the price of Twelve hundred pounds sterling (£1,200 stg.) on the following conditions:—..."

H.'s reply was: "I accept your offer ... to purchase the lodging-house property in Lochgelly belonging to me, together with the fittings and fixtures therein, at the price of £1,200 stg. on the conditions stated in said offer."

Opinion by the Lord President (Kinross) that there was no *consensus in idem*, as the acceptance did not in its enumeration of the items sold include the goodwill.

Opinion contra by Lord Kinnear.

Lord President (at p. 520): "It is also to be observed that the alleged offer and acceptance do not meet each other, and that so far as appears from them, the parties never were *in idem* as to the transaction. ... There is no mention in the acceptance of 'the goodwill of the business carried on in the premises.' It is to be assumed that the defender attached a value to that goodwill, as, *ex facie* of the documents, he stipulated for it. ... The result is that the alleged offer and acceptance do not meet each other, or, in other words, that upon the missives the parties are not *in idem*."

Lord Kinnear (at p. 522): "I cannot see that the parties were not here *in idem*. There was a perfectly distinct offer ... [and] a clear acceptance of an offer clearly identified. I cannot assent to the view that the answer excludes the goodwill of the business from the acceptance. It is not necessary for the acceptance of an offer that every item should be recapitulated, provided the answer, fairly construed, means that the person accepts the offer as it is made; and that appears to me to be the plain meaning of the answer in question. If the pursuer's intention had been to accept the offer for a purchase of the house on the conditions specified, but to reject the proposal to take the goodwill along with it, he must have said so in plain terms. I am therefore not prepared to agree that the letters of offer and acceptance themselves shew that the parties were not *in idem*."

2. On "subject to lease drawn out in due form," see *Stobo Ltd.* v. *Morrisons (Gowns) Ltd.*, below.

Acceptance "subject to contract"

Stobo Ltd. v. Morrisons (Gowns) Ltd.

1949 S.C. 184

S. Ltd. and M. Ltd. were respectively tenants of two shops in Renfield Street, Glasgow. W. Ltd., the owners of both shops, desired to sell them. Before a sale was effected, an arrangement was made between S. Ltd. and M. Ltd. whereby M. Ltd. would make an offer for both shops and, if their offer were accepted, would then sell to S. Ltd. the shop occupied by S. Ltd.

This arrangement was embodied in two letters: (1) an offer, adopted as holograph, from S. Ltd.'s solicitors to M. Ltd. and (2) an improbative reply from M. Ltd. containing the statement: "we accept your offer, on behalf of S. Ltd., to purchase, subject to contract, the shop at present occupied by them."

W. Ltd. accepted M. Ltd.'s offer for the two shops, but M. Ltd. subsequently refused to implement their arrangement with S. Ltd. S. Ltd. brought an action against M. Ltd. for specific implement.

Held that in the circumstances of this case the words "subject to contract," more especially as they occurred in an improbative document, qualified the acceptance and so prevented the arrangement from being treated as a concluded agreement.

LORD PRESIDENT (COOPER) (at p. 191): "The real issue, and it is not an easy one, is whether the letters disclose a concluded agreement, and what effect is to be given to the words 'subject to contract.'

"We were referred to a large number of English decisions dealing with sales and other contracts expressed to have been made 'subject to contract,' 'subject to formal contract,' or in other equivalent terms, and our attention was directed to the difficulty which Professor Gloag seemingly felt—*Contract* (2nd ed.), p. 44—in reconciling these decisions with *Erskine* v. *Glendinning*. I have not derived much assistance from this line of approach. Many of the English decisions belong to the law and practice of vendor and purchaser with which we have no concern. It appears that according to that law and practice the phrases in question have acquired by long usage a technical meaning. . . . That is certainly not true of Scots law and practice; for it is nearly eighty years since such an expression was judicially considered in this Court, and there is no evidence in our conveyancing works or style books to suggest that these formulas are normally employed in Scotland or that they have acquired with us any special meaning or efficacy. Moreover the English decisions do not speak with one voice. . . . Even if it be the case . . . that in England it would now be held that the introduction of the phrase 'subject to contract' or one of its variants automatically excludes concluded agreement, I know of no such rule in Scots law. Further, I see no necessary conflict between the trend of the recent English cases and *Erskine* v. *Glendinning*. . . . An acceptance cannot be read as subject to a suspensive condition merely because the acceptor puts into words what the law would imply as the method in which an agreement, *ex hypothesi* complete, would be carried into legal effect. It follows from that ratio not only that *Erskine* v. *Glendinning* was, in my humble opinion, rightly decided, but that it is distinguishable and does not ... rule the present case.

"The only rules of Scots law which it appears to me to be possible to extract from past decisions and general principles are that it is perfectly possible for the parties to an apparent contract to provide that there shall be *locus poenitentiae* until the terms of their agreement have been reduced to a formal contract; but that the bare fact that the parties to a completed agreement stipulate that it shall be embodied in a formal contract does not necessarily import that they are still in the stage of negotiation. In each instance it is a matter of the construction of the correspondence in the light of the facts, proved or averred, on which side of the border line the case lies. ...

"Now in this case the so-called contract of sale of 66 Renfield Street was a very unusual one, for at the date when it was made the sellers had not acquired the subject of sale, and could not know with certainty on what terms, if at all, they would be able to acquire it. ... Against such a background it is not *prima facie* unlikely that the anticipatory bargain for the subsale of one of the shops should have been treated as only provisional until the full terms of the bargain with the principal seller could be known and until the subcontract could be reduced to formal shape. When in light of these considerations we examine the acceptance ..., we find (*a*) that, though it covers adequately the cardinal points of the intended bargain, it is not exhaustive of details; (*b*) that, though it is sent in reply to a binding holograph offer, it is not itself probative; and (*c*) that it expressly bears to be conditional—the words 'subject to' being suggestive of suspense of commitment. I recognise that grammatically the qualification 'subject to contract' is not inserted at the correct place; but, unless the words are to be given no meaning or effect whatever, I can only read them as a qualification of the acceptance.

"In these circumstances, though the matter is narrow, I am disposed to think that there was no final assent or concluded agreement."

LORD CARMONT (at p. 193): "The defenders' acceptance of the pursuers' offer was made 'subject to contract,' which words *prima facie* qualify the acceptance and operate to prevent the tentative arrangement from being treated as a concluded bargain.

"The question before us is a mere question of construction upon which no light is to be derived from decisions as to the interpretation of other documents in different terms. According to our law there must be an absolute and unequivocal acceptance of the offer, in order to make a contract complete. I do not find in any Scottish case ground for thinking that the words 'subject to contract' must be read as merely importing a stipulation for a formal document embodying the terms already completely agreed to by the parties. *Erskine* v. *Glendinning* ... does not, in my opinion, help the pursuers in the present case. ...

"Taking the case, therefore, as a matter of interpretation of the language used by the defenders, the pursuers have failed to present a relevant case to set up the bargain they seek to enforce."

LORD KEITH (at p. 194): "But for the words 'subject to contract' there is no doubt that the letters ... would have formed complete, although improbative, missives of sale constituting an agreement on which *rei interventus* could be founded. ...

"The present case seems to be a case in which there were such special circumstances as might well have induced the seller to introduce special stipulations into the missives for consideration and acceptance by a prospective purchaser, and this consideration gives special force to the argument that the words 'subject to contract' were intended to suspend concluded agreement until some subsequent minute or agreement of sale was adjusted. I should hesitate to say that such words must in all cases be suspensive of agreement. If everything that was normally required by the circumstances had been agreed, I should be slow to hold that a loophole could thus be given to either party to escape from the conclusion that a completed bargain had been made. But in the present case an opposite conclusion can, in my opinion, be supported. ... In the present case only one of the missives has been adopted as holograph, and the one which has not been so adopted is the one that contains the words 'subject to contract.' This, in my opinion, gives added force to the contention that the words were suspensive of obligation, and, if so, there was no basis on which *rei interventus* could operate."

NOTE

For *Erskine* v. *Glendinning*, see p. 32, above.

Acceptance must be timeous

The Glasgow, &c. Steam Shipping Co. v. Watson

(1873) 1 R. 189

On August 5, 1871, W., a coalmaster, offered to supply a shipping company with steam-coal for one year at 7s. per ton. Negotiations subsequently took place between the parties, and on October 13, 1871, the shipping company sent to W. an acceptance of the offer.

The price of steam-coal had risen by 2s. per ton between August 5 and October 13, and W. refused to recognise the existence of any contract.

The shipping company brought an action of damages against W. for breach of contract.

Held that the offer of August 5 was no longer open for acceptance on October 13, and that W. was therefore not liable for breach of contract.

LORD PRESIDENT (INGLIS) (at p. 193): "Every offer requires to be timeously accepted, and this is particularly the case with such an offer as is here presented, where the material sold is liable to sudden alterations in market price. . . . Now, it is plain, on reading the defender's offer, that it was an offer to supply the coal required from the 5th of August, 1871, to the 5th of August, 1872, and for no other period whatever. But the action as laid represents the period of delivery as the year between 13th October, 1871, and 13th October, 1872, being the twelve months immediately following the date of the alleged acceptance, a totally different period from that which was originally contemplated. . . . No doubt there is no time fixed for accepting, and we are therefore driven to take some reasonable time,—reasonable, that is, in the whole circumstances of the case. But was it ever heard of that, in making an offer of this sort, a period of two months might elapse before acceptance, and that then the contract should begin to run from the date of acceptance, not from the date originally contemplated in the offer?

"But then it is said that, although that might not be a reasonable proposition in ordinary circumstances, the offer might be and was kept open for such a length of time by negotiations between the parties. I am not prepared to dispute that there might be such a case . . . ; but that could only be done by express agreement of parties, the reason manifestly being this, that the contract, when so made, will be a different contract from that which was contemplated by the offer. . . . There was no new proposal that the original offer should be kept open. And therefore I am clearly of opinion that it was not kept open. ... An offer such as this cannot be kept open for acceptance except by the most express agreement between the parties."

LORD DEAS (at p. 195): "There are two fatal objections to the pursuers' claim,—in the first place, the delay in accepting it. ... Offers of certain kinds might be held to subsist for that period,—e.g., an offer to buy or sell a house in ordinary circumstances. But, as regards such an offer as this, to supply an article which at all times fluctuates in price, and which, at the time in question, was rising rapidly in price, it is altogether out of the question to hold it to have been a continuing offer for so long a period as is here contended for. ...

"The second reason is equally conclusive against the pursuers, viz., that the acceptance would make a totally different bargain from that proposed on the 5th of August; for the question at once occurs, whether was the year to run from 5th August or from 13th October, 1871. If the year was to run from 13th October then the completed contract was a contract for a different period of time from that originally contemplated."

NOTE

Cf. Wylie and Lochhead v. *McElroy and Sons* (1873) 1 R. 41: W. & L. were about to erect new stables and invited estimates for the iron-work. On April 24, 1872, McE. & Sons offered to execute the iron-work for a specified sum. W. & L. made no reply until May 27, when they wrote accepting the offer subject to a condition. McE. & Sons did not reply to this communication. Between April 24 and May 27 the price of iron had risen considerably. McE. & Sons declined to proceed with the work, and W. & L. raised an action for damages for breach of contract.

Held that the offer had not been timeously accepted.

Lord Neaves (at p. 43): "Now, the iron business is always subject to considerable fluctuations. Not only does the raw iron, which is the staple of the manufacture, constantly vary in price, but also coke, which is an essential element, and wages, are subject to great fluctuations. Moreover, it is manifest from the proceedings of parties that the iron market was very much agitated during the period in question. It is plain sense, therefore, that any offer depending on this commodity is meant to be immediately closed with or rejected. Any alterations in the market ... might totally alter the terms on which parties would agree.

"... The pursuers' delay until 27th May was utterly unreasonable and unwarrantable. ... Where such a fluctuating commodity as iron is concerned hours must suffice for decision, not weeks or months."

Lord Justice-Clerk (Moncreiff) (at p. 44): "The condition annexed ... could not become binding by mere silence on the part of the person to whom it was addressed."

Completion of contract on posting of acceptance

Jacobsen, Sons, & Co. v. E. Underwood & Son Ltd.

(1894) 21 R. 654

On March 2, 1893, U. Ltd., who had an office in Leith, offered to buy a quantity of straw from J. & Co., Edinburgh. The offer stated, "This for reply by Monday, 6th inst."

On March 6, J. & Co. wrote to U. Ltd. accepting the offer. The letter of acceptance was addressed to U. Ltd., Leith, the name of and number in the street being omitted. It was posted in Edinburgh on the evening of the 6th, but, owing to the insufficiency of the address, did not reach U. Ltd.'s office until the noon delivery, instead of by the morning delivery, on the 7th.

U. Ltd. intimated that as they had not received the acceptance on the 6th the contract was off.

Subsequently U. Ltd. refused to take delivery of the straw, and J. & Co. then brought an action for the difference between the contract price and the price which the straw realised upon a sale.

Held that the offer had been timeously accepted.

Lord Justice-Clerk (J. H. A. Macdonald) (at p. 656): "The defenders maintain that the condition in their letter was not fulfilled; that it could not be fulfilled unless the pursuers' acceptance reached them within what they call 'business hours' on the Monday. ...

"... When a letter of acceptance is posted, it is out of the power of the accepting party. He has committed it to a medium of communication which is bound to hold it and safely deliver it to the other party in due course. The dispatcher of the letter has effectually bound himself the moment he has committed his acceptance to the mail. He has done that act of acceptance which, in the language of Mr Bell in his *Commentaries*, 'binds the bargain.' ... Now, it has been made matter of distinct decision that acceptance by post, that is by posting a letter of acceptance, completes the contract. It is in this case undoubted that acceptance by post was a suitable mode, and indeed was contemplated, and that the defenders' representative expected that the acceptance would so come. I have no doubt in holding (1) that the pursuers were entitled to accept at any time on the Monday, and (2) that they effectually accepted by posting their letter of acceptance on the Monday."

LORD ORDINARY (STORMONTH-DARLING) (at p. 655): "Professor Bell in his *Commentaries* (Lord McLaren's edit. i, p. 344) states the law thus:—'It is the act of acceptance that binds the bargain, and in the common case it is not necessary that the acceptance shall have reached the person who makes the offer. An offer to sell goods is a consent provisionally to a bargain. ... From the moment of acceptance there is between the parties *in idem placitum concursus et conventio*, which constitutes the contract of sale. To this, however, an exception may be made by the offerer limiting it so that the arrival of the acceptance only shall bind the bargain.'

"The rule thus stated by Professor Bell is not limited to the case of an acceptance despatched by post. But authoritative decisions, and particularly the judgment of the House of Lords in *Dunlop* v. *Higgins*, 6 Bell's App. 195, and of the English Court of Appeal in *Household Fire Insurance Company* v. *Grant*, L.R., 4 Exch.Div. 216, have established that where an offer is made which, expressly or by implication, authorises the sending of an acceptance by post, the posting of the letter of acceptance completes the contract, whatever delay there may be in its delivery. In the latter case, indeed, the letter never reached its destination at all. On that special ground Lord Bramwell dissented, but even he conceded that 'where a posted letter arrives, the contract is complete on the posting.' "

NOTE

The English case was doubted in *Mason* v. *The Benhar Coal Co.* (1882) 9 R. 883. M. had completed a circular which stated "I ... hereby express my willingness to take ... shares," but had not completed a second circular sent to him which stated "I ... hereby apply for ... shares." The company, proceeding on the first circular, allotted shares to M. There was a conflict of evidence as to whether he ever received an allotment letter.

Held that M.'s answer to the first circular was not sufficient to bind him to become a shareholder.

Lord Shand (at p. 889): "As to the question whether notice of allotment was received or not, there is a considerable difficulty. ... But it is not necessary to decide the question. I shall only say that, assuming the true inference from the proof to be that delivery is not proved, I should not hold that the contract was completed by the mere posting of the notice of allotment. I should concur on that point in the opinion of Lord Justice Bramwell in the case of the *Household Fire Insurance Company*."

Revocation of offer

Thomson v. James

(1855) 18 D. 1

On November 26, 1853, J. posted to T. an offer to purchase the estate of Renniston for £6,400. On December 1, 1853, T. posted a letter of acceptance, but earlier on the same day J. had posted a letter withdrawing his offer. Both letters were delivered on December 2, 1853.

T. raised an action of implement against J.

Held that a binding contract had been formed.

LORD PRESIDENT (MCNEILL) (at p. 10): "I hold that a simple unconditional offer may be recalled at any time before acceptance, and that it may be so recalled by a letter transmitted by post; but I hold that the mere posting of a letter of recall does not make that letter effectual as a recall, so as from the moment of posting to prevent the completion of the contract by acceptance. An offer is nothing until it is communicated to the party to whom it is made, and who is to decide whether he will or will not accept the offer. In like manner, I think the recall or withdrawal of an offer that has been communicated can have no effect until the recall or withdrawal has been communicated, or may be assumed to have been communicated, to the party holding the offer. An offer, pure and unconditional, puts it in the power of the party to whom it is addressed to accept the offer, until by the lapse of a reasonable time he has lost the right, or until the party who has made the offer gives notice—that is, makes known that he withdraws it. The purpose of the recall is to prevent the party to whom the offer was made from acting upon the offer by accepting it. This necessarily implies precommunication to the party who is to be so prevented.

" . . . I hold that a letter of recall has no effect till the recall has become known to the offeree, or should in due course have become known to him. . . . When an offer is made by letter from a distance through the medium of the post, the offerer selecting that medium of transmission authorises and invites the offeree to communicate his acceptance through the same medium. If the offeree avails himself of that medium of communication, and transmits his acceptance properly addressed through the post-office, and if the acceptance reaches its destination in the due and regular course of that medium of transmission, I am of opinion that the act of acceptance was completed by the putting of the letter into the post-office; and that a letter of recall, which did not arrive till after that act, cannot be held to have interrupted the completion of the contract. . . . There may be extreme or extraordinary cases in which the offerer might not be bound by the fact that the letter of acceptance had been put into the post-office, as for instance, if the mail was totally lost, and the letter never reached its destination; and the offerer, after waiting a reasonable time, and believing that the offer had not been accepted, sold the goods or property in *bona fide* to another. . . . The general rule, as laid down in the case of *Higgins*, is, that the writing and posting of the acceptance completes the contract so as to make it obligatory."

NOTE

The case of *Higgins* referred to is *Dunlop* v. *Higgins* (1848) 6 Bell's App. 195.

Revocation of acceptance

Countess of Dunmore v. Alexander

(1830) 9 S. 190

The Countess of Dunmore who was looking for a new servant heard that Betty Alexander was to leave the service of Lady Agnew. The Countess wrote to Lady Agnew stating that the wages she gave were £12 12s. per annum and requesting information as to Betty's character. Lady Agnew replied that she could recommend Betty, who would gratefully accept the proposed wages. On November 5 the Countess engaged Betty by a letter addressed to Lady Agnew, but on the following day she addressed another letter to Lady Agnew stating that she no longer needed Betty.

Owing to Lady Agnew's absence from home, both the Countess's acceptance and her withdrawal of acceptance were notified to Betty at the same moment.

The Countess refused to take Betty as her servant, and Betty raised an action against her for wages and board-wages for the six months during which she was without a situation.

Held that there had been no completed contract and that Betty was therefore not entitled to the wages claimed.

LORD BALGRAY (at p. 193): "The admission that the two letters were simultaneously received puts an end to the case. Had the one arrived in the morning, and the other in the evening of the same day, it would have been different. Lady Dunmore conveys a request to Lady Agnew to engage Alexander, which request she recalls by a subsequent letter that arrives in time to be forwarded to Alexander as soon as the first. This, therefore, is just the same as if a man had put an order into the post office, desiring his agent to buy stock for him. He afterwards changes his mind, but cannot recover his letter from the post-office. He therefore writes a second letter countermanding the first. They both arrive together, and the result is, that no purchase can be made to bind the principal."

LORD GILLIES (at p. 194): "Lady Agnew received a letter desiring her to engage a servant for Lady Dunmore. She proceeds to take steps towards this by putting a letter into the post-office for the purpose of making the engagement. But, before this letter reaches its destination, her authority to hire the servant is recalled, and, by the help of an express, she forwards the recall, so that it is eventually delivered through the same post with the former letter, and both reach the servant at once. They thus neutralize each other, precisely as in the case put by Lord Balgray of an order and a countermand being sent through one post to an agent."

LORD CRAIGIE dissented on the ground that (at p. 194): "Lady Agnew was ... the mandatory for both parties, the mistress and the servant; she was on the same footing as a person in the well-known situation of broker for both buyer and seller. Every letter between the principals, relative to an offer or an acceptance respectively was, as soon as it reached Lady Agnew, the same as delivered for behoof of the party on whose account it was written. I hold, therefore, that when Lady Dunmore's letter reached Lady Agnew, the contract of hiring Alexander was complete—the offer on the part of Alexander being met by an intimated acceptance on the part of the Countess. No subsequent letter from the Countess to Lady Agnew could annul what had passed by the mere circumstance of its being delivered, at the same time with the first, into the hands of Alexander. I do not think the servant could have retracted after the first letter reached Lady Agnew; and if she was bound, it seems clear that the Countess could not be free."

NOTE

In *Thomson* v. *James* (p. 42, above) the Lord President described this case (at 18 D. p. 13) as "a very peculiar case," while Lord Deas stated (at 18 D. p. 25) that if the decision could be shown to be irreconcileable with the general doctrine that posting of the acceptance operated as an absolute completion of the contract he would be "disposed to abandon the decision, and to adhere to the doctrine."

Ticket: a voucher or a contractual document?

Taylor v. Glasgow Corporation

1952 S.C. 440

Mrs T. went to Woodside Public Baths, Glasgow, to take a hot bath. Having paid the price of 6d., she received a ticket which she was required to hand over to the bath attendant. On the front of the ticket were the words "For conditions see other side" and on the back the words "The Corporation of Glasgow are NOT responsible for any loss injury or damage sustained by persons entering or using this establishment or its equipment."

Mrs T. knew that there was printing on the ticket, but did not read the condition. She alleged that by the negligence of bath attendants she was allowed to fall down an interior stair and suffer serious injury.

She brought an action against the Corporation to recover damages.

Held that the ticket was merely a voucher which Mrs T. would not have been expected to study for conditions.

LORD JUSTICE-CLERK (THOMSON) (at p. 444): "In certain well-known types of case, in particular those relating to carriage and deposit, it is now settled that a reference to conditions, legibly printed on the face of the ticket, is sufficient notice of conditions. The person who buys a railway ticket or a cloakroom ticket is doing a thing which is now recognised by the public in general as entering into a contract which may contain special conditions. The real question is how far this now established rule is to be extended. . . .

". . . 'Tickets' may perform different functions. The ticket in the present case was a domestic check on the defenders' running of their establishment. . . . It also performed the function of a receipt. Further, as the defenders were affording a variety of services, some sort of voucher was necessary in order to ensure that the pursuer got what she paid for and only what she paid for. This latter was the significance of the 'ticket' which would strike the pursuer. . . . It was therefore a convenient, practical method, both from her point of view and the defenders', of passing her into the establishment and thereafter passing her on to the particular facility which she was to be afforded. My view of the evidence is that this voucher aspect of this 'ticket' was the significant aspect, and that, if the pursuer regarded it as a pass or voucher or as a receipt for sixpence which entitled her to be given a hot bath, she was entitled so to regard it. . . .

". . . The Sheriff was right to regard this 'ticket' as in substance a voucher. If so, the pursuer could not be reasonably expected to study it for conditions."

Ticket: condition on back

Henderson v. Stevenson

(1875) 2 R.(H.L.) 71; (1873) 1 R. 215

S. bought a ticket for a voyage on a steamer from Dublin to Whitehaven. On the back of the ticket was printed the following condition: "The company incur no liability whatever in respect of loss, injury, or delay to the passenger or to his or her luggage, whether arising from the act, neglect, or default of the company or their servants, or otherwise." S. did not read this condition, and did not have his attention directed to it by the clerk who issued the ticket.

The steamer was wrecked off the Isle of Man through the fault of the company's servants, and S. brought an action to recover damages for the loss of his luggage which he valued at £70.

Held that the condition had not been imported into the contract of carriage.

LORD CHANCELLOR (CAIRNS) (at p. 74): "The present case is a case in which there was no reference whatever upon the face of the ticket to anything other than that which was written upon the face. Upon that which was given to the passenger, and which he read, and of which he was aware, there was a contract complete and self-contained without reference to anything *de hors*. Those who were satisfied to hand to the passenger such a contract, complete upon the face of it, and to receive his money upon its being so handed to him, must be taken, as it seems to me, to have made that contract, and that contract only with the passenger, and the passenger on his part, receiving the ticket in that form, and without knowing of anything beyond, must be taken to have made a contract according to that which was expressed and shewn to him in that way.

"It seems to me that it would be extremely dangerous, not merely with regard to contracts of this description, but with regard to all contracts, if it were to be held that a document, complete upon the face of it, can be exhibited as between two contracting parties, and without any knowledge of anything besides, from the mere circumstance that upon the back of that document there is something else printed which has not actually been brought to and has not come to the notice of one of the contracting parties, that contracting party is to be held to have assented to that which he has not seen, of which he knows nothing, and which is not in any way ostensibly connected with that which is printed or written upon the face of the contract presented to him."

NOTES

1. Compare *Williamson* v. *The North of Scotland, &c., Navigation Co.*, 1916 S.C. 554, in which the condition had been printed on the face of the steamer ticket, but in the smallest type known. Lord Justice-Clerk (Scott Dickson) (at p. 561): "I think that the defenders have not made out that they did what was reasonably sufficient to give the pursuer notice of the conditions. They adopted a card the size of the familiar railway ticket with its very limited area as their basis, and this compelled them to adopt for printing the condition the smallest type known. ... Nothing ... was done to direct attention to the condition printed on the face of the ticket in small type, which for any passenger must have been difficult to read, and for many passengers impossible to read without artificial assistance and very favourable surroundings."

2. Contrast *Hood* v. *The Anchor Line* (*Hendersons Brothers*) *Ltd.*, 1918 S.C.(H.L.) 143; 1918 S.C. 27. Lord Chancellor (Finlay) (at p. 145): "In the present case the Lord Ordinary and the Second Division found that the Company had done what was reasonably sufficient to give the pursuer notice of the conditions. It appears to me that it is impossible to dissent from this conclusion. The contract was entered into on behalf of the appellant by Mr May as his agent, and the case must be dealt with just as if the appellant in person had done what Mr May did for him. The envelope in which the ticket was handed to Mr May had a conspicuous notice upon its front asking the passenger to read the conditions of the enclosed contract. The ticket itself had on its face a notice in conspicuous type that it was subject to the conditions, and at the foot was printed very plainly in

capital letters, 'Passengers are particularly requested to carefully read the above contract.' "

3. For a railway "pleasure party" ticket, see *Gray* v. *London and North Eastern Railway Co.*, 1930 S.C. 989. The ticket bore on the front, in legible print, "See Back," and on the back, also in legible print, "This ticket is issued subject to the General Notices, Regulations, and Conditions in the Company's current Time Tables and Bills." *Held* that this was reasonable notice.

Lord Justice-Clerk (Alness) (at p. 1001): "Time and again the Courts have held that incorporation of conditions in a railway ticket by reference, and indeed by reference to the company's time tables, is reasonable and sufficient."

4. Exemption clauses in contracts of carriage are now controlled by the Unfair Contract Terms Act 1977 as amended by the Law Reform (Miscellaneous Provisions) (Scotland) Act 1990 (see Appendix A). Even if adequate notice has been given, an attempt to exclude or restrict liability may now fail: by s. 16 (1) of the Act as amended a term or notice purporting to exclude or restrict liability for breach of duty arising in the course of any business is: (a) void if it relates to death or personal injury, or (b) of no effect in other cases unless its incorporation was fair and reasonable.

Incorporation of conditions: course of dealing

McCutcheon v. David MacBrayne Ltd.

1964 S.C.(H.L.) 28

McC., a farm grieve in Islay, when on a visit to the mainland, desired to have the use of his car, and accordingly asked his brother-in-law, McS., a farmer in Islay, to send it over. McS. delivered the car to the shipping company's office, paid the freight and received a receipt.

It was the company's normal practice to require persons shipping goods to sign a "risk note" which incorporated a condition excluding the company's liability for damage to or loss of the goods caused by negligence on the part of the company's servants, but on this occasion, owing to a mistake of the company's official, McS. was not asked to sign a risk note.

As a result of negligent navigation by the company's servants, the *Lochiel*, on which the car was shipped, struck a rock, and the car was submerged in the sea and became a total loss.

In an action by McC. against the company for the value of his car, the company contended that its liability was excluded by the previous course of dealing between itself and McC. in which risk notes had been signed. *Held* that any such course of dealing was irrelevant to the present oral contract.

LORD REID (at p. 33): "The contract was an oral one. No document was signed or changed hands until the contract was completed. . . . The terms of the receipt which was made out by the purser and handed to Mr McSporran after he paid the freight cannot be regarded as terms of the contract. So the case is not one of the familiar ticket cases where the question is whether conditions endorsed on, or referred to in, a ticket or other document handed to the consignor in making the contract are binding on the consignor."

LORD PEARCE (at p. 44): "The defenders rely on the course of dealing. But they are seeking to establish an oral contract by a course of dealing which always insisted on a written contract. It is the consistency of a course of conduct which gives rise to the implication that in similar circumstances a similar contractual result will follow. When the conduct is *not* consistent, there is no reason why it should still produce an invariable contractual result. The defenders, having previously offered a written contract, on this occasion offered an oral one. The pursuer's agent duly paid the freight for which he was asked and accepted the oral contract thus offered. This raises no implication that the conditions of the oral contract must be the same as the conditions of the written contract would have been had the defenders proffered one."

NOTE

In *Grayston Plant Ltd.* v. *Plean Precast Ltd.*, 1976 S.C. 206, G. Ltd., a hiring company, failed to show that a previous course of dealing was sufficient to incorporate conditions making the hirer liable for damage to a crane. On about 12 previous occasions over a period of four years, G. Ltd. had followed up an oral contract of hire with P. Ltd. by sending an acknowledgment of order form, referring to "General Conditions" of hire, a copy of which could be forwarded on request. No copy of the "General Conditions" had ever been sent by G. Ltd. or been asked for by P. Ltd. In written contracts of hire, G. Ltd. enclosed a copy of the "General Conditions," but there had never been a written contract with P. Ltd.

Lord Kissen (at p. 222): "The question in all such cases as the present is whether the party founding on a condition or on conditions in a written contract to modify an oral contract has given reasonable and sufficient notice that such condition or conditions would be implied in subsequent oral contracts....

"On any test, it seems to me that reasonable and sufficient notice has not been given in this case. It would have been very easy to send a copy of the Conditions with the Acknowledgment. Indeed, the pursuers, when they use a written Hire Contract (Offer) not only append the Conditions to it but also draw the intending hirer's attention in a separate notice to Clause 13, which is the Condition on which they found in this case. ... The pursuers must have appreciated the grave import of these Conditions, and, particularly Clause 13."

CHAPTER 3

FORMALITIES FOR CONSTITUTION AND PROOF

NOTE

The Scottish Law Commission in its *Report on Requirements of Writing* (Scot. Law Com. No. 112) has recommended substantial reform of the subject-matter of this chapter.

Obligationes literis: locus poenitentiae

Goldston v. Young

(1868) 7 M. 188

Y. wrote out an offer addressed to himself for the purchase of his shop by G. for £790. G. signed the offer.

Y. then wrote out and signed an acceptance of the offer.

There was no *rei interventus* on the faith of these missives.

G. raised an action for implement of the contract or alternatively for damages.

Held that since the offer was neither holograph of the offerer nor tested, either party was entitled to resile from the contract.

LORD PRESIDENT (INGLIS) (at p. 191): "The letter of acceptance is holograph of the defender, and is signed by him. The pursuer's offer is signed by him, but it is not holograph, the body of the writing being in the handwriting of the defender. . . .

". . . I am of opinion that it is not a good contract. . . . It may be that the defender is taking an undue advantage of the pursuer, but the law is quite settled that where there is not a tested writ or writs constituting the contract, or, failing them, holograph missives, there is *locus poenitentiae* to either of the parties, the subject of the contract being heritage.

". . . It must be kept in view that the contract is *in nudis finibus*,—there is no pretence of *rei interventus*,—and the case therefore depends on principles which have been long ago firmly established."

LORD ARDMILLAN (at p. 192): "We have to consider these documents *in nudis finibus*, for there is nothing of the nature of *rei interventus* or homologation in the case, which must therefore be decided simply on the effect of these documents. Now, the law is well established, and has long been so, that where there has been no *rei interventus*, and documents forming a mutual contract in regard to heritage are not both probative, neither party is bound, since both must be bound, or neither. . . . A writing in regard to heritage which is neither tested nor holograph leaves the obligation open; and if *locus poenitentiae* has not been excluded by *rei interventus*, or something equivalent thereto, the party who subscribes the document is entitled to resile."

LORD KINLOCH (at p. 193): "This being a contract about heritage, the want of a probative deed implies a want of completed agreement. There is no case here of an informal deed perfected *rei interventu*. It is clear that the offer here is not probative, not being written by the party who signs it, nor tested in accordance with the usual solemnities of law. The fact that the document is written by the other party, whatever other inferences that fact may give rise to, will not suffice to make the missive a probative instrument."

Obligationes literis: *proof of agreement restricted to writ or oath*

Walker v. Flint

(1863) 1 M. 417

W. alleged that in May 1860 he entered into an oral agreement with F. by which F. was to let to him certain premises for three years for the purpose of feeding pigs, part of the arrangement being that W. should erect piggeries, which were to remain on the land at the end of the lease.

W. further alleged that he entered into possession and began to erect the piggeries, and that F. frequently saw the progress of the work and remarked that the erections required to be substantial as they had to last for three years or more.

Held that the oral agreement, although followed by *rei interventus*, could not be proved by parole evidence.

LORD JUSTICE-CLERK (INGLIS) (at p. 421): "The leading principle is, that leases, like other heritable rights, can be constituted only by probative writing; and this rule admits of no exception while matters remain entire. But then, if things have been done by the tenant on the faith of the agreement, and in pursuance of it—that is to say, if the agreement is followed by *rei interventus*, there is a rule of law to this effect, that an improbative writing, combined with *rei interventus*, shall be sufficient. The operation of *rei interventus* is sometimes expressed as a bar to *locus poenitentiae*; but the practical effect is that it perfects the contract. ...

"... In what way may the verbal agreement alleged by the complainer be proved? ... It is very necessary to distinguish between the constitution and the mode of proof. The constitution here is ... alleged to have taken place by verbal agreement, followed by *rei interventus*. How is it to be proved? The *rei interventus* may be proved, of course, by parole evidence, and in general can be proved only in that way. But with regard to the verbal bargain, I think it is quite fixed that that can only be proved in one or other of two ways. The first mode is by writing. There is nothing anomalous in saying that a verbal bargain may be proved by writing; for there may be writing sufficient to prove, though not to constitute the agreement. The other mode is by oath."

NOTES

1. Compare *Allan* v. *Gilchrist* (1875) 2 R. 587: A. and his father averred that G. had orally agreed to purchase the stock in trade and goodwill of the baking business and the property of the shop, and that as a result of this oral contract A. had made arrangements for retiring from business. G. refused to implement the contract, and A. and his father raised an action of damages for breach of contract.

Held that, in so far as the contract related to heritage, it could not be proved by parole.

Lord Deas (at p. 589): "I take it to be quite clear that such a proof is altogether incompetent. To instruct a bargain about heritage there must be a probative writ, or the oath of the party. That has been repeatedly decided. It was so held, for instance, in *Walker* v. *Flint*. ... The previous case of *Gowans' Trustees* v. *Carstairs* ((1862) 24 D. 1382) ... was to the same effect."

Lord Ardmillan (at p. 593): "A contract for sale of heritable property cannot be proved by parole."

2. Contrast *Errol* v. *Walker*, below.

Obligationes literis: rei interventus *as proof of agreement*

Errol v. Walker

1966 S.C. 93

E. raised an action of declarator and removing against W. in relation to heritable property at Burghead.

In defence W. averred that he had purchased the property from E., having delivered a probative offer to E.'s solicitor, been put in possession of the property, paid instalments of the price in accordance with the offer, and to E.'s knowledge carried out extensive improvements.

W. admitted that he had received no written acceptance.

Held that W.'s averments, if proved, might be sufficient to imply acceptance, and that it was competent to prove these averments by parole evidence.

LORD STRACHAN (at p. 97): "Counsel for the defender had to surmount two main difficulties. The first of these is that *rei interventus* normally follows on a contract which has been completed, although informally, and its effect is to prevent a party from resiling during the *locus poenitentiae* which is consequent upon the informality of the contract. In this case the argument is that the *rei interventus* completed the contract where no previous contract existed. The second difficulty ... arises from the very well established rule that in cases of this type the constitution of the informal contract can be proved only by the writ or oath of the party who disputes the contract. ...

[Referring to observations in *Mitchell* v. *The Stornoway Trustees*, 1936 S.C.(H.L.) 56] "At page 63 Lord Macmillan, referring to the pleas of homologation and *rei interventus*, said: '... they are invoked not to create an agreement, for that can only be done by writing, but to exclude the right to resile from an informal agreement already in existence.' At page 66 with reference to the case of *Colquhoun* v. *Wilson's Trustees*, he said: '... I do not think that either homologation or *rei interventus* can properly be invoked to give efficacy to informal writings in which any of the essentials of a contract are lacking. There must, in my opinion, be *consensus in idem* as to the essentials of a contract before either of these doctrines can come into play.' ... Lord Macmillan's *dicta* no doubt describe the normal application of the plea of *rei interventus*, but it may be that he did not have in mind another type of case which is referred to by Professor Gloag in his book on contract in the following terms: '... the term *rei interventus* is also applied, though not so frequently, to the case where parties have been in negotiation for a contract, and one of them has acted, and been known and allowed to act, on the mistaken assumption that the negotiations had reached the point of a completed contract' (Gloag on *Contract*, 2nd ed., p. 46). Professor Gloag ... proceeded: '... When *rei interventus* is relied upon in cases where parties have not arrived at any agreement, verbal or written, the rule that actings may bind them to a contract is not an exception to the general rule that contract requires agreement. What is really meant is that the actings in question are evidence that agreement has been actually reached, though it has not been indicated in words or in other way than by the actings, ... they prove that an agreement was reached' (*ibid*. at pp. 46–47). As I see it there must in any event be *consensus in idem* as to the essentials of the contract. ... The difficulty is as to the means by which the existence of *consensus* is to be demonstrated. Lord Macmillan I think went too far in saying that an agreement (regarding heritage) can only be 'created' by writing, for there are cases in which agreements which were partly or wholly verbal have been held to be binding through *rei interventus*. Professor Gloag's statement that actings may be evidence that agreement has been reached is a very important point for the defender in this case. On that view the position would appear to be that while the actings of the defender could never by themselves be evidence of the pursuer's consent yet that consent may be *implied* from actings by or on behalf of the pursuer, and from his having known of and permitted actings by the defender. The question is whether Professor Gloag's statement is adequately supported by authority.

"With regard to the rule that a contract relating to heritage can be proved only by writ or oath it is sufficient to refer to *Walker* v. *Flint* ((1863) 1 M. 417); *Allan* v. *Gilchrist* ((1875) 2 R. 587); and *Dickson on Evidence* ((Grierson's ed.) par. 832). The rule is perfectly well settled. An informal obligation concerning heritage may be constituted verbally and may be binding if followed by *rei interventus*, but although such a contract may be constituted verbally it can be proved only by writ or oath. ... A point of some importance in this case, however, is that proof of *rei interventus* has never been so restricted. It is recognised that *rei interventus* may be proved by parole evidence. In the present case there is a probative writing by the defender, and the contention is that the contract was completed by *rei interventus*, that the actings of the parties are evidence that agreement has been reached. If that be sound in law, it seems to follow that proof of *rei interventus* will be proof of the completion of the contract, and in that event there would, in my opinion, be no reason to restrict the normal method by which *rei interventus* can competently be proved. Apart from that possible ground I see no warrant for relaxing the rule requiring proof by writ or oath of a contract relating to heritage.

[After reviewing the cases cited for the defender] "... The conclusion which I have reached upon a review of all the cases is that the decisions in *Colquhoun* v. *Wilson's Trustees* ((1860) 22 D. 1035), *Ballantine* v. *Stevenson* ((1881) 8 R. 959) and *Keir* v. *Duke of Atholl* ((1815) 6 Pat. App. 317), are authority for allowing an unrestricted proof in the present case. In view of those three decisions and the statement of the law by Professor Gloag, it is in my opinion necessary that the full facts averred should be investigated by parole evidence so that the law may thereafter be correctly applied."

NOTES

1. For *Mitchell* v. *The Stornoway Trustees* and *Colquhoun* v. *Wilson's Trustees*, see below, and for *Walker* v. *Flint* and *Allan* v. *Gilchrist*, see pp. 52–53, above.

2. This case has been criticised as being contrary to the principle that for *rei interventus* or homologation to operate, the parties must first have reached agreement (see David M. Walker, *The Law of Contracts and Related Obligations in Scotland*, 2nd ed., para 13.36). Subsequent Outer House cases, however, have given it some support.

In *Law* v. *Thomson*, 1978 S.C. 343 (O.H.), Lord Maxwell (Ordinary) held that homologation, unlike *rei interventus*, could not of itself create an agreement. In that case the seller of a hotel sought a declarator that there was a binding contract of sale which the purchaser had failed to implement. The purchaser had given no written acceptance of a condition in the seller's offer, but had obtained the keys of the hotel and had applied to the licensing court for a hotel certificate.

The seller contended that by these actings of the purchaser there was homologation which completed the contract between the parties.

The action was dismissed.

Lord Maxwell (at p. 347): "Counsel for the pursuers ... cited no authority for a case in which homologation has been held sufficient to create a contract or a term in a contract. In my opinion homologation in the form simply of actings on the part of one party not said to have had any effect on the other party cannot *per se* create an agreement between the two parties. I think there is a distinction between homologation of that kind and *rei interventus*. *Rei interventus* at least of the kind in *Errol* v. *Walker* involves in some sense a communing between two parties, in that the actings of one party are known to and permitted by the other and those actings are to the prejudice of the party acting. I am unable to see how actings by one party, which in no way impinge upon the other, can entitle the other party to maintain that the party acting had thereby committed himself to a condition in an agreement to which *ex hypothesi* he had not previously expressed agreement."

Law v. *Thomson* was followed by Lord Caplan (Ordinary) in *Rutterford Ltd.* v. *Allied Breweries Ltd.*, 1990 S.L.T. 249 (O.H.): Various negotiations for the sale of a shop in Greenock by A. Ltd. to R. Ltd. ended with an informal reply from A. Ltd. to R. Ltd. and the exchange of draft conveyancing documents. Later A. Ltd. denied that a contract had been concluded, and R. Ltd., in an action for implement of the sale, argued that a contract existed and that, if it was improbative, it had been validated by *rei interventus* and homologation.

Held that (1) *rei interventus* did not operate because the actings relied on were trivial and not sufficiently important and (2) homologation did not operate because there was no prior informal concluded contract in existence. R. Ltd.'s action was therefore dismissed.

Lord Caplan (at p. 253): "The defenders certainly did not formally and expressly accept any offer contained in the letter from the pursuers' solicitors of 11 January, so the question remains whether they perfected a contract by virtue of *rei interventus* or homologation. ...

"... As Lord Maxwell points out in *Law* v. *Thomson*, homologation cannot *per se* create an agreement but can only formalise a pre-existing agreement.

"The position, of course, is different in relation to *rei interventus*, and *Errol* v. *Walker* established that not only can an informal agreement be perfected by *rei interventus* but that *rei interventus* can provide consent to an agreement where an element of consent would otherwise be lacking. ... I think that, if the pursuers could prove that the acts in question amount to *rei interventus*, they would have a valid case. The defenders must be taken to have known of and permitted the preparation by the pursuers of a draft disposition and the relevant conveyancing forms because, in effect, they invited the pursuers to prepare these documents. However, I am not satisfied that what the pursuers claim to have done could ever amount to a change of position sufficiently substantial to be regarded as *rei interventus*."

Obligationes literis: an instance of rei interventus

Colquhoun v. Wilson's Trustees

(1860) 22 D. 1035

W. made a written offer to C. to take a feu of subjects owned by C. and part of which W. held on an unexpired lease.

B., C.'s factor, gave a written acceptance subject to certain conditions.

There was no written agreement or repudiation by W. of these conditions, but W. proceeded to make extensive alterations on the subjects.

W. died suddenly before a feu-contract had been executed.

Held that as W.'s alterations could be ascribed only to a completed contract of feu, they had the effect of making the conditional contract binding on both parties, and that W.'s representatives were therefore bound to enter into a feu-contract.

LORD JUSTICE-CLERK (INGLIS) (at p. 1048): "We have thus an offer by Mr Wilson, upon certain definite terms . . . and we have an acceptance by Mr Boog, but unquestionably an acceptance under conditions. . . . Now that contract, as it stands, was, no doubt, an incomplete contract, because the conditions stipulated by Mr Boog on behalf of Sir James Colquhoun were not assented to in writing by Mr Wilson. And therefore the offer and acceptance not meeting one another, the acceptance not being pure, but *sub modo*, the contract was incomplete until there should be, on the part of Mr Wilson, an assent to the conditions stipulated by Mr Boog, or a departure from those conditions on the part of Mr Boog. Nothing of the kind ever was done in writing, either by Mr Wilson on the one hand, or by Mr Boog on the other. And therefore, on the face of the writings alone, there is unquestionably an incomplete contract. . . . It is incompetent to prove, as part of a contract of this kind, directly by parole evidence, that one of the parties assented or agreed to any one of the conditions of the contract. . . . We thus have . . . the writings standing in the shape of an offer and acceptance, with no written assent to the conditions in the acceptance by the offerer. But then it is a well-known principle of our law, that such a conditional acceptance may be made pure, and the contract, incomplete in itself, may be made effectually binding upon both parties *rei interventu*; and I think the application of legal principle to this case is not attended with any difficulty. The only question is, whether the *rei interventus* was such as can reasonably be ascribed only to the relations created by what the parties intended and considered to be a completed contract of sale? If it be ascribable reasonably and intelligibly to anything else, then it will not validate this conditional acceptance, so as to purify the conditions, and make the contract complete. But, if it be such *rei interventus* as is irreconcilable with any thing else than the completed relation of buyer and seller, with the constitution in the buyer of the full and complete character of proprietor upon a personal title, then it will purify the conditions, and make the contract complete. . . . It seems to me, that what is proved to have been done by Mr Wilson is unintelligible, except upon the footing that he understood that he had already acquired the full rights of proprietor of the subject. And I think it is equally unintelligible that Sir James Colquhoun should have permitted and acquiesced in the proceedings of Mr Wilson, except upon the footing and understanding that he had parted with the estate formally and finally, and that Mr Wilson, and Mr Wilson alone, was thereafter the proprietor. . . . The formation of roads, the pulling down of one garden wall (a valuable one apparently), and the erection of another, and various other operations of that kind, are, it is needless to say, such as no tenant could possibly have taken upon himself to execute, without the permission of the landlord, or some arrangement with the landlord. But without any other permission or title of any kind, except the letters . . . , Mr Wilson does proceed to perform certain acts which are as unequivocally acts of ownership as anything that could well be brought forward. And therefore I think, upon the evidence before us, that the acts of ownership thus performed by Mr Wilson—the extensive operations which he carried through, and was in the course of carrying through at the time of his death on these subjects—do constitute such *rei interventus* as to import that he assented to the conditions contained and referred to in Mr Boog's letter . . . , and that the other party, Sir James Colquhoun, relied upon his having done so. And therefore it appears to me that, by that *rei interventus*, the contract, which was originally conditional and incomplete, became unconditional and complete."

LORD COWAN (at p. 1051): "The letters . . . contain all the *essentialia* of a feu-contract, and followed, as they were, by *rei interventus*, constitute a concluded agreement binding on both parties."

NOTES

1. This case, and in particular Lord Cowan's view, were commented on by Lord Macmillan in *Mitchell* v. *The Stornoway Trustees* (see below).

2. Comments were also made on the case by all three judges in *Errol* v. *Walker* (see p. 54, above): Lord Strachan, agreeing with Gloag's analysis (2nd ed., p. 47), regarded it (at 1966 S.C. p. 100) as "an example of the

category of case where actings amounting to *rei interventus* may bind parties to a contract even where they had not previously arrived at any agreement"; similarly Lord Walker viewed it (at p. 104) "as being one in which it is sought to prove acceptance of a written offer by actings"; Lord Justice-Clerk Grant, however, described it (at p. 106) as a "somewhat dubious case," and thought that it decided merely that since the essentials to the bargain had been set forth in documents, and only some minor conditions remained unadjusted, *locus poenitentiae* had gone, and that there was therefore a concluded contract.

Obligationes literis: *an instance of homologation*

Mitchell v. The Stornoway Trustees

1936 S.C.(H.L.) 56; 1935 S.C. 558

The Stornoway trustees agreed to grant to M. a feu of a triangular piece of ground on which M. was to erect a public garage.

On February 13, M.'s building plans were approved in improbative writing by the trustees, and handed to M. in order that he might attach them to the petition for a lining which he presented to the Dean of Guild Court.

At the proceedings in the Dean of Guild Court the factor of the trustees gave assistance to the burgh surveyor in explaining the details of the building plans, but before the conclusion of these proceedings the trustees withdrew their grant of the feu.

M. brought an action against the trustees to have them ordained to execute a feu-contract.

Held that the trustees were not entitled to resile since their actings and those of their factor in facilitating the proceedings in the Dean of Guild Court homologated the improbative agreement concluded on February 13. (A majority of three out of five held that there had also been *rei interventus*.)

(While this was an affirmation of the judgment of the majority of the Second Division, the Lord Justice-Clerk (Aitchison)'s ground of judgment that the docqueting on February 13 not only constituted but also homologated the agreement was disapproved, since homologation can be effected only by acts occurring after the conclusion of a contract, and Lord Hunter's ground of judgment that the actings of the trustees and their factor before and on February 13 homologated a contract informally entered into on February 1 was disapproved since no contract had been entered into before February 13.)

LORD MACMILLAN (at p. 63): "Although there was admittedly an agreement in writing between the parties on 13th February, that agreement was formally defective inasmuch as it was not embodied in a probative deed or in holograph documents, a solemnity required by the law of Scotland in the case of all obligations relating to land. From such an informal agreement it is open to either party to resile; either party may avail himself of the *locus poenitentiae* which the law in such circumstances allows. But a party desiring to resile may find himself precluded from doing so by what has occurred since the agreement was made. He may have lost his *locus poenitentiae* by reason either of *rei interventus* or of homologation. These are both personal exceptions which on equitable grounds the law permits to be pleaded in answer to the party seeking to disown his contract on the ground of its informality. I may add that the facts requisite to support either of these pleas may be proved *prout de jure*; they are invoked not to create an agreement, for that can only be done by writing, but to exclude the right to resile from an informal written agreement already in existence.

"In the words of Professor Bell, which have now classical authority and have been expressly approved in this House, *rei interventus* 'is inferred from any proceedings not unimportant on the part of the obligee, known to and permitted by the obligor to take place on the faith of the contract as if it were perfect; provided they are unequivocally referable to the agreement and productive of alteration of circumstances, loss or inconvenience, though not irretrievable.' (Bell's Prin., sec. 26). In the language of the same learned author, 'homologation (in principle similar to *rei interventus*) is an act approbatory of a preceding engagement, which in itself is defective or informal, either confirming or adopting it as binding. It may be express, or inferred from circumstances. It must be absolute, and not compulsory, nor proceeding on error or fraud, and unequivocally referable to the engagement; and must imply assent to it, with full knowledge of its extent, and of all the relative interests of the homologator.'—(*Ibid.*, sec. 27). Thus the party who seeks to enforce an informal contract against the party who seeks to disown it may found upon his own actings on the faith of the contract, if these actings have been known to and permitted by the other party, in which case he invokes the doctrine of *rei interventus*; or he may found upon the actings of the party seeking to disown the contract as being actings which imply confirmation of the contract, in which case he invokes the doctrine of homologation. It is obvious that, as Professor Bell says, the principles underlying both doctrines are similar. Thus, knowingly to permit acts to be done by an obligee on the faith of an informal contract may conceivably in some circumstances be reckoned as conduct on the part of the obligor implying his homologation of it; while the same acts, looked at from another point of view, may amount in law to *rei interventus*. The essence of the matter is the occurrence, subsequent to the informal agreement, of acts on the part of either party which would render it inequitable to hold that there was still a *locus poenitentiae* ...

"... It is of the essence of the doctrine of homologation that the homologation must be 'approbatory of a preceding engagement.'....

"In my opinion the only actings of the parties which can be invoked by the respondent in support either of his plea of *rei interventus* or of his plea of homologation are those which relate to the proceedings in the Stornoway Dean of Guild Court.... The appellants were ... not only fully cognisant that the respondent was proceeding with his application to the Dean of Guild Court as owner of the ground, but through their factor assisted in satisfying the burgh surveyor with regard to the building plans. All this, on a fair view of the situation, was inconsistent with the reservation by the appellants of any *locus poenitentiae*.... On 24th February the appellants ... instructed their factor 'to withdraw the grant of the feu made to Mr Mitchell.'

"In my opinion, this attempt by the appellants to disown their agreement came too late. Their conduct between the 13th and the 24th of February was that of parties consenting to the respondent's proceedings in the Dean of Guild Court.... I have come to the conclusion that, by their own conduct and that of their duly authorised factor in relation to these proceedings, the appellants implied their approbation of their preceding engagement and thereby homologated it.

"But I should also be prepared to hold, if necessary, that the respondent's actings in relation to his application to the Dean of Guild Court were in the circumstances sufficient to found a valid plea of *rei interventus*. They were actings 'in the proper pursuance of the agreement and which the other party to the agreement would naturally expect should take place in pursuance of it'—*Gardner* v. *Lucas* ((1878) 5 R. 638), *per* Lord Shand at p. 656.... Both parties attached very considerable importance to the Dean of Guild Court proceedings. In my opinion, they satisfy the not very exacting standard of being 'not unimportant.' ...

"In conclusion, I only wish to add, with regard to the case of *Colquhoun* v. *Wilson's Trustees*, . . . that I do not think that either homologation or *rei interventus* can properly be invoked to give efficacy to informal writings in which any of the essentials of a contract are lacking. There must, in my opinion, be *consensus in idem* as to the essentials of a contract before either of these doctrines can come into play. If *Colquhoun's* case is authority to the contrary, then I desire to reserve my opinion as to its soundness. I observe that, at least in Lord Cowan's view, the parties were in agreement on all the essentials of a feu."

NOTES

1. For *Colquhoun* v. *Wilson's Trustees*, see p. 58, above.
2. See also *Errol* v. *Walker* (p. 54, above).

Obligationes literis: *writ* in re mercatoria

B.O.C.M. Silcock Ltd. v. Hunter

1976 S.L.T. 217

H., the individual principally interested in the company H. (Grain Merchant) Ltd., gave a guarantee to B. Ltd., that he would be personally responsible for payment of sums due to B. Ltd. for animal feedstuffs supplied on credit by B. Ltd. to H. (Grain Merchant) Ltd. The guarantee was contained in a document which had been signed by H. in the presence of one witness.

H. (Grain Merchant) Ltd. failed to pay for feedstuffs to the value of £45,198.91 supplied to it by B. Ltd.

B. Ltd. called upon H. to pay that sum under the guarantee, but H. contended that the guarantee was not binding upon him as it was neither probative nor holograph.

Held that, since the guarantee was a writ *in re mercatoria*, it was binding on H. in spite of its informality.

Opinion of the First Division (LORD PRESIDENT (EMSLIE), LORDS KISSEN and AVONSIDE) (at p. 224): "The defence to the action and the sole justification of the defender's refusal to make payment to the pursuers is the proposition that the document, in terms a comprehensible and ample guarantee, is not binding upon the defender in respect that it is neither holograph nor tested. The pursuers' riposte is that if in general the law of

Scotland requires that a binding guarantee must be holograph or otherwise probative, this guarantee, being a writing *in re mercatoria*, is valid although neither holograph nor formally executed and in any event the informality of its execution has been cured by *rei interventus*. . . .

". . . Counsel for the defender recognised . . . that guarantees are within the class of writings comprehended under the privilege accorded to writings *in re mercatoria*. As the matter is put in Bell's *Commentaries*, vol. 1, p. 342—long accepted as a general canon—'The writings which are held to be comprehended under this privilege, are bills, notes and checks on bankers; orders for goods; mandates and procurations; guarantees; offers and acceptances to sell, or to buy wares and merchandise, or to transport them from place to place; and, in general, all the variety of engagements, or mandates, or acknowledgments, which the infinite occasions of trade may require.' His argument was, however, that not all guarantees satisfy the description of writings *in re mercatoria*. Guarantees granted by a third party to a banker in respect of cash advances to a customer are not so regarded (see *Johnston* v. *Grant* (1844) 6 D. 875). Before a guarantee will be held to qualify as a writing *in re mercatoria* it must be granted in a course of dealing between merchants. Further, before a guarantee will be held to qualify as a writing *in re mercatoria*, it must not only be granted in a course of dealing between merchants but be seen from all the circumstances which surrounded its origin to be an informal writing of the kind which merits its treatment as a mercantile writing. . . . In this case, bearing in mind that it is already clear that the defender was merely in law a third party so far as the transactions between the pursuers and the company were concerned and that the document itself is suggestive of an intention to engage in a formally executed deed, it was argued that it is necessary for the court to reserve judgment on its possible character as a writing *in re mercatoria* until after proof of the circumstances surrounding its granting.

"In our opinion the argument for the defender is without substance. Both the sheriff and the sheriff principal were plainly right in holding that the guarantee of 5 March 1973 was a writing *in re mercatoria*. Our law favours a wide interpretation of the words '*in re mercatoria*.' . . . The guarantee of 5 March 1973 is inextricably associated with, and was an integral part of an admittedly mercantile transaction between merchants and in the absence of authority, and there is none, we regard it as of no significance that the grantor, the defender, was in strict law a third party to the transaction between the pursuers and the company. In any event it may be regarded as well-settled that a guarantee granted by a third party for the express purpose of securing future supplies of goods on credit to a purchaser is a writing *in re mercatoria* (*vide Paterson* v. *Wright*, 31 Jan. 1810, 15 F.C. and the opinion of Lord Glenlee in *Thomson* v. *Gilkison* (1831) 9 S. 520 at p. 522). The proposition has not been questioned for upwards of 150 years and is manifestly so unimpeachable that this is not surprising. That the writing is in formal and precise terms and is signed in the presence of a witness is nothing to the point. . . . It is plain as plain can be from the document itself that the parties did not intend it to be executed in any different way, and certainly did not intend it to be executed as a probative cautionary obligation according to the law of Scotland.

" . . . From the admitted facts in the pleadings of the parties it is inconceivable that the supplies delivered to the company after 5 March 1973 would have been delivered but for the guarantee. Indeed the only inference possible upon the admitted facts is that supply continued after 5 March 1973 on the faith of the guarantee. In these circumstances upon the pleadings alone the fifth plea-in-law for the pursuers ought also to have been sustained."

NOTES

The fifth plea-in-law referred to was to the effect that the improbative nature of the guarantee had been purified by *rei interventus*.

Writ required for proof need not be holograph or tested

Paterson v. Paterson

(1897) 25 R. 144

Mrs P. lent a sum of money to her son John, and John signed a receipt for the amount. John died before he had repaid any of the loan, and Mrs P. brought an action against John's representatives, concluding for payment of £450.

Held that for the proof of the loan the writ did not require to be holograph or tested.

(The decision was by a majority of the whole court (13 judges), *diss.* Lords Young and Adam.)

LORD TRAYNER (at p. 163): "The rule of our law at present is that loan can only be established by the writ or oath of the borrower. There is no question about that. . . . The question is, What kind of writ is necessary to establish loan? and to this question two answers are offered. One is, that the writ to prove a loan must be either holograph or tested, that is, a probative writ; the other is, that any writing which is actually or can constructively be held to be the writ of the debtor will be sufficient. The latter of these answers expresses the view which I hold.

"The rule which limits the proof of loan to the writ or oath of the borrower is not statutory, it is a rule of the common law. ...

"... There is no direct authority in a pure case of the proof of loan (that I have been able to find) in which it is laid down that such proof must be afforded by a probative writ; and there are *dicta* and decisions which, in principle, are to a contrary effect. ... It is a striking fact that if proof by writ of loan must be proof by probative writ, it is the only instance in our law where, proof by writ being necessary, that writ is required to be probative. ... I think our law does not, and never did, require such proof of loan, but that any writ, either actually or constructively the writ of the borrower, is admissible and competent evidence of loan.

"... The question before us is not ruled by authority—... it is still an open question. ... How, on principle and analogy, should the question be determined? I think there can be but one answer to that question. We are quite familiar with the restriction of proof to writ or oath. But in every case to which that restriction is applicable (as in trust, or debts which have undergone the triennial prescription, &c.), the writ necessary as proof need not be probative. I see no reason for making loan the sole case provable by writ or oath where the writ must be probative."

LORD MONCREIFF (at p. 168): "I am of opinion, though with some hesitation, that it is not essential to the proof of loan that the writ or writs founded on *in modum probationis* should be probative. According to our law, loan does not require writing for its constitution, but it can only be proved by writ or oath of the borrower. Now, where either by law or agreement of the parties obligations or rights require writing for their constitution, the writing must be executed according to the solemnities prescribed by the statutes; and in the absence of *rei interventus* or homologation, defects in execution cannot be remedied by the oath of the party; there is *locus poenitentiae*. ...

"On the other hand, where an obligation or right does not require writing for its constitution, and may be proved by writ or oath of party, the general rule is that the writ produced in evidence need not be probative.

"The distinction between these two cases is clear and well recognised, and the fact that loan belongs to the latter category goes very far to solve the present question. Once it is admitted that loan may be proved 'by writ or oath,' we are entitled to inquire what is the meaning of those words when used in regard to other obligations, and when we find that in every other case where proof 'by writ or oath' is competent it is not necessary, in order to satisfy the rule, that the writ or writs founded on shall be holograph or tested, it is legitimate to conclude that loan may be proved in the same way. The strongest example is proof of a verbal lease for years where *rei interventus* has followed. The lease must be proved by writ, but even in that case, which affects heritage, the writ may be of the most informal kind. Any writing, however informal, which can be held to be actually or even constructively the writ of the person sought to be bound, is competent evidence."

LORD KYLLACHY (at p. 172): "Now, the question is, Whether this is a kind of writing to which the old Scottish statutes regulating the authentication of writs apply? ...

"... The category to which the statutes apply would, I think, strike most lawyers as a quite well-known category; that, viz., of written obligations—obligations expressed in writing—the *obligationes literis* of the Roman law. Such written obligations, the statutes declare, shall, unless completed with the prescribed solemnities, be *pro non scripto*. ... But as regards writings or parts of writings which do not express obligations, but merely record facts, the statutes as I read them are silent. The facts recorded may be of importance; they may include express verbal agreements, or facts and circumstances inferring agreements; and they may thus or otherwise involve obligations—obligations arising *ex contractu* or *ex delicto*. But such writings are not written contracts or written obligations. ... They are only pieces of evidence. And accordingly they are, in my judgment, outside the category to which the statutes apply. The distinction thus taken is not a new one. ... It corresponds with the distinction between writings which constitute obligations and writings which merely prove or help to prove them. ...

"... It may, I think, be safely affirmed that there is no other instance in which—the alternative of oath being admitted—a writ (not being itself a written obligation) has been rejected as evidence because improbative. Of course where writ is necessary for constitution, the alternative of oath does not exist."

LORD MCLAREN (at p. 190): "It is common ground that loan of money is not an ordinary consensual contract, and that an alleged loan cannot be proved against the debtor by evidence *prout de jure*. The first question then is, whether writing is necessary to the constitution of a loan, or whether the true principle is that writing under the hand of the debtor is necessary to the proof of loan.

"I do not know that any Court or writer of authority has laid down that the loan of money, like the sale of land, can only be constituted by writing. . . .

". . . It is of course perfectly settled in the law of Scotland that a writing under the debtor's hand, if not necessary to the constitution of the right, is at least necessary to the proof of the contract of loan. In other words, the proof of loan is limited to proof by writ. . . . In every other region of law in which there is a limitation of proof to the writ of the party, the rule is held to be satisfied by the production of a writing signed by the party charged. . . . If then the law requires holograph or tested writ in the case of proof of loan, it would seem that the law is very exceptional in its treatment of claims arising on contracts of loan,—that the law in effect puts obstacles in the way of creditors who are asking back their money which have not been thought necessary or expedient in other cases of proof restricted to writ.

". . . I am not prepared to admit such an exception to the ordinary rules of proof by writ, which undoubtedly include signed letters although neither holograph nor tested, and even entries in account-books kept by the party who is charged with the debt. . . .

"In the view I take of the case, no question arises upon the statutes regulating the authentication of deeds; because the statutes presuppose a deed which either constitutes, transfers, or discharges a right, and do not apply to writings which are only put forward in evidence of a right."

Innominate and unusual contracts

Edmondston v. Edmondston

(1861) 23 D. 995

L.E. averred that an agreement had been entered into between himself and his eldest brother T.E., whereby L.E. would give up his mercantile career, qualify in medicine and then reside permanently with or near T.E. on the island of Unst, while T.E. would leave all his property to L.E.

L.E. implemented his part of the agreement, but on T.E.'s death his will was found to be not in accordance with the agreement.

Held that the agreement, since it fell within the category of innominate and unusual contracts, could not be proved by parole or validated by *rei interventus*.

LORD BENHOLME (at p. 1001): "It is clearly the law of Scotland, not only in regard to heritage, but also in regard to moveables, that innominate contracts, especially such as are of an unusual character, cannot be constituted verbally, or proved by witnesses.

"Nor does it alter the rule that *rei interventus* upon such verbal and innominate contracts is alleged. For the uncertainty as to the terms of an innominate verbal contract renders it impossible to determine what acts can be considered as constituting a partial performance, or *rei interventus* following upon it. ...

"That this is an innominate contract, and one of an unusual kind, cannot be denied. ...

"... The death of the pursuer's brother, who is alleged to have been one of the parties to the contract, puts oath of party out of the question. The pursuer does not propose to prove his contract by any contemporaneous writing. He seemed rather inclined to rest the constitution of the contract, if not purely on parole evidence, on that only, with the aid of inference derived from subsequent correspondence and actings of the parties.

"Such a course of procedure ... involves a hazardous confounding of the alleged *rei interventus* with the terms of the agreement which these actings are said to validate, whereas the former ought to stand, in point of constitution, clear and independent of the latter."

NOTES

1. For another instance of an innominate and unusual contract, see *Garden* v. *Earl of Aberdeen* (1893) 20 R. 896, an action by a tenant against his landlord for loss sustained by the tenant during a 19-years' lease of a farm.

The tenant averred that at a meeting a year before the ish of the lease the landlord had said that if the tenant would remain in the farm to the end of the lease and meantime pay the rent he would at the end of the lease make up to the tenant the loss which he had already sustained and might sustain by his tenancy. The tenant further averred that he had accepted the landlord's proposal by letter.

Held that as this was "an innominate contract of an unusual kind" (*per* Lord Trayner at p. 899), it could be proved only by the defender's writ or oath.

Similarly, in *McCourt* v. *McCourt*, 1985 S.L.T. 335, an alleged agreement between a husband and wife that the wife would transfer her cab-operator's licence to her husband on demand was held to be "not only innominate, but also unusual, anomalous and peculiar, bearing in mind, amongst other factors, that a cab-operator's licence is personal in its nature and of limited duration, and also incapable of transference in any legal sense of the term" (per Lord Hunter at p. 337).

2. Contracts which are innominate but not unusual do not fall into this category. *Forbes* v. *Caird* (1877) 4 R. 1141: C. ran a horse-drawn omnibus daily from Cullen to Portsoy and back, and stabled his horses at F.'s inn in Portsoy. F. brought an action against C. for payment of an account for stabling the horses, and C. averred that it had been agreed that he was to have stable accommodation free of charge in consideration of the omnibus's going to F.'s inn after calling at the Portsoy railway station.

Held that the alleged contract, though innominate, was not of an unusual or anomalous nature, and so could be proved *prout de jure*.

Lord Deas (at p. 1142): "There is no such rule as that no innominate contract can be proved except by writ or oath. But it may be stated to be a rule that a contract of an unusual or anomalous nature can be proved only by writ or oath. For instance, it is so unusual and out of the ordinary course of business for a law agent to work for nothing that a contract to do so will only be allowed to be proved by his writ or oath. But I see nothing to come up to a case of that kind here. It was an important object for the pursuer to have the passengers by the coach brought as customers to his hotel, and there was nothing remarkable or anomalous in the arrangement averred by the defender to have been made."

Forbes v. *Caird* was referred to by Lord President Kinross in *Allison* v. *Allison's Trustees* (1904) 6 F. 496 at p. 500, a case in which a contract which was a combination of partnership and service was held, though innominate, to be not of such an "extraordinary character" that proof was restricted to writ or oath.

Another case illustrating the same point is *Smith* v. *Reekie*, 1920 S.C. 188: S., a fisherman of St. Monance, brought an action against the owners of the steam-drifter *Janet Reekie* for payment of £59 1s., alleging that they had agreed to pay to him a bonus of 1s. a day in consideration of his serving with the crew of the drifter while it was engaged on Admiralty service.

Held that proof was not restricted to writ or oath.

Lord President (Strathclyde) (at p. 192): "It is not enough to exclude parole proof that the contract is innominate; you must further say that it is unusual, anomalous, and peculiar in its terms."

CHAPTER 4

GROUNDS OF INVALIDITY

NOTE

Persons under the age of majority, which was reduced from 21 years to 18 years by the Age of Majority (Scotland) Act 1969, could under the common law challenge within the *quadriennium utile* contracts entered into during minority if enorm lesion could be proved.

The contractual capacity of young persons is now governed by the Age of Legal Capacity (Scotland) Act 1991 (see Appendix A).

Insanity

John Loudon & Co. v. Elder's Curator Bonis

1923 S.L.T. 226 (O.H.)

On March 23 and 28, E., a wholesale merchant in Dundee, ordered goods from L. & Co., a firm of produce agents in Liverpool. On March 31, before any of the goods had been delivered, E. was certified insane, and on April 1, L. & Co. were informed that the contracts must be cancelled.

L. & Co. sued E.'s *curator bonis* for £6,897 7s. 9d. as damages for breach of contract.

E. was proved to have been insane at the time when the orders were given.

Held that the orders were null and void, and that there was therefore no liability for breach of contract.

LORD BLACKBURN (Ordinary) (at p. 227): "The defence to the action is that Magnus Elder was insane at the date of giving the orders and incapable of contracting and that consequently the contracts were null and void. . . .

". . . It is, I think, now beyond question that in Scotland the effect to be given to a contract entered into by an insane person depends upon whether the insane person is at the time when the contract is entered into of mind and capacity to understand and transact the business in question. If so the contract is binding, and if not it is null and void. . . .

"Accordingly, in my judgment, the only question to be decided in this

case is one of fact, namely, what was the mental condition of Magnus
Elder on the dates when the orders were given. ...

[After dealing with the facts disclosed at the proof] "I have accordingly
reached the conclusion without any doubt that at the dates when the two
contracts in question were entered into Magnus Elder must be assumed to
have been quite insane and not of a mind and capacity to understand the
effect of the orders which he was giving. It follows that in my view of the
law the contracts sued upon are null and void and that it is unnecessary for
me to deal with the evidence led by the pursuers on the amount of the
damages they have sustained."

NOTE

The Lord Ordinary referred to *Gall* v. *Bird* (1855) 17 D. 1027, a case
which shows that homologation is not possible where a contract is void
from insanity, whereas it is possible where a contract is voidable on account of facility and circumvention.

Intoxication

Taylor v. Provan

(1864) 2 M. 1226

In the course of a day P. visited T.'s farm and offered to purchase 31 cattle
at £13 10s., £13 15s. and finally at £14 per head, but T. refused to sell as
less than £15.

P. then tried to purchase cattle from two other parties, but was
unsuccessful.

In the evening of the same day P., when the worse of drink, returned to
T. and offered £15 per head. T. accepted the offer.

In an action by T. for the price of £465, P. put forward the defence that
he had been perfectly incapable, from intoxication, of entering into the
contract.

Held that as there was no evidence to show that P. had been totally
incapacitated by intoxication from entering into the contract, the contract
was valid.

LORD JUSTICE-CLERK (INGLIS) (at p. 1232): "The issue between the
parties is not, whether the defender was under the influence of liquor, or
whether he was in such a condition that it would be better for him not to
enter upon business at that time, but whether he was perfectly incapable,

from intoxication, of entering into business transactions, and completing such as he had begun. ... It is impossible to say he was in a state of incapacity from drink. He was in such a condition from drink that he had not all his wits about him; and if that were a sufficient ground for annulling a bargain, I fear we would have plenty of reductions. But something more is required to annul a contract on the ground of incapacity. Now, having read over this evidence, I do not find a single witness who states anything approaching to this,—that the defender was in a total state of incapacity to know what he was about. ...

"The law applicable to the case is clear. Stair says (i, 10, 13),—'Those also who, through fear, or drunkenness, or disease, have not for a time the use of reason, do not legally contract.' Now, I apprehend that the defender must bring himself within this proposition. He must prove that through drink he had not the use of his reason before we can say he has made out his defence."

LORD COWAN (at p. 1232): "Mr Erskine states the law to the same effect. He says,—'Persons while in a state of absolute drunkenness, and consequently deprived of the exercise of reason, cannot oblige themselves; but a lesser degree of drunkenness, which only darkens reason, has not the effect of annulling the contract.'—Ersk. b.i., t.1, sec.16. And Professor Bell gives the same view of the law. ... The question, therefore, is, was the pursuer so drunk as to have been deprived of understanding, and to have been incapable of consent? ...

"Now, in this case ... there is no proof of any such absolute deprivation of understanding as to have rendered the man incapable of consent."

LORD NEAVES (at p. 1234): "The defender states, and his defence could be nothing else, that by reason of intoxication he was incapable of consenting at the time of this contract. Now, intoxication may produce two results,—the one, inability to consent, the other, somewhat of that facility which is of such common occurrence in bargains made after dinner or after liquor. This last condition of mind, if it be followed by fraud, may be a ground, not for holding a contract null, but for reducing it, when it has been followed by lesion. But there is nothing of that kind alleged here. ... If the pursuer had got a greater price from the defender than we was willing to take in the morning, that might have been suspicious. But he does nothing of that sort. He adheres to his former terms. ... On the whole, I have no doubt that the defender has failed to prove the defence that he stated."

NOTES

1. *Pollok* v. *Burns* (1875) 2 R. 497 was a case in which P., described as a "habitual drunkard," was held not entitled to suspend a charge upon a bill. Not only did P. not satisfy the test of incapacity, but he had failed to challenge the bill until six months after it had become due.

Lord Justice-Clerk (Moncreiff) (at p. 503): "Where the plea of intoxication is taken by the person who says he was intoxicated and incapable when he did the act which he wishes to repudiate, he is bound, the moment his sober senses return and he knows what he has done, to take his ground at once. That is essential."

This statement taken by itself would make the contract voidable and not void. The view of the institutional writers referred to in *Taylor* v. *Provan* is to the effect that absence of reason caused by intoxication makes a contract void. See William W. McBryde, *The Law of Contract in Scotland*, p. 145 *et seq.*

2. In *Laing* v. *Taylor*, 1978 S.L.T. (Sh. Ct.) 59, L. sued for payment of a cheque which had been signed by T., when, as T. averred, he was "so drunk ... that his judgment was seriously impaired."

Held, according to Stair and *Taylor* v. *Provan*, that loss of reason was necessary before a contract could be set aside for drunkenness, and that, as there were no such averments in this case, T.'s defence was irrelevant.

Defective expression: patent defect: contract construed by court

Jamieson v. McInnes

(1887) 15 R. 17

McI., desiring to build a tenement, sent out schedules giving the estimated quantities of work required, with a view to tradesmen returning offers.

J. returned one of the schedules for the digger, mason and brick work, with the rate at which he offered to do each item of work filled in and also with a calculation of the cost of each item. The total cost, as J. calculated it in the schedule, was £286 10s. 8½d. In a letter attached to the schedule, J. offered to do the work for that sum, and his offer was accepted by McI.

On completion of the work it was found that J. had under-calculated the cost of one item in the schedule by £32 10s.

The schedules sent out by McI. had had this note appended to them: "The work to be measured when finished and charged at the schedule rates, or others corresponding thereto, as also in proportion to the slump sum in the letter of offer."

Held that the contract was a contract according to the schedule rates, and not a contract for a lump sum, and that J. was therefore not barred by his error from claiming the full sum brought out by his rates.

LORD YOUNG (at p. 20): "The contract ... was not a contract to do the work for a lump sum, but a contract for a sum to be fixed when the work had all been finished, and measured, so as to shew what amount of work was actually done. ... Well, that was what was done here; the work when finished was measured, and the rates were applied to the measurements, and the sum sued for is the balance still due on the sum so brought out. It appears that the pursuer's original calculation ... was an under-estimate to the extent of about £30, and the defender declines to pay the pursuer except under deduction of that sum. The answer which the pursuer makes is, 'Oh, but the error was an *error calculi* in applying the schedule rates to the estimated amount of work to be done, bringing out a smaller total than I was entitled to charge.' 'True,' replies the defender, 'but the error was yours, and I am entitled to have the difference deducted from your account.' I think that is an extravagant proposal."

NOTES

1. This case was followed in *Wilkie* v. *Hamilton Lodging-House Co. Ltd.* (1902) 4 F. 951, relating to a schedule for joiner work which brought out a total sum which was an under-calculation of £151. W. had brought an action against the company for that sum.

2. Another instance of a patent error being corrected by construction of a document occurs in *Glen's Trustees* v. *The Lancashire and Yorkshire Accident Insurance Co. Ltd.* (1906) 8 F. 915: A policy of insurance contained a proviso that the right to recover should be forfeited on the lapse of a certain period "unless" a settlement had been agreed upon or the claim referred to arbitration or "legal proceedings have *not* been taken by the insured."

Held that the word "not" was clearly a grammatical error and that the court was entitled to correct the error and read the clause as if "not" were deleted.

3. Such cases are to be contrasted with cases where one party has made a private error in his calculations, as in *The Seaton Brick and Tile Co. Ltd.* v. *Mitchell* (1900) 2 F. 550: M., by letter, offered to execute certain carpentry work for S. Ltd. for the lump sum of £859. S. Ltd. accepted that

offer. M. later discovered that several items had been inadvertently omitted in the calculation of £859, with the result that his offer had been £326 less than it ought to have been. M. therefore refused to implement the contract, and S. Ltd. raised an action of damages against him.

Held that M. was liable in damages for his breach of contract. If M. had shown the prices for each different item, instead of stating merely the lump sum for the whole work, his error would have been patent and he would not have been bound by the incorrect lump sum.

Defective expression: latent defect: parole evidence admissible to correct error

Krupp v. John Menzies Ltd.

1907 S.C. 903

A formal minute of agreement between M. Ltd., proprietor of the Station Hotel, Mallaig, and Mrs K., manageress of that hotel, provided that the company was to pay Mrs K., in addition to a salary, "one-fifth part of the net annual profits of the business."

Having been manageress of the hotel for five years, Mrs K. brought an action against M. Ltd. for payment of her share of the net profits for that period.

M. Ltd. averred that the verbal agreement between the parties had been that Mrs K. was to receive one-twentieth of the net annual profits and that the words "one-fifth" in the minute of agreement were a clerical error: the clerk had been given as a style an agreement relating to the Palace Hotel, Inverness, in which the share of profits was "one-tenth," had been instructed to insert one-half of that proportion in the agreement with Mrs K., and had miscalculated one-half of one-tenth as one-fifth instead of one-twentieth.

M. Ltd. further averred that this error in the formal agreement had not been discovered by either party until immediately before Mrs K. raised her action.

Held that M. Ltd. was entitled to prove these averments in order that the error might be rectified.

LORD PRESIDENT (DUNEDIN) (at p. 908): "It is a very delicate matter to interfere with a written contract expressed in clear terms, and ... parole proof should not be rashly allowed in such a case. But there are cases in which it would be truly a disgrace to any system of jurisprudence if there was no way available of rectifying what would otherwise be a gross injustice. . . . This case seems to me to have nothing to do with the avoidance or re-formation of the contract. The only question is whether proof is admissible that a document which in ordinary circumstances would be held to express the intentions of the parties does not in fact do so.

"I am clearly of opinion that proof should be allowed."

LORD MCLAREN (at p. 908): "We are not at all in the region of rescinding or re-forming a written contract where one of the parties has been led into error by the fault or negligence of the other party.

"What it is proposed to prove is that the fraction, one-fifth, was inserted in the agreement in place of 5 per cent, the true quantity. This was either a clerical or an arithmetical error, and is *prima facie* subject to correction. We know, for example, that a misnomer is always subject to correction, for on proof of the true name of the person or thing effect is always given to that proof. Then in deeds of conveyance arithmetical errors are subject to correction when it appears on the face of the deed that they are arithmetical errors. In such cases we do not vary the terms of the contract at all, but merely seek to give expression to the true contract as agreed to by the parties."

NOTE

At common law the normal remedy for a latent defect was reduction, and this case was unusual because proof was allowed without reduction being sought.

Anderson v. *Lambie*, 1954 S.C. (H.L.) 43, is an instance of the normal remedy at common law:

A. owned lands in Lanarkshire known as "the lands and estate of Blairmuckhill." The greater part of these lands consisted of the farm of Blairmuckhill, and the remainder was used for colliery purposes and was occupied by the National Coal Board.

A. contracted to sell the farm to L. Owing to an error for which A.'s solicitors were responsible the disposition had the effect of conveying to L. the whole estate instead of only the farm.

A. brought an action for reduction of the disposition.

Held that, as the disposition had not given effect to the agreement between the parties, the disposition fell to be reduced, with the result that the parties would then be bound to implement their obligations under the missives.

A statutory general remedy of rectification of defectively expressed documents is now provided for by sections 8 and 9 of the Law Reform (Miscellaneous Provisions) (Scotland) Act 1985 (see Appendix A).

What is essential error?

Woods v. Tulloch

(1893) 20 R. 477

By a minute of agreement T. sold to coalmasters "the property known as Clayknowes, situated near Greenhill Junction, in the county of Stirling, extending to 132 acres or thereby" for £5,750.

The coalmasters raised an action against T. concluding for reduction of the minute of agreement, averring that they had relied on statements made by T. that the extent of the property was 132 acres and the rental £157, whereas the area was only 125.23 acres and the rental £120 10s., and that they had therefore been under essential error in signing the minute of agreement.

Held that the error was not *in essentialibus* of the contract and that the action was irrelevant.

LORD ORDINARY (KYLLACHY) (at p. 479): "That leaves it only to be considered whether the error here said to be induced amounted to what our law knows as essential error. I do not, I confess, think this question admits of argument. The largest definition of essential error is that contained in Bell's *Principles*, section 11, which, I observe, was accepted and approved by the House of Lords in the case of *Stewart* v. *Kennedy*. But it is quite impossible to bring the alleged error here under any of the heads of that definition. There was no error as to the identity of the subject, or as to the persons contracting, or as to the price, or as to the nature of the contract. The error alleged was as to certain qualities of the subject which, it is impossible to assert, were either expressly or tacitly essential to the bargain. The acreage and rental of an estate are in general no doubt material elements in a sale of land. But they were not more essential here than in every other case of sale. In point of fact, they were less than in the general case, for the sale here was of a mineral estate. How can it be said that the extent of the alleged error, either with respect to the acreage or the rental, made the subject a practically different subject from what was bought and sold? It would really, I think, be difficult to find a better example of what is not in law essential error than the error alleged here."

LORD ADAM (at p. 481): "What the essentials of a contract of sale are is well known. As the Lord Ordinary has said, they are the person, the subject, and the price, but it is not said that the purchasers were in error as to any of these points. That being so, the question is, are the statements in question so material, being innocent, as to affect the mind of the purchaser in such a way as to induce error *in essentialibus*? I agree with the Lord Ordinary that though they may have affected his mind to a certain extent, they cannot be said to have done so to the extent of inducing essential error."

LORD KINNEAR (at p. 481): "There is no such material difference as to justify us in holding that the pursuers have made a relevant statement of error *in essentialibus*."

NOTE

For *Stewart* v. *Kennedy*, see below.

What is essential error? Effect of unilateral error uninduced

Stewart v. Kennedy

(1890) 17 R.(H.L.) 25

S., the heir of entail in possession of an estate in Perthshire, sent to K. a holograph offer to sell the estate at a specified price. The offer included the sentence: "In the event of your acceptance the sale is made subject to the ratification of the Court." K. accepted the offer.

A difference arose between the parties as to the meaning of the words "subject to the ratification of the Court," S. maintaining that they referred to a procedure by which the court would consider whether the terms of the bargain were fair and reasonable, whereas K. maintained that they referred to a different procedure not involving such consideration.

The House of Lords decided that question of interpretation in K.'s favour (1890) 17 R.(H.L.) 1; (1889) 16 R. 421).

S. brought an action of reduction of the missives against K., averring that he had been under essential error as to the "import and effect" of his offer, and that his essential error had been induced by G., K.'s agent.

Held that S.'s error was error *in essentialibus*, that such error was not *per se* a relevant ground for reducing the contract, but that there was a sufficient averment that the error had been induced by G.

LORD HERSCHELL (at p. 27): "It is sought to reduce the contract simply on the ground that the appellant did not intend to make the offer which the Courts have held that he did make. Such a contention is far-reaching in its consequences. It would apply in every case where the parties differed in their construction of an essential part of the contract. After litigating the matter through all the Courts without success, it would always be open to the defeated litigant to reduce the contract, provided he could shew that he understood the contract to bear the interpretation for which he had contended. ...

"... The authorities cited ... shew, I think, that in the case of bilateral obligations it was always considered essential that the error which was said to be taken advantage of by one party to reduce the contract should have been induced by the other party to it."

LORD WATSON (at p. 28): "I concur with all their Lordships [in the First Division of the Inner House of the Court of Session] as to the accuracy of the general doctrine laid down by Professor Bell (Bell's *Prin.* sec. 11) to the effect that error in substantials such as will invalidate consent given to a contract or obligation must be in relation to either (1) its subject-matter; (2) the persons undertaking or to whom it is undertaken; (3) the price or consideration; (4) the quality of the thing engaged for, if expressly or tacitly essential; or (5) the nature of the contract or engagement supposed to be entered into. I believe that these five categories will be found to embrace all the forms of essential error which, either *per se* or when induced by the other party to the contract, give the person labouring under such error a right to rescind it. In the present case no error is alleged except in reference to the nature of the contract of sale constituted by the missives in question, and it is not averred that the same error was entertained by the respondent or his representative, Mr Glendinning.

"Professor Bell does not in his useful treatise deal with the important question, how far in the case of contracts and onerous unilateral obligations an erroneous belief entertained by one party only will give him a right to rescind. Without venturing to affirm that there can be no exceptions to the rule, I think it may be safely said that in the case of onerous contracts reduced to writing the erroneous belief of one of the contracting parties in regard to the nature of the obligations which he has undertaken will not be sufficient to give him the right, unless such belief has been induced by the representations, fraudulent or not, of the other party to the contract. ...

"I am of opinion that the alleged error of the appellant is by itself insufficient to invalidate his consent, but that it will be sufficient for that purpose if it can be shewn to have been induced by the representations of the respondent, or of anyone for whose conduct he is responsible."

NOTES

1. For a case in which *Stewart* v. *Kennedy* was followed, see *Bennie's Trustees* v. *Couper* (1890) 17 R. 782: C. undertook to see paid the amount contained in a bond and disposition in security granted by Goodall. When sued to implement the obligation, C. stated in defence that he had been under essential error in that he had had in mind a property in "Windsor Quadrant," whereas the bond related to a property in "Windsor Circus." *Held* that C. had stated no relevant ground for the setting aside of his obligation.

Lord Justice-Clerk (J. H. A. Macdonald) (at p. 785): "This error was entirely his own error. It was not an error which anyone had done anything to induce. He is not in these circumstances entitled to an issue of essential error in order to prove that he made this error, and so to set aside his obligation. No authority has been cited to us to justify such a contention, and the recent authority (*Stewart* v. *Kennedy*) is to an opposite effect."

2. In *Menzies* v. *Menzies* (1893) 20 R. (H.L.) 108, Lord Watson (at p. 142) gave a wider definition of essential error, but proceeded to confirm the effect of such error: "Error becomes essential whenever it is shewn that but for it one of the parties would have declined to contract. He cannot rescind unless his error was induced by the representations of the other contracting party, or of his agent, made in the course of negotiation, and with reference to the subject-matter of the contract. If his error is proved to have been so induced, the fact that the misleading representations were made in good faith affords no defence against the remedy of rescission."

The House of Lords held that the pursuer, who had, in ignorance of his rights, been induced to enter into an agreement by the representations of his father's law-agent, was entitled to have the agreement reduced.

3. Recent cases on uninduced unilateral error in which *Stewart* v. *Kennedy* was applied are *The Royal Bank of Scotland plc* v. *Purvis*, 1990 S.L.T. 262 (O.H.) and *Spook Erection (Northern) Ltd.* v. *Kaye*, 1990 S.L.T. 676 (O.H.).

In the former case, P. had signed a guarantee as guarantor for money lent by a bank to her husband. In an action against her for sums due under the guarantee, she sought to reduce the guarantee on the ground that she had been under essential error at the time of signing and would not have subscribed the guarantee if she had been aware of its nature. The Lord Ordinary (McCluskey) held that the court could not look to see what was in P.'s mind when she signed and she was therefore bound by the guarantee and not entitled to decree of reduction.

The latter case was an action by purchasers for implement of missives of sale and purchase of heritable property. The sellers had been under the mistaken, but uninduced, belief that the property was subject to a 990-year lease, whereas the purchasers knew that the lease was a 99-year lease. In the action the sellers counterclaimed for reduction of the missives on the ground of essential error. Applying *Stewart* v. *Kennedy*, the Lord Ordinary (Marnoch) dismissed the counterclaim.

4. In *Steuart's Trustees* v. *Hart* (1875) 3 R. 192 reduction of a disposition was granted on the ground of essential error known to the purchaser and taken advantage of by him. S. had sold to H. a plot of ground for £75. S. believed it to be burdened with the cumulo feu-duty of £9 15s., but H. knew that the portion effeiring to it was only 3s., and H. was aware of S.'s mistake. In *Brooker-Simpson Ltd.* v. *Duncan Logan (Builders) Ltd.*, 1969 S.L.T. 304 (O.H.), this was described as a special case which had never been followed.

Unilateral error uninduced: gratuitous deed

McCaig v. Glasgow University Court

(1904) 6 F. 918

Trustees under a testamentary settlement (which did not dispose of the whole of the deceased's estate and which was open to serious challenge on the ground of uncertainty) obtained from the deceased's sister, McC., who would have succeeded on intestacy, a deed of assignation and corroboration by which she homologated the settlement and conveyed her rights in her brother's estate to the trustees.

McC. later brought an action for reduction of the deed of assignation and corroboration on the ground of essential error.

Held that since the deed was gratuitous it was not necessary to aver that the error had been induced by misrepresentation.

LORD ORDINARY (LOW) (at p. 923): "The first issue proposed by the pursuer is whether the pursuer, in granting the deed under reduction, 'was under essential error as to the substance and effect of the deed.' The defenders argued upon the authority of the decision of the House of Lords in *Stewart* v. *Kennedy*, 17 R. (H.L.) 25, that essential error alone was not a ground for reducing a deed. I do not think that that is the import of the judgment in the House of Lords. What was sought to be reduced in that case was a contract, and what was laid down was that a contract could not be reduced on the ground of essential error on the part of one of the parties, unless that error was induced by the other party, or someone acting for him. The same rule would probably apply in the case of onerous unilateral obligations, but I think that it does not do so in the case of a purely gratuitous grant.

"I think that the case of *McLaurin* v. *Stafford* ((1875) 3 R. 265) is an authority for that view. It was said for the defenders that that case had never been followed. It may be that a similar case has never come up for decision, but I know of no reason why the authority of the judgment (which was the unanimous judgment of seven Judges) should be doubted. No doubt the deed in question in this case is not of the same kind as in the case of *McLaurin*, but they have this vital element in common that in both cases the deed was granted gratuitously.

"In form the first issue proposed by the pursuer is that which was adjusted by the Court in *McLaurin's* case, and I think that it ought to be approved. I would, however, suggest that the word 'import' should be used instead of the word 'substance.'

"... It is not any or every misrepresentation or concealment which will justify the reduction of even a gratuitous deed. It might be proved that the pursuer was fully aware of the import and effect of the deed, but was misled in regard to some unimportant details. That would not, I think, entitle her to have the deed reduced."

LORD JUSTICE-CLERK (J. H. A. MACDONALD) (at p. 924) [the pursuer not having been called upon]: "I do not think it necessary to call for any further argument. This case seems to be very similar to that of *McLaurin*. The action is brought to reduce a deed which is said to have been signed under essential error as to its import. The deed was entirely gratuitous, and I think the pursuer is entitled to the two issues in the form allowed by the Lord Ordinary."

NOTE

For *Stewart* v. *Kennedy*, see p. 79, above.

Error in law: general law of the country

Cloup v. Alexander

(1831) 9 S. 448

Messrs Cloup and Pelissie, managers of a company of French comedians, entered into an agreement with A. by which A. was to let to them the Caledonian Theatre of Edinburgh for their performances for five weeks.

Subsequently the managers entered into an agreement with Murray, manager of the Theatre Royal, to perform there during part of the five-week period, and they declined to occupy the Caledonian Theatre.

In an action raised against them by A. they pleaded in defence that when they entered into the agreement with A. they were not aware that by statute the Theatre Royal was the only theatre in Edinburgh in which regular drama, such as their performances consisted of, could be lawfully performed.

Held that ignorance of the law did not entitle them to resile from their contract with A., there being no illegality on the face of the contract.

LORD BALGRAY (at p. 451): "The only question before us is, whether these French gentlemen can refuse implement of their contract with Mr Alexander? Upon examining that contract, I see no illegality on the face of it; and I therefore cannot allow myself to presume that an illegal use of the theatre was intended by either of the parties to the contract. I am for . . . holding the defenders bound by their contract."

LORD GILLIES (at p. 451): "All parties to this contract are presumed to know the law of the country. It is impossible for a foreigner in this country to resile from his contracts by merely pleading that he was ignorant of our laws when he entered into them. Dealing with this question, therefore, as if it were a contract entered into by any of the lieges, I am bound to presume that the legal limits of performance on the stage of the Caledonian Theatre were known to both parties at making the contract, and that it was solely for the performances within these limits that it was let or taken. This presumption may be overcome, if the words of the agreement do not admit of being construed consistently with it; but I see no such *repugnantia* in its terms. . . . Mr Alexander avers that he only let the theatre for such performances as were legal. The contract does not contradict this; and it is of no moment that the defenders allege that they had it then in view to exhibit illegal performances, and afterwards desisted. Suppose that a poacher buys a gun from a gunsmith, who perhaps knows him to have committed poaching before; he carries it away for a twelvemonth, could he then pretend to return it to the gunsmith, and refuse to pay the price for it, because he had meant to make it a means of gain by poaching, but, being afterwards better advised, had made no use of it whatever? The defenders are bound by their contract, which, on the face of it, is of a perfectly legal character."

NOTES

1. For other cases on error in law, see *Stewart* v. *Kennedy* (p. 79, above), and *Laing* v. *The Provincial Homes Investment Co. Ltd.*, below.

2. For gratuitous undertakings, see *McCaig* v. *Glasgow University Court* (p. 82, above), and also Lord Justice-Clerk (Moncreiff) in *Kippen* v. *Kippen's Trustee* (1874) 1 R. 1171, at p. 1179 (a case relating to a marriage-contract): "The general rule is ... that an error in law will not avail to set aside an agreement or contract. A discharge without consideration, in which no other or third party was participant, may stand differently, but I am not prepared to say that even a discharge without consideration, when there are full means of knowledge, will necessarily be set aside upon this ground."

Error in law: interpretation of document

Laing v. The Provincial Homes Investment Co. Ltd.

1909 S.C. 812

Mrs L., the wife of a labourer, entered into a written contract with an investment and building company. The terms of the documents constituting the contract were of considerable obscurity. Mrs L. paid certain sums under the contract, but later brought an action for recovery of these sums and for reduction of the documents, alleging that the terms of the documents were so obscure that there had never been *consensus in idem*.

Held that Mrs L. was not entitled to resile from the contract on that ground, it being for the court to ascertain the true construction of the documents.

LORD KINNEAR (at p. 822): "The Lord Ordinary ... has decerned in the pursuer's favour for the immediate repayment of the money. His general view is that the alleged contract is neither intelligible nor self-consistent, that it cannot be binding from the obscurity of its own terms, and that it is impossible that this pursuer could have understood what it meant. I must say I have some sympathy with the Lord Ordinary's view of the complexity and obscurity of the contract, and also with the sense of equity which leads him to hold that it would not be just to allow an unlearned woman to be bound by an obligation which was perfectly unintelligible to her. But I am afraid that the justice to which we are bound to have regard is justice according to law, and the law does not allow anyone who has executed a written contract to get rid of the liability it imposes by his own bare assertion that he did not understand the meaning of the words to which he put his name. . . .

"The Lord Ordinary says that the terms in which the contract is to be finally expressed are unintelligible. That is a question of construction. When contracting parties bind themselves to certain terms that are put in writing, that means that they are bound according to the true construction of the these terms as they shall be ascertained by the Court, if they themselves differ about it. . . . His Lordship says . . . that this unlearned woman did not understand what she was doing, that she could not have understood the contract as it was presented to her, and therefore that she was not bound by it. But no one who has made a written contract can escape from its obligations by the mere allegation of his own failure to understand the meaning or effect of the terms to which he has expressly assented."

Error as to interpretation of statute is no ground for condictio indebiti

Glasgow Corporation v. Lord Advocate

1959 S.C. 203

Glasgow Corporation for a number of years paid purchase tax on stationery manufactured by them. They did so under the erroneous belief that they were liable to the tax under various Finance Acts.

The Court of Session then decided a case on the interpretation of the statutory provisions in a way which indicated that the Corporation had not been liable for part of the tax, and the Corporation sought to recover it under the *condictio indebiti*.

Held that the *condictio indebiti* did not lie to recover money paid under an erroneous interpretation of a public statute.

Authorities on *condictio indebiti* in cases of error in law *reviewed*.

LORD WHEATLEY (Ordinary) (at p. 214): "The question whether money . . . paid [under an error in law] falls within the *condictio indebiti* is

one which, as far as I can trace, has never been the subject of express decision in Scotland in recent times. There are, however, some early decisions which were prayed in aid by the pursuers as providing an affirmative answer to that question, and these have the further fortification of support from the institutional writers. On the other hand, there are *obiter* opinions in the House of Lords to the contrary effect, and these *obiter dicta* have subsequently been accepted in *obiter* views by Scottish Judges. It is accordingly necessary to examine the history of these pronouncements in order to determine whether the earlier or later views should be followed.
...

"From my review of the history of this question, I am satisfied that the law of Scotland is now, generally speaking, that an error in law does not found an action based on a *condictio indebiti*. It may well be that in matters relating to private agreements and certain relationships exceptions to that rule may be found, but such exceptions do not extend to the general law of the country, including statute law, even if the statute be a taxing statute."

LORD PRESIDENT (CLYDE) (at p. 231): "The argument is founded on the doctrine, firmly fixed in the law of Scotland, of *condictio indebiti*. This doctrine, which comes from the Roman law, gives a right to recover from another money paid under the mistaken belief that it was due—Gloag on Contract, (2nd ed.) p. 60.

"The issue in this case is whether that doctrine applies to a case where the mistake in question is an error in the interpretation of a public general statute. The contention for the Corporation is that the doctrine is an equitable one founded upon considerations of equity; that it is inequitable that one man should profit by the mistake of another and retain the other's property which he acquired without right to it. Upon this view, the right to recover would operate whether the mistake was one of fact or law.

"It has, however, never been authoritatively settled in Scotland whether an error of law, and in particular an error in the interpretation of a public statute, will ground an action based on the *condictio indebiti*. . . .

". . . The question is technically open for this Court to determine on principle. . . . So viewing the matter I have reached the conclusion that the *condictio* does not apply to such a case.

"My main reason is that the doctrine is an equitable one, and it seems to me that in the case of an error in interpreting an Act of Parliament the balance of the equities are in favour of excluding repayment in such circumstances. Where the error is one of fact, it usually affects only the parties to the particular transaction, and not third parties. Equity may well then demand restitution as between these two parties. But where the error is in regard to the interpretation of a public Act of Parliament repayment of a sum paid by one party may very well affect a very large number of others who have made or received payments under a similar misinterpretation. To allow one repayment would necessarily involve allowing all to be repaid, and this would involve a widening circle of interference with transactions which the parties had treated as settled and completed on the law as it was then understood. There seems little equity in enabling B and C and D to secure an unexpected repayment merely because A has succeeded in upsetting the current interpretation of an Act of Parliament under which all of them paid away part of their funds. On a balance of these considerations equity demands finality in payments made in circumstances of this kind.

"Moreover, if equity lies at the root of the doctrine of the *condictio*, original mistake in paying must be excusable—see *Agnew* v. *Ferguson* ((1903) 5 F. 879), Lord Moncreiff at p. 885. It is relatively easy to establish that an error in fact is excusable, as there may be a host of reasons why the fact was unknown, all of which could be justifiable. But the same is not true of a question of law. For there the doctrine of *ignorantia iuris haud excusat* comes into play, and renders the ignorance devoid of that equitable quality which might otherwise have opened the door to the operation of the *condictio*. . . .

"In the whole circumstances therefore, in my opinion, where the error is due to a mistaken construction of an Act of Parliament, payments made under that error are irrecoverable. I am confirmed in this conclusion by the consideration that the law of England which approaches this question from a different angle has now firmly adopted this view."

NOTE

Distinguish *British Hydro-Carbon Chemicals Ltd. and British Transport Commission, Petrs.*, 1961 S.L.T. 280 (O.H.): *Held* that money paid under a mistaken construction of a private commercial contract was recoverable.

Common error: error in law: reduction of discharge

Mercer v. Anstruther's Trustees

(1871) 9 M. 618; affd. (1872) 10 M.(H.L.) 39

One of three daughters sought a reduction of a discharge of all her claims under her parents' marriage-contract. The discharge was contained in the daughter's marriage-contract, and the ground of reduction was that the discharge had been granted under essential error, both the daughter and her father erroneously believing that he was fiar of his deceased wife's estate, whereas he was merely liferenter, the fee having vested in the daughter and one of her sisters.

Held, by a majority of seven judges (*diss.* Lord Deas), that the discharge was reducible, although arising from error in law.

LORD PRESIDENT (INGLIS) (at p. 627): "It is, in my opinion, established by the evidence in this case that neither father nor daughter rightly understood their legal position, and that both of them acted under essential error as to the nature of Mrs Mercer's rights to her mother's estate, and as to the nature and extent of Mr Anstruther's powers over that estate. I am satisfied that Mr Anstruther was fully impressed with the conviction that he had a fee in his wife's estate ..., with a protected succession merely in favour of his children. ... This entirely erroneous, though honest belief, Mr Anstruther impressed on his daughter ..., as the affianced bride of Mr Mercer; and that impression the young lady, reposing the fullest confidence in the business knowledge and honour and the affection of her father, unhesitatingly and unqualifiedly received. ... The error in this case was a very grave and important error in the essentials of the subject-matter with which the father and daughter were dealing as contracting parties. But it has been argued for the defenders that the error was a mistake about a question of law, upon which the ablest lawyers might differ, and that it would be dangerous to allow contracts and transactions to be set aside on the ground of such error. I am not aware that an error *in essentialibus*, as a ground of reduction, must necessarily be an error in fact, and may not be an error in law. On the contrary, one of the most common examples of essential error is where the pursuer of a reduction complains, that when he entered into the contract or arrangement sought to be reduced he was excusably mistaken as to the nature of his legal rights. ... It does not occur to me that the remedy ought to be barred merely on account of the difficulty of the question of law which requires to be solved in order to ascertain what are the true legal rights of the parties complaining. Such an exception from the general rule would be most embarrassing in practice, besides being indefensible in theory, for the admission of the exception would necessitate the adjustment of a scale of difficulties by which each case must be tested so as to ascertain whether it falls within the rule or within the exception. I am of opinion, therefore, that the serious error under which both Mr Anstruther and Mrs Mercer laboured in introducing, and consenting to introduce, a clause of discharge into the marriage-contract of Mrs Mercer, is not the less a good reason of reduction, either because it was an error in law, or because it was an error upon a point of law on which there might be difference of opinion."

LORD KINLOCH (at p. 652): "I cannot doubt of the competency, in our law, of setting aside a deed of discharge granted in essential error as to the character and extent of the rights discharged. It was said that what occurred here was merely an error in law, and where the point of law was one of difficulty. As to the error being one of law, this is no sufficient answer to the reduction of a discharge of legal rights; on the contrary, it is just the essential error proper to that particular case. In a discharge of legal rights, error in law is error in the subject-matter of the transaction. Many cases have occurred in our Court in which a discharge of legal rights was set aside simply because the party was in ignorance or error as to what these rights truly were."

Mutual error excluding consensus: contract void

Wilson v. Marquis of Breadalbane

(1859) 21 D. 957

After negotiations as to sale of cattle, W. sent cattle to B., stating that the price was £15 per head. B. took delivery, but immediately wrote that the price agreed upon had been £13 per head.

Later B. paid W. at the rate of £13 per head, and W. brought an action for the alleged balance.

Held that (1) on the evidence there had been a misunderstanding as to the price, B. supposing that the price had been fixed at £13 per head, and W. that it was to depend on the quality of the cattle; and (2) since the sale had been carried into effect under this misunderstanding, B. had to pay the market value of the cattle, which was proved to be £15 per head.

LORD JUSTICE-CLERK (INGLIS) (at p. 963): "The question which the Lord Ordinary has considered ... is, what was the bargain? ... But there is, I think, another question of great importance, viz., whether there was any contract fixing the price at all? In order to the constitution of a contract of sale, there must be *consensus in idem placitum*. If one party thought that the price was fixed, and the other not, and each believed a different thing to be the contract, there could be no *consensus in idem placitum*. Looking to the whole circumstances, I am quite unable to bring myself to believe that either party has stated what was untrue. My belief is that each is honest in his account of the matter; and that being so, the result I have arrived at is, that there was no contract as to the price. Then what is the legal result? If the question had arisen *rebus integris*, there would have been no contract. The cattle would have belonged to the pursuer, the vendor; and the price to the defender, the vendee. But, *res non sunt integrae*. Both parties went on with the sale. The cattle have been taken, and have been appropriated by the defender. ... Under these circumstances, what is the position of matters? There is no contract price. I think there is nothing for it, but that the defender must pay the value. That is satisfactorily proved to be £15 per head."

NOTE

This case was followed in *Stuart & Co*. v. *Kennedy* (1885) 13 R. 221: In a sale of stone coping S., the seller, and K., the buyer, had a misunderstanding as to what price was to be charged, S. honestly believing that the price was to be 1s.9d. per superficial foot while K. honestly believed that the price was to be 1s.9d. per lineal foot. K. paid £40 for the coping stone supplied and as this was considered to be the market value for it S. was held not entitled to any larger amount.

Lord President (Inglis) (at p. 222): "I think [the Sheriff] is right in holding that the rule of the case of *Wilson* must apply....

"If there is no *consensus in idem placitum*, the effect of course is, that there is no contract at all, and that the parties are as free as they were before they had had any negotiations. But if something has followed, if the contract is partly or wholly performed, you cannot then undo the contract and hold both parties free. Now, here, coping to the extent of 394 feet, or more than half of the whole, had been delivered and received. That being so, *res non sunt integrae*, the contract cannot be resolved or undone, and therefore we must see that there shall be some kind of performance on the other side. To determine what that is to be, we revert to the rule of *Wilson's* case, and hold that the actual value of the subject delivered, as that is ascertained by the market price, is the measure of the defender's liability."

Both *Wilson's* case and *Stuart & Co.'s* case were decided prior to the passing of the Sale of Goods Act 1893, section 8(2) of which required the buyer, where the price was not fixed, to pay a "reasonable" price. For "market value" or "market price" there would now require to be substituted, under the Sale of Goods Act 1979, section 8(2), a "reasonable price." Thus in *Glynwed Distribution Ltd.* v. *S. Koronka & Co.*, 1977 S.C. 1, where there was agreement as to the subjects of sale (hot rolled steel), though not as to the price, there was held to have been *consensus in idem*, and that a "reasonable price," as fixed by the court under section 8(2) of the 1893 Act, had to be paid for the steel delivered.

Such cases—in which there is either no definite price fixed or no agreed price proved—are to be distinguished from cases such as *Steel's Trustee* v. *Bradley Homes (Scotland) Ltd.*, 1972 S.C. 48 (O.H.), where a price is plainly stated in a written contract. The Lord Ordinary (Dunpark) said (at p. 57): "In my opinion it is essential in the interests of business efficacy that the ordinary rule should be that an onerous contract reduced to writing in plain terms should bind the parties thereto."

Unilateral error induced by fraudulent misrepresentation: error as to identity: contract void

Morrisson v. Robertson

1908 S.C. 332

M., a dairyman at Cambusbarron, had brought two of his cows to a market for sale. There he was approached by T., who falsely represented that he was the son of W., dairyman, Bonnyrigg, with whom M. had had business dealings on previous occasions. T. stated that he wished to purchase the cows on behalf of his father. M. believed T.'s statements, and delivered the cows to T. on the usual trade credit.

T. then sold and delivered the cows to R., who purchased them in good faith.

M. raised an action against R. for delivery of the cows, or, alternatively, for payment of their value.

Held that as there had been no sale of the cows by M. to T., R. had no title to retain them.

LORD MCLAREN (at p. 336): "If there had been a contract of sale, then, although the pursuer might have had an action of damages against the person who obtained the goods by fraud, or might have had an action for reducing the sale, yet if in the meantime the property of the cows had passed by lawful subsale to a third person, then the right of that third person, the analogue of the defender in the present case, would be indefeasible. Having acquired the property by purchase from someone who had a lawful title, he would have had a good defence to an action of this nature. But then the case of the pursuer is that there was here no contract of sale. If Telford, the man who committed the fraud, had by false representations as to his own character and credit obtained the cows from the pursuer on credit, then I think that would have been the case of a sale which, although liable to reduction, would stand good until reduced. But then that was not at all the nature of the case. The pursuer never sold his cows to Telford. He believed that he was selling the cows to a man Wilson at Bonnyrigg, whom he knew to be a person of reasonably good credit, and to whom he was content to give credit for the payment of the price. This belief that he was selling the cows to Wilson was induced by the fraudulent statement of Telford that he was Wilson's son. It is perfectly plain that in such circumstances there was no contract between Telford and the pursuer, because Telford did not propose to buy the cows for himself, and because the pursuer would not have sold them on credit to a man of whom he had no knowledge. Neither was there any sale of the cows by the pursuer to Mr Wilson, Bonnyrigg. Wilson knew nothing about them, and had never authorised the purchase; the whole story was an invention. There being no sale either to Wilson or to Telford, and there being no other party concerned in the business in hand, it follows that there was no contract of sale at all, and there being no contract of sale the pursuer remained the undivested owner of his cows, although he had parted with their custody to Telford in consequence of these false representations.

"So much being premised, then I think it follows that as Telford had no right to the cows he could not give a good title to the defender even under a contract for an onerous consideration. He had no better title to sell the cows to any third person than he would have had if he had gone into the pursuer's byre and stolen the cows."

LORD KINNEAR (at p. 338): "The principle is that a contract obtained by fraud is not void but voidable; and since it follows that it is valid until it is rescinded, the rescission may come too late if in the meantime third persons have acquired rights in good faith and for value. But then on the other hand if such third persons have acquired their title through a person who himself did not acquire the goods by virtue of any contract with the true owner, or to whom they were not intentionally transferred by the true owner upon any title, then the purchaser can obtain no better title than the person from whom he acquired, who *ex hypothesi* had no title at all. ...

"... There was no contract at all with Telford. ... If a man obtains goods by pretending to be somebody else, or by pretending that he is an agent for somebody, who has in fact given him no authority, there is no contract between the owner of the goods and him; there is no consensus which can support a contract. The owner, in this case the pursuer, does not contract with the fraudulent person who obtains the goods, because he never meant to contract with him. He thinks he is contracting with an agent for a different person altogether. He does not contract with the person with whom he in fact supposes that he is making a contract, because that person knows nothing about it and never intended to make an agreement; therefore there is no agreement at all."

NOTE

Contrast *MacLeod* v. *Kerr* below.

Unilateral error induced by fraudulent misrepresentation: false name: contract voidable

MacLeod v. Kerr

1965 S.C. 253

K. advertised his Vauxhall Cresta car for sale. Galloway, who gave his name as "L. Craig," called on K., and agreed to pay £375 for the car. He wrote out a cheque for £375, signing it "L. Craig." K. gave Galloway the registration book, and Galloway drove the car away.

The following day K. discovered through his bank that the cheque was one from a stolen cheque book; the cheque was therefore not honoured. K. immediately informed the police.

In the course of the next few days Galloway, giving his name as "K.," negotiated a sale of the car to Gibson, a garage proprietor, for £200.

Later the police took possession of the car from Gibson, and Galloway was convicted of fraud and theft.

An action of multiplepoinding was brought to determine which party was entitled to the car.

Held that the contract between K. and Galloway was not void but voidable, and that the car therefore belonged to Gibson.

LORD PRESIDENT (CLYDE) (after considering *Morrisson* v. *Robertson*) (at p. 256): "In my opinion the decision in *Morrisson's* case is a sound one, and the *ratio decidendi* (namely, error as to the identity of the purchaser) was the correct ratio.

"In the present case, however, the true position is that there was a completed contract of sale of the car by Mr Kerr to Galloway. For there was no dubiety in the present case as to the identity of the purchaser, namely, the man who came in answer to the advertisement. But the seller, Mr Kerr, was induced to enter into the contract by false and fraudulent misrepresentations on the part of Galloway. In law the result is that there was a contract of sale, but it was voidable at the instance of Mr Kerr. . . . In the present case, in my opinion, although this contract with Mr Kerr was voidable, it was not rescinded before Mr Gibson had acquired the car in question from Galloway in perfect good faith and for value. For Mr Gibson knew nothing of Galloway's fraudulent operations. In my opinion, therefore, the car now belongs to Mr Gibson."

LORD GUTHRIE (at p. 258): "In a multiplepoinding raised in the name of the Procurator-fiscal after the criminal proceedings against Galloway were completed, Mr Kerr and Mr Gibson each claimed the ownership of the car. The Sheriff-substitute decided in favour of Mr Kerr, the original owner, and Mr Gibson has appealed against his interlocutor. The Sheriff-substitute held that the car was tainted by a *vitium reale* because Galloway stole it, and therefore that Mr Gibson did not acquire a good title to the car.

"In my opinion the appeal is clearly entitled to succeed. In the first place, I agree with the Sheriff-substitute's view that the contention for Mr Kerr that there had been no contract between him and Galloway, because he was in error as to the person dealt with, is unsound. . . . On 12th February Mr Kerr intended to sell the car to the person present in his premises. It is true that Galloway gave a false name to Mr Kerr, but that lie did not affect the identity of the person who was offering to buy the car from the latter. Galloway did not falsely represent to Mr Kerr that he was another particular person named L. Craig, and Mr Kerr did not think that the man seeking to buy the car was another person than the man actually present in the premises. This case therefore does not fall within the scope of the principle stated by Lord Kinnear in *Morrisson* v. *Robertson* in these terms: 'If a man obtains goods by pretending to be somebody else, or by pretending that he is an agent for somebody, who has in fact given him no authority, there is no contract between the owner of the goods and him; there is no consensus which can support a contract. The owner, in this case the pursuer, does not contract with the fraudulent person who obtains the goods, because he never meant to contract with him.' In this case Galloway did not pretend to be somebody else, and Mr Kerr meant to contract with Galloway. There was therefore no error in the mind of Mr Kerr as to the identity of the person to whom he was selling his car, and an agreement was concluded between him and Galloway for the sale of the car.

"In the second place, I think that the Sheriff-substitute is wrong in stating that Galloway stole the car. Mr Kerr consented to Galloway taking away the car, and therefore there was no theft. Galloway bought the car from Mr Kerr by fraudulent misrepresentations that he would pay the price by cheque, he well knowing that the cheque he gave was worthless, being stolen. But although the contract was induced by fraud, it was nevertheless a contract of sale, under which the ownership of the car passed from Mr Kerr to Galloway. Therefore, as the car was not stolen, it was not tainted by a *vitium reale* which would prevent even a purchaser in good faith from obtaining a title to it good against its owner. The contract, having been induced by fraud, was voidable, not void. Therefore it conferred a title to the car on Galloway, who could transfer the ownership of it to a purchaser in good faith until his title was avoided.

"It was argued for Mr Kerr that the title of Galloway was avoided on 13th February, the day before the car was acquired by Mr Gibson, because on 13th February Mr Kerr had notified the police of the transaction. ... An invocation of the powers of the criminal authorities cannot possibly be the avoidance of a contract entered into under the civil law."

NOTE

For *Morrisson* v. *Robertson*, see p. 92, above.

No general duty of disclosure: essential error not induced by the other party: contract valid

Young v. The Clydesdale Bank Ltd.

(1889) 17 R. 231

David Y., who had been in the habit of granting accommodation bills to his brother Robert for sums under £500, signed a letter addressed to

Robert's bank in which he guaranteed "payment of any advances made, and which may hereafter be made" to Robert.

Subsequently David Y. was sued by the bank on that letter for over £5,000, and brought an action of reduction of it against the bank on the grounds that the bank ought to have informed him at the time of signature that Robert's indebtedness to the bank then amounted to about £5,000 and that he had signed the letter under essential error as to its nature and effect.

Held that there had been no duty on the bank to disclose to a proposed cautioner the state of the principal debtor's account unless information was asked, and that essential error induced not by the other party to the contract but by third parties and by the pursuer's own negligence in failing to read the letter before signing it was not a ground for reduction of the letter.

LORD ADAM (at p. 239): "I do not doubt that this guarantee was signed ... by the pursuer ... without any knowledge of its contents. I do not think that the document was ever read over and explained. I think that what David Young says about it is true, that he had previously granted some accommodation bills to his brother to the amount of between £300 and £400, and that, when taken to the bank to sign this guarantee, he was induced by his brother to believe that he was signing a document which would make him liable to the bank for a sum of a similar amount. He did not know the true nature of the document he was signing, but thought it was a document that would have that effect. I think in that matter he was certainly deceived. He was deceived in the amount for which he was to sign and did sign. . . .

". . . It is well settled that it is not the duty of a bank to give any information to a proposed cautioner as to the state of accounts with the principal. . . . If the cautioner desires to know the state of accounts with the principal it is his duty to ask and to inform himself. . . .

". . . If David Young, relying upon his brother's statement, chose to sign the document without reading, or without looking at what he was signing in order to ascertain what was in it, the consequences must fall upon himself, the bank believing—as they were entitled to believe—that the cautioner knew perfectly well what he was signing. They gave their money on the faith of this document, and it appears to me that that being so, the bank was not and could not be affected by any fraud, or undue concealment in this matter."

LORD SHAND (at p. 244): "There can be no ground of complaint because of concealment by the bank-agent, for nothing is better settled than this, that a bank-agent is entitled to assume that the cautioner has informed himself upon the various matters material to the obligation he is about to undertake. The agent is not bound to volunteer any information or statement as to the accounts, although if information be asked he is bound to give it, and to give it truthfully."

LORD PRESIDENT (INGLIS) (at p. 247): "I desire to state very shortly the ground upon which I am unable to sustain the new plea of essential error. . . .

"I do not doubt that the pursuer was under an error—and a very important error—as to the essence of the document which he subscribed. It is not enough to entitle him to a reduction of this obligation that that error was produced either by outside influence, for which the bank is in no way responsible, or by the negligence of the pursuer himself. I think the error was brought about by both of these means. I think, in the first place, that the pursuer was deceived—and grossly deceived—by his brother and his brother's cashier or clerk. The representations made by them were, I think, of a fraudulent character, and if the bank had been in any way answerable for these representations, I should have been inclined to pronounce judgment against them. But there is no evidence whatever that the bank were in the least degree aware of anything that had passed between the pursuer and his brother and his brother's clerk. . . .

"But I think the pursuer himself was also guilty of great negligence in signing a document of this kind without reading it, or without making himself master of its contents. . . . It was a document about the import of which, if he had read it, he never would have made any mistake. . . . But the pursuer relied entirely upon the representations made to him by his brother and by . . . his brother's clerk, and chose to sign that document without reading it, or otherwise ascertaining what its contents and the nature of its obligations were.

"Now, for the error so brought about nobody can be answerable but the pursuer himself and those who deceived him as to the nature of the obligation he was about to contract. On that short ground I am of opinion that the reasons of reduction . . . cannot be sustained."

Duty of disclosure arising from circumstances: damages for fraudulent concealment

Gibson v. The National Cash Register Co. Ltd.

1925 S.C. 500

G. brought an action of damages against the N.C.R. Co. Ltd. on the ground that the company had sold to him two cash register machines, fraudulently concealing from him the fact that the machines were not new but secondhand.

G. proved that (1) he had desired to buy new machines, (2) the company had held itself out as making and selling new machines, and (3) the machines supplied were secondhand but, by reconditioning, appeared to be new.

Held that G. had established a *prima facie* case of fraud, and that the onus thereafter lay on the company to prove that its agent had disclosed the fact that the machines were secondhand; as the company had failed to discharge that onus, decree in favour of G. *granted.*

LORD JUSTICE-CLERK (ALNESS) (at p. 504): "The pursuer has elected to retain the cash registers which he purchased. He does not seek to rescind the contract, but he contends that, as he was induced to enter into it by the fraud of Mr Nathan, he has suffered loss thereby, and that he is therefore entitled to an award of damages. ...

"... Now, it is of course elementary and indisputable that a pursuer who comes into Court averring fraud against his opponent must prove fraud, if he is to succeed in his action. But onus is not an inflexible thing. It may shift as the case progresses. ... The pursuer's contention is that, while the onus of proving that Mr Nathan did not disclose that the registers which he sold were secondhand originally rested upon the pursuer, there are facts and circumstances in this case, either admitted or proved, which shift the onus, and which impose upon the defenders the necessity of making it plain that their agent disclosed to the pursuer that the registers which he sold were in point of fact secondhand.

"The facts and circumstances on which the pursuer relies in support of his contention are (1) that it is proved, nay, that it is not disputed, that what the pursuer desired to buy were new cash registers; (2) that the defenders hold themselves out to be makers and vendors of such registers; and (3) that what the pursuer obtained from the defenders were second-hand cash registers, which, however, by reason of reconditioning appeared to be new. The pursuer maintains that in these circumstances it was for the defenders to establish that the pursuer was duly informed by Mr Nathan of the secondhand quality of the goods which he supplied. In this contention I think that the pursuer is well founded. . . .

"The issue then appears to be this—Have the defenders discharged the onus, which I hold to rest upon them, of proving that Mr Nathan informed the pursuer that the registers which he was purchasing were secondhand?

"On this matter there is a conflict of evidence. . . .

[After considering the evidence] "I hold therefore that, even if Mr Nathan was a reliable witness, he has not discharged the onus which the circumstances of the case impose upon the defenders. But I further hold that Mr Nathan is not, for the reasons which I have stated, a reliable witness. That being so, the averment on which the defence really rests—that Mr Nathan disclosed to the pursuer that he was selling a secondhand register—is not established. The defenders' case therefore fails."

Duty of disclosure in contracts uberrimae fidei: *insurance*

The "Spathari"

1925 S.C. (H.L.) 6; 1924 S.C. 182

Demetriades, a Greek shipbroker, resident in Glasgow, purchased the SS. *Spathari*, a Finnish ship, at Hull, with the intention of selling her to a syndicate of Greeks in Samos.

Arrangements were made between Demetriades and Borthwick, an impecunious Glasgow shipbroker who was a British subject, that the ship be transferred by the Finnish owners to Borthwick, be registered and insured in Borthwick's name, sail to Samos under the management of Demetriades, and be transferred at the end of the voyage by Borthwick to Demetriades.

At the time when Borthwick insured the ship, Greek ships were uninsurable, or only insurable at exceptionally high premiums. The interest of Demetriades in the ship was not disclosed to the insurance company.

On the voyage the ship sank off the Portuguese coast and became a total loss.

Held that the contract of insurance was void on account of Borthwick's failure to disclose a material fact.

LORD CHANCELLOR (CAVE) (at p. 9): "It is provided by section 17 of the

Marine Insurance Act 1906 that a contract of marine insurance is a contract based upon the utmost good faith, and, if the utmost good faith be not observed by either party, the contract may be avoided by the other party. By section 18 of the same Act it is provided that 'Subject to the provisions of this section, the assured must disclose to the insurer, before the contract is concluded, every material circumstance which is known to the assured,' and further, that 'Every circumstance is material which would influence the judgment of a prudent insurer in fixing the premium, or determining whether he will take the risk.' Now, in this case it cannot be seriously contested that, in the state of the insurance market at that time, the circumstance of the Greek interest in the vessel was a material circumstance which would have influenced the judgment of a prudent insurer in fixing the premium or determining whether he would take the risk. The facts under this head are summed up by the Lord Justice-Clerk [Alness] in a passage in his opinion (1924 S.C. at p. 196) which I will read: 'The "Spathari," ' he says, 'was purchased by Demetriades, who was a Greek. Thereafter, she was no doubt ostensibly transferred to Borthwick, but only for a limited time and for limited purposes. When the "Spathari" reached Greece her ownership was to revert to Demetriades, and she was thereafter to pass into the hands of Greeks. During the voyage to Greece she was to be managed by a Greek, Demetriades. He was entitled to the freight, and he was also liable for the disbursements, apart from insurance. He was, moreover, interested in the cargo. In short, the "Spathari" was infected with the Greek taint throughout. Her past, her present, and her future were permeated by Greek interest. Now, the evidence is clear that, at the date when these insurances were effected, Greek vessels were taboo in the marine insurance world. They were sinking in alarming numbers, and underwriters fought shy of insuring them. If they insured them at all, they did so at exceptionally high premiums. I am quite satisfied, and indeed I do not think that it was disputed, that, if the true facts regarding this vessel, as I have rehearsed them, had been fully disclosed to the underwriters, if what I might term her Greek interest had been laid bare, she would not have been insured at all. That these facts were material I cannot for a moment doubt. That they were not disclosed is matter of admission.'

"It was argued before the Inner House that, if the underwriters desired information on these points, it was their duty to ask for it. But on that plea the learned Lord Justice-Clerk observed (ibid. at p. 197) that, in the state of the marine insurance market with regard to Greek ships at the date when this vessel was insured, no such duty was cast upon the insurers;

and he added that 'as Borthwick was *ex facie* owner of the "Spathari," there was nothing to put the insurers, so to speak, on the scent of a Greek interest, and there was therefore no duty on their part, which it can be said that they neglected to discharge, to make inquiries on that topic. They did not waive inquiry, because there was nothing to put them on their inquiry.' With these observations I entirely agree, and I am of opinion on this ground alone that the action was properly dismissed."

NOTE

The House of Lords also agreed with the Court of Session in holding that there had been actual misrepresentation leading up to the contract of insurance.

Innocent misrepresentation: reduction of agreement to enter into partnership

Ferguson v. Wilson

(1904) 6 F. 779

W., an engineer in Aberdeen, advertised for a partner. F. replied to the advertisement, and after negotiations a minute of agreement was executed by W. and F. by which W. and F. were to enter into partnership.

Some six months later F. raised an action against W. for reduction of the minute of agreement on the ground that he had entered into it under essential error induced by W.'s misstatements as to the profits and pecuniary position of W.'s business.

Held that the minute of agreement fell to be reduced, although there was no evidence that the misstatements had been made fraudulently.

LORD JUSTICE-CLERK (J. H. A. MACDONALD) (at p. 783): "I do not think ... there is good ground for supposing that the defender in making the statements he did was guilty of misrepresentation with fraudulent intent. I think it possible that the defender took a sanguine view, based perhaps on the busy condition in which the works had been, and the increase in the number of employees, that the business was going ahead, and expressed himself in eagerness and not in bad faith. Being anxious to obtain the aid of capital, he may be held to have taken up and expressed a sanguine view without testing it, and I think may have done so without fraud. But it was undoubtedly a misrepresentation—he not knowing the true state of the facts—and representing a view of the facts which was intended by him to be accepted as true, in his knowledge, by those he was dealing with.

"There having been misrepresentation, will it save the defender from a judgment rescinding the contract that no fraud has been proved? I do not think so. The pursuer asks nothing but that it be rescinded, and to that I consider him to be entitled. I adopt the language of Lord Watson in the case of *Adam* v. *Newbigging* ((1888) 13 App.Cas. at p. 320), holding it to apply directly to this case. He says: 'I entertain no doubt that these representations, although not fraudulently made, are sufficient to entitle the respondent to rescind the agreement. ... He relied, and was entitled to rely, upon the assurances which he had received as to the satisfactory condition of the business, until he became aware of the true state of the facts.'"

LORD MONCREIFF (at p. 783): "The pursuer concludes only for reduction—rescission of the contract; he makes no claim for damages. Therefore the case of *Derry* v. *Peek* ((1889) 14 App.Cas. 337), which related to an action of deceit—that is an action of damages on the ground of fraudulent misrepresentation—does not apply. Proof of fraud is not required in this case.

"Therefore if the pursuer has succeeded in proving that he was induced to agree to enter into partnership with the defender by misrepresentations made by the latter on matters material to the contract and facts which were, or should have been known to the defenders, it is immaterial whether the misrepresentations were made innocently or not."

Misrepresentation as distinct from expression of opinion

Flynn v. Scott

1949 S.C. 442 (O.H.)

F. purchased from S. a secondhand Bedford Luton motor van, S. stating that the van was in good running order.

Seven days later the van broke down, and F. intimated to S. his rejection of the van.

Held that S.'s statement had been a mere expression of opinion, not a misrepresentation entitling F. to repudiate the contract.

LORD MACKINTOSH (Ordinary) (at p. 445): "But the pursuer also main-tains that ... he is entitled to reject the van and get his money back, because he says the contract was induced by material misrepresentation made to him by the seller, Mr Scott. The material misrepresentation founded upon is the statement which I have held was made by Mr Scott to the pursuer, namely, that the van was in good running order. Now, in my view, especially in a sale of this type which was a sale of a secondhand motor vehicle, any statement of that kind could only be regarded as an ex-pression of the opinion of the seller, and, if the buyer was not himself suf-ficiently expert or mechanically instructed to satisfy himself as to the condition of the vehicle, then he had only himself to blame if he accepted the seller's expression of opinion on the matter without having it checked by an expert on his behalf. In my view, the statement made by Mr Scott to the pursuer was not in law a representation, but was simply an expression of opinion, and the pursuer cannot found upon that as being a misrep-resentation entitling him to repudiate the contract."

The nature of fraud

Boyd & Forrest v. The Glasgow and South-Western Railway Co.

1912 S.C.(H.L.) 93

A railway company invited tenders for the construction of part of a rail-way line, and showed to intending offerers what purported to be a journal of bores taken along the proposed stretch of line.

B. & F., a firm of contractors, tendered for the work, and as a result a contract was entered into for the construction of the line by B. & F. for the lump sum of £243,090.

During the progress of the work B. & F. found more rock and hard sub-stance in the ground than they had anticipated, and it was discovered that the journal of bores had been compiled by M., the company's engineer, who had mistakenly but honestly altered information supplied by the borers.

Having completed the work, B. & F. sued the railway company for over £100,000—the difference between the cost and the amount payable under the contract—on the ground that they had been induced to enter into the contract by M.'s fraud.

Held that there was no fraud since M. had altered the information sup-plied by the borers only where he honestly believed it to be erroneous.

LORD ATKINSON (at p. 99): "It may be that the wiser and more prudent
thing for Mr Melville to have done in the circumstances would have been
to have recorded the information he received from the borers precisely as
he had received it, and then have appended a note of his own to the effect
that, in his opinion, the borer was in error. . . . Again, it may well be that
the data upon which Mr Melville proceeded to form a judgment, were to
some degree insufficient, even in the case of one of his skill and experience, but if he honestly thought they were sufficient, and, after full consideration, honestly came to the conclusion that the borer was mistaken in
his description of the substances he had found, and that the description
which he (Melville) inserted in the document was the true description,
and further, inserted that description with the object of giving what was,
in his opinion, true information, deliberate lying is, in my view, not only
out of the case, but every element which renders recklessness in statement
equivalent to lying, is absent from it as well. The well-known passage
from Lord Herschell's judgment in *Derry* v. *Peek* ((1889) 14 App.Cas.
337), was cited by Lord Ardwall. It runs thus:—First, in order to sustain
an action of deceit there must be proof of fraud, and nothing short of that
will suffice. Secondly, fraud is proved where it is shown that a false representation has been made (1) knowingly, or (2) without belief in its truth,
or (3) recklessly, careless whether it be true or false. Although I have
treated the second and third as distinct cases, I think the third is but an instance of the second, for one who makes a statement under such circumstances can have no real belief in the truth of what he states. To prevent a
false statement being fraudulent, there must, I think, always be an honest
belief in its truth. And this probably covers the whole ground, for one who
knowingly alleges that which is false has obviously no such honest belief.
Thirdly, if fraud be proved, the motive of the person guilty of it is immaterial. It matters not that there was no intention to cheat or injure the person
to whom the statement was made.'

"If there be any truth in the evidence of Messrs Melville and Mac-
pherson, 'carelessness of whether the description of these substances was
true or false,' the absence of an honest belief 'that their description was a
true and accurate description,' and the making of a statement as true of
that which was, in fact, false, 'without knowing whether it was true or
false,' are all negatived. . . .

". . . To my mind it appears clear that Mr Melville honestly thought he
was stating in the journal of bores the information in fact conveyed to him
by the borers, and that the change he made in the entry was made for the

very purpose of correcting what he honestly believed to be their mis-description of the substance actually found, so that the journal should set forth the absolute truth. ... I think that so far from not knowing or caring whether the statements contained in the journal were true or false, he was anxious to state the truth, and took such means as he honestly considered sufficient for the very purpose of ascertaining what the truth was so that he might set it forth with accuracy.

"It would be a strange way of showing good faith to state the information he received as if he believed it to be true when he, in fact, thought the borers were in error, and yet abstain from correcting their error. I do not think that Mr Melville acted recklessly in any reasonable sense of the word; and am therefore of opinion that the respondents failed to prove that he was guilty of fraud of any kind towards them. Accordingly, I think their case fails upon this point, and that this appeal should be allowed with costs."

Reduction for innocent misrepresentation: restitutio in integrum *must be possible*

Boyd & Forrest v. The Glasgow and South-Western Railway Co.

1915 S.C.(H.L.) 20

Sequel to previous case, above.

B. & F. brought an action against the railway company concluding, in name of recompense, or alternatively in name of damages, for the extra cost of construction, on the ground that they had entered into the contract under essential error induced by misrepresentation, admittedly innocent, of the railway company.

Held that there had been no misrepresentation. *Held* further that B. & F.'s case failed also on the grounds that (1) they had not proved that the alleged misrepresentation had induced them to enter into the contract; (2) they were barred by having proceeded to complete the contract; and (3) assuming there had been misrepresentation, the fact that it was innocent excluded the remedy of damages, while the fact that *restitutio in integrum* was impossible excluded the remedy of reduction of the contract and pay-ment of a *quantum meruit*.

EARL LOREBURN (at p. 23): "It is enough to say that Messrs Boyd & Forrest knew by the end of 1902 all about certain things. They knew the innocent representations by which they had been induced to make the contract, and they knew the reality about the physical condition of the strata. Knowing both, they elected to proceed and to complete the contract. After that they cannot rely upon the discrepancy between those representations and the reality as a basis of any claim either for rescission or for damages, whether it be called recompense or compensation, or by any other form of words."

LORD ATKINSON (at p. 25): "Now, where a special contract ... has been entered into to execute, for a lump sum, the works therein mentioned, the right to be paid on a *quantum meruit* does not arise out of that contract, but out of a new contract springing into existence on the extinction of the old one. The two contracts cannot co-exist. .... I am inclined to the opinion that the entering into a new agreement to pay the pursuers for the work they have done on a *quantum meruit* basis has not been proved in the present case. The law of Scotland does not, as far as I have been able to ascertain, differ from the law of England on this subject. Having regard to the view I take upon the other questions raised in this case, it is unnecessary for me to pronounce a definite opinion on this point. ...

[After considering whether there had been misrepresentation] "I think, therefore, that the pursuers' case wholly fails upon this their main point; but even if I were in error in that view I should still be clearly of opinion that they are not entitled to have this contract set aside, inasmuch as *restitutio in integrum*, in the true sense of that phrase, is now absolutely impossible.

"The pursuers cannot take back what they gave, their work, though they might restore what they got, the money they received; that, however, is precisely what they are not required to do. The work was done; the parties cannot in any sense be restored, in relation to this contract, to the position they occupied before the contract was entered into. If they had succeeded on their allegation of fraud, they could have got damages in an action for deceit sufficient to cover their loss; but they have not sued for damages either for deceit or breach of contract, and they cannot get damages for an innocent representation made outside the contract, though inducing to it,—*Derry v. Peek* ((1889) 14 App.Cas. 337)."

LORD SHAW OF DUNFERMLINE (at p. 36): "Until this case I have not for many years heard it doubted that rescission is not a remedy open to any litigant when matters are not entire and when *restitutio in integrum* is impossible. I do not find myself able fully to comprehend that view of the case which would treat the situation as one equivalent to possible restitution by a process of adjustment of accounts. The railway is there, the bridges are built, the excavations are made, the rails are laid, and the railway itself was in complete working two years before this action was brought. Accounts cannot obliterate it, and unless the railway is obliterated *restitutio in integrum* is impossible. ...

"Nor do I think that there is a remedy in damages for an innocent misrepresentation."

LORD PARMOOR (at p. 42): "I desire to guard myself against giving any sanction to the view that the respondents would have been entitled to claim a reduction of the contract even if it had been proved that they entered into the contract under essential error induced by the innocent misrepresentation of the appellants. Innocent misrepresentation connotes not wrongdoing but an innocent act, and the question is which of the two innocent parties should suffer. The remedy of reduction is not in general available unless the party seeking reduction is able to place the party against whom it is sought in substantially the same position as he occupied before the contract. In substance there must be *restitutio in integrum*. As incidental to the remedy of reduction, and in order to work the remedy out to a just result, there may be a giving back and a taking back on both sides; but whatever such adjustment may involve, it must clearly be distinguished from damages. ...

"In the present case *restitutio in integrum* is impracticable in any form."

NOTE

This case must now be read in the light of section 10 of the Law Reform (Miscellaneous Provisions) (Scotland) Act 1985 which abolished the rule that damages could not be recovered unless fraud was proved (see Appendix A).

Reduction for fraudulent misrepresentation: doctrine of restitutio in integrum *is not to be applied too literally*

Spence v. Crawford

1939 S.C.(H.L.) 52

S., a director of a private company, Glencairn Metals Ltd., sold his shares in the company to C., a fellow-director.

Later S. brought against C. an action for reduction of the contract on the ground of fraudulent misrepresentations made by C. as to the company's condition.

C., as well as denying the fraud, contended that in any event reduction could not be granted because S. could not make *restitutio in integrum*. In support of this contention C. founded on the facts that (1) the company's capital had been increased since the sale and if the shares were returned S. would not have the same controlling interest in the company as he formerly had, and (2) in accordance with the contract of sale C. had relieved S. of an obligation undertaken by S. in respect of the company's bank overdraft and to do so C. had had to sell securities at a serious loss.

Held that (1) fraud had been proved and (2) *restitutio* could be effected by repayment by S. to C. of the price paid for the shares with interest (less a sum representing the loss sustained by C. on the securities which he had had to sell), payment by C. to S. of the dividends on the shares, and retransfer of the shares by C. to S.

LORD THANKERTON (at p. 69): "The normal type of case in which the question has arisen is one where the pursuer is purchaser and seeks to recover the price on restoration of the subject purchased, and the question in issue is whether the pursuer by his treatment of the subject purchased, while in his possession, has so treated it that it is no longer identifiable in any reasonable sense. I should add that the alteration of the subject purchased might also have been caused by circumstances outside the control of the pursuer, such as the conversion of shares into shares of an essentially different character. . . .

"It is well established that the doctrine is not to be applied too literally. . . .

[After referring to English cases] "The above cases were all examples in substance of a purchaser seeking relief against a vendor, but in the present case the position is reversed. . . .

" . . . In my opinion, there may well be a different conclusion according as the misrepresentations are fraudulent or not. While the decision in any case must turn on the terms of the contract under reduction and the facts of the particular case, I may say broadly that, in my opinion, the defender who, as purchaser, has been guilty of fraudulent misrepresentation is not entitled in bar of restitution to found on dealings with the subject purchased which he has been enabled by his fraud to carry out. . . .

" . . . In a case of innocent misrepresentation, it may well be that an alteration of the holdings in the company, made on the footing that the contract was valid, might, under certain circumstances, prove a bar to restitution."

LORD WRIGHT (at p. 76): "On the basis that the fraud is established, I think that this is a case where the remedy of rescission, accompanied by *restitutio in integrum*, is proper to be given. The principles governing that form of relief are the same in Scotland as in England. The remedy is equitable. Its application is discretionary, and, where the remedy is applied, it must be moulded in accordance with the exigencies of the particular case. ... The Court must fix its eyes on the goal of doing 'what is practically just.' How that goal may be reached must depend on the circumstances of the case. But the Court will be more drastic in exercising its discretionary powers in a case of fraud than in a case of innocent misrepresentation. ... There is no doubt good reason for the distinction. A case of innocent misrepresentation may be regarded rather as one of misfortune than as one of moral obliquity. There is no deceit or intention to defraud. The Court will be less ready to pull a transaction to pieces where the defendant is innocent, whereas in the case of fraud the Court will exercise its jurisdiction to the full in order, if possible, to prevent the defendant from enjoying the benefit of his fraud at the expense of the innocent plaintiff. But restoration is essential to the idea of restitution. To take the simplest case, if a plaintiff who has been defrauded seeks to have the contract annulled and his money or property restored to him, it would be inequitable if he did not also restore what he had got under the contract from the defendant. Though the defendant has been fraudulent, he must not be robbed nor must the plaintiff be unjustly enriched, as he would be if he both got back what he had parted with and kept what he had received in return. The purpose of the relief is not punishment, but compensation. The rule is stated as requiring the restoration of both parties to the *status quo ante*. ... The Court can go a long way in ordering restitution if the substantial identity of the subject-matter of the contract remains. ... Certainly in a case of fraud the Court will do its best to unravel the complexities of any particular case, which may in some cases involve adjustments on both sides.

"In the vast majority of cases of the transfer of property it is a purchaser who is seeking to reduce the contract on the terms of restoring on the one hand what he has purchased, and on the other hand of being repaid the purchase price with all proper allowances and accounts. The present case is peculiar in that it is a vendor who seeks rescission. But the principles must be the same."

Reduction impossible after sale to third party

Edinburgh United Breweries Ltd. v. Molleson

(1894) 21 R.(H.L.) 10; (1893) 20 R. 581

M. entered into a minute of agreement for the sale to D. of the Palace Brewery for £20,500, the price being based on profits as shown in the books of the business.

Shortly afterwards D. agreed to sell the brewery to E. Ltd. for £28,500, and a disposition was granted directly to E. Ltd. by M.

Two years later it was discovered that the books had contained false entries as to profits, and E. Ltd., in its own name and as D.'s assignee, and D. raised an action against M. for reduction of the contract between M. and D., and of the disposition by M. to E. Ltd., E. Ltd. offering restitution *in integrum*.

Held that (1) as E. Ltd. had not been a party to the contract between M. and D., E. Ltd. had no title to sue; and (2) as D. had no interest in the property after the disposition by M. to E. Ltd., he had no title to reduce the contract.

LORD WATSON (at p. 16): "The contract sought to be set aside, which was implemented by a conveyance to the company, was a contract to which Mr Molleson and Mr Dunn were the only parties. There was no privity between Molleson and the company, and in conveying to them Molleson simply fulfilled the obligation, which he had undertaken to Dunn, to make a conveyance to his nominee. The deed of conveyance is the only contract between Mr Molleson and the company. By the ordinary rule of law, the moment a conveyance is accepted as in implement of the obligations of a contract, the original contract is at an end, and the conveyance constitutes the only contract between the parties.

" ... Now, what is the position of Mr Dunn? He made a remunerative sale, and he has no interest in the brewery, which was the subject of these dealings; and if he made a valid contract of sale to the company to be followed by a conveyance in virtue of his contract with Mr Molleson, it humbly appears to me that his title to challenge this transaction with the respondent came to an end the moment the conveyance was completed ....

"Therefore, it appears to me that Mr Dunn as a pursuer is out of the case; he had no title in his own right, and I do not see how his concurrence can in the least degree aid the title of the company."

Reduction possible after rescission of subsequent assignation: date from which rescission takes effect

Westville Shipping Co. Ltd. v. Abram Steamship Co. Ltd.

1923 S.C.(H.L.) 68; 1922 S.C. 571

A. Ltd. had entered into a contract with Dublin Shipbuilders Ltd. for the building of a steamer.

A. Ltd. then assigned the contract to W. Ltd., making, in good faith, certain representations as to the stage of construction.

W. Ltd. then assigned the contract to B. Ltd., making the same representations.

B. Ltd., having discovered by inspection at the shipbuilding yard that the representations were false, brought an action in England against W. Ltd. on August 17 for rescission of their assignation. W. Ltd. consented to decree and the final order was pronounced on December 11.

Meantime W. Ltd. on November 5 brought an action in the Court of Session against A. Ltd. for reduction of the first assignation.

Held that (1) W. Ltd.'s title to sue, which had been abrogated by the second assignation, revived upon the rescission of that assignation; and (2) it was not affected by the fact that the action of reduction was brought prior to the actual granting of decree in the English action.

LORD DUNEDIN (at p. 71): "The second point is that the action is barred by the fact of the subsale. So long as the subsale stood, this would of course be so. . . . No one can be allowed to maintain a contract between him and another and at the same time to reduce another contract on which alone his title to make that contract depended. That was the position of Dunn in *Molleson's* case. Dunn proposed to stick to his contract with the United Breweries Co., and at the same time to reduce the original contract. But here the subcontract no longer exists. It has been put out of the way by the decision in the English Courts. . . . The respondents have been put back into their original position, *i.e.*, as purchasers under the contract with the appellants. Why then should they not reduce that contract if they have relevant grounds to do so?

"The only point remaining is founded on date. . . . The original title to set aside a contract induced by misrepresentation was quite good. It is true that for the moment there seemed a good answer, namely: 'You have parted with the subject of the contract and therefore you have lost your interest,' but the moment that the instrument by which they had so parted was swept away the original title was then in all its force."

LORD ATKINSON (at p. 73): "Where one party to a contract expresses by word or act in an unequivocal manner that, by reason of fraud or essential error of a material kind inducing him to enter into the contract, he has resolved to rescind it and refuses to be bound by it, the expression of his election, if justified by the facts, terminates the contract, puts the parties *in statu quo ante*, and restores things, as between them, to the position in which they stood before the contract was entered into. It may be that the facts impose upon the party desiring to rescind the duty of making *restitutio in integrum*. If so, he must discharge that duty before the rescission is, in effect, accomplished; but, if the other party to the contract questions the right of the first to rescind, thus obliging the latter to bring an action at law to enforce the right he has secured for himself by his election, and the latter gets a verdict, it is an entire mistake to suppose that it is this verdict which by itself terminates the contract and restores the antecedent status. The verdict is merely the judicial determination of the fact that the expression by the plaintiff of his election to rescind was justified, was effective, and put an end to the contract."

NOTE

For *Molleson's* case see *Edinburgh United Breweries Ltd.* v. *Molleson* (p. 111, above).

Fraudulent misrepresentation: damages without rescission

Smith v. Sim

1954 S.C. 357 (O.H.)

Sim, proprietor of the Market Arms, Montrose, advertised his business for sale. Smith, relying on statements as to turnover supplied to him by Sim's solicitors, purchased the business for £21,600.

Shortly after entering on possession, Smith alleged that Sim had been guilty of fraud in having falsely represented the turnover at a figure about twice that which it had been, and without offering to rescind the contract of sale sued for damages of £10,000.

Held that the action of damages was competent.

LORD WHEATLEY (Ordinary) (at p. 359): "Defender's counsel . . . contended that, where there was alleged fraudulent misrepresentation, the only remedy open to the pursuer was to rescind the contract and sue for damages, where the circumstances justified such a course, and that it was incompetent to maintain the contract and at the same time sue for damages . . . .

"In my opinion, the pursuer's argument that the action is competent is well founded. It receives its initial support from a passage in Stair (I, ix, 14), and while that passage may . . . be in general terms, it was founded upon by Lord Curriehill in the case of *Graham* (*Graham* v. *Western Bank* (1865) 3 M. 617 at p. 628) in arriving at the conclusion that this was a competent optional remedy open to a pursuer who claims to have been defrauded. . . . The whole history of judicial opinion seems to be in favour of the competency of such an action. . . . In the case of *Manners* (*Manners* v. *Whitehead* (1898) 1 F. 171) Lord President Robertson stated that he found it impossible to discover in the action an action of rescission and agreed with the Lord Ordinary, Lord Kyllachy, that it was an action of damages for deceit and nothing else, thereby accepting the competency of such a latter type of action. In the same case Lord McLaren also accepted the competency of such an action. . . . The passage in the judgment of Lord Justice-Clerk Alness in *Smart* (*Smart* v. *Wilkinson*, 1928 S.C. 383 at p. 388), where he expressed the view that an action of reparation would be open to a person who claimed that he had suffered damage as a result of the fraudulent misrepresentations of another person with whom he had entered into a contract, was . . . an *obiter dictum*. . . . Nevertheless it is yet a further step in the acceptance of this principle by Judges of eminence. At the end of the day the defender's counsel were left with the case of *Bryson & Co.* (*Bryson & Co. Ltd.* v. *Bryson*, 1916, 1 S.L.T. 361 (O.H.)), and they nailed their colours to its mast. Unfortunately for them, that case, far from being an authority in support of their argument, is an authority against them. An analysis of the case discloses that the pursuer's claim was laid in the alternative, the first leg being an *actio quanti minoris*, and the second leg an action of damages based on fraudulent misrepresentation. Lord Anderson held that the first leg was incompetent, but in terms accepted the competency of the second form of action. . . .

"In the light of that anthology of judicial opinion I hold that it is the settled law of Scotland that an action of damages in a case such as the present is competent without rescission of the contract."

NOTES

1. For *Smart* v. *Wilkinson*, see p. 253, below.

2. In *Bryson & Co. Ltd.* v. *Bryson* Lord Anderson said (at p. 364): "If there has been in the contract some fraud on the part of the seller I think it is well settled that the buyer has a choice of two remedies: first, rescission of the contract involving the return of the subject-matter of the sale and a claim of damages; and second, a claim of damages without rescission or restitution."

Extortion: mere inadequacy of consideration does not of itself invalidate agreement

McLachlan v. Watson

(1874) 11 S.L.R. 549

McL., who had in 1868 taken a lease of the George Hotel, Glasgow, entered into an agreement with W., whereby, in consideration of W.'s advancing money and granting guarantees to the extent of over £5,000 in respect of McL.'s transactions, McL. undertook to pay to W. an annual bonus of £600 for the 10 years of the lease.

McL. died in 1872, having for the first four years of the lease applied the profits in part payment of the sums due for the establishment of the business; he had therefore been unable to pay the bonuses to W., but had, each half-year, granted a promissory note to W. for £300.

McL.'s widow, as his executrix, brought an action against W. to reduce the agreement and the eight promissory notes on the ground that the agreement was unequal, extortionate, and unfair.

Held that in the absence of fraud mere inadequacy of consideration was not sufficient as a ground of reduction.

LORD ORDINARY (MACKENZIE) (at p. 550): "There can be no doubt that the defender made a very hard bargain with Mr McLachlan. But mere inadequacy of consideration will not, *per se*, invalidate the agreement. Such inadequacy will, no doubt, form a very important element in considering the question whether there has been fraud."

LORD ARDMILLAN (at p. 551): "It is said that the agreement was unequal, extortionate, and unfair—such as equity cannot recognise, and law ought not to enforce. It appears to me that the defender Mr Watson did make a bargain very favourable to himself, and pressing very severely on

McLachlan. In other words, the consideration in respect of which Mr McLachlan undertook the obligation to pay to Mr Watson £600 a year for 10 years was very inadequate. But then it is quite settled, and I think rightly settled, that in the absence of fraud mere inadequacy of consideration is not sufficient to sustain reduction of an agreement between parties capable of contracting. This has been matter of decision, and has been frequently stated by high judicial authority. ...

"The fact of inadequacy of consideration, if gross and manifest, is, however, important in regard to the ulterior question of fraud, and fraud is here alleged.

" ... Giving, as I think, due weight to the inequality and inadequacy, I have still arrived at the conclusion that fraud has not been proved. I can see no proof of fraud. ... It may well be true, and I am disposed to think it is true, that the price paid for this support was extremely high. But not on that ground can we reduce this written agreement, clearly expressed, perfectly understood, and deliberately subscribed. ... It is indeed possible that Mr McLachlan might have obtained in other quarters, and on more favourable terms, the funds which he required. It is not quite clear that he could. But if he was not deceived or defrauded by Mr Watson, and if, knowing the meaning of this agreement, he signed it, and acted on it, then the mere fact that he might have made a better arrangement cannot sustain this action.

" ... I have some sympathy with the pursuer. I think this has been a hard bargain. I think the consideration was inadequate. But I cannot find proof of fraud, deception, or misrepresentation."

NOTE

Contrast exceptional cases:

Young v. *Gordon* (1896) 23 R. 419: Miss Janet Young, formerly a schoolmistress, kept furnished apartments at Claremont, Bridge of Allan. She had granted to G. two promissory notes, payable on demand, for £100 and £24 16s. She was unable to pay when a demand was made and asked for delay. In return for a delay of 24 hours G. prevailed on her to grant three promissory notes, one for £100 and two for £75 each. Enforcement of these was refused.

Gordon's Administrator v. *Stephen*, 1902, 9 S.L.T. 397 (O.H.): In 1893 S. had granted to G. a promissory note for £25. Each quarter, the promissory note was renewed and on each occasion G. claimed £8 interest, with the result that by the end of six years G. had paid about £198 in all and the promissory note was still outstanding. Enforcement of the promissory note was refused. S., an Aberdeenshire crofter 70 years of age, was described as "a very simple and timid old man, unacquainted with the ways of the world, and very ill fitted for dealings with such a man as Gordon."

Force and fear: threatened violence: contract void

Earl of Orkney v. Vinfra

(1606) Mor. 16,481

In relation to a claim made by the Earl of Orkney against V. for payment of "2,000 merks," V. contended that the contract was null because it had been "extorted by fear and dead-dome": he stated that the Earl had summoned him to his castle in Zetland and had commanded him to subscribe the contract which had already been subscribed by the Earl, and that on V.'s refusing to do so "the said Earl was so offended, that with terrible countenance and words, and laying his hand upon his whinger, he threatened with execrable oaths to bereave this Vinfra of his life, and stick him presently through the head with his whinger, if he subscribed not, and so for just fear he being compelled to subscribe it, the same was null."

The Earl, on the other hand, argued that "there was no fact nor deed libelled, but only boisterous words which could not be thought just fear."

Held that the exception of fear was "very relevant."

Force and fear: fear of lawful consequences not sufficient

Priestnell v. Hutcheson

(1857) 19 D. 495

A husband, by antenuptial contract of marriage, conveyed certain heritable property to his wife in liferent. The firm in which he was a partner became deeply involved in debt to a bank, and the property was disponed to the bank. The wife sought to reduce the disposition on the grounds of force and fear and essential error, averring that her husband had come hurriedly into her bedroom, when she was unwell, and told her that the bank threatened him with diligence and ruin unless she signed the disposition, that, if she did not sign, he would, to avoid imprisonment, flee the country, leaving her and her family to do as they best might, that the bank agent then came with the disposition, and that she signed it without reading it or having it explained to her.

Held that these averments were insufficient to support force and fear, but that, as regarded the averment of essential error, proof before answer should be allowed.

LORD DEAS (at p. 499): "Although, translating the language of the Roman law, we couple together force and fear as one ground of reduction, the act of force is truly, as Lord Stair observes (i, 9, 8), only one means of inducing fear, the true ground of reduction being *extortion*, through the influence of fear, induced in the various ways, of which he gives instances, partly from the civil law and partly from our own law—such as the fear of torture, fear of infamy, fear of danger to life, and so on. It would be very difficult, and it is not here at all necessary, either by definition or description, to point out all the means by which, and which alone, such fear may be induced, on the part of a married woman, as the law will recognise as sufficient to void her solemn deed. Certain it is, on the one hand, that it is not every sort of fear—or rather it is not the fear of consequences of every sort, which will void such a deed; and, on the other hand, that fear of particular consequences may be sufficient in the case of a married woman, though of full capacity, which would not be sufficient in the case of a man of full capacity, and that these consequences need not necessarily be injury to herself, either in her person or character, but may be injury to her husband or to her children, the fear for whose safety may be stronger even than the fear for her own. But while I state these propositions in a general form, I do not attempt to define or describe what must be the nature of the consequences feared, in order to render them relevant to support reduction of the deed. . . .

". . . The grounds of fear must be such as the law recognises as relevant to void a solemn written deed; and here the only fear alleged is fear of consequences, which it was quite lawful for the bank to hold out, and equally lawful for the husband to communicate to his wife, as well as to tell her what he himself might thereupon feel constrained to do, in order to avoid imprisonment and gain a livelihood; and when the wife, to avoid the consequences thus impending, agreed to sign the deed, it would be more correct to say that she acted from affection than that she acted from fear; and although affection may no doubt induce fear for the person who is its object, yet if the fear so induced be merely the fear of (or in other words, the desire to avoid) such consequences as are stated here, all which might have ensued without illegality on the part of anybody, this is not the sort of fear which we can hold relevant to void a formal and delivered deed. The bank threatened nothing which was unlawful, and the husband held out nothing which was unlawful, for he only said he would be constrained to leave the country, which might be a very natural course for him to take to avoid imprisonment, and seek a livelihood. . . . In a reduction on the ground of force and fear, I hold it necessary to specify the things said and done in such a way as to enable the Court to judge whether they really amount to force and fear in the eye of law, very much as in a case of fraud it must be specifically stated in what the alleged fraud consists. Here, I think, the specification, in place of supporting, destroys the charge."

LORD ORDINARY (BENHOLME) (at p. 498): "The authorities in our law upon this subject are happily very few."

NOTES

1. This leading case was followed in *Hunter* v. *Bradford Trust Ltd.*, 1977 S.L.T. (Notes) 33 (O.H.): Two sisters were in financial difficulties and entered into a minute of agreement with a property trust company to take over certain heritable property, pay to the sisters £8,500 and one-half of the net profits (if any) on realisation. The night before the sale by auction was to take place, a director of the company discovered that the minute of agreement ought to have provided for £8,500 to be deducted from the proceeds to be paid to the sisters. He refused to allow the roup to proceed until the sisters signed an amended minute of agreement. The sisters, having brought an action to reduce the second minute of agreement, averred that they had signed it because of force and fear, *i.e.* the threat that if they had not signed it, the roup would have been cancelled.

Held that the averments relating to force and fear were not relevant.

Lord Migdale (at p. 34): "Mr Denham [one of the defenders' directors] threatened to cancel the roup if the pursuers would not sign an amending agreement. . . . No doubt the pursuers were seriously perturbed about the attitude of their banker and other creditors. That was the element of fear. The threat and the only threat made by Mr Denham was to cancel the roup fixed for the next day. There was nothing illegal in this. The defenders were, in terms of the first agreement, the persons who were to sell the property. True they were bound to do so as early as possible but the only persons required to arrange for the disposal of the property were the defenders. If they decided to cancel the roup fixed for a particular day they were entitled to do so. Mr Denham's threat was accordingly not one of an unjustifiable or unwarrantable act. Such a threat could not form the basis of an action of reduction on the ground of force and fear.

" ... If the only threat is a threat to do a lawful act, the plea of force and fear must fail."

2. In *Hislop* v. *Dickson Motors (Forres) Ltd.*, 1978 S.L.T. (Notes) 73 (O.H.), H., who had been employed by D. Ltd. as cashier-bookkeeper, was suspected by D. Ltd. of embezzlement. H. admitted having taken money and agreed to repay it. Her employers obtained from H. a signature to a withdrawal form for H.'s savings bank account and also the key of her car. At a subsequent meeting, her employers, having discovered that H. also had a current account, obtained her signature to a blank cheque in their favour. The employers withdrew all the money at the credit of both accounts.

H. claimed reduction of the withdrawal form and the cheque and return of the car, on the ground of force and fear.

On a consideration of the evidence the Lord Ordinary (Maxwell) held (at p. 76) that the signature of the withdrawal form and the handing over of the key to the car were voluntary acts done when H.'s mind could not be said to have been overpowered, but that the signing of the blank cheque at the second meeting could not reasonably be considered a truly voluntary act on H.'s part, but "was rather the submission to pressure which might in the whole circumstance well have overpowered the mind of a woman of normal firmness finding herself in such a situation. While the pursuer in fact signed the cheque, I consider that the abstraction by the defender of the funds in her current account is more akin to a forceful seizure of those funds than a voluntary payment of them by her."

Facility and circumvention: old age

Cairns v. Marianski

(1850) 12 D.919 and 1286

F. died in 1846 at the age of 93 leaving two daughters, of whom the younger had married C. in 1832 and the elder had married M. in 1839. Mr and Mrs M. had resided with F. from shortly after their marriage until F.'s death.

Mrs C., on her father's death, raised an action to reduce, on the ground of facility and circumvention, certain documents subscribed by F. in favour of M.

The jury found that there had been both facility and circumvention.

Held that the verdict of the jury should not be set aside as contrary to the evidence.

LORD JUSTICE-CLERK (HOPE) in charging the jury (at p. 922): "The issue in this case proposes two distinct questions. 1st. Whether at the date when the subscriptions &c. were adhibited, Fairservice was of weak and facile mind, and easily imposed upon; and, 2d. Whether the defender, taking advantage of his weakness and facility, did, by fraud or circumvention, or intimidation, obtain these subscriptions, &c., or any of them, to the lesion of the granter? . . .

". . . The words facile, and easily imposed upon, are very flexible terms. A certain degree of weakness is certainly required, but the degree may depend very much on the means employed to obtain the signatures. There may be such weakness of mind from old age, such timidity of character, such dread of violent scenes, as will warrant the setting aside of these documents. One man of sound intellect may be able to resist violence of temper, dread of family disturbance, and so on, while another of even greater intellect may, from old age, or want of nerve, be incapable of resisting the same degree of violence."

On the defender's motion for a new trial:

LORD MONCREIFF (at p. 1291): "I am of opinion that no new trial ought to be granted. It is maintained that there was no evidence of facility. It may be that, on the evidence, it does not appear that the deceased was so defective in intellect that his deeds generally could be reduced, as the deeds of a man incapable from mental defect. But that is not the nature of this case. The case is, that though he had not lost his understanding generally, he was, *quoad* this defender, in a state of even more than that ordinary facility. . . . It is true that there is not here any direct evidence of fraudulent practice at the moment of executing any of the particular writs under reduction. But the facts established can leave no doubt in any reasonable mind that they never could have been executed except under the influence, and by the effect, of fraudulent practice—by deception and intimidation of the grossest kind; and then there is here what I think equivalent to direct evidence of undue influence and intimidation employed, by taking advantage of the very peculiar relation in which the parties stood to one another.

"The man was on the verge of ninety. From the mode of living into which he was in a manner compelled, at all events reduced, by the defender, he came to be entirely under his command and control; and, in the result, the defender comes out, from having absolutely nothing in the world, a comparatively very rich man, by means of merely colourable deeds or writings of the deceased, obtained without any consideration whatever.

"... I am satisfied that the verdict is according to the truth and justice of the case; and as we know that it was satisfactory to the Judge who presided in the trial, I am of opinion that no sufficient cause has been shewn for sending the cause to any other trial."

LORD MEDWYN (at p. 1292): "The weakness which might be established, instead of being of the ordinary case of incapacity from weakness or defect of intellect, might rather exist from the timidity incident to the old age of a nervous man of a feeble body, under the influence of a man of violent temper living in family with him, and constantly watched by him in all his actions, and who had such power over him as to induce him to write what was required of him, and fear to complain of it afterwards."

LORD COCKBURN (at p. 1294): "It was laid down by the Judge at the trial, that in the issue facility did not necessarily and exclusively mean defect of understanding, but also meant that facility, consisting of mere weakness, which makes extreme age liable to be controlled by intimidation. This direction was quite sound, and accordingly no exception was taken to it.

"Now, I never saw the combination of this weakness and of intimidation more clearly proved. Under this evidence I could have pronounced no other verdict."

LORD JUSTICE-CLERK (HOPE) (at p. 1295): "The substance of the explanation given to the Jury ... was, that the expressions 'weak and facile,' and 'easily imposed upon,' are flexible terms, intended to cover cases of a very different character, and may embrace the case of a very old man whose intellect may not be weak, if at all impaired, but who may be easily frightened—timid and nervous from age—afraid of violence—compelled from dread, and from the desire of ease, and the helplessness and dependence of age, to submit to the ascendancy of another, and incapable of exercising resolution so as to resist violence of temper. ...

"... Of course extreme age renders the effect of intimidation on the nerves more complete; and to exclude challenge in such a case because the understanding might be unimpaired, or nearly so, would be unjust, and against the actual truth of the case."

Facility and circumvention: cautioner dissuaded from consulting law-agent

Sutherland v. W.M. Low & Co. Ltd.

(1901) 3 F. 972

T., who was insolvent, being pressed by L., one of his creditors, to obtain security for a debt, asked S., his brother-in-law, a 78-year-old retired butler, to become cautioner in a bond for the amount of the debt. S. refused to do so without consulting his law-agent.

T. informed L. of S.'s refusal, and L. told T. to tell S. that it was unnecessary to consult a law-agent and that he would never be required to pay anything if he signed.

T. told this to S., and S. then signed the bond without consulting his law-agent. The fact that T. was insolvent was not disclosed to S.

S. was charged to pay the sum in the bond.

Held that the cautionary obligation fell to be reduced.

LORD YOUNG (at p. 979): "What we have to consider, then, is this, whether the pursuer—looking to the evidence as to his condition, his age, infirmity, and facility—should have been asked by any honest man to sign this bond for an insolvent brother-in-law without consulting his man of business. Ought we not, on the principles of justice which we administer in this Court, to restore the man into the position in which he was before he was induced to put his name to this deed? I think these considerations of justice require that the pursuer should be restored, by the reduction of the deed, to the position in which he was before he was induced to sign it. If Low had had no connection with the proceedings connected with the granting of the deed—if he had taken the deed *in bona fide*—it might not have been possible to restore the pursuer without inequity to Low. . . . But . . . my opinion is . . . that Low is himself responsible for the way in which the pursuer was induced to do what honestly he ought never to have been required to do."

LORD MONCREIFF (at p. 980): "The question which we have to decide is really now narrowed to a very narrow and very sharp one. It is now admitted . . . that Sutherland was facile, and that he was induced to grant the bond of caution through the circumvention of Robert Thomson. The only question we have to decide is, whether the defender Low is affected by the fraud and circumvention used by Thomson in procuring this deed. I think that the case is a special one. . . . The case we have to deal with is . . . that of a creditor who, not content with calling on his debtor to furnish security, himself interferes in the selection of the cautioner and puts unfair pressure on the cautioner, instructing the debtor to dissuade him from taking steps for his own protection which, if taken, would certainly have prevented him from becoming a cautioner. In such a case I think the creditor forfeits all the benefit which enures to a creditor who abstains altogether from interference in such a matter. In the present case, therefore, the only question we have to consider is, whether in making his representations to Sutherland and preventing him from consulting his own agent Thomson was acting as the hand or agent of Low; and on that point I have not the slightest doubt. I think the evidence ... amply instructs that it was at Low's instigation that Thomson returned to Sutherland and induced him to abstain from seeing his own law-agent before signing this deed."

LORD JUSTICE-CLERK (J. H. A. MACDONALD) (at p. 980): "In this case the man was certainly hopelessly insolvent, and, whether he went first instigated by Low, or on the suggestion of Low, he came back from Sutherland with the knowledge that Sutherland would not act as he desired him to act without laying the matter before his law-agent. Now Low, I think it is proved on the evidence, told Thomson there was no need for Sutherland to go to an agent. I think no honest man of intelligence would have given that advice. He gave plainly, I think, dishonest advice. I think he must have known perfectly well that if his advice was not acted upon, and the person to whom the advice was given did see an agent, no bond would ever have been granted. Therefore the only other question is whether Thomson in pressing that advice on the cautioner was acting for Low. I think it is satisfactorily made out that he was."

Facility and circumvention: specification is required

Mackay v. Campbell

1967 S.C.(H.L.) 53; 1966 S.C. 237

C., the owner of the islands of Taransay and Gaskir in the parish of Harris, suffered a leg injury as a result of a fall in the old schoolhouse on Taransay.

While in Lewis Hospital where his leg was operated on, C. signed missives of sale by which he agreed to sell his islands, together with the livestock and moveable property thereon, to M. for £16,000.

C. failed to implement these missives, and M. raised against C. an action in which he concluded for decree ordaining C. to execute a disposition of the heritable subjects.

C. sought to have the missives reduced, averring that when he signed them he had, to M.'s knowledge, been in a weak and facile state of mind, afraid that he might die and in any event believing that he would never be able to walk properly and look after his islands again, that M., making no attempt to reassure C. that his fears were groundless, took improper advantage of C.'s false belief, and that the value of the islands was at least 50 per cent. more than the price in the missives.

Held that there were no relevant averments of circumvention, since all the facts averred were consistent with honesty on M.'s part.

LORD GUEST (at p. 61): "In assessing the relevancy of the appellant's averments three matters have to be considered: (1) weakness and facility, (2) circumvention, and (3) lesion. These three factors are all interrelated and they must be looked at as a whole and not in separate compartments. The strength of averments on one matter may compensate for the weakness of averments upon other matters.

"So far as lesion is concerned, the Division have held that there are relevant averments of lesion and in this I think they were right. Indeed, it was not challenged by the respondent. . . .

"But this does not take the appellant very far. There are no specific averments of the respects in which his mind was weak and facile. It is not said that his false belief in the severity of his illness and the consequences of his accident were so irrational as to lead to the conclusion that his sense of judgment was impaired. It is not suggested that he was suffering from any form of senile or other mental decay. A mere averment that he was in a weak and facile state of mind, without further specification, is not, in my view, sufficient. I am very doubtful whether there are relevant averments of facility; they are certainly not so strong as to relieve the appellant of the necessity of averring and proving circumvention.

" 'Circumvention signifieth the act of fraud, whereby a person is induced to a deed or obligation by deceit'—Stair, I, ix, 9. Bell's *Dictionary* ((7th ed.), p. 181) puts the matter thus: 'Circumvention; deceit or fraud.' This is not a case where the person upon whom the circumvention has been practised is dead or *incapax*, as may be in the case of the reduction of a testamentary document. In such a case if facility or weakness of mind is satisfactorily averred and the deed is impetrated in favour of the impetrator or his relatives, there is probably no need to aver or prove any specific act of circumvention. Indeed it may not be possible to do so, because the act would be in secret. Circumvention would in such circumstances be assumed. Such were the cases of *Clunie* v. *Stirling* (1854) 17 D. 15) and *Horsburgh* v. *Thomson's Trustees* (1912 S.C. 267). But this is a different case. The injured party is alive and a party to the action. To succeed he must aver some facts and circumstances from which circumvention can be inferred. There is a notable lack of anything suggestive of deceit or dishonesty on the part of the respondent or his solicitor. . . . Upon the pleadings as they stand, all the facts are quite consistent with honesty on the part of the respondent and his solicitor. None of the averments are, in my view, facts from which circumvention or fraud can be inferred."

NOTES

1. The Court of Session decided that it was competent to sue for implement of only one part of a composite contract for the sale of both heritage and moveables. On this point Lord Justice-Clerk (Grant) said (at p. 248): "It was argued, however, that when one has a composite contract for the sale of both heritage and moveables, it is incompetent to sue for implement of only one part of the contract. It is to be noted here that the pursuer, though asking for a disposition alone, is tendering the *whole* purchase price, which covered (and by the missives was apportioned equally between) both heritage and moveables. I am unable to see why he should not be entitled to proceed in this way and no authority was cited to us which would appear to support a contrary view. If A buys from B a house with all its contents for a lump (but apportioned) sum, and B proceeds to sell off the contents elsewhere, it does not seem to me that A is thereby precluded from raising an action of implement *quoad* the heritage alone."

2. The Court of Session also decided that an averment that the islands had an incalculable sentimental value for the defender in that he had inherited them from his father and had lived and worked all his life on Taransay was not a relevant averment of such "special hardship" as would dissuade the court from pronouncing a decree *ad factum praestandum*. On this, the Lord Justice-Clerk said (at p. 248): "The defender's fifth plea in law in regard to 'hardship' seems to me to be even more hopeless. By the end of Mr Milligan's speech it was clear that it was a very lame duck indeed—by the end of the case it was dead. We were referred to the passage in *Gloag on Contract* (2nd ed.), *sub voce* 'Disproportion of Interest to Loss Inflicted' at pp. 251-252. The cases there cited, on which the defender relies, are very special and are wholly different in their facts from the present. I need go no further than to refer to *Gloag* at p. 655,

where he cites the classic *dicta* of Lord Watson in *Stewart* v. *Kennedy* ((1890) 17 R.(H.L.) 1 at p. 9), which despite any erosion there may have been in other spheres, still express, in this particular aspect, the law of Scotland (in contradistinction to that of England) as it survives today. The defender's fifth plea fails."

The *dicta* referred to are quoted below (p. 221) under the heading "specific implement."

Undue influence: parent and child

Forbes v. Forbes's Trustees

1957 S.C. 325 (O.H.)

Mrs F. had, when aged 25, entered into an antenuptial contract of marriage, whereby she contributed the whole of the trust funds, amounting to £150,000. In doing so she had acted on the advice of her father, in whom she had complete confidence.

More than 13 years after the marriage she brought an action for reduction of the contract on the ground of undue influence.

Held that, as her father had been acting solely in her interests and had no adverse personal interest, his influence could not be regarded as undue.

LORD GUTHRIE (Ordinary) (at p. 330): "The general effect of the evidence is, therefore, that the pursuer's father was her trusted adviser in matters of business, and exercised a fairly strict control of her expenditure even after her majority; that he was afraid lest her estate should be dissipated; that in genuine devotion to her interests he urged her to have a marriage contract; that notwithstanding her unwillingness he insisted upon his proposal, and that she reluctantly acquiesced to avoid displeasing him; that the instructions for the preparation of the deed were given by him to her solicitor, and that he revised the drafts; that having fallen in with his wishes, she was content to leave these matters in his hands, and that she signed the deed—in his absence—without question or demur; finally, that the only advice she received about the contract came from her father.

"... It is obvious that whether or not a transaction has been brought about by undue influence will depend on the circumstances of the particular relationship between the person exercising it and the person subjected to it, and the precise nature of the particular transaction. ... The meaning and effect of undue influence may not be the same in the law of contract as in the law of wills. . . . Where there is a confidential relation-ship, such as agent and client or parent and child, I think that the *dictum* of Lord President Clyde in *Ross* v. *Gosselin's Executors*, 1926 S.C. 325, at p. 334, applies, whether the question arises in connexion with a will or with a contract. The Lord President said: 'The essence of undue influence is that a person, who has assumed or undertaken a position of quasi-fiduciary responsibility in relation to the affairs of another, allows his own self-interest to deflect the advice or guidance he gives, in his own favour.' This statement accords with the opinion of Lord President Inglis in *Gray* v. *Binny* (1879) 7 R. 332, the leading case in Scotland on undue influence in connexion with an *inter vivos* deed. In that case a mother, with the assistance of the family solicitor, obtained from her son, aged twenty-four, a deed of consent to disentail for a grossly inadequate con-sideration, by taking advantage of the son's ignorance of his rights and his confidence in them. The Lord President said (at p. 342): 'It is not enough, however, for the pursuer of such an action as this to prove that he has given away valuable rights for a grossly inadequate consideration, and that he has been betrayed into the transaction by his own ignorance of his rights, without proving deceit or unfair dealing on the part of those who take benefit by his loss. But in order to determine what kind and amount of deceit or unfair practices will be sufficient to entitle the injured party to redress regard must always be had to the relation in which the transacting parties stand to one another. If they are strangers to each other, and deal-ing at arm's length, each is not only entitled to make the best bargain he can, but to assume that the other fully understands and is the best judge of his own interests. If, on the other hand, the relation of the parties is such as to beget mutual trust and confidence, each owes to the other a duty which has no place as between strangers. But if the trust and confidence, instead of being mutual, are all given on one side and not reciprocated, the party trusted and confided in is bound, by the most obvious principles of fair dealing and honesty, not to abuse the power thus put in his hands.' . . .

"In my opinion, an onerous contract entered into by a party of full age cannot be reduced on the ground that his consent was the result of undue influence exercised upon him, unless the influence was exerted to the detriment of that party by or on behalf of the other party to the deed in breach of a duty arising out of a fiduciary or quasi-fiduciary relationship. . . . There is no case in Scotland where a contract has been held voidable on the ground of undue influence, where the influence has been exerted in genuine devotion to the interests of the person influenced. There is no Scottish case where it has been held that a contract can be reduced when the undue influence has not been exercised by or on behalf of the other party to the agreement.

"Counsel for the pursuer founded strongly upon an English case, *Bullock* v. *Lloyds Bank* [1955] Ch. 317. . . .

" . . . The meaning placed on the words 'undue influence' in that case does not accord with the signification placed upon them in the Scots decisions. . . . It is, as is settled by such cases as *Gray* v. *Binny* and *Ross* v. *Gosselin's Executors*, essential to the conception of 'undue influence' in the law of Scotland that there has been a breach of fiduciary or quasi-fiduciary duty, confidence acquired and abused. . . . The pursuer cannot succeed by relying on the decision in *Bullock*. If that case were accepted and followed in Scotland, it would look suspiciously like the extension of the benefits of the doctrine of minority and lesion to persons of full age and capacity. A distinction must be drawn between undue influence and bad advice.

"It is averred by the pursuer that she at no time received 'independent advice' on the position. . . . Her counsel repeatedly urged that the absence of 'independent advice' was a circumstance inferring undue influence by the pursuer's father. I confess that I do not appreciate this submission in the circumstances of the present case. Where a parent bargains with a child so that his personal interests are involved, and the child is, therefore, deprived of the natural protection of reliance upon his parent's advice and assistance, then there is clearly a duty upon the parent to obtain independent advice for the child so that the child's interests shall be fully protected. . . . But, where a father is acting solely in the interests of his child and has no adverse personal interest, he is entitled to urge his views to the child, and is under no duty to send the child to consult another as an appellant advisory tribunal. . . .

"In *Gray* v. *Binny* Lord Shand outlined the circumstances which create a cause of action on the ground of undue influence. He said (at p. 347): 'The circumstances which establish a case of undue influence are, in the first place, the existence of a relation between the granter and grantee of the deed which creates a dominant or ascendant influence, the fact that confidence and trust arose from that relation, the fact that a material and gratuitous benefit was given to the prejudice of the granter, and the circumstance that the granter entered into the transaction without the benefit of independent advice or assistance.' Therefore, since the essential question is whether there has been breach of fiduciary or quasi-fiduciary responsibility, what is relevant is whether the person in such a position has obtained a benefit, by abuse of the trust reposed in him, to the prejudice of the person who ought to have been protected. Therefore, in my opinion, the Dean of Faculty was well founded in his submission that the pursuer had not proved, and had not attempted to prove, any relevant loss or prejudice, since she had not proved or sought to prove that her father had obtained any corresponding benefit. Here a material and gratuitous benefit was not obtained to the prejudice of the granter, and, therefore, an essential element in the cause of action has not been proved.

"In any event, I am of opinion that, in the criticism made by counsel for the pursuer of the terms of the contract, there is a good deal of wisdom after the event. ... In *Gillespie & Sons* v. *Gardner*, 1909 S.C. 1053, a case dealing with a transaction between a law-agent and his client, Lord President Dunedin said (at p. 1061) that 'in judging the fairness of a bargain you must put yourself as best you can into the position of the parties at the time, you must not judge with the wisdom of after events.' ... The fact is that the hardships of which the pursuer complains are not the natural and probable consequence of her father's advice, but are the results of the continuous fall in the value of the pound since 1945 and the high cost of living combined with heavy taxation. Therefore, even if the loss and prejudice which were urged by her counsel are relevant in the absence of corresponding benefit to her father, I do not think that it has been established that they flow from the deed into which she entered.

" ... I think that the inducing cause of the attempt to reduce the marriage contract is the economic circumstances of our time, and that the attack made after his death upon his activities on his daughter's behalf in 1941 is simply an endeavour to obtain legal grounds for evading the consequences of these conditions."

Undue influence: solicitor and client: contract voidable

McPherson's Trustees v. Watt

(1877) 5 R.(H.L.) 9

W., law-agent for McP.'s trustees, offered to purchase on behalf of his brother, Dr W., four houses in Aberdeen which the trustees desired to sell.

Unknown to the trustees W. had arranged with his brother to take over from him two of the houses on paying one-half of the price.

Dr W. brought an action for implement of the contract of sale, and McP.'s trustees raised an action of reduction of the missives.

Held that W. stood in a confidential relation to the trustees, and that non-disclosure of the fact that he was purchasing partly for himself was fatal to the validity of the transaction.

LORD O'HAGAN (at p. 17): "An attorney ... must be prepared to shew that he has acted with the most complete faithfulness and fairness; that his advice has been free from all taint of self-interest; that he has not misrepresented anything or concealed anything; that he has given an adequate price, and that his client has had the advantage of the best professional assistance which, if he had been engaged in a transaction with a third party, he could possibly have afforded; and although all these conditions have been fulfilled, though there has been the fullest information, the most disinterested counsel, and the fairest price, if the purchase be made covertly in the name of another without communication of the fact to the vendor, the law condemns and invalidates it utterly. There must be *uberrima fides* between the attorney and the client, and no conflict of duty and interest can be allowed to exist. ...

"There are only two questions in the case—Was Mr Watt the agent of the appellants for the purposes of the sale? And, if he was, did he conceal the fact that to a large extent the purchase was for himself, though nominally made for his brother? If these questions be answered in the affirmative, as I think they ought to be, the transaction cannot be maintained."

LORD BLACKBURN (at p. 24): "Then came the question ... is the contract to be set aside in the case of Dr. Watt as well as in the case of John Watt junior? My Lords, I have come to the conclusion (I am sorry for it, because I think it presses hardly upon Dr. Watt) that the contract is one entire contract for all the four houses as a lump thing, and if we were to say that one part of it should be set aside and the other part enforced we should really be making two contracts of it. It follows that if we say that it ought to be set aside in the case of John Watt junior it must be set aside altogether, and consequently the appeal must be allowed *in toto*."

NOTE

Opinions may differ as to whether cases such as this involving transactions between solicitor and client are properly brought under the heading "undue influence," instead of being regarded solely as applications of the principle of the law of agency that an agent must not, without his principal's consent, himself transact with his principal on agency matters (no inquiry as to fairness or unfairness being allowed). The question depends on the definition attributed to "undue influence"; see the review of authorities in *Forbes* v. *Forbes's Trustees* (p. 127, above), and the comment on

McPherson's Trustees v. *Watt* by Lord President Dunedin in *Gillespie & Sons* v. *Gardner* (Note to *Aitken* v. *Campbell's Trustees*, below).

Undue influence: solicitor and client: contract valid

Aitken v. Campbell's Trustees

1909 S.C. 1217

A., a builder, entered into various building speculations along with C., his law-agent, under agreements by which C. helped to finance the transactions and participated in the profits.

The speculations were successful, and resulted in large profits for C.

Later A. brought an action for reduction of the agreements and for repayment of certain of the profits on the ground that C. had taken advantage of his position as law-agent to induce A. to enter into unfair bargains to A.'s disadvantage.

Held that in view of the circumstances of the parties at the time when the agreements were made, including the risks undertaken by C., the agreements were fair and reasonable, and were therefore not liable to reduction.

LORD PRESIDENT (DUNEDIN) (at p. 1225): "The law as laid down, the general terms of which cannot now be gone back upon, is that a contract of any sort between a client and his agent must be scrutinised in a way that a contract between two third parties would not be. . . . You have to find out whether the general relationship of law-agent and client exists, and then, if you find it does exist, you must apply the strictest scrutiny to the contracts. Well, here I do not think there can be any question for one moment that the general relationship of law-agent and client did exist. . . .

" . . . If the building speculation had gone wrong instead of going right, [C.] would have found himself liable for £10,000, and that being so, I cannot say that it has been proved that the remuneration to the defender was excessive or could not be supported by the criterion which we laid down in the case of *Gillespie* v. *Gardner* (1909 S.C. 1053). That is to say, would another law-agent have advised it, or if the proposition had been made by a third party, would this same law-agent have advised it to his own client?

[Referring to another transaction] " . . . The bargain has certainly turned out to be an exceedingly good one for Campbell, a better bargain than one would think a bargain in the ordinary case would be. But after mature consideration of the matter I have come to the conclusion that . . . , viewed as at the time, it was fair and reasonable, and could be supported. ... I think it is quite certain that Campbell, in this transaction, ran a very considerable risk. ... [He] had practically saddled himself with financing this man through the contract. ... Now, under all these circumstances I come to the conclusion that the bargain was not a bad one, as at the time, for people without capital, and in the view that although everything did turn out well, things might have turned out badly."

NOTE

Gillespie & Sons v. *Gardner* related to a profit made by a law-agent out of transactions with a firm of builders. In this case also the bargain was held to have been fair and honest, and beneficial to the interests of the clients. Lord President (Dunedin) stated (at p. 1061): "Where you have the law-agent and the client entering into a contract about things which do not fall within the matters covered by a law-agent's remuneration, yet in respect of the fiduciary position and in respect of what the law considers the superior position of the law-agent in the matter of knowledge over his client, that bargain will not be supported unless the law-agent can shew that the bargain was fair and entered into without concealment of any kind. Concealment will vitiate even if there is no unfairness. The case of *McPherson* v. *Watt* is a very good instance of that. But where there is no concealment there is no absolute nullity in a bargain made between law-agent and client. If the law-agent can shew that it was fair then the bargain will be supported."

Pacta illicita: *contract void by statute: purchaser liable for market value*

Cuthbertson v. Lowes

(1870) 8 M. 1073

C. sold to L. two fields of potatoes at the price of £24 per Scots acre. L. obtained delivery of the potatoes, but did not pay the full purchase price.

C. brought an action for the unpaid balance.

Held that since the contract was void under the Weights and Measures Acts it could not be enforced by the court but that C. was entitled to recover from L. the value of the potatoes at the time when they had been removed from the fields.

LORD PRESIDENT (INGLIS) (at p. 1074): "In the first place, where the Legislature has imposed the penalty of forfeiture of goods which are the subject of a prohibited contract, there can be no doubt that the loss falls upon one of the parties only, but then the other is not allowed to retain or resume possession of the goods forfeited, for in such a case they belong to the Crown.

"Again, it is quite clear that whatever may be the result as affecting the parties, a court of law cannot entertain an action for implement of a contract which the Legislature has expressly declared to be illegal, for the court can do nothing contrary to the clear terms or necessary implication of an Act of Parliament.

"There is another class of cases, those in which statutory enactments have been formed for the protection of purchasers against the frauds of traders, and in these cases the statutory penalty being directed against one of the parties only for the protection of the other, he alone must suffer the consequences of a breach of the enactment.

"In the present instance, however, the statutes founded upon by the defender are directed against both of the parties—the buyer is equally prohibited with the seller; and the prohibition, or statutory nullity of the agreement is obviously not designed for the protection of either of them, but to enforce a measure of public policy.

"But, my Lords, if the defender's contention were well founded, one of the parties would make a large gain at the expense of the other, upon whom the whole loss would fall. The defender seeks to retain the pursuer's potatoes without paying anything for them, on the ground that the Court cannot take cognisance of an agreement which by the statutes is declared to be null and void. I cannot readily yield assent to a proposition which would be productive of a result so inequitable, and I am of opinion that we are not constrained to do so. No doubt the Court cannot enforce performance of an illegal contract, and *in turpi causa melior est conditio possidentis*, but there is no turpitude in a man selling his potatoes by the Scotch and not by the imperial acre; and although he cannot sue for implement of such a contract, I know of no authority, in the absence of *turpis causa*, to prevent the pursuer from recovering the market value of the potatoes, at the date when they were delivered to the defender. That is not suing upon the contract."

NOTE

Contrast *Jamieson* v. *Watt's Trustee*, below.

Pacta illicita: *contract illegal by statute: claim for payment unenforceable*

Jamieson v. Watt's Trustee

1950 S.C. 265

The Defence Regulations 1939 declared certain construction work unlawful if done without a licence.

W. instructed J., a joiner, to execute joinery work on a cottage in Banff. J. applied for and obtained a licence for expenditure of £40 upon the work.

On completion of the work he rendered an account for £114 8s. 6d.

W. admitted his obligation to pay £43 7s. 7d. (£3 7s. 7d. being admittedly a reasonable margin of error), but refused to pay the remainder on the ground that the Regulations had been contravened.

Held that J. was not entitled to payment for work not covered by the licence since his claim depended on his breach of a statutory regulation, and accordingly that the equitable doctrine of recompense was inapplicable.

LORD JUSTICE-CLERK (THOMSON) (at p. 271): "The pursuer in incurring the items in respect of which he sues was in breach of the Regulation. That being so, Is he to be permitted to invoke the aid of the Courts to enforce his claim for payment?

"To this question the law of England in a long series of cases culminating in *Bostel Brothers* ([1949] 1 K.B. 74), which deals with this very Regulation, replies in an unequivocal negative. It does so on the ground of public policy. I am satisfied that in Scotland the answer is the same. The decision of the House of Lords in *Stewart* v. *Gibson* ((1840) 1 Rob.App. 260) puts the matter beyond doubt. If a pursuer cannot maintain his cause of action without establishing that he acted in breach of a statute, the Courts will not listen to him. This proposition was not directly controverted either by the Sheriff-substitute or by the appellant. The case advanced for the pursuer invoked the doctrine of recompense. ... It was submitted that in the interests of commercial morality the Court was bound to intervene to prevent the defender obtaining an advantage to which he was not entitled. ...

"The appellant's argument in the end of the day came to rely on *Cuthbertson* v. *Lowes*. There, statutes intended to secure uniformity of

weights and measures contained a provision that agreements with reference to any weight or measure established by local custom . . . should be
'null and void.' . . . It was held that the contract could not be enforced but
that the defender was not entitled to retain the potatoes without accounting to the pursuer for their value at the date at which they came into
his possession. I regard *Cuthbertson* as a special case turning on its own
circumstances. The effect of the statute was to make the contract void,
and, as Gloag points out (2nd ed., p. 550), a distinction can be drawn between agreements which the law will not allow to operate as contracts and
contracts which are contrary to law. The position in *Cuthbertson* was that
the contract did not operate, and, as a result, there was nothing to prevent
the Courts from regulating the rights of parties. It is different where, as in
the present case, one party to a contract comes forward to seek relief in
respect of his own breach of a regulation committed in the carrying out of
the contract."

LORD MACKAY (at p. 275): "The chief and only reliance came to be a
case decided in 1879, *Cuthbertson* v. *Lowes*.

"I have been interested to understand and to explain this judgment,
standing alone and never yet followed. . . .

"What then is the true place and effect of *Cuthbertson* v. *Lowes*? On a
full and careful reading of the reported matter for our apprehension, I
have come to think there are not one but many ways of refusal to give it
any effect contrary to the many years of law stretching out on either side
of it. The real embarrassment of riches is to sever out any one ground of
distinction sufficient for *Cuthbertson* but which saves the general proposition, as unshaken in our law.

"Firstly, I feel for myself that here is one case where a faulty headnote
in a rubric has contributed to decades of misunderstanding. The first
among the headlines is 'Sale—*Pactum Illicitum*.' Now I find that the statutes concerned, two of the Weights and Measures Acts, do not in fact
pronounce the words 'illicit' or 'illegal,' but merely make certain bargains 'null and of no effect.' . . .

" . . . The authority which has not ever, so far as known, been followed,
seems thus to be a precedent of that kind that it can only now be held authoritative for its very own case—a sale 'by the Scots acre.' Moreover, the
whole statutory basis of such limited decision has, since 1878 and 1897,
been repealed, so that the exact case can probably not recur.

"There is, then, a call upon us for a decision now, that, according to our

Scots law, in any case of proper and full illegality, whether it is pronounced in matter of contract or in the matter of operation, there is no room for avoiding the bar to a Court's aid by reason of the illicit character, by applying a *quantum meruit* or (better) a *quantum lucratus est* method of affording some relief to the person *versans in illicito*. I do so give my decision. . . .

" . . . My firm opinion is that the doctrine is as much a Scottish as an English one, and cannot be shaken by any proper reading of *Cuthbertson*."

LORD JAMIESON (at p. 278): "The main controversy turned on the pursuer's argument that he was entitled to payment *quantum meruit* for the work done. It was founded on the case of *Cuthbertson* v. *Lowes*. The case appears to stand by itself, and the researches of counsel did not bring to light any case in which it had been judicially commented on. . . . Professor Gloag draws a distinction between contracts the illegality of which rests merely on a statutory avoidance, which renders them unenforceable but does not make them illegal in the wider sense of depriving the parties of any rights against each other enforceable by law, and contracts involving an element of illegality, as distinguished from mere statutory avoidance, the effect being to debar the parties concerned from the right to appeal to Courts of Justice—*Gloag on Contract* (2nd ed.), pp. 550, 585. The present case, I think, clearly falls under the second category. What the pursuer did is in terms declared to be unlawful by a regulation passed in defence of the realm and fenced with severe penalties. The case is, therefore, entirely different from *Cuthbertson*, where, as Lord President Inglis pointed out, there was no turpitude in entering into the contract."

LORD PATRICK (at p. 280): "The pursuer's request for a remedy was founded solely on the case of *Cuthbertson* v. *Lowes*. This case is rightly put by Gloag into the very special category of cases where an act was unobjectionable at common law and is subsequently declared void by statute, there being no statutory declaration of illegality—*Gloag on Contract* (2nd ed.), p. 550. . . . The distinction is again emphasised by Gloag on page 585 when he considers the effect of illegality. He points out that, where a contract involves an element of illegality, the effect is to debar the parties concerned from the right to appeal to the Courts of Justice. In this respect he distinguishes contracts declared to be illegal from contracts merely declared by statute to be void. . . . He points out, with reference to contracts declared to be illegal, that the necessary consequence of the refusal of judicial assistance in the expiation of rights resulting from an illegal agreement is that the party who has gained an advantage keeps it. ...

"It was suggested that on this matter the law of Scotland was not so severe as the law of England. There is no warrant for the suggested distinction between the laws of the two countries—*Stewart* v. *Gibson*.

"The case of *Cuthbertson* v. *Lowes* cannot therefore justify us in enforcing a claim for recompense arising out of the breach of an Act and Regulations wholly different in outlook and effect from the statutes with which that case was concerned."

Pacta illicita: *contract illegal at common law:* melior est conditio defendentis

Laughland v. Millar, Laughland, & Co.

(1904) 6 F.413

L., a director of the Sunnyside Rivet Co. Ltd., had entered into an agreement with the managers of the company to the effect that if the managers should receive a bonus of £700 from the company on the sale of its business, L. should receive £200 from the managers.

The managers received the bonus of £700 but refused to pay the £200 to L., and when L. raised an action against them for payment they pleaded that as the agreement had been concealed from the shareholders, it was an immoral contract and not binding in law.

Held that the contract was illegal and could not be enforced, and that the maxim *melior est conditio defendentis* applied.

LORD ADAM (at p. 416): "Was this a corrupt agreement by a director with the managers? I do not think it is anything else but a corrupt agreement. It is a combination between the managers and the director of this Company to get into their possession a sum belonging to the shareholders. That is the nature of the transaction, and if that is the nature of the transaction the question is, can such a corrupt agreement be sued upon? ... My humble opinion is that a corrupt agreement such as this cannot be sued upon. Just put it the other way. If the pursuer had got the money into his hand, then I do not think the defenders, if they had sued him for it, could have recovered from him any more than he can recover from them."

LORD MCLAREN (at p. 417): "The question is, these parties having made a corrupt bargain for profiting at the expense of the Company, whether one of these parties to the bargain can sue the other for its fulfilment. I am very clearly of opinion that the right of action in such a case does not exist. It is quite unnecessary to review the authorities, because there is no point in the law of contract which is more firmly established than that when a contract is open to the objection that it is either against public policy, or is a dishonest attempt to defraud a third person, then the one party cannot sue the other, but the property or fund in question must remain in its existing position."

LORD KINNEAR (at p. 418): "Now, the matter of the destination ... of the price was a matter for the shareholders, because it was their money, and I do not see that the defenders and the pursuer had any right or duty to enter into a contract about it at all. The pursuer's business was to advise the shareholders. ... According to the pursuer's own statement, it was his plain and obvious duty, in bringing the matter before the shareholders, to tell them that if they paid £700 to the defenders there was an agreement between them and him that he was to get £200. ... A contract of this kind according to our law is ineffectual. It cannot be enforced, and the law to that effect is stated very clearly, not only by Mr Bell in his *Principles* [35] ... but by Stair and Erskine, and by all the institutional writers. These writers, no doubt, give a number of illustrations of what they understand by a contract *contra bonos mores*, and I do not think there is to be found among them the case of a director of a joint stock company taking a commission to the prejudice of his shareholders, but that is only because cases of that kind had not arisen when either Stair or Erskine or Bell wrote so frequently as they have unhappily arisen now. ... I think it clear that the pursuer has alleged a contract which he has no right in law to enforce against anybody."

NOTE

Barr v. *Crawford*, 1983 S.L.T. 481 (O.H.) was an action for recovery of money which Mrs B. alleged that she had paid to influence a licensing application. She averred that she had been told by C., the Provost of Falkirk, that to save the licence 10 people would have to be bought, including lawyers and police, for £10,000.

Held that this sum was a bribe, and action *dismissed*.

Contracts in restraint of trade: employment

Stewart v. Stewart

(1899) 1 F. 1158

R.S. owned a photographic business in Elgin and employed his brother, E.S., as assistant in the business. E.S. signed an agreement by which he bound himself not to start or carry on the business or trade of a photographer either in Elgin or within 20 miles of that town.

When, a year later, E.S. admitted that he intended to carry on business as a photographer in Elgin, R.S. sought to interdict him.

Held that the restraint was reasonably necessary for the protection of R.S. and was therefore enforceable.

LORD JUSTICE-CLERK (J. H. A. MACDONALD) (at p. 1163): "It remains only to consider whether effect can be refused to the agreement in respect that it involves a restraint of trade, which is illegal, as being contrary to public policy. I am unable to see that there is any ground for coming to that conclusion. The agreement imports no restriction on any business except that of photography, and that only in Elgin and the immediately neighbouring district. Such a restriction leaves it open to the defender to carry on any business he pleases, including photographic business, anywhere throughout the world except in a small town in the north of Scotland and a circle of twenty miles round it. I cannot hold that either as regards the defender's own interests as a citizen or as regards the interests of the public in that district, there is anything that can be called unreasonable in restraint of trade, or more than a reasonable protection to the other contracting party. .... I think that a more reasonable case could hardly be imagined than the present. A photographer in a small town is desirous that his brother should not set up a rival business beside him and avail himself of the knowledge of the business and the customers of the existing establishment in which he has been an employee. That appears to me to be a most reasonable ground for such an agreement, not unduly restrictive of the liberty of the appellant to carry on business, and not detrimental to any interest in the community."

NOTES

1. In *Ballachulish Slate Quarries Co. Ltd.* v. *Grant* (1903) 5 F. 1105, Lord Moncreiff said (at p. 1115): "In the case of *Stewart* we had occasion to consider fully the law applicable to conditions in restraint of trade, and the circumstances in which such conditions will receive effect, and the

authorities bearing on the subject. The general law is not doubtful. Put shortly, such a condition (especially if partial as regards area) will receive effect if it is not unreasonable, having regard to the subject-matter of the contract and the interests of the party in whose favour it is made, and not contrary to public policy."

2. See also *Watson* v. *Neuffert* (p. 172, below).

3. In *The Scottish Farmers' Dairy Co. (Glasgow) Ltd.* v. *McGhee*, 1933 S.C. 148, Lord President Clyde said (at p. 152): "By the law of Scotland a prohibition against competition by the servant is not less admissible than a prohibition against using or divulging trade secrets or against canvassing or enticing customers, provided always the master can show that—in the circumstances of his particular business—the prohibition against competition is not wider than is necessary to protect his legitimate interests. The mere exclusion of competition never can be—in itself—a legitimate interest."

4. A worldwide restriction on a former employee who had acquired trade secrets was held to be not unreasonable in *Bluebell Apparel Ltd..* v. *Dickinson*, 1978 S.C. 16.

D., who had been an assistant manager with B. Ltd., manufacturers of "Wrangler" jeans, was, by his contract of employment, restricted from disclosing trade secrets and for a period of two years after the end of his employment from performing any services for any competitor. D. left his employment with B. Ltd., and took up employment with Levi Strauss & Co., manufacturers of "Levi" jeans and a major competitor of B. Ltd.

Held that since the real interest of B. Ltd. was to prevent even unintentional disclosure of their trade secrets to a competitor by a former employee, there was nothing unreasonable in a restriction designed to prevent such an employee from becoming employed by a competitor at all during the short period of the restriction.

5. There is an example of an unreasonable restriction in *Dallas McMillan & Sinclair* v. *Simpson*, 1989 S.L.T. 454 (O.H.).

A contract of copartnery of a Glasgow firm of solicitors prohibited a partner from carrying on business as a solicitor within 20 miles of Glasgow Cross.

Lord Mayfield (at p. 456): "In my view the restraints on the respondent not being able to practise at all in any capacity were greatly in excess of those required to protect the legitimate interests of the petitioners. I find it difficult to conclude that it was necessary for the protection of the petitioners' interests that the respondent should not practise in any capacity, for example, in East Kilbride, Hamilton, Motherwell or Airdrie to mention a few sizeable centres. He could not, for example, even carry out the function of duty legal aid solicitor. It would prevent the respondent from operating in fields of law in which the petitioners may not be concerned."

Contracts in restraint of trade: sale of business

Dumbarton Steamboat Co. Ltd. v. MacFarlane

(1899) 1 F. 993

A firm which had carried on business as carriers in the Dumbarton area sold the business, including the goodwill, to the D. Co. Ltd. MacF. and L., the partners of the firm, were to be employed by the D. Co. Ltd., and undertook to seek to procure for the company the benefit of the firm's custom and also not to "carry on or be concerned in any separate business of a like or similar kind in the United Kingdom for a period of ten years."

Some three years later, MacF., having been dismissed from the D. Co. Ltd.'s employment, began business on his own account in the Dumbarton area.

Held that (1) MacF. could be interdicted from canvassing the former customers of the firm, (2) the restriction against carrying on business anywhere in the United Kingdom was unreasonable and therefore unenforceable and (3) the court could not remodel the restriction so as to confine it to a more limited area.

LORD JUSTICE-CLERK (J. H. A. MACDONALD) (at p. 996): "I am satisfied upon the evidence adduced that the appellant gave ground for complaint to the respondents, to whom he had sold his business, by so dealing with and canvassing former customers of his as to interfere with the rights of the complainers as purchasers from him of his business. ... The appellant was, of course, entitled to any business that might be voluntarily and without any inducement or solicitation on his part placed in his way by those who chose to be his customers. ... And if all he had done had been to do such business as he was spontaneously employed to do by persons choosing without solicitation to consign goods to his care for transit, I do not think there could have been any ground for complaint. But it is, I think, quite plain that he went beyond this, and in certain cases tried to induce business against the legitimate rights of the complainers, as purchasers from him. In other words, he, not by general advertisement of his business, but by particular invitation or solicitation, endeavoured to gain over old clients to do business with him again. And it is, I think, proved that on some occasions he conveyed goods which had been specially marked for conveyance by the respondents. I think the Sheriffs were right in holding that he had given ground for interdict being granted to restrain him from so proceeding."

LORD TRAYNER (at p. 997): "Two questions have been raised under this appeal for our decision,—the first and perhaps the most important of which is, whether the restraint imposed on the defender (by his agreement with the pursuers) from carrying on the business of a carrier within the United Kingdom for ten years is valid and enforceable. The Sheriff has decided that it is not, and in that decision I concur. The business which the defender sold to the pursuers was the business of a carrier between Dumbarton and the Vale of Leven and Glasgow, and it was for the pursuers' protection in carrying on that business that the restriction or restraint now sought to be enforced was put on the defender. I think that restraint was unreasonable having regard to the subject-matter of the contract in which it is introduced. Its unreasonableness appears from this, that it would prevent the defender from carrying on business as a carrier, between say Liverpool and Manchester, or between Galashiels and Selkirk, both localities so distant from the place or places where the pursuers carry on the business bought by them that rivalry or competition between them and the defender is entirely out of the question. A restraint operating over so wide an area is greatly more than necessary for the pursuers' protection, and cannot therefore, in my opinion, be sustained. . . .

"The pursuers said that they would be satisfied if the defender was interdicted from carrying on the business of carrier between Glasgow and Dumbarton. But that was not contracted for. If the restraint, as the parties themselves expressed it, is not valid, then I think it must be disregarded. The Court cannot remake the contract for the parties. . . .

"On the other hand, I agree with the Sheriff that interdict should be pronounced against the defender in terms of the second part of the prayer of the petition. I think it is established that the defender has been directly soliciting the business of persons who were his customers,—that is, customers of the business which he sold to the pursuers,—and endeavouring to get them to withhold their orders from the pursuers and to give them to him. This is against the good faith of his contract with the pursuers, and in violation of his duty and the pursuers' rights."

LORD MONCREIFF (at p. 998): "I hold it proved that the defender has canvassed or solicited orders from customers of the old firm of Mac-Farlane & Company, the goodwill of which he sold to the pursuers. ...

" ... As the business which was sold by the defender to the pursuers was of a very limited character, the restriction which would prevent him from carrying on the business of carrier in any part of the United Kingdom, however remote from Dumbarton and unconnected with the Dumbarton trade, is excessive, and should not receive effect. I also agree that the Court has no power to remodel the restriction and confine it to a more limited area."

Contracts in restraint of trade: severable restrictions

Mulvein v. Murray

1908 S.C. 528

Mulvein, boot and shoe factor, Maybole, engaged Murray as a retail traveller under an agreement by which Murray bound himself "not to sell or to canvass any of the said George Mulvein's customers, or to sell or travel in any of the towns or districts traded in by the said George Mulvein for a period of twelve months from the date of the termination of this engagement."

Murray, having terminated his engagement by giving the requisite notice, took up a similar position with a boot and shoe manufacturer in Ayr, and Mulvein brought an action for interdict.

Held that (1) the restriction on selling to or canvassing Mulvein's customers was reasonable and valid, (2) the other restrictions were unreasonable and invalid and (3) the reasonable restriction could be severed from the others and so was enforceable.

LORD ARDWALL (at p. 533): "Originally at common law all such agreements as that under consideration in the present case were void as being made in restraint of trade and contrary to public policy. To this general rule exceptions have been from time to time admitted in certain cases, on the ground that the restraint imposed in these cases was reasonable and proper on a consideration of the contract between the parties.

"It is a question of circumstances in each particular case whether the restraint imposed is reasonable or not, and the main point to be considered in each case is whether the restraint is or is not wider than is necessary for the reasonable protection of the party desiring to enforce it.

"With regard to the agreement in question, I am of opinion that the first part of it in which the defender 'bound himself not to sell to or to canvass any of the said George Mulvein's customers' is a valid provision, and is separable from what follows. But the contract also binds the defender not 'to travel in any of the towns or districts traded in by the said George Mulvein for a period of twelve months from the date of the termination of this engagement.' The limitation in time which is applicable to both the clauses I have quoted, is quite reasonable, but I am of opinion that the latter clause I have quoted imposes an unreasonable restraint upon the defender. It is too wide and too vague. For all that appears the pursuer may have traded in every district in Scotland and England too, and I may add that the word 'district' is in itself a very vague term, as it is not a known geographical division of either town or country. In short, this provision leaves the defender entirely in the dark as to what towns or districts he is precluded from selling or travelling in, and so far as its terms are concerned it might embrace the whole country, should it turn out that Mulvein had traded in each district thereof, whatever that may mean. . . . I am of opinion that an agreement of this sort in restraint of trade should at least be definite and distinct, and in such terms as that the person who is coming under the restraint should know what he is binding himself to refrain from doing. . . .

"But further, I am of opinion that the second clause I have quoted is invalid inasmuch as it is a restraint against selling or travelling for any purpose in any of the towns or districts mentioned. Now I think it was wholly unnecessary for the protection of the pursuer that the defender should be prohibited from selling or travelling for any purpose whatever in these towns or districts, and was unreasonable in respect that the defender had a right to engage in any sort of business for himself, provided he did not interfere with the pursuer's class of business in such towns or districts."

NOTE

Restrictions were also held to be severable in *Hinton & Higgs (UK) Ltd.* v. *Murphy*, 1989 S.L.T. 450 (O.H.).

M.'s contract of employment included unreasonably wide restrictions covering persons who had been customers of his employers prior to M.'s period of employment. It also provided that confidential information about the employers would not be given to other persons. This latter restriction was held to be severable from the former and enforceable.

CHAPTER 5

INTERPRETATION AND SCOPE

Written contract: prior communications and deleted words not to be looked at

Inglis v. Buttery & Co.

(1878) 5 R.(H.L.) 87; (1877) 5 R. 58

B. & Co. entered into a contract with I. for the execution by I. of certain alterations and repairs on a steamship. The contract was embodied in a memorandum of agreement signed on behalf of both parties.

In the memorandum the following words had been deleted before signature, but remained legible: "but if any new plating is required, the same to be paid for extra."

The plating of the hull was found to be very defective, and had to be replaced by new plating to enable the vessel to be classed at Lloyds.

The parties differed as to whether the renewal of the plating was within the contract.

Held that upon a sound interpretation of the terms of the contract, I. was bound to supply the new plating, but that the court was not entitled to look either at letters passing between the parties before the memorandum was executed or at the deleted words.

LORD GIFFORD (dissenting in the Court of Session) (at p. 68): "The question is, whether the cost of very extensively renewing a large portion of the old plating of the hull ... is or is not included in the slump contract price ..., or whether that renewal forms extra work, the cost of which must be paid for by Messrs Buttery in addition to the contract price admittedly due by them. ...

"I am of opinion, in the first place, that the contract between Messrs Buttery and Messrs Inglis is a written contract, and is not to any extent a parole or verbal contract, and I agree with the Lord Ordinary that the contract consists, and consists exclusively, of the formal memorandum of agreement. ...

"Now, I think it is quite fixed, and no more wholesome or salutary rule relative to written contracts can be devised, that where parties agree to embody and do actually embody their contract in a formal written deed, then in determining what the contract really was and really meant a Court must look to the formal deed and to that deed alone. This is only carrying out the will of the parties. The only meaning of adjusting a formal contract is that the formal contract shall supersede all loose and preliminary negotiations, that there shall be no room for misunderstandings which may often arise and which do constantly arise in the course of long and it may be desultory conversations, or of correspondence or negotiations in the course of which the parties are often widely at issue as to what they will insist in and what they will concede. The very purpose of a formal contract is to put an end to the disputes which would inevitably arise if the matter were left upon verbal negotiations or upon mixed communings, partly consisting of letters and partly of conversations. The written contract is that which is to be appealed to by both parties, however different it may be from their previous demands or stipulations, whether contained in letters or in verbal conversation. There can be no doubt that this is the general rule, and I think the general rule strictly and with peculiar appropriateness applies to the present case. The deed which we have to interpret as the contract consists of the memorandum and specifications, and of nothing else. . . .

"The next question, however, is a more difficult question, for the contract itself . . . exhibits . . . a very important deletion. . . . It is admitted that these words were deleted by consent and agreement of both parties before the contract was signed by the parties as their final and mutual deed. The deletion is authenticated by a marginal note . . . , which marginal note is initialled by both parties, and there is no dispute that the deleted words do not form part of the written agreement, that is, the deletion must be given effect to. But the deleted words, though deleted, can still be read under the deletion . . . , and the contention of Messrs Buttery is, that although the words are deleted and not to be read as part of the contract they can still be read and looked at for the purpose of interpreting and giving a meaning to the words which are undeleted, that is, to the contract as it at present stands. . . .

" . . . I think that when parties who are about to sign a formal deed agree that certain words shall be deleted before signing it the meaning of such agreement is that the deleted words shall not be read to any effect whatever. Deletion, however executed on the paper, means entire deletion and blotting out. The words are to be abolished, and held *pro non scripto*, just as if they had never been there. The deed is to be read without them, the agreement come to is an agreement without the words, and I see neither reason nor authority for holding that although both parties stipulate that the words shall form no part whatever of the agreement they are yet to be read as interpreting it, that is, really as part of it, or as an explanatory note embodied therein.

"Surely an agreement to delete means an agreement to delete effectually and to all intents whatever. It is not an agreement partially to delete or to delete *ad hunc effectum tantum*, and not as to other effects. . . . Deletion means utter abolition, or it means nothing."

LORD HATHERLEY (at p. 90): "There has been a good deal of evidence adduced with the view of expounding the contract, not for the purpose of explaining the meaning of a particular technical phrase used in the contract, which is a purpose for which it is quite legitimate to use external evidence, but where the words of the contract are not themselves in any way technical, but are plain and simple language, at all events so plain and simple as to require no aid of testimony specially to explain them, in that case it is not legitimate to introduce parole testimony to say what the meaning of the contract is.

"Nor can I think . . . that it is legitimate to look at those words which appear upon the face of the agreement with a line drawn through them, and which are expressly by the intention of all the parties to the agreement deleted, that is to say, done away with and wholly abolished. I think it is not within the legitimate rules of evidence to examine those words because you happen to be able to read them, and find that they have been once there although they are expunged now. It is not legitimate to read them and to use them as bearing upon the meaning of that which has become the real contract between the parties, namely, the final arrangement of the document which we must now proceed to construe."

LORD O'HAGAN (at p. 98): "I do not think that the case is to be decided at all either with reference to the deleted words or with reference to the evidence as to communings or writings before or after the completion of the contract. . . .

"With reference to the deleted words, I think . . . that it is of great importance that it should be understood that there is no doubt on that point in the mind of any one of your Lordships. When those words were removed from the paper which at that time presented the full contract between the parties, those words being removed ceased to exist to all intents and purposes, and whether it was possible, as in point of fact it was, to read them in consequence of their simply having a line drawn through them, or whether they were absolutely obliterated, appears to me not to make the smallest difference in the case. The contract was complete after the deletion. The parties had had a confluence of will, and had come to identity of decision, and the removal of those words took away absolutely from that contract any sort of explanation or condition which might have been introduced into it by them. . . .

"I need say no more than has been already said as to the impossibility of allowing the class of evidence of what is called communings, that is to say, negotiations, whether those negotiations or communings occurred before the contract was completed or afterwards. The contract must stand by itself, and must be construed according to its own words and what is contained within its own four corners."

LORD BLACKBURN (at p. 102): "I read about twenty lines of Lord Gifford's judgment, as expressing in extremely clear words exactly what I think myself. He says—'Now, I think it is quite fixed . . . [as on pp. 146–147, above] . . . and of nothing else.' Now, my Lords, I agree in every word of that, and I do not see that I can express it better."

LORD GORDON (at p. 105): "Lord Gifford, I venture to think, has expressed more correctly the views which ought to regulate this case."

NOTES

1. Similarly, in *Norval* v. *Abbey*, 1939 S.C. 724, the court held that a prior letter containing conditions of let but not referred to in the contract of lease could not competently be referred to in a question between the tenants and a purchaser for the purpose of adding to or modifying the terms of the lease.

Lord Wark referred (at p. 728) to "the well-known rule of *Inglis* v. *Buttery & Co.* . . . that, where parties agree to embody, and do actually embody, their contract in a formal written deed, the Court, in determining what the contract was, must look to that deed and that alone. That rule is of much earlier standing in the law of Scotland. It was regarded as settled law by Lord Justice-Clerk Inglis in *McGregor* v. *Lord Strathallan* ((1862) 24 D. 1006), where it was held that averments by a tenant of a separate verbal agreement with his landlord about matters not contained in the formal lease were irrelevant, even if the agreement were alleged to be coeval with the lease. . . .

" . . . It is, in my view, essential that a condition, to be effectual against a singular successor, should be part of the lease; and, where there has been a formal lease, it is, in my opinion, incompetent to have recourse to earlier informal writings to add to, or modify, the terms of the formal document."

Lord Jamieson (at p. 734): "The letter is not in the proper sense collateral to the lease constituted by the formal probative documents, but is being put forward by the appellants as containing additional terms of let which they seek to add thereto. The rule that, when parties have embodied the terms of their contract in a formal deed, it alone can be looked at to expiscate the contract to the exclusion of all prior communings is well settled, and to allow proof to set up the letter would be to act contrary to the well-established rule."

See also *Lee* v. *Alexander* (p. 152, below).

2. *Steuart's Trustees* v. *Hart* (1875) 3 R. 192 is also authority for the point that when a contract has been embodied in a formal deed it is not competent to modify its terms by parole evidence that the intention of the parties was different from that set forth in the deed.

Lord Deas (at p. 200): "Where a regular and formal disposition has been executed and delivered it is incompetent, by our law and practice, to interfere, as the Lord Ordinary has substantially done, in the way of reforming the contract. There are many decisions refusing such a remedy."

Lord President (Inglis) (at p. 201): "The Lord Ordinary repels the defender's third plea, which is that 'the transaction in question having been concluded by formal deed, it is not competent to modify or contradict the same by extrinsic evidence.' I think that plea was well founded and ought not to have been repelled."

3. In *Hamilton & Baird* v. *Lewis* (1893) 21 R. 120 the court held that it was incompetent to prove by parole evidence an alleged verbal agreement to vary the terms on which an action had been compromised in a joint minute signed by counsel.

Lord President (J. P. B. Robertson) (at p. 121): "The parties in this action settled the case by joint minute, signed by counsel, and the terms of the minute are quite unambiguous. It constituted a contract upon which the party entitled to implement was justified in taking decree.

"The case now made is that a meeting between the parties took place in a London hotel, at which it was verbally agreed that a different mode of payment should be accepted by the pursuers from that proposed in the joint minute, and a parole proof is asked.

"There is no warrant for allowing a party to get over a solemn contract by parole proof of communings of this sort."

4. In *Lavan* v. *Gavin Aird & Co. Ltd.*, 1919 S.C. 345, the rule of law that a written obligation cannot be modified by a verbal agreement, except when followed by actings inconsistent with the obligation, was applied to

an obligation contained in a decree of court. This was an action by a debtor for recall of arrestments used on a small-debt decree for a lump sum; the pursuer alleged a verbal agreement under which the creditors had agreed to accept payment by weekly instalments instead of by a lump sum; he sought to prove that agreement *prout de jure* in respect that it had been followed by *rei interventus*, viz., payment and acceptance of certain instalments.

Held that, as the payment of instalments was not inconsistent with the debtor's remaining under obligation to pay in terms of the decree, it did not constitute *rei interventus* qualifying the obligation, and accordingly that the debtor was not entitled to prove by parole evidence the alleged verbal agreement to vary the terms of the decree.

Lord Justice-Clerk (Scott Dickson) (at p. 348): "As I understand it, the law with regard to the discharge or modification of obligations constituted by writing depends upon authorities which have been quite well settled for a long period, certainly since the decision in the case of *Kirkpatrick* v. *Allanshaw Coal Co.* ((1880) 8 R. 327), and amounts to this: where there is a written agreement constituting obligations between the parties, these obligations can neither be discharged nor modified by a verbal agreement unless that agreement has been followed by actings inconsistent with, or contradictory to, the original obligation. ...

" ... The authorities to which we were referred, beginning with the *Countess of Argyle* ((1583) Mor. 12,300), show, to my mind, that an obligation constituted by decree cannot be more easily discharged by subsequent actings of the parties than a contractual obligation. And in order to get rid of even a contractual obligation by a verbal agreement, I think you must have two things:—In the first place, an averment of an agreement inconsistent with the written obligation; and, secondly, actings upon that agreement which are inconsistent with the original obligation."

5. Parole evidence is not excluded where the *validity* of a contract is challenged: *e.g.* Lord President (Normand) said in *Bell Brothers (H.P.) Ltd.* v. *Aitken*, 1939 S.C. 577 at p. 585: "The rule of law that the construction of a written contract cannot be modified by parole evidence has no application to a case like the present [involving error induced by misrepresentation], and I consider that the law is correctly stated by Mr Gloag in the second edition of his book on *Contract* (at p. 365): 'Rules as to interpretation of written contracts do not apply to cases where the question really is whether the contract is binding on the parties. So parole evidence is admissible to prove that one or other party never gave any assent, or

that his assent was obtained by misrepresentation, fraud or other improper means.' "

See also *Krupp* v. *John Menzies Ltd.* (p. 76, above).

Formal conveyance superseding previous contract

Lee v. Alexander

(1883) 10 R.(H.L.) 91

A completed disposition of certain superiorities proceeded on the narrative that it was granted in consideration of an agreement between the parties.

The Court of Session held ((1882) 10 R. 230) that it was competent to refer to the agreement for the purpose of clearing up an ambiguity in the disposition.

Held (*rev.* that judgment) that the execution of a formal conveyance, even when it expressly bears to be in implement of a previous contract, supersedes that contract *in toto*, and the conveyance thenceforth becomes the sole measure of the rights and liabilities of the contracting parties.

LORD WATSON (at p. 96): "I do not think there is any ambiguity in the language of the disposition of December 1879 which can justify a reference, for the purpose of controlling the language, to an antecedent agreement. ... According to the law of Scotland, the execution of a formal conveyance, even when it expressly bears to be in implement of a previous contract, supersedes that contract *in toto*, and the conveyance thenceforth becomes the sole measure of the rights and liabilities of the contracting parties.

NOTES

1. *Butter* v. *Foster*, 1912 S.C. 1218, illustrates the same point.

B. sold the estate of Faskally, Perthshire, to F. under articles of sale which contained certain conditions as to the rights of B. and F. respectively in the rents. The disposition which followed contained an assignation of rents in the usual statutory form.

Held that the rights of the parties in the rents were regulated by the disposition to the exclusion of the conditions contained in the articles of sale.

Lord Mackenzie (at p. 1225): "There is a preliminary question here as to whether the articles of sale may be referred to, but I think, on the cases of *Lee* v. *Alexander* and of *Orr* v. *Mitchell* ((1893) 20 R.(H.L.) 27), there can only be one answer on that point. The case of *Jamieson* v. *Welsh* ((1900) 3 F. 176), which was founded upon, was plainly a different case, because there the terms of the disposition did not exhaust the contract between the parties. Accordingly, I think there is no question that it is upon the disposition that the rights of the parties must depend."

2. Parties may agree that the ordinary rule shall not apply—*Fraser* v. *Cox*, 1938 S.C. 506.

Lord President (Normand) (at p. 515): "Normally, of course, . . . the only document which would fall to be construed, and the only document which the Court would look at, would be the formal disposition which had been granted and taken. It would entirely supersede all prior negotiations, including the missives themselves. The authority for that is the case of *Lee* v. *Alexander* among others. But I think that it is competent for the parties to agree, before the disposition is granted, that a term which will be included in the disposition shall fall to be construed as it stood in the missives which preceded the disposition and would normally be wholly superseded by it. As Lord Low said in the case of *Young* v. *McKellar Ltd.* (1909 S.C. 1340 at p. 1346), 'A contract of sale is intended to supersede all prior negotiations by stating precisely what the agreement at which the parties have ultimately arrived is, and a disposition granted in implement of a contract of sale is intended to supersede that contract by giving the purchaser a complete title to the subjects. Therefore neither party can, while holding to this bargain, be allowed to modify or interpret the contract of the disposition, as the case may be, by reference to that which the contract or the disposition was intended to supersede. If, however, the parties choose to make a special agreement which renders the ordinary rule inapplicable, it is quite lawful for them to do so. And that, in my judgment, is what has been done in this case.' "

3. See also *Edinburgh United Breweries Ltd.* v. *Molleson* (p. 111, above), *Norval* v. *Abbey* (Note 1 to *Inglis* v. *Buttery & Co.*, p. 149, above), and *Houldsworth* v. *Gordon Cumming* (p. 159, below).

4. Since in recent years missives have become longer and more complex, a series of cases has come before the courts concerned with the question of whether the missives are entirely superseded by the subsequent disposition (the general principle of *Lee* v. *Alexander*, also now referred to as the "single-contract theory") or whether they are in part to survive the disposition (being exceptions to the general rule and usually now being fortified by a "non-supersession" clause in the missives or in the disposition or in both).

The cases have been confined to the sheriff courts and the Outer House of the Court of Session, except that the first of the series, *Winston* v *Patrick*, 1980 S.C. 246, was an Inner House case.

In *Winston* v. *Patrick* a clause in missives stated: "The seller warrants that all statutory and local authority requirements in connection with the erection of the subjects of sale and any additions, extensions and alterations thereto have been fulfilled." The purchasers obtained a disposition on payment of the purchase price, but later raised an action of damages for breach of contract on the ground that the sellers had failed to construct an extension in accordance with the warrant obtained from the buildings authority.

Held that on a proper interpretation the clause in the missives was an obligation on breach of which the purchasers could found only until the disposition was delivered.

Lord Justice-Clerk (Wheatley) (at p. 249) [After quoting the general rule as stated by Lord Watson in *Lee* v. *Alexander*]: "It was also accepted that there were exceptions to that general rule. Examples of these were (*a*) where the missives incorporated obligations in relation to moveables which would not be appropriate to be included in a disposition of heritage, (*b*) where in the missives there was a collateral obligation distinct from the obligation to convey the heritage, and (*c*) where there was an agreement in writing either in the missives or in a separate document or in the disposition itself that a personal obligation included in the missives would subsist and remain in force even if it was not included in terms in the disposition."

In *Pena* v. *Ray*, 1987 S.L.T. 609 (O.H.), where a clause in the missives provided that they were to subsist only for three months after the date of entry the purchaser was held not entitled, on raising an action after the time-limit, to damages for the seller's failure to provide a completion certificate in respect of renovation work. On the other hand, where there was a similar time-limit, a clause in the missives which fell into the category of an independent enforceable agreement, was legitimately relied on in an action brought within the time-limit: *Fetherston* v. *McDonald*, 1988 S.L.T. (Sh. Ct.) 16, and *Fetherston* v. *McDonald (No. 2)*, 1988 S.L.T. (Sh. Ct.) 39.

The view taken by different Aberdeen sheriffs in *Finlayson* v. *McRobb*, 1987 S.L.T. (Sh. Ct.) 150, and *Wood* v. *Edwards*, 1988 S.L.T. (Sh. Ct.) 17, was that "the only effective method whereby parties may agree that non-collateral obligations in missives shall survive a disposition is to incorporate an agreement to that effect in the disposition itself" (*per* Sheriff R.J.D. Scott at 1988 S.L.T. (Sh. Ct.), p. 20). That view was, however, not followed in *Jones* v. *Heenan*, 1988 S.L.T. (Sh. Ct.) 53, and *Bourton* v. *Claydon*, 1990 S.L.T. (Sh. Ct.) 7. Usually, the non-supersession clause is in the missives only. An exception was *Tainsh* v. *McLaughlin*, 1990 S.L.T. (Sh. Ct.) 102, where the non-supersession clause appeared in both the missives and the disposition.

Authorities were fully reviewed in *Jamieson* v. *Stewart*, 1989 S.L.T. (Sh. Ct.) 13, and *Taylor* v. *McLeod*, 1990 S.L.T. 194 (O.H.).

In *Jamieson* v. *Stewart*, J., the purchaser of a house in Dumbarton, claimed damages from the sellers, S., for an alleged breach of a term in the missives to the effect that the central heating system was and would be in good working order as at the date of entry. The missives also included a non-supersession clause. The disposition made no mention of the central heating system or of the warranty in the missives concerning it.

Having obtained entry, J. alleged that the central heating system was in a dangerous and defective condition and that the remedial work cost £618. J.'s claim for the recovery of that sum was based on the warranty contained in the missives.

Held that the parties had clearly provided in the missives that delivery of the disposition would only fulfil those parts of the missives directly covered by its terms and that the evidence relating to the missives was competent and relevant.

Sheriff Principal P.I. Caplan (at p. 15): "I may begin the expression of my own views by observing that I agree with the submission made to me by the pursuer's solicitor that there is nothing in this area of the law intended to inhibit the right of parties to enter into such contracts as they see fit provided of course that they express their agreement in clear and proper form. The critical question is always 'What did the parties intend?' ...

"The cornerstone of the conveyancing rule is often said to be the dictum of Lord Watson in *Lee* v. *Alexander*. ...

"There is nothing in the authorities I have discussed so far to indicate that the conveyancing rule under discussion is to be regarded as absolute or incapable of yielding to the clear will of the parties. ...

"... [T]he implication of condition 6 [the warranty as to the central heating] need not depend upon inference because it has to be read along with condition 18 [the supersession clause]. That condition provides quite specifically that conditions not directly covered by the disposition will remain in full force and effect for a period of 28 days from its delivery. Thus the parties have deliberately and clearly provided that delivery of the disposition will only be taken as fulfilling those parts of the missives which are directly covered by its terms."

The facts in *Taylor* v. *McLeod* were similar. The sellers' undertaking in the missives to have the central heating system and a lift put into full working order was held to be a collateral and personal obligation which survived the disposition.

Lord Milligan (at p. 199): "What cl. 26 does involve is twofold, namely first, warranting that appliances will be in full working order at the date of entry and, secondly, undertaking that so far as they are not, the purchasers can have them put in such order at the sellers' expense. It is to be noted that in the present action the pursuers found only on the second part of the clause, which involves a personal obligation on the sellers to reimburse the purchasers for the cost of repairs necessary to put appliances into full working order. In my opinion, such an obligation is a 'collateral obligation' distinct from the obligation to convey the heritage, to use the terms of exception (b) in *Winston's* case. Accordingly I consider that the present case falls within an accepted exception to the general rule of the single contract theory and that the obligation to reimburse for the cost of repairs survives the disposition notwithstanding that it is not repeated therein. Furthermore, I consider that exception (c) in *Winston's* case also applies in the present case. Clause 26 of the missives is apt, in my opinion, to bring the present case within that exception."

Written contract: incompetent to prove by parole evidence that party was acting as agent.

Lindsay v. Craig

1919 S.C. 139

An investor, L., purchased from a chartered accountant, C., 150 shares and paid the price for them.

In an action by L. against C. for transfer of the shares or repayment of the price, C. denied liability, averring that he had been merely an agent for a disclosed principal.

Held that, on the terms of a receipt which had been issued by C. to L., C. was personally liable to implement the contract and that it was incompetent for him to adduce parole evidence to show that he was merely an agent.

LORD PRESIDENT (STRATHCLYDE) (at p. 143): "The passage quoted in the Lord Ordinary's opinion from Lord McLaren's note in Bell's *Commentaries* appears to me to be a correct and apposite statement of the law of Scotland applicable to the subject-matter in hand."

LORD ORDINARY (HUNTER) (at p. 141): "The position is summed up by Lord McLaren, I Bell's *Com.* (7th ed.), 540. In dealing with that matter he says: 'In the case of written contracts, the question who is the party to, or personal obligant directly bound by, the contract is determined by the writing, which cannot be contradicted or varied by extrinsic evidence. The general presumption is, that the party executing the contract intends a personal liability, unless it appear expressly on the face of the contract that he does not contract personally; and words of description merely, denoting his character of agent, and not exclusive of personal liability, are insufficient for this purpose.' "

Written contract: proof of collateral agreement by parole evidence.

William Masson Ltd. v. Scottish Brewers Ltd.

1966 S.C. 9

M. Ltd. entered into a contract for the sale of the Hop Inn, Aberdeen, to S.B. Ltd. Clause 11 of the contract provided that "outstanding obligations" in respect of repairs or renewals to the premises were to be borne by M. Ltd. At the time when the missives were being signed S.B. Ltd.'s representative orally undertook to relieve M. Ltd. of liability under an agreement for the hire of a new sign.

Subsequently S.B. Ltd. rejected the new sign, and the signmakers recovered damages from M. Ltd.

In an action by M. Ltd. against S.B. Ltd. for damages for breach of the oral undertaking, S.B. Ltd. maintained that parole evidence of the undertaking was inadmissible because the undertaking contradicted clause 11.

Held that since the missives dealt only with the property sold and not with the sign, which did not belong to M. Ltd., the undertaking as to the sign did not contradict clause 11, and could be proved by parole evidence.

LORD PRESIDENT (CLYDE) (at p. 13): "The argument is that . . . any such verbal contract was immediately thereafter superseded by the written acceptance of the missives and in particular article 11 thereof. The argument is based on the contention that the contract regarding the new inn sign with the Franco-British Electrical Company was one of the contracts to which article 11 applied. This argument is based on the well-known principle that a written contract supersedes preliminary negotiations. . . .

"[The neon sign] agreement was an agreement between the pursuers and the manufacturers of the sign to construct a sign which would always remain the property of the manufacturers, but which they would hire to the pursuers. The sign therefore never formed part of the property belonging to the pursuers and never could do so. The pursuers could not sell it and could not assign their rights under the agreement regarding it to the defenders without the manufacturers' consent. This agreement, therefore, was not one which was capable of being transferred. It was in fact a purely personal agreement between the pursuers and the manufacturers. . . . It was not an agreement or contract, therefore, in my view to which article 11 applies. It did not affect the subjects which passed under the missives. . . .

"But in any event, in my view, article 11 qualifies the obligations to which it applies by limiting them to 'outstanding' obligations only. As I read it, this article is intended to relate to cases for the supply of additions or improvements which had been already made to the assets being sold under the missives, but which had not yet been paid for. If the agreed price of £36,000 for these assets was a fair one, it was obviously inequitable that the defenders should pay twice over for such additions or improvements. . . . But the new sign, and the agreement relating to it, could not fall into this category at all. For the new sign was not yet there. It did not and never would form an asset of the business. It was not, and never could be, a fitting or fixture appertaining to the business and it was quite obviously no part of the goodwill of the business. In my view accordingly article 11 does not apply to it. It would follow, therefore, that the contract in regard to the new sign was outside the ambit of the missives, and it would indeed have been quite an inappropriate item to incorporate thereunder. For the missives dealt with articles and subjects which were the property of the pursuers. Arrangements regarding articles which were or were to be hired to the sellers formed no part of what passed under the missives, and owing to the difference in their character properly formed the subject of a separate agreement, which in fact was a verbal one.

" . . . Apart altogether from the assets transferred under the missives a separate and distinct verbal arrangement was made in regard to the three items which could not be transferred in property, namely, the juke box and the internal telephone, which were both hired to the pursuers, . . . and thirdly, the agreement for the new neon sign for which they also verbally agreed to relieve the pursuers of liability. On the defenders' construction of article 11 it is quite unintelligible how or why the defenders took over liability for the hire of the juke box or the telephone, as they undoubtedly did. For if article 11 was wide enough to supersede the verbal agreement regarding the new sign, inevitably it was wide enough to supersede the verbal agreement regarding the juke box and the internal telephone, which was made at the same time."

Latent ambiguity: parole evidence competent

Houldsworth v. Gordon Cumming

1910 S.C.(H.L.) 49

C., the owner of the estate of Dallas in Morayshire, had entered into missives for the sale of it to H.

When the conveyance was being prepared the parties disagreed as to the boundary, C. maintaining that he was bound to convey only the lands delineated on a plan which had been used by the parties in their prior negotiations but was not referred to in the missives and H. claiming the lands as possessed by C. under the titles.

Held that (1) the evidence of prior negotiations was competent to identify the subject sold and (2) the parties had agreed to the sale of the estate as shown on the plan.

LORD CHANCELLOR (LOREBURN) (at p. 52): "In the dealings between these parties I think the sale was on the plan. ...

"If your Lordships take this view, it concludes the case in favour of the appellant. In any other view I should have felt great difficulty in holding that there was a *consensus in idem*. It is not enough for the parties to agree in saying there was a concluded contract if there was none, and then to ask a judicial decision as to what the contract in fact was. That would be the same thing as asking us to make the bargain, whereas our sole function is to interpret it. My own view, however, is that there was a consensus."

LORD KINNEAR (at p. 54): "This appears to me to be a question as to the identification of the subject-matter of an admitted contract, or, in other words, it is a question of fact to be determined by evidence. ...

" ... If a question arises as to the description to be inserted in a disposition, the first thing to be settled is what is the exact subject sold; and that is to be determined, not by the existing titles, but by the contract of sale, interpreted, as every document whatsoever must, more or less, be interpreted, by reference to the surrounding circumstances.

"The evidence which has been adduced for this purpose is said to be inadmissible; but . . . I am very clearly of opinion that it was perfectly relevant and was rightly admitted by the Lord Ordinary. I concede that the letters specified in the summons make a complete and final contract, and it follows that in accordance with the well-known rule of law the terms therein expressed cannot be contradicted, altered, or added to by oral evidence. But it is just as well settled law that evidence may be given not to modify but to apply the contract by identifying any person or thing mentioned in it which requires identification; and I see no difference in this respect between the admissibility of a map or plan of the estate and that of any other item of evidence, so long as the plan is not used for the purpose of importing additional or different terms, but only to prove the external facts to which the contract relates.

" . . . The material fact is that beyond all question Sir William Gordon Cumming intended to sell the estate of Dallas, as delineated on the plan . . . , and that that intention was made clear to the buyer."

LORD SHAW OF DUNFERMLINE (at p. 62): "In *Keith* v. *Smyth* ((1884) 12 R. 66, 74) a reference to a plan was made in the titles of certain heritable subjects. On that Lord President Inglis observes: 'There being no boundaries expressed in the dispositions, I apprehend it is clear that the plans are referred to for the purpose of shewing the boundaries, and, in the second place, for the purpose of shewing the extent or measurement of the ground.'

"This, which is true with regard to executed deeds of conveyance, is also similarly true with regard to a contract of sale of heritable property. The parties . . . each maintain that they were both agreed, and the question is whether they agreed upon a sale *per* plan or *per* titles. We have had the advantage of a most careful treatment of that subject by Lord Mackenzie, who heard the witnesses. He has come to the conclusion that the subject of sale was *per* plan. . . . I cannot see my way to differ from the conclusion arrived at by the Lord Ordinary."

Plain language: custom of trade

Tancred, Arrol & Co. v. The Steel Co. of Scotland Ltd.

(1890) 17 R.(H.L.) 31; (1887) 15 R. 215; (1889) 16 R. 440

A steel company entered into a written contract with the contractors for the Forth railway bridge to "supply the whole of the steel required" for the bridge subject to certain terms and conditions one of which was—"The estimated quantity of steel we understand to be 30,000 tons, more or less."

The steel company brought an action against the contractors for declarator that the contractors were bound to take from the steel company the whole of the steel required in the construction of the bridge and for damages on the ground that the contractors had obtained some steel from elsewhere.

The contractors pleaded that by the custom and practice of the iron and steel trade the contract was to be regarded as for 30,000 tons of steel, the words "more or less" meaning that the quantity delivered should not exceed or fall short of the estimated quantity by more than 5 per cent.

Held that the contractors were bound to take from the steel company the whole of the steel required for the bridge, the mention of 30,000 tons being merely by way of estimate.

LORD CHANCELLOR (HALSBURY) (at p. 33): "The contract is for the supply on the one hand, and the acceptance on the other, of the whole of the steel required for the Forth Bridge. ... The words are as plain as the English language can make them, they are to 'supply the whole of the steel.' Well, that standing by itself ... seems to me to be about as plain as anything can be.

"The next suggestion has reference to the words 'the estimated quantity of steel we understand to be 30,000 tons more or less.' Now, let us see in the first instance whether these words in their natural and ordinary meaning control, cut down, or in any way affect the language of the first part of the contract—'We hereby offer to supply the whole of the steel required by you for the Forth Bridge.' ... No answer appears to me to have been given to a question which was more than once propounded to the learned counsel—if that meant 30,000 tons, neither more nor less ..., why did not the parties say so? Instead of saying 'We hereby offer to supply the whole of the steel required by you for the Forth Bridge,' why did they not say 'We offer to supply 30,000 tons, more or less, for the Forth

Bridge?' From first to last I heard no answer given to that interrogatory. Then it stands that there is a word here used which is apt and fitting, and no other word that I can suggest is more apt or more fitting to convey that meaning of the contract, that the respondents were to be the suppliers of the whole of the steel required for the Forth Bridge. . . .

"The only other observation which I wish to make upon this part of the case, is that the language, as it appears to me, speaks for itself. It is not language of contract—the parties do not contract anything—it is a statement of what they understand to be the fact. . . . It strikes me that both the parties knew perfectly well what they were doing, and they used very fitting and proper language in order to express their meaning. . . .

"Now, the next point insisted upon is that we can cut down and over-ride this contract, and the language in which it is conceived, by some sort of custom. . . . I think the principle is the same in both countries; you may translate the words of a contract, you cannot vary or alter it."

LORD WATSON (at p. 37): "Except by denying all effect to the plain language of the obligatory clause, it is simply impossible to treat the estimate of quantity as being other than a statement of what would probably be required."

LORD PRESIDENT (INGLIS) (at 16 R. p. 450): "Now, the words, 'the whole of the steel required' are certainly very emphatic. It is difficult to understand that the parties could have meant something less than the whole of the steel which is according to the specification of the principal contract necessary for the construction of the bridge. Surely the words 'whole of the steel' would never have been used unless that was in the contemplation of the parties. . . .

". . . I think the contract could not have admitted of the slightest doubt as to its meaning if it had not been for some words which are used at the very end of the conditions . . . , and upon which indeed the whole argument of the parties turns. The words are these—'The estimated quantity of steel we understand to be 30,000 tons, more or less.' Now, it is contended that that limits the words of obligation to supply and of obligation to take to 30,000 tons or thereabout. It appears to me that these are not words of contract at all, but the expression of an understanding; and it was certainly most natural and convenient that there should be some such understanding between the parties. . . . I come without any hesitation to the conclusion that these words do not in any way limit the legal obligation in this contract, and that the pursuers are entitled to supply and the defenders are bound to take the whole quantity of steel required by the specification of the principal contract to be supplied for the purpose of constructing the Forth Bridge."

NOTE

P. & W. MacLellan Ltd. v. *Peattie's Trustees* (1903) 5 F. 1031 illustrates the same point.

Iron and steel merchants undertook in writing to deliver certain rails "in about two weeks' time." The rails were delivered, but not within the time specified, the undertaking being dated September 7, 1901, and the delivery being averred to have been about the end of October. In an action brought by the merchants for the balance of the price of the rails the purchasers averred that owing to the delay in delivery they had suffered damage to the extent of the sum sued for. The merchants averred in reply that in accordance with a well-known custom of trade the contract was subject to extension as regards time.

Held that the averments with regard to custom of trade were not relevant.

Lord McLaren (at p. 1034): "If parties have agreed to supply goods within a definite time, they must be held to their contract."

Lord Ordinary (Pearson) (at p. 1033): "Where there is a time limit it must be observed."

Trade terms: evidence as to course of dealing admissible

Von Mehren & Co. v. The Edinburgh Roperie and Sailcloth Co. Ltd.

(1901) 4 F. 232

Rope manufacturers agreed to supply a broker and merchant with "all" his "requirements" in Manila rope for one year at a fixed price.

During the currency of the contract there was a steep rise in the market price of Manila rope, and thereafter the manufacturers refused to implement an order on the ground that the word "requirements" was to be interpreted as confined to the buyer's trade in Manila rope in Iceland and the Faroe Islands.

The buyer brought an action for damages for breach of contract.

Held that (1) evidence as to the course of dealing between the parties for the previous six years was admissible in the interpretation of "requirements," and (2) in view of the facts disclosed the order in question could not fairly be regarded as having been within the contemplation of the parties when the contract had been made, and the defenders were therefore not in breach of contract in refusing to implement the order.

LORD PRESIDENT (J.B. BALFOUR) (at p. 238): "The question which we have to decide is what is the proper construction to be placed upon the word 'requirements,' as used in these letters. That word is ambiguous, and, in particular, it may mean either all that the purchasers may demand, or all that they may need in the prosecution of their business, or some department of it. The pursuers . . . maintained that the words comprehend all that they could sell in any part of the world, or in any class of business, whether carried by them previously or not, with or without solicitation, either to other wholesale merchants like themselves, or to middlemen or retail dealers, or to shipbuilders or shipowners who would use the rope. . . . The defenders, on the other hand, allege that the only trade in which they knew the pursuers to be engaged, or in which they believe them to have been engaged, at the date of the contract, or at any other time, was the importation to this country of the products of the Faroe Islands and Iceland, and the exportation to these islands of, *inter alia*, fishing lines, sailcloth, and Manila rope.

"The contract in question was entered into in continuation of a course of dealing which had existed between the parties for about six years previously. . . . The defenders allege that, throughout their dealings with the pursuers, the words 'all your requirements' were intended and understood by both parties to mean, and did mean, the pursuers' requirements for their Faroe and Iceland trade, and for no other trade or purpose. It seems to be clear from the letters which passed between the parties—at all events, down to the letters upon which the present question arises—that the Faroe and Iceland trade was the only one which was *in intuitu* of either the pursuers or the defenders. . . .

"The Lord Ordinary (Low) allowed a proof, with the view of ascertaining what the parties meant by the term 'requirements,' saying, *inter alia*, . . . 'In a contract either side is always entitled to know the circumstances with reference to which the contract is made.' It does not appear to me to be doubtful that where, as in the present case, a term which might have two or more meanings is used in a mercantile contract, it is competent to prove the circumstances surrounding the parties, the character of their business, and the previous course of dealing (if any) between them, for the purpose of determining the true construction of the language used.

"I think that the result of the proof is to establish that all the supplies

..., furnished by the defenders to the pursuers under the five contracts which immediately preceded that under which the present question arises, were exclusively for the Faroe Islands and Iceland. None of the supplies were for wholesale merchants of the same class as the pursuers, or for supplying dealers or customers in any other places than the Faroe Islands or Iceland—in other words, the trade carried on between them from 1893 was exclusively a Faroe and Iceland trade. The quantities of the different articles were not specified in any of the contracts, apparently because the trade with the Faroe Islands and Iceland was, in the knowledge of both parties, of a comparatively small and manageable volume."

NOTES

1. A similar decision was reached in the interpretation of "require" in *The North British Oil and Candle Co.* v. *Swann* (1868) 6 M. 835.

By an agreement between a coal-master and a company which manufactured coal oil, the coal-master was bound to supply as much cannel coal (within certain limits) as the company should "require."

Held that this did not mean as much as the company should demand but as much as the company should require for the purposes of its manufacture.

2. A different interpretation of "usual requirements" is illustrated by *Blacklock & Macarthur* v. *Kirk*, 1919 S.C. 57.

Manufacturers who had agreed to supply a glazier with his "usual requirements" of putty were held liable in damages for failing to supply increased quantities required for glazing work undertaken in connection with munition factories, since the words "usual requirements" did not import any restriction as to quantity but only a restriction as to the character and *locus* of the glazier's business (which was not changed).

Lord President (Strathclyde) (at p. 63): "It may be difficult to define the meaning of the expression 'usual requirements'; but I think the Court will never find any difficulty in distinguishing between honest business and factitious business. We have an excellent example of the latter in the case of *Von Mehren & Co.* v. *Edinburgh Roperie and Sailcloth Co.* In this case I come to the conclusion that 'usual requirements' means just the ordinary needs of the defender as a tradesman in the use of the material he was compelled to employ in his business, and that it has no direct relation to quantity; further, that the 189 tons, which he certainly needed for carrying on his business, was the measure of 'his usual requirements' for the year 1915, and that the pursuers were under their contract bound to supply that quantity."

Trade terms: proof restricted to their usage in the trade

Sutton & Co. v. Ciceri & Co.

(1890) 17 R.(H.L.) 40; (1889) 16 R. 814

S. & Co. quoted for the shipment of "alabaster goods, furniture, &c., but not for goods described as statuary."

Certain terra-cotta figures, the property of C. & Co., were damaged in transit.

Held that S. & Co. were liable as carriers, having failed to show that the terra-cotta figures fell within the exception of "goods described as statuary."

LORD HERSCHELL (at p. 40): "Dealing for the moment with the exception contained in the letter . . . , the burden clearly rests upon the appellants of shewing on this part of the case that these goods which were damaged fall within the language of their letter as "goods described as statuary."

"Upon the question whether they would be, or ought to be, or could be so described, there was a considerable amount of evidence given— evidence of three kinds: of dealers in such works, artistic evidence, and the evidence of those connected with the carriage of goods. I cannot think that any of that evidence is material except the evidence of the sense in which that word would be understood by those engaged in the carriage of goods. Indeed, it may be said, strictly speaking, that the proposition would need to be limited still further, and that it would only be the evidence of those engaged in the carriage of goods from abroad to this country that would be material.

"It seems to me that we have nothing to do with the artistic definition of 'statuary.' "

LORD WATSON (at p. 43): "The present case appears to me to illustrate the impropriety of permitting general evidence to be led as to the meaning of words of contract without a distinct averment on record as to the particular words to which the proof is to be directed, and the precise technical or trade meaning which the person making the averment desires to attribute to them. The consequence of disregarding that rule is, that the bulk of the evidence in this case, whilst it might be of some use to a person about to compile a dictionary, is not of the slightest use in construing the contract of the parties. . . . I entirely agree . . . that the appellants have failed to shew that these articles, the value of which is now in controversy, are included in the word 'statuary' as understood in the carrying trade."

Implied term must yield to contrary express term

Duthie & Co. Ltd. v. Merson & Gerry

1947 S.C. 43

D. & Co. Ltd., fish salesmen, Lossiemouth, had been in the habit of allowing a discount to buyers, but eventually intimated to the buyers that the discount was to cease.

M. & G., a firm of buyers, nevertheless, continued to deduct discount when making payments.

D. & Co. Ltd. brought an action against M. & G. for payment of £57 18s. 4d., the amount which they alleged had been wrongfully retained as discount.

M. & G. contended that there was a custom of trade as to the discount and that the salesmen were not entitled to terminate the custom without the consent of the buyers.

Held that a custom of trade merely adds an implied term to a contract in which the contrary is not expressed and that the buyers must be treated as having bought under the express condition imposed by the sellers that discount was no longer allowed.

LORD PRESIDENT (NORMAND) (at p. 50): "The rule is that an implied condition or term, whether derived from a custom of trade or in any other way, must necessarily yield to a contrary express condition or term in any future contract entered into between the parties. It was thus open to the respondents to decline to sell their fish under the implied condition which had prevailed up to December 1944, and the withdrawal of this implied condition did not need the appellants' consent."

LORD RUSSELL (at p. 51): "The defenders aver and plead that their right to make that deduction is based upon a long-standing custom of trade or commercial usage which has operated in the fish market at Lossiemouth since about 1890 and has regulated all transactions in the sale of white fish between sellers and buyers. They maintain that that custom or usage applied to each of the transactions covered by the present action and operated so as to introduce into each of the contracts of sale an implied term authorising the discount in question. . . .

". . . I am of opinion that the sellers' express and unambiguous intimations of discontinuance of the discount negatived the right of the defenders thereafter to maintain that the allowance of a discount continued to be an implied term of contracts entered into subsequent to that date. I consider that no such implied term could be read into a contract in face of an express contrary stipulation communicated *ab ante* by one party to the contract to the other party."

Ejusdem generis *principle applied*

The Abchurch Steamship Co. Ltd. v. Stinnes

1911 S.C. 1010

The steamship *Abchurch* was chartered by S., a coal exporter, to load a cargo of coal at Methil to be taken to Rouen.

A demurrage clause in the charterparty excepted from the time specified for loading a number of causes of delay, including "floods, riots, storms, detention by railway or cranes, stoppage of trains, accidents to machinery or any other unavoidable cause preventing the loading."

Delay was caused by failure to obtain a berth, and the steamship company brought an action against S. for demurrage.

Held that the cause of the delay was not covered by the words "any other unavoidable cause."

LORD PRESIDENT (DUNEDIN) (at p. 1015): "I think it has been again and again said that such general words following words of specification are to be construed on what is called the *ejusdem generis* principle; and construing the words 'other unavoidable cause' upon the *ejusdem generis* principle, I do not find that they would bring in the want of a berth, because I think all the things that are given before are things which point at what I may call some class of breakdown in arrangements, and do not go to such a thing as is really part of the ordinary routine of the port—that you will always be kept waiting if there are other people in front of you."

LORD KINNEAR (at p. 1016): "It was argued that the causes specifically enumerated are not of one *genus*, and that, therefore, the rule cannot be applicable to the general words, because we cannot find one common characteristic of the enumerated causes. I do not think that is sound, because, in the first place, the general words must be subject to some restriction since they are expressly brought into the clause to provide for exceptions, and not for a general rule. And if they were to be interpreted in their most universal sense, the specific enumeration of exceptions would be futile, and the general rule would be swept away—there would be no meaning in it. The clause, in that view of it, would have been properly framed by excepting all causes of detention except the fault or negligence of the charterer. I must say also that I concur with your Lordship in finding no great difficulty in discovering a common characteristic of all the enumerated causes which is not to be found in the actual cause of the delay—the congestion of traffic in the harbour—because, although there are a great variety of causes, they resemble one another in this, that they are all accidental causes arising from the state of the weather, or from the breaking down of machinery, or from strikes or lock-outs, or stoppages of a colliery, all of which would obstruct the ordinary and lawful working of the harbour upon the assumption that the harbour is perfectly ready to receive the ship. It seems to me that the actual cause was different from all these, and that it is within the general intention of the contract to put the risk of such unavoidable delay upon the charterer."

NOTE

Another argument put forward unsuccessfully for S. was that since failure to obtain a berth resulted in failure to obtain the use of a crane the cause of delay came within "detention by . . . cranes."

Lord President (Dunedin) (at p. 1014): "I think that it is straining the words to call the cause of delay here detention by cranes. I do not know that there is any better test than the use of ordinary language. If anyone connected with the matter had been asked what was it that delayed the ship in loading, the plain answer would have been—because she could not get a berth. . . . I think it is quite clear that detention by cranes points to something quite different, namely, something connected with the crane itself."

Lord Kinnear (at p. 1015): "We must read the language [the parties] use according to the ordinary natural sense of the words. And I do not think that anybody making a contract for the failure of a ship to obtain a berth, owing to the congestion of traffic at a certain port, would describe that contingency as a 'detention by cranes.' "

Ejusdem generis *principle excluded*

The Admiralty v. Burns

1910 S.C. 531

The Earl of Hopetoun granted a lease of a farm within the lands of Rosyth to B. A clause in the lease reserved to the landlord "full power at all times to take off land from any part or parts of the subjects hereby let for the purpose of planting, feuing, or letting on building leases, or for making, altering, or widening roads, or for making railroads or canals, or for any other purpose."

Later the Earl disponed the lands of Rosyth to the Admiralty for the purpose of the construction of a naval base, and the question arose of whether the Admiralty were entitled, under the clause referred to, to resume a small portion of B.'s farm for the erection of buildings and plant in connection with the naval base.

Held that the terms of the clause, and in particular the general words "for any other purpose," were sufficiently wide to cover the resumption proposed.

LORD KINNEAR (at p. 538): "Now, there are two observations which occur to me upon the construction of the clause itself. In the first place, with reference to the language of the clause, I observe that the general words which are intended to cover the purposes unspecified are not only in themselves wide enough to cover the particular purpose in question, but that they are as wide as the form of language can make them, because the words of the reservation are 'full power to take off land,' for certain purposes, 'or for any other purpose.' I do not think it is proper in the construction of a clause to deny all force to terms such as the word 'any.' 'Any purpose' does not, in ordinary language, mean for certain purposes or for purposes of a certain kind; it means any other purpose, whatever it may turn out to be. 'Any purpose' is any you please. . . .

"But the second observation is perhaps of more importance, and it is this, that if you are to limit general words by holding that they must cover only things that are *ejusdem generis* with preceding specific words, you must find that these specific words themselves are *ejusdem generis* with one another. The question is, whether the enumerated purposes have such a common characteristic as to make a *genus*, because if they have not, the contract does not disclose a particular category by reference to which the general words are to be limited. Now, I confess I have great difficulty in seeing what is the common characteristic which is said to be expressed in all the specific purposes for which the landlord is to resume the land under this contract. . . . I confess I do not see what the *genus* is, which is to limit the construction of these last general words."

NOTE

For Lord Kinnear's first observation, compare *Glasgow Corporation* v. *Glasgow Tramway and Omnibus Co. Ltd.* (1898) 25 R.(H.L.) 77.

A contract, bearing to be a "lease," between the Corporation of Glasgow and a tramway company included the condition that the company should pay to the Corporation "the expense of borrowing, management, &c., and this provision shall be so construed as to keep the Corporation free from all expenses whatever in connection with the said tramways."

Held that the company was bound to relieve the Corporation of landlord's taxes.

Lord Chancellor (Halsbury) (at p. 77): "The words 'free from all expenses whatever in connection with the said tramways" appear to me to be so wide in their application that I should have thought it impossible to qualify or cut them down by their being associated with other words on the principle of their being *ejusdem generis* with the previous words enumerated.

" 'Expenses,' I presume, is itself a very general word; but the construction which limits that word would be strange indeed which would strike out the word 'all' and the word 'whatever' from the sentence."

Lord Herschell (at p. 79): "Nothing could be wider than 'all expenses whatever'; they seem to me necessarily to exclude any limitation of the expenses to those *ejusdem generis* with expenses of 'borrowing' or 'management.' If the sums sought to be recovered have to be paid by the appellants, will they be 'expenses in connection with the said tramways'? I cannot doubt it."

Electio est debitoris

Christie v. Wilson

1915 S.C. 645

Held in the interpretation of a lease that the landlord, and not the tenant, had the option of choosing by which of two alternative methods the landlord would fulfil the obligation undertaken in the lease to supply extra water.

LORD DUNDAS (at p. 651): "Where a person undertakes to do one or other of two things, I consider that the option, as a general rule, lies with him as to the method of performing his obligation. I see nothing in the language of article 6 which should take the case out of the general rule; and no authority was cited to us which seemed to me to point in any way to such a result. At the outset of the matter, therefore, I think the option plainly lay with the landlord, and not with the tenant."

LORD MACKENZIE (at p. 654): "Clause 6 is in these terms: 'The proprietor agrees to supplement the present water supply so as to make it adequate, or otherwise to lay a pipe from the well beside the steading, and, if need be, to provide a pump therefor so as to bring water up to the dwelling-house. . . .' This clause contains a proper alternative, and according to all the authorities cited it is for the debtor and not the creditor to choose the mode of performance."

Interpretation preferred which made contract enforceable

Watson v. Neuffert

(1863) 1 M. 1110

W., a corn-factor in Leith, engaged N. as his clerk under an agreement which provided that N. was not, either while in W.'s service or after leaving it, to "accept any other situation" or "engage directly or indirectly in any business" on his own account in Leith or its neighbourhood.

After leaving W.'s service, N. commenced business, including the trade of corn-factor, on his own account in Leith, and W. sought to have him interdicted from doing so.

N. pleaded that the restriction, being without limitation either as to time or as to description of employment, was unreasonable and unenforceable.

Held that the restriction was to be interpreted as limited to the trade of corn-factor, and was accordingly reasonable and enforceable.

LORD JUSTICE-CLERK (INGLIS) (at p. 1112): "I do not think there is any difficulty about the law of this case. There can be no doubt that, according to the law of Scotland, a paction against the liberty of trade is illegal; and that agreements, by which a man binds himself that he will not carry on trade of any kind though limited in space, or a particular trade if unlimited in space, are both equally bad in law. But then it is equally settled in the law of Scotland, that there may be a good agreement, that a man shall not carry on a particular trade in a particular place. That was settled so long ago as 1735, in the case of *Stalker* v. *Carmichael* ((1735) Mor. 9455). The case arose out of a copartnery in the bookselling trade in Glasgow. That city was then thought too narrow for two booksellers at a time; and therefore it was agreed, that after the expiry of three years, either of the partners 'refusing to enter into a new contract upon the former terms, should be debarred from any concern in bookselling within the city of Glasgow.' A reduction of the contract was brought by one of the partners, but the Court held, that the debarring clause was a lawful paction, and not contrary to the liberty of the subject.

"That is a case where the agreement not to trade was confined to a particular place, and to the particular business of bookselling. If the present case falls within that principle, the agreement is good. If, on the other hand, the restriction is unlimited either as regards the nature of the trade or the space to which the prohibition applies, the agreement is bad in law. The whole question here, therefore, is a question of construction. . . . On a consideration of the whole circumstances, I have come to an opinion satisfactory to my own mind, that the contract is to be read according to the limited construction put upon it by the complainer, and therefore that it is a lawful contract. . . .

". . . I am disposed to read this contract in what appears to me the fair and reasonable sense, and to hold that the respondent is restrained from accepting any situation during the currency of the contract, and also from directly or indirectly carrying on any business on his own account, as a corn-factor in Leith or its neighbourhood. If that be the meaning of the contract, its legality is beyond question."

LORD COWAN (at p. 1114) concurred: "*In dubio*, that interpretation of a contract was to be rejected which made it illegal. The respondent must have intended, when he entered into this contract, to come under some sort of obligation, and it could not be taken off his hands now, when he had obtained the advantage which the contract held out to himself, and acquired a full knowledge of the complainer's business. . . . His Lordship . . . had no doubt in holding [the letter] to mean that the respondent was restricted from becoming a rival of the complainer in his own trade, by engaging in business as a corn-factor in Leith or the neighbourhood. There was no doubt that an unlimited restriction on trade was illegal."

LORDS BENHOLME and NEAVES (at p. 1114) concurred in holding that, "according to a sound interpretation of the contract, the restriction was applicable only to the trade of a corn-factor, or a similar trade in Leith or the neighbourhood."

Indemnity clause construed contra proferentem

North of Scotland Hydro-Electric Board v. D. & R. Taylor

1956 S.C. 1

A firm, T., contracted to carry out certain work in the North of Scotland Hydro-Electric Board's transformer sub-station at Abernethy. One of the conditions of the contract was: "4. The contractor shall indemnify the Board against all claims from third parties arising from his operations under the contract."

In the course of the work one of T.'s employees was injured by an electric shock, and recovered damages from the Board on the ground that the accident had been due solely to the Board's negligence.

The Board thereafter brought an action against T. for indemnification in terms of the clause in the contract.

Held that the Board was not entitled under the contract to be indemnified against claims based on its own negligence.

LORD JUSTICE-CLERK (THOMSON) (at p. 7): "The law has ... in certain circumstances set a limit to the scope of such a clause of indemnity. A party is to be indemnified against a claim for which he would be legally responsible in virtue of his own negligence only if it is clear that the other party consented to the situation. Our own doctrine of construction *contra proferentem* is consistent with the views recently expressed both in the Court of Appeal and in the Privy Council. [The Lord Justice-Clerk then quoted from *Alderslade* v. *Hendon Laundry Ltd.* [1945] K.B. 189 and *Canada Steamship Lines Ltd.* v. *The King* [1952] A.C. 192.]

"... I do not see how it can be said that the clause under consideration rests on negligence and nothing else.... There is enough to be gathered as to the scope of the contract to show that the relationship between the parties might readily give rise to claims by third parties on grounds independent of the Board's negligence....

"The Court should not be astute so to construe an exemption clause as to relieve a party of the results of his own negligence. The answer must be found in the contract itself, read, no doubt, against the general background. That general background is not very satisfactorily sketched in, but ... there is enough to show that the relationship of the parties was such as to give rise to claims by third parties independently of the Board's negligence. And I think further that the clause, read against the general background, yields possible heads of damage other than that of negligence which cannot be described as either fanciful or remote."

LORD PATRICK (at p. 9): "There remains the . . . question: whether the head of damage contemplated in the indemnity clause may be based on some ground other than the negligence of the employers' servants, in other words whether a reasonable content can be found for the indemnity clause if claims caused by the negligence of the employers' servants are excluded from its scope. . . . I have come to the opinion that sensible content can be found for this indemnity clause without construing it as covering claims caused by the negligence of the employers' servants, and that it should not be construed as covering such claims."

NOTES

1. A similar indemnity clause came before the House of Lords in *Smith* v. *U.M.B. Chrysler (Scotland) Ltd.*, 1978 S.C.(H.L.) 1.

S. Ltd., electrical contractors, agreed to carry out maintenance work at a factory occupied by U. Ltd. The contract included an indemnity clause by which S. Ltd. undertook to indemnify U. Ltd. of "any liability . . . whatsoever" for personal injury or for damage to property arising out of or in the course of the work.

An electrical fitter employed by S. Ltd. was injured, and made a successful claim, based on negligence, against U. Ltd. The question then arising was whether U. Ltd. was entitled to be indemnified by S. Ltd.

Held that the indemnity clause was not to be interpreted in such a way as to exempt U. Ltd. from a liability based on the negligence of itself or its servants.

Lord Fraser of Tullybelton (at p. 12): "Mr Cullen [senior counsel for the respondents] argued that paragraph (*b*) in the present indemnity clause contained language which 'expressly' entitled the respondents to indemnity against the consequence of their own negligence. . . . The argument was that the words 'any liability, loss, claim or proceedings whatsoever' amounted to an express reference to such negligence because they covered any liability however caused. . . . I do not see how a clause can 'expressly' exempt or indemnify the *proferens* against his negligence unless it contains the word 'negligence' or some synonym for it. . . . The word 'whatsoever' occurs in paragraph (*b*) of Clause 23 here, but in my opinion it is no more than a word of emphasis and it cannot be read as equivalent to an express reference to negligence. . . . In the present case I am clearly of the opinion that there is no express provision that the respondents are to be indemnified against the results of their own negligence."

2. An exclusion-of-liability clause in a lease was interpreted to the same effect in *Evans* v. *Glasgow District Council*, 1979 S.L.T. 270.

The clause provided: "The proprietor/s shall not be liable for any loss or damage caused by or arising from the bursting or leakage of any service pipes or tanks or flooding from within or without the premises or from any other cause whatsoever during the currency of the let."

E., the tenant, suffered loss and damage to his printing and stationery business as a result of vandalism, and brought an action for damages for negligence against the proprietor on the ground that, because of demolition of adjoining property, vandalism was a risk which the proprietor ought to have taken reasonable care to prevent.

The proprietor pleaded that the exclusion-of-liability clause operated to defeat E.'s claim.

Held (1) there was doubt as to whether the clause was wide enough to cover negligence on the proprietor's part and therefore the clause had to be construed against the proprietor; and (2) as it could not be said that the clause had no content unless liability for negligence was excluded, the proprietor could not by relying on the clause escape any liability to E.

3. In *Graham* v. *The Shore Porters Society*, 1979 S.L.T. 119 (O.H.), a clause in a contract of carriage exempting the carriers from losses arising from accidental fire was construed as restricted to statutory liability under the Mercantile Law Amendment Act Scotland 1856 and not as extending to liability arising out of the carriers' breach of contract in not providing a reasonably fit van.

Lord Grieve (at p. 121): "The words used in condition 7 contain no reference to a breach of contract on the defenders' part. There is thus no express language used in the condition to which due effect can be given in order to relieve the defenders of their liability for damage to their customer's goods by fire caused by a breach of contract on their part. . . .

". . . As common carriers they would be liable to their customers if goods which they were carrying were accidentally damaged by fire. This was a liability which they could not normally take steps to prevent by their own actings, unlike damage resulting from their breach of contract, or their negligence. It is accordingly reasonable to assume that they would take steps to exempt themselves from their statutory liability for accidental damage to their customers' goods as a result of fire. That in my opinion is what the defenders sought to do, and succeeded in doing by condition 7."

4. Indemnity clauses and exclusion-of-liability clauses are now controlled, over a wide range of contracts, by the Unfair Contract Terms Act 1977 (see Appendix A).

Insurance contract construed contra proferentem

Kennedy v. Smith

1975 S.C. 266

On taking out a car insurance policy, S. had signed an abstinence declaration containing the statement: "I am a total abstainer from alcoholic drinks and have been since birth."

The policy provided that the insurance company would not be liable for any claim arising while the insured was "under the influence of intoxicating liquor," or for any claim arising while the car was being driven by "the insured having consumed intoxicating liquor prior thereto in breach of the abstinence declaration."

On the return journey from a successful bowling club outing, S. was persuaded to drink a pint, or perhaps a pint and a half, of lager in a public-house. Some 15 minutes afterwards S.'s car, with S. at the wheel, went out of control on a dual carriageway, crossed the central reservation, and collided with a road sign, with the result that the two passengers in the car were killed.

The widows of the two passengers claimed damages from S., and a decree was pronounced against S. for an agreed amount of damages.

The insurance company, however, refused to indemnify S., on the grounds that at the time of the accident S. had been "under the influence of intoxicating liquor" and "in breach of the abstinence declaration."

Held that the insurance company was bound to indemnify S. because (1) it had failed to prove that S. had been "under the influence of intoxicating liquor" at the time of the accident and (2) the abstinence declaration did not cover future conduct of the insured.

LORD PRESIDENT (EMSLIE) (at p. 275): "For the defender the submission under reference to exception 5 (*a*) is simple to state. There were no sufficient proved facts capable of supporting the inference that at the time of the accident the pursuer was 'under the influence of intoxicating liquor,' as these words are properly to be understood. They mean, as the

Lord Ordinary accepted, 'under such influence of intoxicating liquor as disturbs the balance of a man's mind.' ...

"For the defender the submission was that Statement (2) is no more than a warranty of the defender's position at the time of the proposal and since birth, and there is nothing in the Policy itself to cast doubt upon this construction. This is clear from the tenses used and it would have been easy, if the third party had intended it to contain a promise for the future, to have said so in clear and simple terms. ...

"For the third party counsel urged us to find a warranty for the future in Statement (2), notwithstanding the tenses used. ...

"Although in the course of the hearing counsel for the parties referred us to a number of cases in which construction of particular Statements or Answers in proposal forms was in issue, I do not find reference to these to be helpful. What I do find helpful, however, is to remind myself of the approach which the Court ought to take to construction of statements, like Statement (2), incorporated in proposal forms and the like. ...

"... If insurers seek to limit their liability under a policy by relying upon an alleged undertaking as to the future, prepared by them and accepted by the insured, the language they use must be such that the terms of the alleged undertaking and its scope are clearly and unambiguously expressed or plainly implied and that any such alleged undertaking will be construed, *in dubio, contra proferentem.*

"In my opinion approaching the question of construction in this case as it must be approached I am, with respect to the Lord Ordinary, quite unable to construe Statement (2) as he has done and as the third party urged me to do. The statement does not require to be given a future promissory content to make it intelligible. It is quite intelligible if it is read literally for, no doubt, the risk during the period of insurance is reduced if at the outset the proposer is a Total Abstainer since it may reasonably be hoped that he is unlikely to abandon his principles. It would have been simple to include in the statement, if this had been intended, that the insured shall continue to be a Total Abstainer for the period of the insurance. ... In short I am quite unable to read Statement (2) as an undertaking not to drink in the future when this could so readily have been said and was not."

LORD AVONSIDE (at p. 280): "The respondent contends that the declaration suffices to cover the future conduct of the signer. The respondent insures only total abstainers and that at a favourable rate. It is believed and anticipated that a total abstainer will remain one by reason of principle or habit and it is on that basis of belief and understanding that the respondent issues its policies to those who have made a satisfactory declaration of abstinence. I accept that this may very well be the belief and, indeed, the experience of those who conduct the affairs of the respondents. But that is not the question. The true question is whether the terms of the declaration are to be construed against the insured in such a manner that a lapse by him leads immediately to contravention of the declaration.

"In my opinion it does not. It has been said time and again that if insurers wish to lay down a condition which can be expressed clearly and simply then they must do so. . . . In the present case the declaration by the appellant clearly refers to his position at its date and previously. . . . If the respondent had wished to make future abstinence a feature of the declaration of total abstinence they could easily have done so. That was not done and futurity cannot be brought in by any attempt to raise some kind of implication."

NOTES

1. Another instance of an insurance contract being construed *contra proferentem* is *Davidson* v. *Guardian Exchange Assurance*, 1979 S.C. 192.

D.'s car, comprehensively insured with G., was damaged by fire. G. elected to repair the car, but owing to delay in the completion of the repairs D. claimed damages from G. for breach of contract. G., although conceding that they were obliged to repair the car within a reasonable time, founded on an exception clause in the policy which provided that the company was not to be liable for loss of use.

Held that on a proper construction of the policy the exception clause qualified the extent of indemnity under the policy but did not exclude liability for loss of use arising out of breach of the contract of insurance itself.

Lord Kissen (at p. 198): "The basis of the submission by defenders' counsel was that this was a commercial agreement and had therefore to be construed broadly. That basis is clearly incorrect. This was a policy of insurance framed and printed by the defenders and, if there was any ambiguity, the construction had to be *contra proferentem* [Gloag on Contract, 2nd ed., p. 400]. The argument for the defenders was that repairs would obviously take time, that the pursuer would be deprived of the use of his car during that time, that a claim for loss of use of the car was excluded by the Exceptions clause and that, therefore, all claims for loss of use, whether caused by breach of contract or not, were excluded. This argument ignores the fact that the claim by the pursuer is based on breach of contract. The Policy is not concerned with breach of contract. The risks insured against are defined . . . and the Exceptions clause limits and qualifies the extent of the indemnity against those risks only. Normal loss of use during repair of the car would be excepted because the Exceptions clause limits the indemnity in the risk. Loss of use, due to a breach of contract, is not covered by the Exceptions clause and, indeed, the Policy does not deal with breach of contract. The Policy was the occasion for the breach of contract, on which the pursuer sues, in that the breach was caused by the manner in which the defenders attempted to carry out their contractual obligation of repair but the Policy is otherwise irrelevant to the pursuer's claim."

2. The Unfair Contract Terms Act 1977 (see Appendix A) does not apply to contracts of insurance.

Doctrine of fundamental breach

Pollock & Co. v. Macrae

1922 S.C.(H.L.) 192

P. & Co., engineers, Glasgow, contracted to build and install a set of motor marine engines for M., a Stornoway fishcurer. The contract contained the following clause: "5. All goods are supplied on the condition that we shall not be liable for any direct or consequential damages arising from defective material or workmanship, even when such goods are supplied under the usual form of guarantee."

Held that this clause, while it would have protected the engineers where parts of engines were defective, was of no avail where there had been a complete breach of contract owing to a series of defects which made the engines practically unserviceable.

LORD DUNEDIN (at p. 198): "The usual function of a specification is, as its name denotes, to specify exactly what the seller is to deliver to the buyer. It is also usual that it should contain clauses protecting the seller from the effect of causes over which he has no control, and which may hinder or render impossible the performance of the contract. Such are strike clauses, clauses as to the supply of material from other sources, clauses as to the effect of weather, such as frost, &c. But it is not usual that it should in addition contain conditions which amount to a counter-stipulation on the part of the buyer that he will forgo the ordinary remedies which the law gives him in the event of breach of contract. Such conditions to be effectual must be most clearly and unambiguously expressed, as is always necessary in cases where a well-known common law liability is sought to be avoided. Illustrations of the necessity may be found in numerous cases where carriers have sought to limit or avoid their liability.... Reading the clauses in this light, I am of opinion that, although they excuse from damage flowing from the insufficiency of a part or parts of the machinery, they have no application to damage arising when there has been total breach of contract by failing to supply the article truly contracted for."

NOTES

1. The doctrine of fundamental breach was applied in *W. L. Tinney & Co. Ltd.* v. *John C. Dougall Ltd.*, 1977 S.L.T. (Notes) 58 (O.H.).

In a claim for damages for breach of a contract for the sale of seed potatoes, the question was whether the sellers could rely on the following term in the contract of sale: "It is specifically provided and agreed that compensation and damages payable under any claim or claims arising out of this contract under whatsoever pretext shall not under any circumstances amount in aggregate to more than the contract price of the potatoes forming the subject of the claim or claims."

Amongst the cases referred to by the Lord Ordinary (Wylie) were *Pollock & Co.* v. *Macrae* and *Suisse Atlantique Société d'Armement Maritime S.A.* v. *N.V. Rotterdamsche Kolen Centrale* [1967] 1 A.C. 361.

Lord Wylie held that, if the purchasers proved their alleged case of fundamental breach, the sellers could not, as a matter of law, rely on the quoted term.

He said (at p. 58): "I am satisfied that, if the clause which seeks to exclude or to limit liability is to apply in the case of fundamental breach of contract, and such protection is to be afforded to the party guilty of such failure as would entitle the other party to the contract to rescind it, it must be spelled out in the clearest possible terms. I respectfully agree with the view expressed by Lord Wilberforce in *Suisse Atlantique* ..., at p. 432 where his Lordship says that where it is a question of contractual intention whether a particular breach is covered or not 'the Courts are entitled to insist, as they do, that the more radical the breach the clearer must the language be if it is to be covered.' "

2. At common law, however, the language of the parties may be sufficient to exclude the application of the doctrine of fundamental breach.

Such language was held to have been used in a contract with ship repairers in *Alexander Stephen (Forth) Ltd.* v. *J. J. Riley (U.K.) Ltd.*, 1976 S.C. 151 (O.H.).

The conditions of the contract provided that, apart from liability for defective workmanship and for damage directly caused by negligence, the repairers were not to be liable to the customer "even if the circumstances arise in which the customer is entitled to terminate the repair contract by reason of a fundamental or other repudiatory breach on the part of the contractor."

Lord Kincraig (Ordinary) (at p. 156): "Where ... parties use the words 'fundamental breach' in a written contract, which is to be governed by the law of Scotland, the phrase must be taken to have been intended to have the same meaning as 'material breach.' ...

[After referring to the speeches of Lords Reid and Upjohn in the *Suisse Atlantique* case] "It surely must be possible, unless there is a substantive rule of law to the contrary, for parties to agree how their rights are to be regulated if one of the parties is in such fundamental breach of contract as entitles the other to rescind and thus end the contract, and to do so in the same document which embodies the obligations of the parties during the subsistence of the contract. I was referred to no such substantive rule in the law of contract in Scotland, and in my judgment that law allows parties to contract as they may deem fit, and to contract in such a way as to limit their liability, even in cases of so-called fundamental breach, or, to put it in phraseology more familiar to Scots lawyers, in cases where there has been a material breach of contract by one of the parties which entitles the other to rescind the contract."

3. In *Ailsa Craig Fishing Co. Ltd.* v. *Malvern Fishing Co. Ltd.*, 1982 S.C. (H.L.) 14, the House of Lords, affirming the judgment of the Court of Session, held that a clause of limitation of liability did not require to be judged by the specially exacting standards applied to exclusion and indemnity clauses, and that the clause of limitation of liability in the case was clear and unambiguous and effective to limit liability even for negligence.

Lord Fraser of Tullybelton (at p. 58): "The appellants were the owners of the fishing vessel 'Strathallan' which sank while berthed in Aberdeen Harbour on 31st December 1971, at a time when Securicor were bound, under the contract with the [Aberdeen Fishing Vessel Owners'] Association, to provide security cover in the Harbour. Her gallows fouled the vessel moored next to her on the starboard side, called the 'George Craig,' which also sank. ...

"The question whether Securicor's liability has been limited falls to be answered by construing the terms of the contract in accordance with the ordinary principles applicable to contracts of this kind. The argument for limitation depends upon certain special conditions attached to the contract prepared on behalf of Securicor and put forward in their interest. There is no doubt that such conditions must be construed strictly against the *proferens*, in this case Securicor, and that in order to be effective they must be 'most clearly and unambiguously expressed'—see *Pollock & Co.* v. *Macrae*. . . .

"There are later authorities which lay down very strict principles to be applied when considering the effect of clauses of exclusion or of indemnity. . . . [Lord Fraser then referred to the principles applied in *Smith* v. *U.M.B. Chrysler (Scotland) Ltd.* (see NOTE 1 to *North of Scotland Hydro-Electric Board* v. *D. & R. Taylor*, p. 175, above).] In my opinion these principles are not applicable in their full rigour when considering the effect of clauses merely limiting liability. Such clauses will of course be read *contra proferentem* and must be clearly expressed, but there is no reason why they should be judged by the specially exacting standards which are applied to exclusion and indemnity clauses. The reason for imposing such standards on these clauses is the inherent improbability that the other party to a contract including such a clause intended to release the *proferens* from a liability that would otherwise fall upon him. But there is no such high degree of improbability that he would agree to a limitation of the liability of the *proferens*, especially when . . . the potential losses that might be caused by the negligence of the *proferens* or its servants are so great in proportion to the sums that can reasonably be charged for the services contracted for. It is enough in the present case that the clause must be clear and unambiguous. . . .

". . . The question remains whether in its context [the clause limiting liability] is sufficiently clear and unambiguous to receive effect in limiting the liability of Securicor for its own negligence or that of its employees. In my opinion it is. It applies to any liability 'whether under the express or implied terms of this contract, or at common law, or in any other way.' Liability at common law is undoubtedly wide enough to cover liability including the negligence of the *proferens* itself, so that even without relying on the final words 'any other way,' I am clearly of opinion that the negligence of Securicor is covered."

4. The need for recourse to the doctrine of fundamental breach was significantly reduced by the Unfair Contract Terms Act 1977 (see Appendix A).

Condition regarded as satisfied where party bound has done all he can to satisfy it

Mackay v. Dick & Stevenson

(1881) 8 R.(H.L.) 37; (1880) 7 R. 778

M., who was involved in excavation work for a railway line, contracted to buy from D. & S., engineers, a steam excavator on condition that at a trial the machine was proved capable of digging out a specified amount of earth in a day of 10 hours. For this trial M. was to provide a "properly opened up face" at the Carfin cutting.

When the machine was ready the Carfin cutting was not sufficiently advanced for the application of the machine, and the machine was tested at another cutting. It broke down in the course of the test, was repaired by D. & S., and the following month sent to the Carfin cutting. There it again broke down.

D. & S., alleging that M. had not provided a "properly opened up face," brought an action for the price of £1,115.

Held that since D. & S. had been prevented from fulfilling the condition precedent through the fault of M., the condition was to be regarded as having been satisfied, and that D. & S. were therefore entitled to the price.

LORD BLACKBURN (at p. 40): "I think I may safely say, as a general rule, that where in a written contract it appears that both parties have agreed that something shall be done, which cannot effectually be done unless both concur in doing it, the construction of the contract is that each agrees to do all that is necessary to be done on his part for the carrying out of that thing, though there may be no express words to that effect. ... Now, applying this principle to the present case, both agree that the machine shall be tested at Carfin, and therefore the pursuers agreed that they would bring the machine to the Carfin cutting, and there erect it on the defender's land, and there do their part in working it till there had been a fair test; and the defender agreed that he would do his part; and even if there had been no express mention in the letters of a properly prepared face, the nature of the thing shews that he agreed to let the pursuers have access to a part of the cutting, put by the defender in such a condition that the machine could be fairly tested by working at it, and to assist in working it there until there had been a fair test."

LORD WATSON (at p. 45): "The terms of the contract seem to me to imply very plainly that it was incumbent on the appellant, and not upon the respondents, to provide 'a properly opened up face' for the trial of the machine. . . . The respondents were only entitled to receive payment of the price of the machine on the condition that it should be tried at a proper working face provided by the appellant, and that on trial it should excavate a certain amount of clay or other soft substance within a given time. They have been thwarted in the attempt to fulfil that condition by the neglect or refusal of the appellant to furnish the means of applying the stipulated test; and their failure being due to his fault, I am of opinion that, as in a question with him, they must be taken to have fulfilled the condition. The passage cited by Lord Shand [in the Court of Session] from Bell's *Principles* (section 50) to the effect that, 'If the debtor bound under a certain condition have impeded or prevented the event, it is held as accomplished. If the creditor has done all that he can to fulfil a condition which is incumbent on himself, it is held sufficient implement,' expresses a doctrine, borrowed from the civil law, which has long been recognised in the law of Scotland, and I think it ought to be applied to the present case."

Presumption against joint and several liability

Coats v. The Union Bank of Scotland Ltd.

1929 S.C.(H.L.) 114; 1928 S.C. 711

C., M. and R. purchased 2,250 shares in a company for £69,750, and a bank agreed to advance £39,750 "on joint loan" to the three purchasers, the balance of the price being provided by them in equal portions, and the bank holding the shares in security of the advance.

C., M. and R. paid for the shares by granting their individual cheques to the sellers for £10,000 each, and by drawing joint cheques, signed by them all, on the bank for the £39,750 advanced.

The bank paid this amount to the sellers, and opened a joint overdraft account in the name of C., M. and R.

The value of the shares fell, and the bank intimated to C. that it held him liable for the whole amount of the loan.

C. brought an action for declarator that he was liable only for one-third of the loan and that on payment of one-third he was entitled to a transfer of one-third of the shares.

Held (*aff.* judgment of First Division) that C. was liable for one-third of the loan only; but (*rev.* judgment of First Division) that C. was not entitled to receive a transfer of one-third of the shares since under the arrangement for the pledge of the shares, the bank was entitled to treat the whole of the shares as security for the whole amount advanced.

VISCOUNT HAILSHAM (at 1929 S.C.(H.L.) p. 119): "By the law of Scotland, differing in this respect from the law of England, joint debtors are regarded *prima facie* as incurring a *pro rata* liability only; but this *prima facie* presumption may be rebutted. The law is stated in Gloag on Contract, (2nd ed.) at p. 198, as follows: 'As a mere general rule, subject to many exceptions and yielding to expressions indicative of an intention to the contrary, obligations are construed as involving rights and liabilities *pro rata*, so that one of two creditors can exact payment of a half only; one of two debtors is liable in the same proportion only.' *Prima facie*, therefore, a request for a joint loan would import an undertaking to repay only a proportionate part of the amount advanced. The question which is to be determined is whether the documents in this case, read as a whole, and the method by which the transaction was carried out, contain evidence sufficient to rebut the presumption and to prove that the intention of both parties was that Mr Coats should be liable for the whole of the debt.

"The argument for the Bank was based almost entirely upon the fact that the transaction was carried through by means of a cheque signed by all three borrowers. They pointed out that, by virtue of the Bills of Exchange Act 1882, each of the drawers of a cheque was liable for the full amount of the cheque to a holder in due course; and they said that the cheque was an integral part of the transaction, and that by signing it Mr Coats assumed liability for the whole amount, and therefore he must be treated as having made himself liable to the Bank to the full extent of the advance.

"I cannot regard this argument as well founded. It is no doubt true that, if the cheque had not been honoured, Mr Coats would have been liable for its full amount to a holder in due course; but I think that the Bank was quite wrong in its claim to be regarded as a holder. The Bank was the drawee of the cheque; the cheque was duly honoured . . . ; and thereupon the cheque was discharged by payment in due course by virtue of section 59 (1) of the Bills of Exchange Act. Any claim by the Bank as a holder of the cheque must therefore fail. . . .

"In the present case it may well be that, if there had been no independent arrangement for a loan, the fact that the loan transaction was carried out by means of a joint cheque drawn on the Bank might have afforded an inference that the transaction was intended to impose a several liability upon each of the drawers for the full amount of the cheque. But in fact the terms of the loan are set out in the letter of the 21st of December . . . ; and the cheque was merely a piece of machinery for carrying out these terms. I cannot think that any man who was asked to sign the letter of the 21st of December would have imagined that the mere fact that that letter referred to a loan cheque was sufficient to change the character of the transaction from the joint loan for which the letter asked into a loan for which each of the signatories was to be severally liable *in solidum*. . . .

". . . Has Mr Coats the right to redeem his 750 shares by payment of his one-third share of the joint loan? This seems to have been treated by the First Division as almost a necessary consequence of their decision that the liability on the loan was only *pro rata*. I do not think that that assumption is justified. The terms of the letter of pledge are that the shares shall be held as collateral security for any advance made by the Bank to the borrowers; the Bank is authorised to realise such shares at any time for the purpose of repaying the amount due to the Bank; and, in my judgment, the proper and necessary inference from the language used is that the Bank was entitled to treat the whole of the shares deposited as being security for the whole of the amount advanced. I see no inconsistency between the personal liability of each of the borrowers being limited to the amount which they respectively required and the shares of each of them being deposited as a security for the whole amount of the debt jointly incurred."

LORD ATKIN (at 1929 S.C.(H.L.) p. 126): "I agree . . . that the contractual documents in this case do not displace the *prima facie* presumption that the obligation undertaken by the three contracting parties was an obligation to pay *pro rata*. I also agree . . . that the security given covers the whole of the debt, and is not to be treated distributively as covering the relative proportion due from each of the contracting parties. . . . It is possible that . . . the fact of the payment having been made on a cheque may have some bearing on the question whether the obligation of the parties to the bank was joint and several or *pro rata*; but, inasmuch as a banking transaction by way of drawing on a bank account would ordinarily be carried out by cheque whether the obligation of the drawers was to be joint and several or *pro rata*, the effect of the cheque would appear somewhat colourless. In the present case it seems to me plain that the cheques were only ordinary business means of carrying out a transaction defined in other prior documents, and their existence cannot affect the decision."

LORD ORDINARY (CONSTABLE) (at 1928 S.C. p. 717): "The general rule or presumption undoubtedly is that a joint obligation imports only *pro rata* liability."

LORD PRESIDENT (CLYDE) (at 1928 S.C. p. 722): "By the law of Scotland (differing in this respect, as I understand, from the law of England) a joint obligant—that is, a person who joins with others in undertaking an obligation (*e.g.*, to pay or to repay a sum of money)—does not, by the fact that he so joins, incur an obligation *in solidum* to the creditor in the obligation. If he is bound merely as an obligant along with others, or *per expressum* 'jointly' with others, he incurs no obligation to the creditor beyond payment, or repayment, of a *pro rata* part of the joint debt. Thus, if three persons bind themselves—either simply or 'jointly'—to pay or to repay a sum of £300 to a creditor, all the creditor gets against them is a right to recover £100 from each. It is only when a joint obligant is bound 'jointly and severally' with others that the creditor can recover against him *in solidum*.

"The question to which category a particular obligation belongs depends either on special rules of law or on the terms in which the obligation is conceived. Thus, joint and several liability is implied by the law of Scotland in certain classes of obligations and under certain instruments. This implication rests either on the nature of the obligation itself (*e.g.*, if the subject of the obligation is indivisible); or on the legal character of the relations between the co-obligants (*e.g.*, in partnership, where each partner is liable for the whole debts of the firm); or on the custom of merchants (*e.g.*, the joint and several liability of the drawers and acceptors of a bill of exchange for the engagements they undertake by signing the bill) .... In all obligations not covered by a special rule of law, the presumption is against joint and several liability. Further, in written obligations (not falling under any of the particular classes just referred to)—and particularly in written obligations for the payment or repayment of money—co-obligants are not bound *in solidum*, but only *pro rata*, unless they are bound in so many words 'jointly and severally,' or by some other expression importing joint and several liability—*e.g.*, 'as full debtors.'...

"... In my opinion the documents and correspondence are consistent only with a *pro rata* obligation on the part of the pursuer, and negative the undertaking by him of any joint and several liability."

NOTES

1. For comments on the meaning of "jointly and severally" see *Fleming* v. *Gemmill*, 1908 S.C. 340:

Lord McLaren (at p. 345): "The word 'severally' implies that against whatever number of defenders a man proceeds, each is liable for the whole sum sued for, and the word 'jointly' or 'conjunctly' secures to those against whom the decree is made operative the right of rateable relief against the persons who have not paid."

Lord Pearson (at p. 345): "The expression 'jointly and severally' was originally part of the language of obligations, and imported a reserved right on the part of the creditor of two or more persons in a divisible obligation, to hold them bound either each for his own share or each for the whole."

2. In obligations *ad factum praestandum* each is bound for the whole and liable in damages for breach of the obligation: *Rankine* v. *The Logie Den Land Co. Ltd.* (1902) 4 F. 1074.

Jus tertii

Blumer and Co. v. Scott and Sons

(1874) 1 R. 379

B. & Co., shipbuilders, sold an unfinished ship to E. & Sons under an agreement by which delivery was to be not later than February 1872 "delays of engineers, and every other unavoidable cause excepted."

B. & Co. then entered into an agreement with S. & Sons, engineers, for the supply of engines for the ship, the agreement providing that the engines were to be finished to the satisfaction of B. & Co.'s overseer.

The engines were not delivered until October 1872.

B. & Co. and E. & Sons raised an action for damages against S. & Sons.

Held that B. & Co., being protected from liability by the clause in their contract with E. & Sons, were not entitled to damages since they had suffered no loss, and that E. & Sons had no claim because they had not been parties to the contract for the supply of the engines and the terms of that contract had not conferred a *jus quaesitum tertio* on them.

LORD PRESIDENT (INGLIS) (at p. 384): "The two contracts are ... wholly different. In the one Blumer and Co. are bound to Ellis and Sons, in the other Scott and Sons are bound to Blumer and Co. It appears to me, therefore, impossible to hold that Ellis and Sons had any right to sue on the contract between Blumer and Co. and Scott and Sons, or had any right to claim damages for loss suffered by them in consequence of any alleged breach of contract on the part of Scott and Sons.... There remains the alternative conclusion by which Blumer and Co. try to recover damages said to have been suffered by themselves along with those said to have been suffered by Ellis and Sons. It is of importance to observe that this is not an action of relief, and Blumer and Co. can have no hope of turning it into such an action, because when they were offered an opportunity of changing their present claim into an action of relief of damages for which they were liable to Ellis and Sons, they failed to avail themselves of it. It is clear, unless Blumer and Co. are responsible to Ellis and Sons for these damages, that they can have no claim against Scott and Sons for them. Unless they can be made liable themselves for them they can have no claim against Scott and Sons. We see the explanation of their refusal . . . ; it is that Ellis and Sons have no claim against Blumer and Co. under their contract, and, therefore, unless such a claim could be made, Blumer and Co. can have no claim against Scott and Sons for relief. The alternative conclusion will thus not do either."

LORD ARDMILLAN (at p. 385): "There is no doubt that Blumer and Co. are entitled to recover from the defenders whatever damages they can instruct as due to themselves in consequence of delay by the defenders in fulfilment of the contract to supply the engines. . . .

"Still further, if Blumer and Co. have incurred liability to Ellis and Sons for damage resulting from delay in furnishing the ship, that delay being caused by the defenders' delay in supplying the engines, then Blumer and Co. might have claimed from the defenders relief from their obligation or liability to Ellis and Sons. . . . This action has not been framed so as to enforce such a claim of relief, or so as to recover damages on such a footing. . . . Blumer and Co. do not seek relief, and naturally so, for they have protected themselves against liability to Ellis and Sons for damage caused by 'delays of engineers.'

"To me it is very clear that . . . Blumer and Co. have no direct action against the defenders for damage done, not to themselves, but to Ellis. . . .

"The second question raised is attended with more difficulty. I refer to the direct conclusion for damages . . . which the pursuers, Ellis and Sons, maintain against the defenders.

"Now, Ellis and Sons are not parties to the defenders' contract with Blumer and Co., and the defenders are not parties to Blumer and Co.'s contract with Ellis. There is thus, on the face of the proceedings, no privity of contract between Ellis and Sons and the defenders; and, not only so, but Ellis and Sons have contracted to discharge from liability the party who contracted with them, viz., Blumer and Co., in respect of any damage by delay caused by engineers.

"... On the face of the contract sued on, the only contract to which the defenders are parties, Ellis and Sons, who did not contract with the defenders, have no right of action.

"But it has been suggested ... that there is here *jus quaesitum tertio*—in other words, that out of the contract between Blumer and Co. and the defenders there arises a right to Ellis to enforce this claim of damages....

"Undoubtedly there is a legal doctrine known as *jus quaesitum tertio*, resting on principles which have been to some extent introduced from the Roman law. It is, when rightly understood and applied, a sound and equitable doctrine. But, after careful consideration of the contracts in this case, and of the averments on record, and of the authority of Lord Stair, and of the decisions referred to reported in Morison's *Dictionary*, and of the recent authorities of *Peddie* v. *Brown* ((1857) 3 Macq. 65), and of *Finnie* v. *The Glasgow and South-Western Railway Co.* ((1857) 3 Macq. 75), I am clearly of opinion that there is no *jus quaesitum tertio* in this case. The opinion of Lord Chancellor Cranworth, and the opinion of Lord Wensleydale, in the House of Lords, in these two last-mentioned cases, appear to me to be valuable and conclusive authorities on the question before us.

"According to Lord Stair it is only where there is in a contract some 'article in favour of a third party' which cannot be recalled by one or both of the contractors that there is *jus quaesitum tertio*, and this doctrine is specially recognised and approved of by Lord Cranworth and Lord Wensleydale. The right may truly be conceived in favour of a third party, and may therefore be enforced by that third party, although he be not named in the contract; but the stipulation of which the benefit can thus be transferred to him must rest on an agreement between the contracting parties—that the stipulation shall be performed in favour and to the satisfaction of the third party. Even if not named, the third party may be entitled to adopt the agreement, and enforce it by action. But in such a case it must be clear that both the contracting parties intended so to secure him, and that they could not, separately or together, revoke the stipulation. If not named, he must, at least, be described, and it must be clearly apparent that the stipulation was intended to be in reference to him, and for his benefit. Now, in the present case, Ellis and Sons are not named or described in the contract with the defenders Scott, nor are the defenders taken bound to deliver the engines to Ellis and Sons, nor at the place of their business, nor are the defenders bound to furnish them to the satisfaction of Ellis and Sons.... The supposed right of Ellis, founded on as *jus quaesitum tertio* arising out of the contract between Blumer and Co. and the defenders, could have been revoked and put an end to by the parties to the contract, which is said to contain the stipulations out of which his right emerges. It is obvious that this does not satisfy the definition of *jus quaesitum tertio* given by Lord Stair, and adopted in the House of Lords.

"... The position of the parties is simply this: The party who alleges that he has suffered injury has no contract with the defenders, and no right of action against them. The party who has a contract with the defenders, and has a right of action thereon, has not suffered the damage now in question, because he has protected himself from liability by a clause in his own contract. I do not disguise that there may be some hardship in this matter as regards Ellis and Sons, supposing them to have suffered this damage. It looks like a wrong without a remedy. But the answer and the explanation is, that Ellis and Sons have by their own act deprived themselves of their remedy, for they have regulated the liability in this matter."

NOTES

1. See also *Edinburgh United Breweries Ltd.* v. *Molleson* (p. 111, above).

2. In *Henderson* v. *Robb* (1889) 16 R. 341 Lord President Inglis said (at p. 343): "I am of opinion that the pursuer has no title to sue. He is doing that which has been found over and over again to be incompetent, trying to sue his debtor's debtor."

Lord Adam said (at p. 345): "It is very clear on principle, and is perfectly settled, that a creditor cannot directly sue his debtor's debtor."

Jus quaesitum tertio: *co-feuars*

Hislop v. MacRitchie's Trustees

(1881) 8 R.(H.L.) 95

A superior feued ground for the building of five villas which were to form one side of Gayfield Square, Edinburgh. All the feu-contracts contained building restrictions, which were, however, not uniform but adapted to the situation of each villa. There was no reference to any general building plan, but all the buildings were required to be the same distance from the street in front of them. There was no undertaking by the superior in any of the feu-contracts to impose restrictions on adjoining feuars.

Various violations of the building restrictions took place, including the building of a warehouse in front of No. 1 Gayfield Square, but, when H., a coach-builder who owned No. 2 Gayfield Square, proceeded to build on to the front of his house a glass showroom for carriages, MacR.'s trustees, the owners of No. 4, acting "with consent and concurrence" of the superior, sought to interdict H.'s operations as being in violation of his feu-contract.

Held that (1) the restriction in H.'s feu-contract did not create a *jus quaesitum tertio* in favour of MacR.'s trustees, but was merely a condition of tenure between superior and vassal, and (2) since the trustees had no title whatever, as distinct from a defective title, the objection to their title was not obviated by the consent and concurrence of the superior to whom alone the right of action truly belonged.

LORD CHANCELLOR (SELBORNE) (at p. 97): "The restrictive provision as to building in Dick's feu-contract was not, in any sense, *jus quaesitum tertio*; it was merely a condition of tenure between superior and vassal. The fact of several feuars of neighbouring plots of building land in the same street holding from a common superior, does not, by itself, entitle one of those feuars to claim the benefit of restrictions in the feu-contract of another, unless some mutuality and community of rights and obligations is otherwise established between them; which can only be done by express stipulation in their respective contracts with the superior, or by reasonable implication from some reference in both contracts to a common plan or scheme of building, or by mutual agreement between the feuars themselves. Here there are none of those things. It follows that the respondents ... have no interest of their own, no right or cause of action against the appellant. They are strangers to the contract in which the restrictions which they seek to enforce are contained."

LORD BLACKBURN (at p. 99): "A great deal of house property in Scotland is held under feus containing in the feu-charters restrictions as to what is to be done. Such restrictions are, *prima facie*, enforceable only by the superior, who alone is a party to the contract of feu....

"I ... think that in the case now at the bar there is nothing to indicate that restrictions were imposed for the benefit of the co-feuars, beyond the fact that the feus were all given out nearly at the same time, and that some of the conditions inserted in the feus are similar to each other. That, and the fact ... that the houses are built so as to produce a considerable degree of uniformity, are all the respondents' counsel could point out as tending to shew that the restrictions were originally imposed for the benefit of the co-feuars."

LORD WATSON (at p. 101): "It is settled by a series of decisions in the

Courts of Scotland that every one of a class of feuars deriving their title from a common superior may have an implied right or *jus quaesitum* to enforce conditions occurring in contracts between the superior and his co-feuars to which he was not a party. In some cases it is made a matter of express stipulation by the superior, in contracting with his vassals, that each of them shall have that right.. . .

"Both parties, in their argument at the bar, assumed, and rightly assumed, that in order to the constitution of such a *jus quaesitum*, it is essential that the conditions to be enforced shall appear in all the feu-rights, that they shall in all cases be similar, if not identical, and of such a character that each feuar has an interest in enforcing them. But the respondents carried their argument so far as to maintain that these considerations, where they are found to co-exist, sufficiently indicate that the conditions of feu were intended for the mutual benefit of all the feuars, and must therefore be held to confer upon each feuar a right of action against his co-feuars for the enforcement of these conditions. . . .

"The fact of the same condition appearing in feu-charters derived from a common superior, coupled with a substantial interest in its observance, does not appear to me to be sufficient to give each feuar a title to enforce it. No single feuar can, in my opinion, be subjected in liability to his co-feuars, unless it appears from the titles under which he holds his feu that such similarity of conditions and mutuality of interest among the feuars either had been or was meant to be established. According to the tenor of the feu-disposition, or feu-contract, as the case may be, the feuar and his superior are the only parties to it; and I am of opinion that no *jus quaesitum* can arise to any *tertius* except by the consent of both these contracting parties. That being so, unless the feuar, either in express words or by implication, gives his consent to the introduction of a *tertius*, the superior cannot as against him create any such interest, by imposing the same conditions to which he has submitted upon another feu in his vicinity. . . .

"In the present case, the respondents' title to sue appears to me to fail in two essential particulars. The titles to the appellant's feu are of older date than those of any other of the five lots in question, with the exception of lot 3, which was originally included in the same feu-contract. . . . That deed lays no obligation upon the superior to observe any limitation in building upon the adjacent ground, or to impose any such limitation upon those to whom he might subsequently feu or dispone it. . . . There is not a single expression which can reasonably be held to indicate the superior's intention to restrict the adjoining feuars, and still less to imply that he meant to come under an obligation to that effect. Again, the several restrictions as to building contained in the titles of the appellant and the respondents do not, in my opinion, so resemble each other as to raise the inference that they were intended to be mutual. . . .

"I have accordingly come to the conclusion that the respondents had and have no title, in their own persons, to raise and insist in the present action. That leaves the question whether their right to sue, which I assume to be *nil*, has been validated by the consent and concurrence of their superiors, to the effect of entitling them to decree in the terms of the prayer of the note of suspension and interdict.

". . . I know of no authority for holding that, according to the law or practice of Scotland, a person who has no right or title whatever can sue an action, provided he obtain the consent and concurrence of the party to whom alone such right or title belongs."

NOTE

In *Murray's Trustees* v. *Trustees for St. Margaret's Convent*, 1907 S.C.(H.L.) 8; (1906) 8 F. 1109, Lord Kinnear, with whom the other judges of the First Division concurred, applied Lord Chancellor Selborne's test and held that no *jus quaesitum tertio* had been created. The appeal to the House of Lords was confined to the other point raised in the case—construction of the phrase "building of an unseemly description" in a bond of servitude.

Jus quaesitum tertio: *irrevocability*

Carmichael v. Carmichael's Executrix

1920 S.C.(H.L.) 195

C. took out a policy of assurance upon the life of his son, Ian, then aged nine years. The policy provided that, during Ian's minority, C. would be entitled to the surrender value of the policy and that, if Ian died before attaining majority, the premiums would be repaid to C., but that, if Ian attained majority and he or his assigns continued to pay the premiums, the sum assured should be paid on his death to his executors. As an alternative, Ian was entitled at majority to exercise certain options including conversion of the policy into a cash payment or a fully-paid policy.

Ian attained majority but died before the next premium fell due and without having exercised any of the options. He knew of the existence of the policy, but it had not been delivered or intimated to him by his father. Ian, by holograph will, left his whole estate to his aunt Miss McColl.

Held in a competition between C. and Miss McColl that, although the policy had never been delivered to Ian either actually or constructively, its terms, taken in conjunction with the whole circumstances of the case, showed that Ian had acquired a *jus quaesitum* under it, and, accordingly, that the proceeds fell to Miss McColl.

LORD DUNEDIN (at p. 197): "Had Ian Carmichael a *jus quaesitum tertio* under the policy which passed the proceeds thereof to his executrix?

"I think it very necessary to begin by pointing out that the expression '*jus quaesitum tertio*' is, in different cases and different circumstances, used in a varying sense, or, perhaps I might better say, is looked at from a different point of view. The one sense is meant when the question being considered is simply whether the *tertius* C has the right to sue A in respect of a contract made between A and B to which contract C is no party. The controversy then arises between C, who wishes to sue, and A, who denies his title to do so. It is here that there is a sharp technical diversity between the laws of England and Scotland. In England, no matter how much the contract contained provisions for behoof of C, C could never sue at law. In equity he could sue, but he could only sue if, by the terms of the contract, he could successfully maintain that A was constituted a trustee in his favour. In Scotland, if the provision is expressed in favour of C, he can sue, and this is often designated by saying 'He has a *jus quaesitum tertio*.' Probably the reason of the difference indicated lies in the simple fact that in Scotland law and equity were never separate. Another familiar illustration of the same class of difference will be found in the right of an assignee in Scotland to sue in his own name, a right which at common law in England apart from statute he did not possess. But, as already stated, in all this class of cases the controversy is between A and C: B is either no longer existent or is, so far as he is concerned, quite willing that C should exact his rights. Examples of this first class of controversy may be found in such cases as *Finnie* v. *Glasgow and South-Western Railway Co.* ((1857) 3 Macq. 75), *Henderson* v. *Stubbs* ((1894) 22 R. 51), and *Love* (1912 S.C. 1078). The other sense of the expression is when the emphasis is, so to speak, on the *quaesitum*, and when the controversy arises not between C and A but between C and B. In such a case A is willing to perform his contract, and the contract in form provides that A shall do something for C, but B, or those who represent B's estate, interfere and say that B and not C is the true creditor in the stipulation. Of this second class are the deposit-receipt cases such as *Jamieson* v. *McLeod* ((1880) 7 R. 1131), *Crosbie's Trustees* v. *Wright* ((1880) 7 R. 823) (examples of different results according to the evidence), and insurance policy cases such as *Hadden* v. *Bryden* ((1899) 1 F. 710) and *Jarvie's Trustee* v. *Jarvie's Trustees* ((1887) 14 R. 411).

"It is needless to say that the present case is one of the latter category. No question is raised by the Insurance Company. They are willing to pay the £1,000. The question is, to whom are they to pay it? Moreover, so far as the form of the stipulation is concerned, it is clear that the creditors are the executors, administrators, or assigns of the person whose life is assured, *i.e.*, of the son, for to them alone is payment expressed to be made....

"Here I must first deal with an argument of the appellant which, if sound, would be conclusive, but which, in my opinion, attempts too much. It is, that the terms of the document alone are sufficient to create the right. Doubtless she thought to support this argument by a very great authority, the words of Lord Stair (*Inst.* I. x. 5), which, if taken literally, and according to what I may call the natural grammar, would go the whole length. Lord Stair says: 'It is likewise the opinion of Molina, and it quadrates *with* our customs that when parties contract, if there be any article in favour of a third party, at any time, *est jus quaesitum tertio*, which cannot be recalled by *either or both* of the contractors, but he may compel either of them to exhibit the contract, and thereupon the obliged may be compelled to perform.' That would mean that the moment you find from the form of the obligation that there was a *jus* conceived in favour of a *tertius* it proved that that *jus* was *quaesitum* to that *tertius*. I do not think Lord Stair meant to lay down such a proposition. If he did, and if your Lordships were to say he was right in so doing, then you would overrule not only the long string of comparatively modern cases as regards deposit-receipts ... but also the older authorities as to bonds, destinations in titles to land, and insurance policies.... Speaking for myself, I should decline to be a party to such a holocaust of accepted authorities in the law of Scotland; but I do not think Lord Stair meant any such thing. It was pointed out by Lord Ardmillan in *Blumer & Co.* v. *Scott & Sons* ((1874) 1 R. 379, at p. 387), and accepted by Lords Dundas and Mackenzie in this case, that the transposition of the words '*est jus quaesitum tertio*' and the words 'which cannot be recalled by either or both of the contractors' would make the proposition agree with the decided cases. Irrevocability would be a condition, not a consequence, of the expression of the *jus* in favour of the *tertius*. Perhaps the ambiguity arises from Lord Stair putting his sentence partly in Latin and partly in English.... But the real reason for supposing that Lord Stair did not mean the larger proposition is the fact that he quotes four cases on which he founds what he is saying, and not one of these would warrant this larger proposition.... I ... reject the argument for the appellant that the mere terms of the document prove her case.

"Taking now Lord Stair's dictum in the other sense, in which I hold it to be sound, what it comes to is this, that irrevocability is the test; but the mere execution of the document will not constitute irrevocability. It is obvious that if A and B contract and nothing else follows, and no one is informed of the contract, A and B can agree to cancel the contract....

"... There must therefore be something more than the form of the document forming the contract and conceived in favour of the *tertius* to effectuate irrevocability. This something may be provided in different ways, for, after all, it is a question of evidence. Now the most obvious evidence is the delivery of the document to the *tertius* himself. The delivery of a deposit-receipt taken to the *tertius*, or the endorsement of a deposit-receipt taken to the depositor and the handing of the receipt to the *tertius*, are familiar examples. In place of delivery of the document to the *tertius* there may be a dealing with the document in such a way as to put it out of the power of the original contractors to deal with it. This may be effected by a registration for publication, *i.e.*, in the Books of Council and Session. There the deed, once registered, is left, and cannot be recalled. The case of *Cameron's Trustees* (1907 S.C. 407), where it was held that a *jus quaesitum* was not established, is no exception to this reason, for in my judgment in that case I was careful to point out that the Register of Sasines is not like the Books of Council and Session. It is only by a modern and statutory fiction that a conveyance has any place there, and that only as a copy, the effect of which is made equivalent to the registration of an instrument of sasine. Not that registration in the Register of Sasines might not be conclusive, for in some cases it would be equivalent to delivery....

"This, however, does not exhaust the ways in which irrevocability may be shown. Intimation to the *tertius* may be quite sufficient.... This is clearly recognised by the Second Division in the case of *Burr* v. *Commissioners of Bo' ness* ((1896) 24 R. 148), where the want of intimation of the resolution to increase the pursuer's salary made his claim fail.

"There is also the class of cases where the *tertius* comes under onerous engagements on the faith of his having a *jus quaesitum*, though the actual contract has not been intimated to him. This is at the root of a feuar being able to enforce building restrictions against a co-feuar; the conditions under which such a *jus quaesitum* may be inferred being set forth with great detail in the well-known judgment of Lord Watson in [*Hislop* v. *MacRitchie's Trustees*].

"I have gone through these various ways in which the intention that a vested *jus tertio* should be created can be shown, but, after all, they are only examples and not an exhaustive list, for in the end it is a question of evidence, and the only real rule to be deduced is that the mere expression of the obligation as giving a *jus tertio* is not sufficient. . . .

"Now, in examining the evidence, while . . . the terms of the document are not conclusive, that does not mean that they are not to be considered. On the contrary, they form a very important piece of evidence. . . .

". . . I have already called attention to the actual terms, but there is something more. We are entitled, I think, to look to the nature of the insurance effected, the incidents which are connected with it, and the objects which . . . are sought to be attained. So doing, I find a contract which makes a marked distinction between the period up to the majority of the life assured and the period thereafter. . . . After majority the whole scheme alters, the grantee no longer engages to pay the premiums, but the life assured is given several options. . . . These options given to the life assured, but not to the grantee, are strangely inconsistent with the idea of there being no vested right in the life assured. . . . Then comes the fact that the son undoubtedly knew of the assurance, a knowledge which it is legitimate to conclude came through his father, though the proof falls short of direct communication. . . .

"Taking all the circumstances together, I come to the conclusion that we have here the evidence necessary, when taken along with the terms of the document, to show that an irrevocable *jus quaesitum* was constituted in favour of Ian Carmichael; that the proceeds of the policy which, by the conception of the contract, fall to be paid to his executors truly belong to them; and that, therefore, the present appeal should be allowed."

LORD SHAW OF DUNFERMLINE (at p. 205) referred to *Crosbie's Trustees* v. *Wright* ((1880) 7 R. 823) as follows: "I should like to say . . . that I have during nearly all my working life looked upon the case of *Crosbie's Trustees* v. *Wright* as a leading and unimpeachable authority. It is so for two reasons. In the first place, it disposes effectively of the plea that delivery of a written document is an absolute essential in all cases where the question is whether a right has been acquired by the third person named as the grantee therein. Delivery is no doubt of high importance, but its absolute essentiality in all cases can no longer be affirmed. 'I do not think,' says

Lord Mure (at p. 832), 'that it has ever been held that actual delivery, in the strict sense of that expression, was necessary, provided there was distinct evidence of an intention to make a donation.'...

"But, in the second place, the high value of *Crosbie* is this, that it shows the extreme importance of attaching the greatest weight to the terms of the document itself which, so to speak, vouches the transaction. These are, in the language of Lord President Inglis (at p. 826), 'very important elements of evidence.' "

NOTES

1. For *Blumer and Co.* v. *Scott and Sons, Burr* v. *Commissioners of Bo'ness*, and *Hislop* v. *MacRitchie's Trustees*, see pp. 189, 2 and 192 above, respectively.

2. *Lamont* v. *Burnett* (1901) 3 F. 797 provides another instance of a *jus quaesitum tertio*.

L. was the proprietor of the Royal Hotel, Crieff. B. sent to L.'s agent an offer to purchase the hotel for £7,000. In a covering letter B. stated: "Further, I will be pleased to give to Mrs L. a sum not less than one hundred pounds as some compensation for the annoyance and worry of the past few days, and for her kindness and attention to me on my several visits to Crieff."

L.'s agent accepted the offer "as supplemented by" the letter.

B. paid £7,000, but declined to pay the £100, and Mrs L. brought an action against him for that amount.

Held that Mrs L. was entitled to the sum sued for, since the acceptance had created a *jus quaesitum tertio* in her for the £100 mentioned in B.'s letter.

3. See also *Morton's Trustees* v. *The Aged Christian Friend Society of Scotland* (p. 3, above).

Assignability

Cole v. C.H. Handasyde & Co.

1910 S.C. 68

S. sold to H. a quantity of black grease. Although S. had an expert knowledge of the qualities of black grease, he did not manufacture the grease but dealt as a merchant only, and this was known to H.

Before the grease had been delivered, S. executed a trust deed for his creditors in favour of C., and C. tendered delivery of the grease to H., who refused to accept it.

C. raised an action of damages for breach of contract. H. maintained that he had entered into the contract in reliance upon the personal skill of S., and that the contract was not assignable.

Held that the contract referred nothing to the skill or experience of the seller, and was therefore assignable.

LORD PRESIDENT (DUNEDIN) (at p. 73): "Nobody doubts that the law as to whether a contract is assignable or not depends upon whether, as the expression goes, there is the element of *delectus personae* in it or not. Now, I think by way of illustration there are three stages to be taken. The highest and easiest example of a contract in which there is *delectus personae* is where the contract is one for a personal service of a peculiar nature. Nobody supposes that in a contract with A or B to paint a picture or write a book it is possible for A or B to say—'I will get somebody else to paint you the picture or write you the book, and that must satisfy you, and you must pay me the price.' Next you have another class where the *delectus personae* is not so clear. I mean the case of manufactured articles. It may quite well be that an article is of such a character and quality and the reputation of the manufacturer such that, when you contract for a thing from so-and-so, you really imply that the article is to be made by so-and-so. For instance, a contract for a gun from Purdie would not be well implemented by giving you a gun bought in the ordinary market in Birmingham. There are of course cases where it is not very easy to determine on which side the matter falls, but these are cases where the difficulty lies in the application of the law to the particular circumstances. But when we come away from manufacturers, and that is the case here, and when you come to a contract with a person who does not himself manufacture and does not profess to—a contract for goods of a certain description ...—then it seems to me that you may go on and contract in one form or another. You may either say, 'I contract with you that you shall supply me with goods as to which you shall do something, or as to which you shall satisfy yourself in such-and-such a way,' and then you really incorporate into your contract for the goods a contract also for the personal services of the person with whom you contract. Or, on the other hand, you may contract for an article, and then stipulate that the article is to be of a certain standard which is specified in the contract, and say no more. It seems to me that in the latter case the whole element of *delectus personae* is gone.

"Now, I turn to the contract in question. . . .

"... I am unable to see how in this there is any question of *delectus personae* at all. It seems to me that the contract is assignable."

LORD KINNEAR (at p. 75): "The principle which we call *delectus personae*, as I understand it, applies when a person is employed to do work or to perform services requiring some degree of skill or experience. And it is therefore to be inferred that he is selected for the employment in consequence of his own personal qualifications. Such a contract is not assignable by him to a third person who may or may not be competent for the work. But this is not a contract of that nature at all. It is a contract for the purchase of a certain commodity, and although we are told that the seller was specially skilled to judge of the qualities of the commodity in question, the contract refers nothing to his skill or experience, but, on the contrary, provides for inspection and lays down a totally different standard according to which the goods are to be delivered and accepted.... I agree that there is no room for the principle of *delectus personae*, and therefore the objection to the pursuer's title cannot be sustained."

NOTES

1. In *Stevenson & Sons* v. *Maule & Son*, 1920 S.C. 335, the court held that a contract to beat a carpet contained no *delectus personae*, and that therefore when the carpet was accidentally destroyed in the premises of a subcontractor who had been selected without negligence, the contractor was not liable.

Lord President (Strathclyde) (at p. 343): "The contract to beat an ordinary carpet, which this was, may be performed vicariously. To beat a carpet does not require, and it is not here alleged to require, any special skill or experience. It is not averred that the defenders were employed to beat this carpet in reliance on their special skill or experience as carpet beaters. There is no *delectus personae* in this contract."

2. In *Dampskibsaktieselskapet Aurdal* v. *Compania de Navegacion La Estrella*, 1916 S.C. 882, Lord Salvesen said (at p. 891): "There is no element of *delectus personae* involved in the sale or purchase of a ship."

3. Another case in which there was held to be no *delectus personae* is *Asphaltic Limestone Concrete Co. Ltd.* v. *Glasgow Corporation*, 1907 S.C. 463 (paving streets).

4. A case providing an instance of purely personal service is *Hoey* v. *MacEwan and Auld* (1867) 5 M. 814 (clerk to firm of accountants).

Assignatus utitur jure auctoris

The Scottish Widows' Fund v. Buist

(1876) 3 R. 1078

In 1871 M. took out a life policy for £1,000. The policy contained a stipulation that if it afterwards appeared that there had been any untrue statement in the assured's declaration as to his age or state of health, the policy would be void.

In 1872 M. assigned the policy to B. and others, and the assignation was duly intimated to the insurance company.

In 1875 M. died at the age of 30, and the assignees applied to the insurance company for payment of the sum in the policy.

The company raised an action of reduction on the ground that M. had in his declaration knowingly made false statements as to his state of health.

Held that these false statements were a relevant ground of reduction as against B. and others, who were onerous assignees.

LORD PRESIDENT (INGLIS) (at p. 1082): "It appears to me to be long ago settled in the law of Scotland—and I have never heard of any attempt to disturb the doctrine—that in a personal obligation, whether contained in a unilateral deed or in a mutual contract, if the creditor's right is sold to an assignee for value, and the assignee purchases in good faith, he is nevertheless subject to all the exceptions and pleas pleadable against the original creditor. That is the doctrine laid down in all our institutional writers, and it has been affirmed in many cases. But it seems to be said that this doctrine admits of some exceptions. Now, that I entirely dispute. I think the true view of the law is that these things that are called exceptions are classes of cases to which the doctrine does not apply. The doctrine does not apply to the transmission of heritable estate; the doctrine does not apply in the sale of corporeal moveables. But within the class of cases to which the doctrine is applicable—I mean the transmission to assignees of a creditor's right in a personal obligation—I know of no exception to the application of the doctrine.... In a question between the debtor in a personal obligation and the assignee of the creditor, the assignee is open to all the objections that would have been pleadable against the cedent....

"I hold it therefore to be clearly established that in all cases of personal obligation, whether constituted by unilateral deeds or mutual contract, this doctrine is universally applicable."

LORD DEAS (at p. 1084): "The party who takes an assignation to a contract must take it as it is; and if he has the means of ascertaining everything about it, and does not do so, I am of opinion that whatever may be said of other and different cases, the assignee is, in that case, in no better position than the cedent."

CHAPTER 6

BREACH OF CONTRACT

Mutuality

Graham & Co. v. The United Turkey Red Co. Ltd.

1922 S.C. 533

G., appointed in February 1914 as a commission agent for the sale of certain cotton goods dealt in by a company, agreed not to sell similar goods derived from other sources.

At first he observed this condition, but from July 10, 1916, onwards he was in breach of it.

In November 1917 he terminated the contract, and brought an action of accounting against the company for the balance of commission alleged to be due to him for the whole period of his agency.

Held that G. was not entitled to an accounting for the period after July 10, 1916, as he was then in material breach of his contract and therefore could not sue upon the contract, but was entitled to an accounting for the period prior to that date.

LORD JUSTICE-CLERK (SCOTT DICKSON) (at p. 541): "*Turnbull's* case ((1874) 1 R. 730) has, so far as I know, always been accepted in our Courts as sound. ... Even before *Turnbull's* case the same principle ... had been stated by Lord Justice-Clerk Inglis in the case of *Johnston* v. *Robertson* ((1861) 23 D. 646, at p. 656) thus: '... In a mutual contract, where one party seeks performance of the stipulations in his favour, he must show that he has given or tendered performance of his part of the contract. Every action on a mutual contract implies that the pursuer either has performed, or is willing to perform, his part of the contract; and it is, therefore, always open to the defender to say that under the contract a right arises also to him to demand performance of the contract before the pursuer can insist in his action.' "

LORD SALVESEN (at p. 545): "The defenders ... rely upon the opinion of the Lord Justice-Clerk [Moncreiff] in the case of *Turnbull*, where he says (at p. 738): 'I understand the law of Scotland, in regard to mutual contracts, to be quite clear—(1st) that the stipulations on either side are the counterparts and the consideration given for each other; (2nd) that a failure to perform any material or substantial part of the contract on the part of one will prevent him from suing the other for performance.' Similar views were expressed by Lord Benholme and Lord Neaves. The former said (at p. 739): 'It is very important that we should express our determination to abide by the well-established rule of Scotch law that in mutual contracts there is no ground for separating the parts of the contract into independent obligements, so that one party can refuse to perform his part of the contract, and yet insist upon the other performing his part. The unity of the contract must be respected.' And Lord Neaves said (at p. 739): 'It is a general principle that all the material stipulations in a contract forming a *unum quid* are mutual causes.' Now, the pursuers' counsel frankly admitted that the condition . . . was a material part of the contract. . . . In the subsequent case of *Ramsay* v. *Brand* ((1898) 25 R. 1212), which applied to a building contract, the Lord President [J.P.B. Robertson] said (at p. 1214): 'In judging of this question, it is necessary to bear in memory the law applicable to it. No man can claim the sum stipulated to be paid on the completion of certain specified work unless he has performed that work *modo et forma*, and this applies to building contracts just as much as to other contracts.' Accordingly, in that case it was held that the contract price sued for was not due, except under deduction of the full amount which would be necessary in order to enable the proprietor of the house to take down those parts which had been erected disconform to the contract, and complete the work in accordance with the contract. . . . This case was followed by the Second Division in *Steel* (1907 S.C. 360). . . .

"Now, it is quite true that these decisions are not in terms applicable to a contract of agency. But the general statement of the law in *Turnbull* v. *McLean* makes the rule the same wherever there are mutual stipulations and any material stipulation has been violated by the party who is suing on the contract. It does not follow that he necessarily forfeits all claim, but it puts upon him the onus of proving the extent to which the other party has been *lucratus* by the services he has rendered, instead of putting upon the defenders the onus of showing the amount of loss which has flowed from their agent's breach of duty. . . . I am unable to concur in the Lord Ordinary's view that an agent who deliberately violates a material part of the contract under which he is appointed, and which alone entitles him to commission at the stipulated rate, shall have exactly the same rights of action against his principals, in the matter of compelling them to lodge accounts, as if he had throughout honestly performed all the stipulations of the contract incumbent upon him."

LORD ORMIDALE (at p. 549): "While in most of the cases cited the contracts in question were not contracts of agency, the principle of law enunciated in the opinions of the Judges who decided them ... is clearly applicable, the principle, namely, that a person who has broken a contract cannot sue upon it. ...

" ... I cannot agree with the Lord Ordinary that the pursuers in any view were entitled to a *quantum meruit* and that the *quantum* would be found to be just what was sued for as commission. If the defenders were benefited at all by the services of the pursuers after July 1916, the question would be not *quantum meruit* the pursuers, but *quantum lucrati* the defenders, and the burden of the proof would be on the pursuers."

LORD HUNTER (at p. 552): "If A contracts to build a house or to do some piece of work according to certain requirements, he cannot claim payment under the contract unless he has complied with the material obligations undertaken by him. The most apt illustrations of this rule are probably to be found in building contracts. In *Ramsay* v. *Brand* Lord President Robertson said (at p. 1214): 'No man can claim the sum stipulated to be paid on the completion of certain specified work unless he has performed that work *modo et forma*, and this applies to building contracts just as much as to other contracts.' At another part of his opinion he says: 'when contractors do not stick to their contracts they not only unmoor themselves from their contract rights, but they drift into much less certain and much less definite claims.' In that case, however, the Court gave the building contractor, who had deviated from plans agreed upon, the contract price under deduction of the cost of bringing the building into conformity with the plans. In *Steel* v. *Young* (1907 S.C. 360) it was held that a contractor, who had, in breach of his contract, substituted milled lime for cement mortar, was not entitled to sue for the contract price. Lord Low said (at p. 365): 'The general rule is that a building contract, like any other contract, must be performed *modo et forma*, and if the builder departs from the contract he loses his right to sue for the contract price.' These cases were considered in the House of Lords in the more recent case of *Forrest* (1916 S.C.(H.L.) 28); but, although some of the Judges expressed doubt as to their soundness, they were not overruled and are binding upon this Court.

"... In my opinion ... it is impossible to treat the clause as to remuneration as separable from, and independent of, the agents' obligation as to not selling the goods of rival traders. I do not think it can be said that, if they had reserved to themselves liberty to act for competitors in trade of the defenders, they would necessarily have received the commission stipulated in the contract.... From July 1916 the pursuers appear to me to have been continuously acting in breach of obligations to the defenders that affected their claim to commission, and during that period they are therefore not entitled to found upon the contract as giving them a claim to remuneration, whatever may be their claim independent thereof. I think, therefore, that the Lord Ordinary's interlocutor should be altered by confining the period for an accounting to the time prior to July 1916."

NOTES

1. *Turnbull* v. *McLean & Co.* (1874) 1 R. 730: McL. & Co., coal-merchants, contracted to supply T. with coal, the price to be settled monthly. T. refused to pay for the coal of a past month or even to make a payment to account.

Held that McL. & Co. were justified in rescinding the contract.

Lord Benholme (at p. 739): "In this case I am of opinion that Turnbull unduly refused to pay the price of what he had received, and therefore could not compel McLean and Company to go on supplying coals in terms of the contract. McLean and Company were thus justified in rescinding the contract."

Lord Neaves (at p. 739): "The case is to be decided on the principle of mutual contract. Turnbull wrongfully refused to pay for the past month's deliveries, and therefore McLean and Company were entitled to rescind the contract."

2. For *Johnston* v. *Robertson* and *Ramsay & Son* v. *Brand*, see pp. 247 and 259, below, respectively.

3. See also *Dingwall* v. *Burnett* (p. 249, below).

4. *Macbride* v. *Hamilton and Son* (1875) 2 R. 775: M. entered into a contract with H. & Sons to make and fit up in H. & Son's premises certain pieces of machinery by a certain date. When M. sued for the contract price, H. & Son resisted payment on the ground that M. had failed to execute the work within the time agreed on and had thereby caused them loss exceeding the sum sued for.

Held, on the principle that one party is not entitled to enforce performance if he has himself violated an express condition, that H. & Son were entitled to have their claim of damages liquidated in the action at M.'s instance and set off against the contract price.

Lord President Inglis (at p. 780): "The general proposition is clear, that where a party seeks to enforce a contract he must shew that he has performed, or been ready to perform, his part of the contract."

Lord Ardmillan (at p. 783): " I do not think this case comes strictly under the legal category of compensation. It rather presents itself to my mind as falling under the principle that one of the parties to a mutual contract cannot enforce it against the other if he has violated it himself."

5. In *Sharp* v. *Rettie* (1884) 11 R. 745 (relating to a merchant ship) Lord President Inglis said (at p. 751): "It is always competent when one party sues the other upon a contract entered into between them, for the latter to say—'You broke the contract, and instead of my being in debt to you, you are in debt to me.' "

Anticipatory breach: repudiation inferred from conduct

Forslind v. Bechely-Crundall

1922 S.C.(H.L.) 173

Cobbold, the proprietor of a timber-covered property at Kinloch Rannoch, entered into an agreement for the sale to B. of 11 lots of growing timber. Under the agreement B. was not entitled without Cobbold's written consent to carry out cutting or removal operations on more than four lots at one time.

In May 1918 B. entered into a contract with F., a timber merchant who supplied timber to shipyards, for the felling and delivery on rail to F. of the timber in lot 6, B. undertaking to begin "at once" to fell the trees and arrange about cartage to rail. F. paid £5,000 to account.

More than four lots of timber on the estate were then partly cut, and Cobbold refused to allow the cutting of lot 6 to proceed.

When, in October, Cobbold withdrew his objection, B. refused to deliver any of the timber to F. until an account connected with a totally different transaction had been settled. He also sought to excuse non-delivery by the bad condition of the roads and of the railway.

After a prolonged correspondence, F. in April 1919, by which time no timber from lot 6 had been delivered, brought an action against B. for repayment of the £5,000 and for damages for breach of contract.

Held that B.'s conduct justified F. in believing that B. did not intend to fulfil his part of the contract, and amounted to repudiation of the contract, and that F. was therefore entitled to the repayment and to damages.

VISCOUNT HALDANE (at p. 179): "The law on the subject is not obscure. In Scotland, as in England, it is that the pursuer is dispensed from waiting for the arrival of the stipulated period for performance, if the defender has intimated in advance an intention to refuse to perform his obligations under it, and the pursuer elects to treat this as an entire breach and to act on it. If the defender has behaved in such a way that a reasonable person would properly conclude that he does not intend to perform the obligations he has undertaken, that is sufficient. The defender's words and the state of his mind are less important than the intention to be gathered from what he does, as evidenced by his attitude."

LORD DUNEDIN (at p. 190): "There is a case decided by this House which has not received the attention it deserves from the fact of its being only reported in the Scottish reports (*Carswell* v. *Collard* ((1893) 20 R.(H.L.) 47). I cite it because I think Lord Chancellor Herschell put the true criterion which is to be applied to the facts in a case where a party to a contract says he is entitled to be free of it owing to repudiation on the other contractor's part. Lord Herschell says (at p. 48): 'Of course, the question was not what actually influenced the defender, but what effect the conduct of the pursuer would be reasonably calculated to have upon a reasonable person.' Applying this criterion to the facts of the present case I take the same view as that expressed by Lord Haldane, which is also the view of the Lord Ordinary.

"I think that, if I may use the expression, the respondent assumed such a shilly-shallying attitude in regard to the contract that the appellant was entitled to draw the inference that the respondent did not really mean to fulfil his part of the contract timeously, although he might, if he found it suited him, go on to deliver timber. Such conduct, I think, amounted to a repudiation which entitled the appellant to say he would no longer be bound."

LORD SHAW OF DUNFERMLINE (at p. 190): "Where one party to a contract treats the non-performance by the other of the latter's obligations as equivalent to a repudiation of the contract, then (1) the conduct so treated must not be in some incidental or accidental particular, but it must fundamentally affect the fair carrying out of the bargain as a whole; and (2) the burden of proving that it does so rests upon the person putting forward that plea. . . .

". . . If, in short, A, a party to a contract, acts in such a fashion of ignoring or not complying with his obligations under it, B, the other party, is entitled to say: 'My rights under this contract are being completely ignored and my interests may suffer by non-performance by A of his obligations, and that to such a fundamental and essential extent that I declare he is treating me as if no contract existed which bound him.' The accent of the psychology is not upon the mind of the person who is defiant or heedless of his obligation, but, as Lord Herschell [in *Carswell* v. *Collard*] put it, upon the mind of the person who is suffering from the defiance. In business over and over again it occurs—as, in my opinion, it occurred in the present case—that procrastination is so persistently practised as to make a most serious inroad into the rights of the other party to a contract. There must be a stage when the person suffering from that is entitled to say: 'This must be brought to an end. My efforts have been unavailing, and I declare that you have broken your contract relations with me.' These points are in practice points of fact; the question whether the stage has been reached when procrastination or non-performance may be so construed is an inference of fact upon which I should be slow to disturb the verdict of a jury or a Judge of first instance.

"I refer also to the judgment of my noble and learned friend, Lord Dunedin, in *Wade* v. *Waldon*. I entirely agree with him when he says: 'It is familiar law, and quite well settled by decision, that in any contract which contains multifarious stipulations there are some which go so to the root of the contract that a breach of those stipulations entitles the party pleading the breach to declare that the contract is at an end. There are others which do not go to the root of the contract, but which are part of the contract, and which would give rise, if broken, to an action of damages.' And I add that, in my own opinion, it is abundantly clear in the present case that the breach of contract by the respondent satisfied the first of these propositions."

NOTE

For *Wade* v. *Waldon*, see p. 223, below.

Anticipatory breach: unaccepted repudiation and action for contract price

White & Carter (Councils) Ltd. v. McGregor

1962 S.C.(H.L.) 1

W. Ltd. supplied street litter bins to local authorities, and was allowed to attach to the bins plates carrying advertisements. The company derived its profit from payments made to it by the advertisers.

McG. was a garage proprietor in Clydebank. In June 1957, Ward, McG.'s sales manager, made a contract with W. Ltd. for the display of advertisements of the garage business for a period of three years. When

McG. heard of this later the same day, he at once wrote to W. Ltd. to cancel the contract.

W. Ltd. refused to accept the cancellation, prepared the necessary plates and exhibited them on the bins from November 1957 onwards.

W. Ltd. sued for the contract price.

Held that W. Ltd. was entitled to perform the contract and claim the contract price, and was not obliged to accept McG.'s repudiation and sue for damages.

LORD REID (at p. 11): "The general rule cannot be in doubt. It was settled in Scotland at least as early as 1848, and it has been authoritatively stated time and again in both Scotland and England. If one party to a contract repudiates it in the sense of making it clear to the other party that he refuses or will refuse to carry out his part of the contract, the other party, the innocent party, has an option. He may accept that repudiation and sue for damages for breach of contract, whether or not the time for performance has come; or he may, if he chooses, disregard or refuse to accept it and then the contract remains in full effect.

"In *Howie* v. *Anderson* ((1848) 10 D. 355) Anderson sold shares to be delivered on 8th January 1847; on 31st October 1846, his agent intimated to Howie that he refused to go on with the transaction. Howie refused to accept this repudiation. Anderson pleaded that Howie ought to have gone into the market and bought other shares on 31st October, but it was held that damages must be awarded on the price ruling on 8th January. ...

"I need not refer to the numerous authorities. They are not disputed by the respondent, but he points out that, in all of them, the party who refused to accept the repudiation had no active duties under the contract. The innocent party's option is generally said to be to wait until the date of performance, and then to claim damages estimated as at that date. There is no case in which it is said that he may, in face of the repudiation, go on and incur useless expense in performing the contract, and then claim the contract price. ...

"Developing this argument, the respondent points out that, in most cases, the innocent party cannot complete the contract himself, without the other party doing, allowing or accepting something, and that it is purely fortuitous that the appellants can do so in this case. In most cases, by refusing co-operation, the party in breach can compel the innocent party to restrict his claim to damages. Then it was said that, even where the innocent party can complete the contract without such co-operation, it is against the public interest that he should be allowed to do so. ...

"... It may well be that, if it can be shown that a person has no legitimate interest, financial or otherwise, in performing the contract rather than claiming damages, he ought not to be allowed to saddle the other party with an additional burden with no benefit to himself. If a party has no interest to enforce a stipulation, he cannot in general enforce it: so it might be said that, if a party has no interest to insist on a particular remedy, he ought not to be allowed to insist on it. And, just as a party is not allowed to enforce a penalty, so he ought not to be allowed to penalise the other party by taking one course when another is equally advantageous to him. If I may revert to the example which I gave of a company engaging an expert to prepare an elaborate report and then repudiating before anything was done, it might be that the company could show that the expert had no substantial or legitimate interest in carrying out the work rather than accepting damages. I would think that the *de minimis* principle would apply in determining whether his interest was substantial, and that he might have a legitimate interest other than an immediate financial interest. But if the expert had no such interest, then that might be regarded as a proper case for the exercise of the general equitable jurisdiction of the Court. But that is not this case. Here, the respondent did not set out to prove that the appellants had no legitimate interest in completing the contract and claiming the contract price rather than claiming damages. ... It is, in my judgment, impossible to say that the appellants should be deprived of their right to claim the contract price merely because the benefit to them, as against claiming damages and re-letting their advertising space, might be small, in comparison with the loss to the respondent: that is the most that could be said in favour of the respondent."

LORD HODSON (at p. 26): "It is settled as a fundamental rule of the law of contract that repudiation by one of the parties to a contract does not itself discharge it. See Viscount Simon's speech in *Heyman* v. *Darwins Ltd.* ([1942] A.C. 356 at p. 361), citing with approval the following sentence from a judgment of Scrutton L.J. in *Golding* v. *London and Edinburgh Insurance Co. Ltd.* ((1932) 43 Ll.L.Rep. pp. 487 and 488): 'I have never been able to understand what effect the repudiation of one party has unless the other party accepts the repudiation.'

"In *Howard* v. *Pickford Tool Co. Ltd.* ([1951] 1 K.B. 417 at p. 421), Asquith L.J. said: 'An unaccepted repudiation is a thing writ in water and of no value to anybody: it confers no legal rights of any sort or kind.' These are English cases, but that the law of Scotland is the same is, I think, clear from the authorities of which I need only refer to one, namely,

Howie v. *Anderson*, where language to the same effect is to be found in the opinions of the Lord President and Lord Moncreiff.

"It follows that, if, as here, there was no acceptance, the contract remains alive for the benefit of both parties, and the party who has repudiated can change his mind, but it does not follow that the party at the receiving end of the proffered repudiation is bound to accept it before the time for performance and is left to his remedy in damages for breach.

"Mr Bennett, for the respondent, did not seek to dispute the general position of law to which I have referred, but sought to argue that, if, at the date of performance by the innocent party, the guilty party maintains his refusal to accept performance, and the innocent party does not accept the repudiation, although the contract still survives, it does not survive so far as the right of the innocent party to perform it is concerned but survives only for the purpose of enforcing remedies open to him by way of damages or specific implement.

"This produces an impossible result; if the innocent party is deprived of some of his rights, it involves putting an end to the contract except in cases, unlike this, where, in the exercise of the Court's discretion, the remedy of specific implement is available.

"The true position is that the contract survives and does so not only where specific implement is available. When the assistance of the Court is not required, the innocent party can choose whether he will accept repudiation and sue for damages for anticipatory breach, or await the date of performance by the guilty party. Then, if there is failure in performance, his rights are preserved.

"It may be unfortunate that the appellants have saddled themselves with an unwanted contract, causing an apparent waste of time and money. No doubt this aspect impressed the Court of Session, but there is no equity which can assist the respondent. It is trite that equity will not rewrite an improvident contract where there is no disability on either side. There is no duty laid upon a party to a subsisting contract to vary it at the behest of the other party so as to deprive himself of the benefit given to him by the contract. To hold otherwise would be to introduce a novel equitable doctrine that a party was not to be held to his contract unless the Court in a given instance thought it reasonable so to do. In this case, it would make an action for debt a claim for a discretionary remedy. This would introduce an uncertainty into the field of contract which appears to be unsupported by authority, either in English or Scottish law, save for the one case upon which the Court of Session founded its opinion and which must, in my judgment, be taken to have been wrongly decided."

NOTES

1. The case referred to in the last sentence quoted from Lord Hodson's speech was *Langford & Co.* v. *Dutch*, 1952 S.C. 15.

2. The House of Lords' decision, which reversed the judgment of the Court of Session (1960 S.C. 276), was by the narrow majority of 3 to 2, with Lord Tucker merely concurring with Lord Hodson, and Lords Morton of Henryton and Keith of Avonholm dissenting. Its soundness has been doubted on the ground that it ignores the principle of mitigation of damages (*e.g.*, David M. Walker, *Principles of Scottish Private Law*(4th ed.), Vol. II, p. 163).

3. *White & Carter (Councils) Ltd.* v. *McGregor* was followed in *Salaried Staff London Loan Co. Ltd.* v. *Swears and Wells Ltd.*, 1985 S.C. 189: S. & W. were tenants in a commercial lease for 35 years. The ish prescribed by the lease was August 1, 2011. By letter in March 1982 S. & W. purported to "renounce" the lease, vacated the premises and handed the keys back to the landlords' factor. The landlords raised an action against S. & W. for rent up to February 1983.

Held that they were entitled to payment, as S. & W. made no averments which would justify the court in concluding that it would be manifestly unjust and unreasonable to allow the landlords this remedy.

Specific implement

Grahame v. Magistrates of Kirkcaldy

(1882) 9 R.(H.L.) 91; (1881) 8 R. 395

In 1879 G., suing as a member of the community, obtained an interdict against Kirkcaldy magistrates prohibiting them from erecting stables or other buildings on a small portion of what was formerly the south links of Kirkcaldy, called the Volunteers' Green, which was held by the magistrates for behoof of the inhabitants as a bleaching-green and place of recreation.

At the time when the interdict had been applied for, the magistrates had already executed a considerable portion of the work, and before the interdict was granted the stables had been completed at a cost of £2,000.

In 1880 G. raised an action to have the buildings removed and the ground restored to its former state.

The magistrates offered to make over to the community another piece of ground of double the size.

Held that (1) notwithstanding the prior judgment in the interdict process it was still open to the court to ordain the offer of the magistrates to be accepted in lieu of specific implement, in respect that the offer was *res noviter*, and (2) the offer of the magistrates was one that should be accepted.

LORD WATSON (at p. 91): "It appears to me that a superior Court, having equitable jurisdiction, must also have a discretion, in certain exceptional cases, to withhold from parties applying for it that remedy to which, in ordinary circumstances, they would be entitled as a matter of course. In order to justify the exercise of such a discretionary power there must be some very cogent reason for depriving litigants of the ordinary means of enforcing their legal rights. There are, so far as I know, only three decided cases, in which the Court of Session, there being no facts sufficient to raise a plea in bar of the action, have nevertheless denied to the pursuer the remedy to which, in strict law, he was entitled. These authorities seem to establish, if that were necessary, the proposition that the Court has the power of declining, upon equitable grounds, to enforce an admittedly legal right; but they also shew that the power has been very rarely exercised.

"The earliest case is that of *Macnair* v. *Cathcart* ((1802) Mor. 12,832). ...

"The next case is that of *Sanderson* v. *Geddes* ((1874) 1 R. 1198). ...

"The last authority to be found in the books is *Begg* v. *Jack* ((1875) 3 R. 35). ...

"In each of these three cases the object of the action was to recover possession of the pursuer's estate of feu, and to oust the party by whom it had been invaded. ... The appellant sues, neither as the owner of land, nor as the proprietor of a dominant tenement, and as such in right of a servitude. He does not even sue as the owner of property within the burgh of Kirkcaldy, but as one of the community of the burgh. The right and interest of a burghal proprietor, whose property is near to or abuts upon the South Links, differs in degree from the right and interest of a person whose connection with the burgh is dependent upon residence alone. The interest of the one may be proprietary in this sense, that an alteration in the condition of the Links will affect, not his personal convenience merely, but the value of his property into whose hands soever it may come. The right and interest of the other is personal and transient, and cannot be distinguished from that of the rest of the inhabitants of the burgh. This suit is truly an *actio popularis*, inasmuch as it is brought for the vindication of a right common to all the inhabitants, and in disposing of it the Court must, according to my apprehension, consider, not the interest of the individual pursuer, but the interest of the general community.

"Now, it is conceded in this case that the respondents have, contrary to the right of the community, spent nearly £1,900 of their ratepayers' money in erecting stables upon a portion of the South Links, nearly a quarter of an acre in extent. The stables are required for police purposes, and the outlay would have been unobjectionable had it not been made upon the links. The respondents have since acquired about half an acre of ground at some distance from the Links for a present payment of £250, and an annual feu-duty of £14 14s. 7d., which they offer to dedicate to the use of the community in lieu of the present site of the stables. The learned Judges of the Second Division were very clearly of opinion (and so far I have no difficulty in agreeing with them) that, although the appellant asserts the contrary, it would be much more for the advantage of the community to accept the substituted ground, and allow the stables to stand, than to ordain the stables to be pulled down, seeing that in that case they must be rebuilt elsewhere at the expense of the burgh rate-payers, who may be taken as fairly representing the bulk of the community. ...

"The difficulty which I have felt in regard to the interlocutor under appeal arises from the circumstance, which is not noticed in any of the opinions delivered in the Court below, that before the present action was instituted the appellant had obtained decree in a process of suspension and interdict directed against the respondents in relation to the erection of these stables. ...

"As between the appellant and the respondents, the judgment of the 19th of June 1879 is now *res judicata*. It was not disputed at the bar that the final decree prohibitory in a process of suspension and interdict draws back to the date of the application, and strikes against everything that has been done by the respondents after that date. ... The rule of the law of Scotland is *pendente lite nihil innovandum*; and whatever a party chooses to do after the matter is litigious he does at his own risk. The ordinary and legal result of the final interdict is, that the party who has obtained it has a right to apply for and obtain a judicial order to undo that which has been so done; and it has always been regarded as a necessary consequence of that right that the order for removal must be extended to that which had been erected before the litigation began.

"If the judgment of the 19th of June 1879 had been a decree capable of being put into execution without the intervention of the Court, it would have been too late to consider whether these buildings ought or ought not to be taken down; but the appellant has no means of enforcing it, except by a new application to the Court for an order of removal. Even in that application it is, in my opinion, too late for the respondents to resist the granting of the order upon considerations which either were, or might have been, competently pleaded by way of answer to the note of suspension and interdict. . . . If, however, there be *res noviter* affecting the relative position or rights of the litigants which have emerged since the date of the final judgment, the Court is not only entitled, but bound, to take cognisance of them, and to consider whether, in the altered circumstances of the case, the decree previously granted ought or ought not to be enforced.

". . . It is with great difficulty that I have ultimately come to the conclusion that the circumstances of the present case are sufficient to justify a refusal of the remedy which the appellant asks. In arriving at that conclusion I have been mainly influenced by these considerations: first, that the community of the burgh, whose rights are at stake, has an interest on both sides of the present litigation; and, secondly, that the tender of a substituted piece of ground is, in this sense, *res noviter*, that the ground was not the property of the burgh or under the control of the corporation at the time when the appellant obtained decree of interdict. Were the appellant seeking to enforce a decree which he held in his own private right and interest, I do not think the considerations of inconvenience and pecuniary loss to the respondents arising from the position in which they had placed themselves, by their own acts, would have afforded a relevant answer to his demand in the present action. But these considerations assume a very different answer when the necessary result of disregarding them will be to inflict that loss and inconvenience upon the community whose interest the appellant represents. In the peculiar circumstances of this case, I do not think it is too late to consider the interest of the community, and I agree with the Court below that their interests will be better served by giving them the field recently acquired by the corporation in exchange for the portion of the Links of which they have been deprived, instead of granting an order which will have the practical effect of charging the community, or the common good of the burgh, with the whole expense of taking down the stables and re-erecting them upon a new site."

LORD O'HAGAN (at p. 98): " I adopt the words of Lord Gifford in *Begg* v. *Jack*—'There is an equitable power vested in the Court in virtue of which, when the exact restoration of things to their previous condition is either impossible or would be attended with unreasonable loss and expense quite disproportionate to the advantage it would give to the successful party, the Court can award an equivalent. In other words, they can say upon what equitable conditions the building should be allowed to remain where it is, although it has been placed there without legal right.' That opinion is supported by several Scotch decisions of undoubted authority, and seems to me quite in accordance with sound principle and the practice of English Courts of equity; and, if it be sustainable, the facts of the case abundantly justify the decision of the Court of Session."

NOTES

1. In *Skerret* v. *Oliver* (1896) 23 R. 468 Lord Kincairney (Ordinary) held that specific implement was not an appropriate remedy where a minister of a congregation of the United Presbyterian Church had been suspended from office.

Lord Kincairney said (at p. 485): "The question remains, whether the remedy demanded, viz., the remedy of reduction and of restoration to the position existing before the sentence of suspension was pronounced, is a remedy which the Court ought to grant, or is in use to grant in similar cases.

"That question I have now come to think should be answered in the negative. It is a remedy which has not yet been granted in Scotland in any question about the sentence of a voluntary Church. It was asked in *McMillan* v. *The Free Church*, and it was refused. ...

"The remedy sought in this case is of the nature of specific performance. ... Now, there are many contracts of which specific performance will not be ordered. Possibly the most obvious and familiar example is a promise of marriage, which of course is not enforceable, and there are the whole classes of contracts of hiring and service ..., which, generally speaking, will not be enforced specifically, but which will support only a claim of damages in the event of non-fulfilment."

In *Lawrie* v. *James Brown & Co. Ltd.*, 1908 S.C. 705, Lord Ardwall said (at p. 712): "A contract of service, as is pretty well settled, is not a contract of which a Court of law will decern specific implement."

2. In *Moore* v. *Paterson* (1891) 9 R. 337 it was the opinion of the judges of the First Division that in the circumstances of the case, if the pursuer had had a title to sue (which he was held not to have), damages and not specific implement would have been the appropriate remedy.

Lord Shand said (at p. 351): "There now remains the question whether in any case the pursuers would be entitled to specific implement or to damages merely. The general rule of our law is that when a party has it in his power to fulfil an obligation which he has undertaken the Court will compel him to do so. But it must always be in the discretion of the Court to say whether the remedy of specific implement or one of damages is the proper and suitable remedy in the circumstances. In the present case there are several considerations which seem to me to shew that the pursuers are not entitled to the remedy of specific implement for which they ask. In the first place, a great peculiarity of the case is that Mr Paterson undertook an obligation with reference to property which was not his own. Both parties must be assumed to have had in view the possibility that Mr Paterson might be unable to fulfil his undertaking, and that such an agreement could only be enforced in terms if the use of the strip could be got on terms not altogether extravagant and unreasonable. Now, what are the facts? . . . What are the terms on which McEwan proposes to sell this comparatively small portion of the ground for which he paid in all £142. He offers to take £1,500 in addition to the expenses of the former action, as taxed between agent and client, which I suppose may be a considerable sum. Mr McEwan has certainly recognised the practical value of the maxim that the buyer's necessity is the seller's opportunity. . . . That plainly is a case in which we cannot decree specific implement. If Mr McEwan had demanded £10,000 I suppose the pursuers could hardly have pressed their claim for specific implement, and his actual demand seems to me for all practical purposes to be equally objectionable. I am therefore of opinion . . . that even if the pursuers had a title to maintain the action, their claim must be one of damages and not for specific implement."

3. On the difference between Scots and English law, see *Stewart* v. *Kennedy* (1890) 17 R.(H.L.) 1; (1889) 16 R. 421. (For an outline of the facts, see *Stewart* v. *Kennedy* (1890) 17 R.(H.L.) 25. (p. 79, above).)

Lord Herschell (at p. 5): "I do not think it would be of any advantage to devote time to an analysis of the English decisions, or to inquire whether a Court of equity in England would require a decree for specific performance under the circumstances which are alleged to exist in the present case. For I think if that proposition could be established it would afford no guide to the conclusion which ought to be arrived at where a decree for specific implement is sought in the Courts of Scotland. Specific performance was not a remedy to which a party was entitled at common law in England. To obtain it he was compelled to resort to the separate jurisdiction of the Court of Chancery, which at times refused its assistance, even where a legal right was established, leaving the party who invoked it to his ordinary legal remedies. In Scotland, on the contrary, specific implement is one of the ordinary remedies to which a party to a contract is entitled where the other party to it refuses to implement the obligation he has undertaken. ... I do not of course mean to say that it would not be open to maintain there that in the circumstances of a particular case it would be inequitable to enforce that remedy, but a party to a contract certainly does not establish that proposition by shewing that he imagined its legal effect and operation to be other than they are."

Lord Watson (at p. 9): "I do not think that upon this matter any assistance can be derived from English decisions; because the laws of the two countries regard the right to specific performance from different standpoints. In England the only legal right arising from a breach of contract is a claim of damages; specific performance is not matter of legal right, but a purely equitable remedy, which the Court can withhold when there are sufficient reasons of conscience or expediency against it. But in Scotland the breach of a contract for the sale of a specific subject such as landed estate gives the party aggrieved the legal right to sue for implement, and although he may elect to do so, he cannot be compelled to resort to the alternative of an action of damages unless implement is shewn to be impossible. ... Even where implement is possible, I do not doubt that the Court of Session has inherent power to refuse the legal remedy on equitable grounds, although I know of no instance in which it has done so. It is quite conceivable that circumstances might occur which would make it inconvenient and unjust to enforce specific performance of contract of sale, but I do not think that any such case is presented in this appeal. The fact that the construction of a term in the contract is attended with doubt and difficulty, evidenced it may be by the different meanings attributed to it by Courts or individual Judges, ought not in my opinion to prevent its receiving its full legal effect, according to the interpretation finally put upon it by a competent tribunal. The argument that in this case a decree for specific performance would necessarily impose upon the appellant the duty of performing a long series of personal acts under the supervision of the Court does not appear to me to have a solid basis in fact. The acts which such a decree enjoins would be entirely within his power, and practically might be performed *uno flatu*, viz., by his signing a conveyance in favour of the respondent, and at the same time giving instructions to his agents to take the necessary steps for obtaining its approval by the Court."

Lord Macnaghten (at p. 11): "In the present case I do not think there is anything unreasonable in holding Sir Douglas Stewart to his bargain. No English decision was cited which lends any colour to the suggestion that if this question had arisen in England specific performance would be refused. But I must say that I think the Lord Advocate was well founded in his observation that if any such case could be produced it would be no guide to the decision of the present question. In England the remedy of specific performance is an extraordinary remedy. It is always a matter of discretion, and defences are admitted in a suit for specific performance which are inadmissible according to the doctrines and practice of the Courts of Scotland, where specific performance is part of the ordinary jurisdiction of the Court."

4. On implement of one part of a contract, see *Mackay* v. *Campbell* (p. 124, above).

5. Specific implement is available as a remedy to enforce an undertaking to subscribe for shares in a company: *William Beardmore & Co. Ltd.* v. *Barry*, 1928 S.C. 101; affd. 1928 S.C.(H.L.) 47.

P. addressed a letter to the directors of a company stating "I agree at any time upon request by you to subscribe for or find subscribers to your satisfaction for 48,000 . . . preference shares." No such request was made during P.'s lifetime, but after P.'s death the directors called upon P.'s executrix to implement the agreement.

Held that there were no facts and circumstances to exclude the remedy of specific implement.

Lord Justice-Clerk (Alness) (at p. 108): "The learned Dean of Faculty contended . . . that the conclusion for specific performance in this action is incompetent. That contention necessitates consideration of the law of Scotland with regard to a claim for specific performance. I do not think it is too much to say that our law, differing from the law of England, favours such a claim. I know of no better judicial statement relating to the matter than is to be found in Lord Watson's judgment in *Stewart* v. *Kennedy* ((1890) 17 R. (H.L.) 1, at p. 9). . . . Now it cannot be contended in this case that implement of the defender's obligation is unjust, and I am unable to affirm that it is inexpedient. I can see no valid reason why the defender should not be required to implement the obligation which the deceased, had he lived, would plainly have been bound to obtemper. There are, in this case, no special facts and circumstances averred which, as a matter of equity, would exclude the remedy which *prima facie* is within the pursuers' rights. . . . The defender can qualify no prejudice or hardship or difficulty if she should be required to carry out her author's obligation."

The only question pressed in the House of Lords was whether the obligation undertaken by P. was binding on his executrix. *Held* that the obligation was not personal to P., and that it therefore transmitted in the ordinary way against his executrix.

Rescission: breach of non-material stipulation

Wade v. Waldon

1909 S.C. 571

In March 1907 Wade, a comedian whose stage-name was "George Robey," and Waldon, a theatrical manager, entered into a written agreement by which in March 1908 Wade was to perform at the Palace Theatre, Glasgow. A term incorporated into the agreement required artistes to give 14 days' notice prior to their performances and to supply "bill matter" at the same time.

Wade neither gave the required notice nor supplied bill matter, and Waldon refused to allow him to perform.

Wade claimed £300 as damages for breach of contract.

Held that Wade's breach of contract was not sufficiently material to entitle Waldon to rescind the contract, and Waldon was therefore liable to Wade in damages for refusing to allow Wade to perform.

LORD PRESIDENT (DUNEDIN) (at p. 576): "The whole point then is, is this stipulation one of such a kind that a breach of it would entitle the defender without more ado to declare the contract at an end? It is familiar law, and quite well settled by decision, that in any contract which contains multifarious stipulations there are some which go so to the root of the contract that a breach of those stipulations entitles the party pleading the breach to declare that the contract is at an end. There are others which do not go to the root of the contract, but which are part of the contract, and which would give rise, if broken, to an action of damages.

"... It is quite in the power of parties to stipulate that some particular matters, however trivial they may be, yet shall, as between them, form conditions precedent. If they have said so, then their agreement in the matter will be given effect to, but where they have not said so in terms, as is the case here, then the Court must determine, looking to the nature of the stipulation, whether it goes to the essence of the contract or not. ...

"I am very clearly of opinion that this is a stipulation which does not go to the root of the contract."

LORD MCLAREN (at p. 577): "Mr Wade was in breach of contract to a limited extent in respect that he neglected to give notice within fourteen days and to send bill matter. But it is not the law, and it would be very unworkable if it were the law, that every breach of contract, however trifling, would entitle the other party to bring the contract to an end, and to get out of his bargain. The question always is whether a stipulation which has been broken is of the essence of the contract. I think the omission to send notice did not in substance amount to a breach of contract entitling the other party to rescind. It is clear that Mr Wade was in a position to fulfil, and meant to fulfil, his part of the contract."

NOTES

1. This case was followed in *Blyth* v. *Scottish Liberal Club*, 1982 S.C. 140.

B., employed by a club as managing secretary, had failed, on instructions, to attend a meeting of the club's review committee and to take minutes of a meeting of the club's management committee. He was dismissed on the ground of these two breaches of his contract of employment.

Held that B.'s breaches were material and therefore entitled the club to dismiss him.

2. *Wade* v. *Waldon* and *Blyth* v. *Scottish Liberal Club* were referred to in *Ghaznavi* v. *BP Oil (UK) Ltd.*, 1991 S.L.T. 924.

G. had entered into a user's agreement with BP by which, in garage premises owned by BP, G. would sell only BP's brands of motor fuel. When G. discovered that stocks were insufficient to meet customers' needs, G. ordered a small quantity of fuel from another source. BP served notices terminating the agreement on the basis of G.'s breach of contract.

Held that sale of the unauthorised fuel was a contravention of the Trade Descriptions Act 1968 and was therefore serious.

3. For an instance where parties stipulated that particular matters were to be material, see *Dawsons Ltd.* v. *Bonnin*, 1922 S.C.(H.L.) 156 (aff., but on different grounds, 1921 S.C. 511).

This was an action for payment under a policy of insurance of a motor-vehicle. The answer in the proposal form as to the place at which the vehicle was usually garaged had been wrong. The policy provided that the proposal form "shall be the basis of this contract and be held as incorporated herein."

Held that this made statements contained in the proposal fundamental to the contract, irrespective of whether they were material or immaterial, and that the false statement therefore rendered the policy void.

Viscount Cave (at p. 169): "It seems to me impossible for a Court to say that statements which the parties themselves have described in the policy as incorporated in and forming the basis of the contract are wholly immaterial to the contract. ... In these circumstances it appears to me to be irrelevant to consider the conflicting evidence in the case as to whether a misstatement as to the place of garage is, in the ordinary sense, material or not. The parties have agreed that it shall be deemed material, and that concludes the matter."

Lord Dunedin (at p. 169): "I think that the evidence shows that the misstatement was not in fact material to the assessment of the premium. . . .

"Was then the statement as to the usual place of garage material? I pointed out in the case of *Wade* v. *Waldon* that there may be in contracts certain stipulations which go to the root of the contract, a breach of which entitles the other party to hold the contract at an end; and that there are other stipulations which do not go to the root, and only give rise, if broken, to actions of damages. At the same time I . . . pointed out that it was within the power of parties to contract that particular matters, however trivial, might form conditions precedent. Have the parties so contracted in this case? That raises the pure question, as yet I think undecided—When certain statements are said to be the 'basis of the contract and incorporated therewith,' is that equivalent to saying that these statements are held to be contractually material?

"After much consideration . . . I have come to the conclusion that it is. I think that 'basis' cannot be taken as merely pleonastic and exegetical of the following words, 'and incorporated therewith.' It must mean that the parties held that these statements are fundamental—*i.e.*, go to the root of the contract—and that consequently, if the statements are untrue, the contract is not binding."

Rescission: payment of price by stipulated date may be non-material

Rodger (Builders) Ltd. v. Fawdry

1950 S.C. 483

F. agreed to sell the estate of the Haining to R. Ltd. for £18,250, 10 per cent. of the price being paid at the date of the signing of the missives, and the remainder at November 11, 1947, the date of entry.

No payment was made at November 11, and a fortnight later F. warned R. Ltd. that unless the balance of the price was paid by November 28 the sale would be regarded as void.

Payment was not made by that date, and F. immediately entered into missives with Bell, who accepted without investigation F.'s statement that the first contract was at an end.

A disposition followed on these second missives, and was recorded without delay.

R. Ltd. brought an action for reduction of the second missives and the disposition.

Held by Lord Sorn (Ordinary) (whose judgment on this point was not challenged in the Inner House) that F. was not entitled to rescind the contract with R. Ltd. since failure to pay by a stipulated date is not in general a ground for rescinding a contract for the sale of heritage, and that in this case there had not been such unnecessary or unjustifiable delay as entitles a seller to impose a time-limit within which a failure to pay allows him to rescind the contract.

LORD SORN (at p. 492): "The law which governs the question at issue was not to any material extent in dispute and may be shortly stated. In a contract for the sale of heritage, where it is stipulated that the price is to be paid on a particular date, payment of the price on the appointed date is not, in general, an essential condition of the contract, and failure to pay on that date does not entitle the seller to rescind. But payment of the price by a fixed date may be made an essential condition of such contract. If there is unnecessary or unjustifiable delay on the part of the purchaser in paying the price, the seller may limit a time within which payment must be made, and, provided the time limited is a reasonable one in the circumstances, failure to pay within that time will be treated as breach of an essential condition entitling the seller to rescind. ... It follows from this that, where there has been delay in paying the price on the part of a purchaser, the question of whether that delay has been necessary, or whether it has been justifiable, must depend for its answer upon the particular circumstances of the case, including the previous attitude of the parties towards each other and the communications which have passed between them. The reasonableness of the time limit itself must also be a question depending on the particular circumstances. ... The conclusion to which I come ... is that ... there had by 25th November been no unjustifiable delay and that the situation did not warrant the sending of an ultimatum. This makes it unnecessary for me to consider as a separate point the question whether, had the time been ripe for an ultimatum of some kind, the time limit itself was reasonable, but, if that question had arisen, I should have been inclined to think that the time allowed was, in the circumstances, unreasonably short. ... It is not always an easy matter to advise a seller who is standing out of his price, but it seems to me that there is room for a broad distinction between two possible types of case. In the one, there is no reason to doubt that the money will ultimately be forthcoming and in such cases, while pressure may be applied, it is right that patience should be shown, before matters are brought to a head—it being remembered too that, after entry, interest is running on the price. In the other type of case, there is reason to doubt whether the money will be forthcoming and, in that case, the setting of a time limit may be more readily resorted to. What will justify doubt must always be a question of circumstances."

LORD JAMIESON (at p. 498): "The Lord Ordinary has held that Mr Fawdry was not entitled to attempt to rescind the pursuers' contract with him. Mr Fawdry has not reclaimed against the Lord Ordinary's finding, and the reclaimers, Mr and Mrs Bell, have made no attack, and I think could not successfully have made one, on that part of the Lord Ordinary's judgment."

NOTE

In the Inner House the case proceeded on the footing that there was a subsisting contract between the pursuers and F., and the decision was that Bell had not been entitled to rely on F.'s assurance that the prior contract was no longer in existence, and that failure to make the necessary inquiries was sufficient *per se* to deprive him of the character of a *bona fide* purchaser.

Lord Jamieson (at p. 499): "In such circumstances the law is not in doubt. If an intending purchaser is aware of a prior contract for the sale of the subjects, he is bound to inquire into the nature and result of that prior contract, and his duty of inquiry is not satisfied by inquiry of the seller and an assurance by him that the contract is no longer in existence. If he merely obtains such an assurance, he cannot rely on the missives or on a disposition following thereon. ... Fraud in the sense of moral delinquency does not enter into the matter. It is sufficient if the intending purchaser fails to make the inquiry which he is bound to do. If he fails he is no longer *in bona fide* but *in mala fide*."

Damages: inconvenience and trouble, but no pecuniary loss

Webster & Co. v. The Cramond Iron Co.

(1875) 2 R. 752

C. Co. agreed to supply piping to W. & Co., cotton manufacturers, for use in their mill.

There was a delay of some three months before sound pipes were delivered.

W. & Co. claimed £300 damages for the loss which they averred they had sustained by the delay. They failed to prove that they had suffered any specific pecuniary loss, but proved that they had had considerable inconvenience and trouble before obtaining delivery of the sound pipes.

Held that W. & Co. were entitled to moderate damages (£10) for the inconvenience and trouble.

LORD PRESIDENT (INGLIS) (at p. 753): "The Lord Ordinary has found, first, that a contract was made between the pursuers and defenders, and secondly that the contract was broken. ... The breach of contract was in respect of time only. ... In these circumstances the pursuers are entitled to damages for breach of contract to the extent to which they have sustained damages, but to no greater extent. It lies on them to shew wherein they have sustained damage. ...

"... The contract and the breach of it are established. That leads of necessity to an award of damages. It is impossible to say that a contract can be broken even in respect of time without the party being entitled to claim damages—at the lowest, nominal damages. In directing a jury I should have stated that principle, and told them that if they were satisfied that the pursuers were not put to any serious inconvenience they might give the smallest imaginable sum, but if they thought that, though no specific damage had been proved, the pursuers had been put to serious inconvenience and trouble, then their duty was to give something more substantial. This latter view occurs to me as the one which is applicable here. The correspondence shews that this affair caused considerable annoyance and trouble to the pursuers, and I propose to fix the damages at £10."

LORD ARDMILLAN (at p. 754): "I think there has been a failure on the part of the defenders to implement their contract. The pipes were not delivered in due time. ... If special or actual damage had been proved to have been caused by the failure the defenders would, to that extent, have been liable. But I am of opinion that no such damage has been proved. ...

"But the stoppage of the main mill, and the delay in fitting up and working the turbine wheel, was not caused by the delay or the fault of the defenders, and in regard to the claim for damages on that ground I think that no actual damage has been proved. At the same time a breach of contract by the defenders is necessarily a wrong to the pursuers, and a wrong for which some amount of damages may well be claimed. There must have been, to some extent, inconvenience, annoyance, and anxiety, even in regard to the main mill and the turbine wheel. The damage could not have been great, but, failure having been proved, some damage is due. . . .

"On the whole matter, I think that a small sum of damage, such as your Lordship suggests, should be awarded."

Damages: one action only

Stevenson v. Pontifex & Wood

(1887) 15 R. 125

In 1884 P. & W., engineers in London, supplied a Pontifex refrigerating machine to S., ice-merchant in Glasgow, under a contract which provided that P. & W. would not without S.'s consent supply, within the next five years, any machine which they knew was to be erected within 10 miles of the Cross of Glasgow and which was intended to be used for making ice for sale.

In 1885 in contravention of this undertaking P. & W. supplied a machine to V. who thereafter manufactured ice for sale in competition with S.

In 1886 S. brought an action of damages against P. & W. for that breach of contract. The action was compromised.

In 1887 S. raised another action against P. & W. for damages, averring that V. had continued to compete with him, had undersold him in the market and so reduced his profits.

Held that P. & W. could not be sued in a second action for further damages arising out of the same breach.

LORD PRESIDENT (INGLIS) (at p. 129): "The defence is in substance that the claim now made is satisfied and discharged by the interlocutor of Lord Lee in the former action giving effect to the tender and acceptance. I am of opinion that this defence must be sustained.

"The cause of action in the previous summons was breach of contract and consequent damage. The breach consisted of the single act of supplying one machine to Verel & Company, and I am of opinion that a single act amounting either to a delict or a breach of contract cannot be made the ground of two or more actions for the purpose of recovering damages arising within different periods but caused by the same act. On the contrary, I hold the true rule of practice based on sound principle to be, that though the delict or breach of contract be of such a nature that it will necessarily be followed by injurious consequences in the future, and though it may for this reason be impossible to ascertain with precise accuracy at the date of the action or of the verdict the amount of loss which will result, yet the whole damage must be recovered in one action, because there is but one cause of action. The most familiar illustration of this rule is to be found in actions for injury to the person, in which the practice is invariable.

"Where the breach of contract or delict complained of consists not of one but of a series of acts the rule is different. Thus, if one contracts to deliver a certain quantity of goods during each month in the ensuing year, and fails to perform in the first or second month, that is in itself a distinct breach of contract, and if the purchaser sues for damages for that breach he cannot in the same action claim for an apprehended breach in subsequent months, for the obligant may perform his contract for the future, and if he fails in any subsequent month, that is a fresh breach of contract, for which a separate action will lie.

"So also an operation *in suo* which creates a nuisance to one's neighbour may be followed by long continued loss and damage to that neighbour, and yet it may not be necessary to recover the whole damage in one action; because he who commits the nuisance is under a constant legal obligation to abate it, and so long as he fails in performing that legal obligation he is every day committing a fresh nuisance."

LORD MURE (at p. 130): "It is incompetent for the pursuer now to bring a second action founded upon the same breach."

LORD ADAM (at p. 130): "There was only one wrongous act on the part of the defenders, and in my opinion, as soon as the act was committed, the right of action to recover all damages arising from it arose. I agree with your Lordships that the pursuer is bound to recover all the damages to which he can lay claim in the one action. The pursuer says that he is entitled to have successive actions of damages for his alleged losses, as they may arise from time to time over an indefinite period. It may be true that where a person is obliged to have recourse to one action and to one only the amount of damages may vary under different circumstances, but of that we have daily experience and cognisance, for instance, in actions of damages for personal injuries arising from fault. It is always impossible to ascertain accurately what sum of damage will cover the injury or loss, but, although the amount of damages awarded may be to some extent speculative, yet the evil thus resulting is far less than would be the evil of allowing successive actions of damages from time to time arising from the same originating cause. How many actions are there to be—and are they to be brought at the rate of one every six months, or every year? That would lead to an intolerable state of matters. In this case we have had one action, which covered the period down to July 1886. We now have a second, which is founded upon the same wrongous act, brought nine months later. A proceeding such as this is quite unknown to our law, and ought to receive no encouragement."

NOTE

This case was followed in *Aberdeen Development Co.* v. *Mackie, Ramsay & Taylor*, 1977 S.L.T. 177 (O.H.).

Developers (A.) had built 50 houses to the design of architects (R.). A. raised an action for declarator against R. that the design was materially defective and that R. was liable to make reparation to A. for loss sustained or to be sustained by A. as a result of this breach of contract. A. claimed that the loss which they would sustain would be in respect of claims against them by original purchasers who still owned houses and might make claims; A. also claimed damages of £15,000 as the cost of repairing the one house in respect of which a claim had already been made.

Held that the declarator was incompetent and irrelevant because it was an attempt to allow different actions to be raised for losses flowing from one breach of contract.

Lord Maxwell (at p. 180): "It is possibly arguable that, as matter of policy, the rule in *Stevenson* v. *Pontifex & Wood*, is too sweeping and overharsh on pursuers in a case such as the present, but that is not a matter for me. The rule in my opinion is unequivocal, is binding on me in this court, is applicable to the present case and precludes the declaratory conclusion."

Damages: foreseeability

A/B Karlshamns Oljefabriker v. Monarch Steamship Co. Ltd.

1949 S.C.(H.L.) 1; 1947 S.C. 179

A Swedish firm chartered the *British Monarch* to convey a quantity of soya beans from Manchuria to Sweden. The charterparty provided that the ship should be seaworthy and contained a clause that anything done in compliance with the orders of the British Government should not be deemed a deviation. At the time when the charterparty was entered into there was a grave risk of war in Europe and that risk was recognised by the shipowners.

The ship ought to have arrived at its destination before the outbreak of war, but was still at sea owing to unseaworthiness which had existed at the commencement of the voyage. Under orders of the British Government the ship proceeded to Glasgow, and the cargo of beans was transhipped to Sweden in Swedish vessels.

The Swedish firm claimed damages from the shipowners.

Held that as it was the ship's initial unseaworthiness which had caused the delay and the direction of the ship to Glasgow, the shipowners were liable to the Swedish firm for the cost of the transhipment.

LORD WRIGHT (at p. 18): "I agree . . . with the unanimous decision of all the Judges below that the claim for the damages is justified. It in truth gives effect to the broad general rule of the law of damages that a party injured by the other party's breach of contract is entitled to such money compensation as will put him in the position in which he would have been but for the breach. In that respect this case is singularly clear, because the contract entitled the respondents to have the beans delivered at Karlshamn and the damages claimed and awarded represent simply the sum necessary to effect that result, namely the cost of transhipment from Glasgow to Karlshamn. . . . The extra cost incurred for transhipment was the proper subject of monetary compensation. The respondents have made no claim for interference with their business. The damages awarded are not special or remote but are the damages naturally and directly resulting from the appellants' breach of contract within the rules of *Hadley* v. *Baxendale* ((1854) 9 Ex. 341 at p. 354). . . . There was indeed in 1939 the general fear that there might be war. . . . Risks consequent on the prolongation of the voyage must have been in contemplation both by the shipowners and the shippers. The question whether damage is remote, or 'natural' and direct, can in general only be decided on a review of the circumstances of each special case. Remoteness of damage is in truth a question of fact. . . .

". . . The question in a case like the present must always be what reasonable business men must be taken to have contemplated as the natural or probable result if the contract was broken. As reasonable business men each must be taken to understand the ordinary practices and exigencies of the other's trade or business. . . .

"But a question of remoteness in another connexion and in another sense has been raised. That is in reference to remoteness in the sense of causal connexion. The claim here is for damages for unseaworthiness which, it is said, caused delay on the voyage, and the delay exposed the vessel to being directed by order of the Admiralty. ... Unseaworthiness must generally, perhaps always, in a sense be a 'remote' cause. ... From its very nature it must always, or almost always, operate by means of and along with the specific and immediate peril. That is because the essence of unseaworthiness as a cause of loss or damage is that the unseaworthy ship is unfit to meet the peril. ... Causation in law does not depend on remoteness or immediacy in time. ... Unseaworthiness is a decisive cause or, as it is called, a dominant cause. If it is not expressly excepted, the shipowner cannot excuse himself by any specific exception for a loss for which he is himself responsible, because he is responsible for unseaworthiness. ...

"... I think the common law would be right in picking out unseaworthiness from the whole complex of circumstances as the dominant cause."

LORD DU PARCQ (at p. 29): "Damage arises 'according to the usual course of things' if, in the circumstances existing at the date of the contract, both parties to it, supposing them to have considered the probable effects of a breach of the contract, with due regard to events which might reasonably be expected to occur, must be assumed as reasonable men to have foreseen such damage as at least a serious possibility. ... If it be once granted that there was a real, and known, danger of war at the date of the contract, ... the diversion of the ship which caused such grave loss to the respondents followed in the usual course of things from the delay and the unseaworthiness which caused it.

"In order that the respondents might succeed in establishing their case, it was not necessary, in my opinion, that the parties to the contract should be shown to have contemplated the outbreak of war as something certain and unavoidable. They are not to be supposed to have had the gift of prophecy. It is enough if they may reasonably be assumed to have contemplated a war, and the likelihood that it would lead to such an embargo as was in fact imposed, as a real danger which must be taken into account."

NOTE

In *Haberstich* v. *McCormick & Nicholson*, 1975 S.C. 1, where solicitors delivered to purchasers of a cottage a disposition which they knew to be defective, the purchasers, having improved the cottage and offered it for sale, were held entitled in damages to the difference between the price which the cottage would have fetched untainted by the defect in title (£5,000) and the price actually obtained (£3,500), *i.e.* £1,500.

Lord President (Emslie) (at p. 10): "Before settlement, it can hardly be disputed that the defenders ought to have had in contemplation that the pursuers might sell the cottage before the expiry of the prescriptive period and that if they did so, they would discover that they had to accept a price lower than that which would then have been paid for subjects untainted by the consequence of a breach of contract on the defenders' part. The reduction in price which the pursuers had to accept at the sale can fairly and reasonably be regarded only as a consequence which arose naturally from the defenders' breach of contract itself."

Damages: special circumstances not made known

Steamship "Den of Ogil" Co. Ltd. v. Caledonian Railway Co.

(1902) 5 F. 99

The *Den of Ogil*, a steamship of 4,000 tons lying at Plymouth, had broken one of her pistons. Another piston had been cast at Port-Glasgow and was sent by passenger train from Port-Glasgow to Plymouth, the railway company being informed that the carriage was urgent and that delay would cause detention of the ship, but not being informed of the size of the ship, that it had a crew of 57 on board or that the casting was a piston.

There was a delay of between three and four days in delivery, and the shipowners sued the railway company for damages, including outlays and loss of profit caused by the detention of the ship, amounting to £300.

Held that the railway company was not liable for the loss of profit but only for part of the outlays (estimated at £50) caused by the delay.

LORD ORDINARY (LOW) (at p. 99): "The defenders do not dispute that they were in breach of their contract, and the question at issue is, what is the measure of damages which falls to be applied in such a case?

"The pursuers claim the loss which they have sustained on account of the detention of the vessel, which includes the expenses incurred while she was lying at Plymouth, and the profit which she would have earned if she had not been detained. The defenders on the other hand maintain that they are not liable to make good such loss, because it does not represent the damages arising naturally, and in the ordinary course of things, from the breach of contract.

"I did not understand the pursuers to dispute that if the contract with the defenders was simply to carry the piston to Plymouth, without any notice of the special circumstances, the defenders would not be liable to pay for the detention of the vessel, but they maintain that the defenders were given such information in regard to the circumstances that the damages claimed must be supposed to have been in the contemplation of both parties when they made the contract as the probable result of the breach of it.

[After reviewing the evidence] " ... Assuming that knowledge of the circumstances would render the defenders liable for the damages claimed, I am of opinion that that knowledge would require to be full and precise, and the evidence in my opinion negatives the idea that such full and precise knowledge was in fact communicated. ... Practically all that McGregor [the stationmaster at Port-Glasgow] knew was that the early delivery of the article which he was asked to forward was so important that the senders were willing to pay the high rate charged for carrying it by passenger train. If he had known the exact circumstances he might very well have considered it prudent to take special precautions against delay. ...

"I therefore think that it is impossible to say that when the defenders agreed to carry the piston they had such accurate knowledge of the circumstances that they must be presumed to have had in view that the result of their failure to carry out their contract would be that a large merchant ship, which was otherwise ready to proceed upon a voyage, would be detained at great expense to her owners."

LORD PRESIDENT (KINROSS) (at p. 104): "The material point, in my judgment, is that the defenders were apprised that the consequence of failing to forward the casting to Plymouth at the time contracted for would be to delay the sailing of the 'Den of Ogil' until it had arrived; or, in other words, that the non-fulfilment of the contract of carriage would infer the detention of the 'Den of Ogil.' The fact that the carriage was urgent was also evident from the piston being sent by a passenger train at a high rate of charge. The defenders were thus, in my view, affected with notice that the transit was urgent, and that the effect of its not being punctually fulfilled would be to delay the sailing of the 'Den of Ogil.' But, on the other hand, it does not appear that the defenders were informed that the 'Den of Ogil' was so large a steamer having such a numerous crew.

"Under these circumstances the question comes to be, what is the measure of the damages which the defenders are liable to pay for their admitted breach of contract? One of the claims made by the pursuers is for the loss of profit caused by the detention of the 'Den of Ogil' for about three days, and I am of opinion that this is not a legitimate head of claim, for the reasons explained by Lord Justice Mellish in the case of *'The Parana'*

((1877) L.R. 2 P.D. 118). But while I think that the pursuers are not entitled to loss of profit, I consider that they have right in name of damages to a part at least of any outlays which were rendered necessary by the detention of the steamer while awaiting the arrival of the piston at Plymouth, and which became unprofitable in consequence of that detention. If the defenders had been made aware of the size of the 'Den of Ogil' and the number of her crew, I think that the pursuers would have had a strong claim for the whole of such outlays during the period of detention, as it has been said that in such cases the measure of the damages is the amount of the loss which might naturally be expected by the parties in the state of knowledge which they had when they entered into the contract to result from a breach of it. A part, therefore, at all events of the wages of the crew while waiting at Plymouth for the piston, after, by the terms of the contract of carriage, it should have arrived there, seems to me to be a legitimate charge against the defenders, and also a part of the cost of provisions, stores, &c., consumed by them, or necessarily used in the vessel during the period of detention.

"It further appears that the fires of the 'Den of Ogil' were banked in order that she might be ready to start immediately upon the piston being fitted in after its arrival, and I think that part, at all events, of the cost of the coal so consumed during the period between the time at which, by the terms of the contract, the piston should have arrived, and the time at which it actually did arrive, forms a legitimate item of charge against the defenders, as well as a part of any other outlays rendered necessary by the delay, and not otherwise useful or available for the purposes of the ship. The Lord Ordinary says that it seems to him that the damages must be limited 'to the extra cost to which the defenders were put in fitting in the piston by reason of the delay in delivery, and any expenses which they incurred in waiting for and seeking to recover it.' This statement would seem to include the items which I have indicated appear to me to form proper heads of claim, but the Lord Ordinary has assessed the total damage at £10, and I am of opinion that this sum is inadequate. I think that £50 should be awarded in name of damages."

Damages: mitigation: onus of proof

Connal, Cotton & Co. v. Fisher, Renwick & Co.

(1882) 10 R. 824

R. contracted to carry 50 tons of white-lead for C. from the Tyne to Montreal, the freight amounting in all to £27 10s.

R. failed to secure a ship, and declined to carry the goods. C. sent the goods via Liverpool for a total cost of £113, and sued R. for the difference between that sum and the freight contracted for.

Held that the onus was on R. to show that the mode of conveyance adopted by C. was more expensive than was necessary, and that as R. had failed to show this, he was liable for the sum sued for.

LORD PRESIDENT (INGLIS) (at p. 828): "The pursuers say that the defenders broke their contract, and that the defenders are liable to pay the difference in the cost of carriage, however great it may be. To this the defenders reply, not that they did not break their contract, for the breach of it is admitted on record, but that the mode adopted by the pursuers of having the white-lead conveyed was too expensive, and that it ought to have been conveyed at a cheaper rate. Now, I do not think that it lies on the pursuers to show that in the circumstances, and especially having regard to the time of year, the carriage of the goods could not have been accomplished more cheaply. . . .

". . . If the defenders had seen their own interest they would have tried to get the goods conveyed in the cheapest way they could, but instead of that they left the pursuers without any option. They had to send their goods to those with whom they had contracted in Canada; and they say they did so in the best and cheapest way they could. It turned out a very expensive way certainly, but it lay on the defenders, if they meant to allege that in defence, to prove that it could be done more cheaply. There is no such proof here, for I cannot give any weight to the loose statement of their manager as to the cost for which the goods could have been sent. He is their only witness. He says he thinks certain things could have been done, but the defenders were bound to prove as matter of fact that the goods could have been sent at a lower cost, and this they have failed to do."

Damages: mitigation: extraordinary exertions not required

Gunter & Co. v. Lauritzen

(1894) 31 S.L.R. 359 (O.H.)

L., a merchant in Denmark, contracted to supply to G. & Co. at Aberdeen a cargo of Danish hay and straw, warranted to be in sound condition on delivery. L. was aware that G. & Co. were buying for the purpose of resale.

The cargo on arrival was disconform to warranty and was rejected by the sub-purchaser.

G. & Co. brought an action against L. for damages for breach of contract, claiming as part of the damage the loss of profit on the subsale, and proved that at the time and place of delivery there was no market for goods of the same kind and quality as those contracted for, and that they were not on public sale at the time, or quoted in any public market list open to their inspection.

L. averred in defence that goods to the amount required might have been obtained by G. & Co. in three separate parcels from private sellers in this country.

Held that G. & Co. were under no duty to take other than ordinary measures to replace the goods, and were entitled to the whole profit they would have obtained on a resale.

LORD STORMONTH DARLING (Ordinary) (at p. 360): "The only defence which is now put forward is . . . to the effect that the pursuer could at the time of delivery have bought in Scotland, and particularly at Leith or Grangemouth, Danish hay and straw at a price less than he had agreed to pay the defender. I am of opinion that this defence is not made out. It is clear in the first place, on the principle of *Hadley* v. *Baxendale* ((1854) 9 Ex. 341), that the damage which the defender was bound to make good in the event of his breaking the contract, was such as might be held to have been in contemplation of the parties at the time of making the contract, and in this case the damage contemplated was the loss of profit on the re-sale. The defender says that there is an equitable limitation to this rule to the effect that the purchaser, before he can recover such loss of profit, must show that he has taken every means to supply himself with similar goods, and unless he does so he is barred from recovering. That may be the equitable rule where the goods are of a kind currently bought and sold in the open market at the time and place of delivery. If the purchaser can go into the market and supply himself with goods of the same quality and at a price not greater than that in the contract, then he would suffer no damage, for he would be able to fulfil his contract with the sub-purchaser. But the goods in question were of a very special kind; they were specially consigned from a foreign country, and it is the result of the evidence, in my opinion, that at Aberdeen, which was the port of delivery, there was not a market for these goods at the time at all. The defender had led evidence to show, that by hunting all over the country, the pursuers might have found out that there were small parcels of Danish hay and straw at Leith and other places, which he might have picked up by private treaty; but none of these parcels were on public offer at the time, or quoted in any public market list which was open to the pursuers' inspection. In these circumstances I think there was no duty on the purchaser to make extraordinary exertions to supply himself with goods elsewhere. This is the ground on which I decide the case, but I am by no means satisfied on the proof that it could have been possible for the pursuer, even if it had been his duty, to obtain the goods at a cost less or no greater than the prices he had agreed to pay the defender."

Liquidate damages or penalty: sum proportionate to extent of failure held to be liquidate damages

Lord Elphinstone v. The Monkland Iron and Coal Co. Ltd.

(1886) 13 R.(H.L.) 98

Tenants in a mineral lease undertook to level and soil over slag hills by a certain date under a "penalty" "at the rate of £100 per imperial acre for all ground not so restored, together with legal interest thereon, from and after the date when the operations should have been completed until paid."

Held that this was a stipulation for liquidate damages and not for a penalty.

LORD WATSON (at p. 106): "The payments stipulated in the 12th article are, in my opinion, liquidated damages, and not penalties. When a single lump sum is made payable by way of compensation, on the occurrence of one or more or all of several events, some of which may occasion serious and others but trifling damage, the presumption is that the parties intended the sum to be penal, and subject to modification. The payments stipulated in article 12 are not of that character; they are made proportionate to the extent to which the respondent company may fail to implement their obligations, and they are to bear interest from the date of the failure. I can find neither principle nor authority for holding that payments so adjusted by the contracting parties with reference to the actual amount of damage ought to be regarded as penalties."

LORD CHANCELLOR (HERSCHELL) (at p. 107): "The agreement does not provide for the payment of a lump sum upon the non-performance of any one of many obligations differing in importance. It has reference to a single obligation, and the sum to be paid bears a strict proportion to the extent to which that obligation is left unfulfilled. There is nothing whatever to shew that the compensation is ... extravagant in relation to the damage sustained. And provision is made that the payment is to bear interest from the date when the obligation is unfulfilled. I know of no authority for holding that a payment agreed to be made under such conditions as these is to be regarded as a penalty only; and I see no sound reason or principle, or even convenience, for so holding."

LORD FITZGERALD (at p. 108): "The law of Scotland ... seems in this respect to agree in principle with the law of the rest of the United Kingdom; or it would be more correct to say that the law of Scotland in this respect existed in full force and equitable effect whilst we were struggling against the hard and technical rules of our common law.... We may take it, then, that by the law of Scotland the parties to any contract may fix the damages to result from a breach at a sum estimated as liquidated damages, or they may enforce the performance of the stipulations of the agreement by a penalty. ...

"I am clearly of opinion ... that the sum of £100 per imperial acre for all ground not restored, though described in one part of the 12th article as 'the penalty therein stipulated,' is not a penalty, and represents stipulated or estimated damages. It is satisfactory also to be able to make out from the uncontroverted evidence that the sum is not exorbitant or unreasonable."

NOTE

There are observations on the distinction between liquidate damages and penalty in *Robertson* v. *Driver's Trustees* (1881) 8 R. 555.

This was an action by a joiner for the balance of a contract price. The employer pleaded that he was entitled under a penalty clause to a deduction of £2 per day for each day the work had remained unfinished after a stipulated date.

Held that in the circumstances, the various stipulations as to time being inconsistent with the work being completed on the date fixed, the claim for liquidate damages could not be enforced.

Lord Young (at p. 562): "Where there is a distinct time bargain and a stipulation by the parties that if the contractor fail to complete the contract within the time distinctly limited, he shall be liable for a certain sum of money for every day or week during which it remains incomplete, the Court will generally give effect to that bargain if it be reasonable that damages be paid. But if, again, the penalty be truly a penalty—that is, a punishment—the Court will not allow that, because the law will not let people punish each other. They may contract that the one will be bound to reimburse the other for any loss caused, but not for punishment. Anything beyond compensation, which is a reasonable enough penalty, is punishment, and will not be enforced. That is the result of all the decisions. The word 'penalty' is sometimes used to express liquidate damages, and, again, what is called liquidate damages is really penalty. The Court will look into the circumstances of each case, without being influenced by the term used, and having ascertained the truth, will act accordingly. In this case, in the circumstances, I do not think this penalty should be enforced."

Liquidate damages or penalty: reasonable pre-estimate of loss held to be liquidate damages

Cameron-Head v. Cameron & Co.

1919 S.C. 627

A firm of timber merchants entered into a contract with the proprietor of the estate of Inverailort in Inverness-shire whereby they bought standing timber under the condition: "The wood to be cleared away by 1st April, 1918, under a penalty of 10s. (Ten shillings) a day until such is done."

In April 1919, the wood not having been completely cleared away, the proprietor brought an action against the timber merchants for payment of one year's "penalty" at the stipulated rate.

Held that (1) under the contract the damages accrued *de die in diem*, and that, accordingly, the proprietor was not bound to delay her action until the contract had been completely executed by the timber merchants; and (2) although the sum was described in the contract as a penalty, yet, as it was a reasonable pre-estimate of the loss and not a mere random figure, and, further, was not averred by the timber merchants to be exorbitant, it fell to be regarded as liquidate damages and not as a penalty.

LORD SALVESEN (at p. 632): "In my opinion this so-called 'penalty' is really in the nature of a pre-estimate of damage. Nothing is said against the reasonableness of the sum that the parties have fixed, having in view the kind of damage which it was anticipated the proprietrix would suffer from a breach of this contractual obligation. The main damage, I take it, was the loss of privacy or amenity, which might conceivably affect the subjects equally over the whole period when operations were going on. ... It seems to me that, as regards the main subject of damage—loss of amenity—it might be substantially the same so long as any of this wood remained unremoved from the premises of the owner of the land. Accordingly, I have come to the conclusion that we must treat this agreement for a penalty as if the words 'liquidate damages' had been used instead.

"The only other question is: Can the pursuer bring the action now for payment of the sum contracted to be paid for each day's delay, or must she wait until the contractor in his own time thinks fit to remove the last trees that he has purchased?

"The Court can always prevent any improper multiplication of proceedings, but I cannot hold that the proprietrix here is acting improperly in bringing an action after the expiry of a year for a sum calculated at ten shillings a day for that year. According to the true intention of the contract, I think the ten shillings were to become immediately exigible, and that the contract is to be construed as if it had contained an express clause to that effect. The other construction—that, while there was a stipulation as to the payment of this sum per day, the amount was not to be exigible until the contract was completed—does not seem to me to be according to the true intention of the parties."

LORD SKERRINGTON (at p. 635): "I should be slow to say that the parties did not mean what they said when they described the ten shillings a day as a 'penalty.' I think that they intended to protect the interests of the seller by providing the purchaser with a strong motive for punctually fulfilling his contract. But that consideration by itself does not make this stipulation unenforceable. The question still remains, as Lord Robertson pointed out in the *Clydebank* case ((1904) 7 F.(H.L.) 77 at p. 84), whether the one party had no interest to protect by that clause, or whether that interest was palpably incommensurate with the sum agreed on. In other words, if this ten shillings a day is a random sum, the Court will not enforce payment; on the other hand, if it represents a reasonable pre-estimate of the loss which the pursuer might suffer by delay in having her ground cleared, then the stipulation ought to be enforced. In my view it was a stipulation not merely in the interests of the seller but also in the interests of the purchasers, because one object was to protect the purchasers against possible claims of an exorbitant kind which they might find it difficult to meet.

"... The subject-matter of this contract is one which made it peculiarly appropriate that the parties should, in their several and separate interests, assess the damages in advance. ... The damage ... is obviously difficult to translate into pounds, shillings, and pence. Accordingly, it was reasonable on the part of the contractors to fix a specific sum as the damages which should be recoverable in respect of a breach of this particular stipulation.

"There is nothing in the circumstances, so far as we know, to suggest that ten shillings a day was at all exorbitant. ... The fact that the agreed-on sum is so much per day goes far to show that what the parties had in mind was not a random sum but a true estimate of conventional damages. ...

"The only other question is whether this penalty was intended to become due from day to day, or whether it was not to accrue as a debt until the contract had been completely executed by the purchasers. ... The purpose which the parties had in view would be defeated, if the penalty could not be exacted immediately but was to be payable only if and when the purchasers thought fit to complete their contract."

NOTE

For "the *Clydebank* case," see below.

Liquidate damages or penalty: stipulated sum held to be liquidate damages, where pre-estimate of loss was impossible

Clydebank Engineering and Shipbuilding Co. Ltd. v. Yzquierdo y Castaneda

(1904) 7 F.(H.L.) 77;(1903) 5 F. 1016

Shipbuilders in Clydebank by two contracts undertook to supply in all four torpedo-boat destroyers to the Spanish Government within periods varying from 6½ to 7¾ months from the date of the contract.

The contracts included this clause: "The penalty for late delivery shall be at the rate of £500 per week for each vessel not delivered by the contractors in the contract time."

All the vessels were delivered many months late, and the Spanish Government brought an action against the shipbuilders for in all £75,500, calculated in accordance with the "penalty" clause.

Held that the sum of £500 per week was to be regarded as liquidate damages and not as penalty, and that the Spanish Government was therefore entitled to an amount (held after a proof to be £67,500) calculated according to that rate.

LORD CHANCELLOR (HALSBURY) (at p. 77): "Two objections have been made to the enforcement of that payment. The first objection is one which appears upon the face of the instrument itself, namely, that it is a penalty, and not, therefore, recoverable as a pactional arrangement of the amount of damages resulting from the breach of contract. It cannot, I think, be denied—indeed, I think it has been frankly admitted by the learned counsel—that not much reliance can be placed upon the mere use of certain words. Both in England and in Scotland it has been pointed out that the Court must proceed according to what is the real nature of the transaction, and that the mere use of the word 'penalty' on the one side or 'damages' on the other, would not be conclusive as to the rights of the parties. It is, I think, not denied now that the law is the same both in England and in Scotland. . . .

"We come then to the question, What is the agreement here? and whether this sum of money is one which can be recovered as an agreed sum as damages, or whether, as has been contended, it is simply a penalty to be held over the other party *in terrorem*—whether it is, what I think gave the jurisdiction to the Courts in both countries to interfere at all in an agreement between the parties, unconscionable and extravagant, and one which no Court ought to allow to be enforced.

"It is impossible to lay down any abstract rule as to what it may or may not be extravagant or unconscionable to insist upon without reference to the particular facts and circumstances which are established in the individual case. I suppose it would be possible in the most ordinary case, where people know what is the thing to be done and what is agreed to be paid, to say whether the amount was unconscionable or not. For instance, if you agreed to build a house in a year, and agreed that if you did not build the house for £50, you were to pay a million of money as a penalty, the extravagance of that would be at once apparent. Between such an extreme case as I have supposed and other cases, a great deal must depend upon the nature of the transaction—the thing to be done, the loss likely to accrue to the person who is endeavouring to enforce the performance of the contract, and so forth. It is not necessary to enter into a minute disquisition upon that subject, because the thing speaks for itself. But, on the

other hand, it is quite certain, and an established principle in both countries, that the parties may agree beforehand to say, 'Such and such a sum
shall be damages if I break my agreement.' The very reason why the parties do in fact agree to such a stipulation is that sometimes, although undoubtedly there is damage and undoubtedly damages ought to be
recovered, the nature of the damage is such that proof of it is extremely
complex, difficult, and expensive. . . .

"It seems to me, when one looks to see what was the nature of the transaction in this case, it is hopeless to contend that the parties only intended
this as something *in terrorem*. Both parties recognised the fact of the importance of time; it is a case in which time is of the essence of the contract
and so regarded by both parties, and the particular sum fixed upon as
being the agreed amount of damages was suggested by the defendants
themselves, and to say that that can be unconscionable or something
which the parties ought not to insist upon, that it was a mere holding out
something *in terrorem*, after looking at the correspondence between the
parties, is, to my mind, not a very plausible suggestion. . . . I think there is
no ground for the contention that this is not pactional damage agreed to
between the parties . . . at the time the contract was entered into."

LORD DAVEY (at p. 81): "As to the first question, it is . . . a question, not
of words or of forms of speech, but of substance and of things, namely,
whether a clause like the one in question provides for liquidate damages
or for a penalty strictly so called in the sense of punishment irrespective of
the damage sustained.

"Now, it appears to me that a very useful rule for guiding the Court in
this matter has been laid down for us in this House by Lord Watson and
Lord Herschell, L.C., and the other noble and learned Lords who took part
in the decision of the case of *Lord Elphinstone* v. *Monkland Iron and
Coal Co.* . . .

"I therefore conceive that it may be taken as an established principle in
the law of Scotland that, if you find a sum of money made payable for the
breach, not of an agreement generally, which might result in either a trifling or a serious breach, but a breach of one particular stipulation in an
agreement, and when you find that the sum payable is proportioned to the
amount, if I may so call it, or the rate of the non-performance of the agreement—for instance, if you find that it is so much per acre for ground
which has been spoilt by mining operations, or if you find, as in the present case, that it is so much per week during the whole time for which the
delivery of vessels beyond the contract time is delayed—then you infer

that *prima facie* the parties intended the amount to be liquidate damages and not penalty. I say *'prima facie'* because it is always open to the parties to shew that the amount named in the clause is so exorbitant and extravagant that it could not possibly have been regarded as damages for any possible breach which was in the contemplation of the parties, and that is a reason for holding it to be a penalty and not liquidate damages notwithstanding the considerations to which I have alluded.

"... In *Forrest & Barr* v. *Henderson & Co.* ((1869) 8 M. 187) the Lord President Inglis says this: '... The question whether it is exorbitant or unconscionable is to be considered with reference to the point of time at which the stipulation is made ...' ...—that is to say, in regard to any possible amount of damages or any kind of damage which may be conceived to have been within the contemplation of the parties when they made the contract.

"I hold it to be perfectly irrelevant and inadmissible for the purpose of shewing the clause to be extravagant, in the sense in which I use that word, to admit evidence ... of the damages which were actually suffered by the Spanish Government. I agree that it was for the very purpose of excluding that kind of evidence that the parties determined to have the damages liquidate in this manner by naming a specific sum, and it appears to me that the learned counsel have been doing the very thing which the parties intended to prevent by the way in which they have framed their contract."

LORD ROBERTSON (at p. 84): "This clause sought to be enforced is not a general penalty clause, but a specific agreement that sums of money, graduated according to time, shall be paid as penalties for delays in delivering these vessels. Now, the Court can only refuse to enforce performance of this pecuniary obligation, if it appears that the payments specified were—I am using the language of Lord Kyllachy—'merely stipulated *in terrorem*, and could not possibly have formed' 'a genuine pre-estimate of the creditor's probable or possible interest in the due performance of the principal obligation.'

" ... The question remains, Had the respondents no interest to protect by that clause, or was that interest palpably incommensurate with the sums agreed on? It seems to me that to put this question in the present instance is to answer it. Unless injury to a State is as matter of law inexpressible in money, Spain was or might be deeply interested in the early delivery of these ships and deeply injured by delay.

"To my thinking, Lord Moncreiff has, in two sentences, admirably stated the case: 'The subject-matter of the contracts, and the purposes for which the torpedo-boat destroyers were required, make it extremely improbable that the Spanish Government ever intended or would have agreed that there should be inquiry into, and detailed proof of, damage resulting from delay in delivery. The loss sustained by a belligerent, or an intending belligerent, owing to a contractor's failure to furnish timeously warships or munitions of war, does not admit of precise proof or calculation; and it would be preposterous to expect that conflicting evidence of naval or military experts should be taken as to the probable effect on the suppression of the rebellion in Cuba or on the war with America of the defenders' delay in completing and delivering those torpedo-boat destroyers.' "

Liquidate damages or penalty: "penalty" held to be liquidate damages and available as a defence: mutuality

Johnston v. Robertson

(1861) 23 D. 646

J. contracted with the Parochial Board of Latheron to erect a poor-house for £1,742. By the contract J. undertook to complete the work on or before March 31, 1856, under a "penalty" of £5 for every week during which the work remained unfinished after that date.

J. brought an action against the Board for an alleged balance of the contract price and also for payment for extra work.

The Board alleged that, since the work had not been completed by March 31, 1856, J. was, under the penalty clause, liable to the Board for a greater sum than the sum sued for.

Held that (1) the stipulated "penalty" was liquidate damages and not penalty; and (2) in a mutual contract the principle applicable was that one party was not entitled to enforce performance without showing that he had himself performed his part of the contract.

LORD JUSTICE-CLERK (INGLIS) (at p. 655): "The mere use of the word 'penalty' is not conclusive as to the true character of the stipulation. A consequence may be a penalty, although it is not called so; and, on the other hand, it may not be a penalty, though it receives that name. And, therefore, I do not attach much importance to the circumstance, that this £5 per week is called a penalty.

"It is always material, in questions of this kind, to consider whether the thing to be provided against by the so-called penalty is essential in the view of the contracting parties, or one or other of them. In this case, it is clear that the time when it was agreed the works were to be completed was a matter of the highest importance, because the parochial board, so long as their poor-house was unfinished, required to provide accommodation for their paupers elsewhere; and, therefore, they stipulated that the work should be concluded by a fixed day, and that by that time the work should be in such a state of completeness that they could then enter on the premises.

"The next inquiry is, whether the stipulation is a reasonable and appropriate mode of enforcing that obligation to complete the work by the date specified, and whether it is so conceived, that the penalty stipulated may be proportionate to the loss suffered by the party seeking to enforce the obligation?

"Now, payment of a sum for every week after the stipulated time during which the work was not completed, was a very suitable and appropriate remedy for the loss the parochial board might suffer by the delay. It would enable them to provide accommodation for their paupers elsewhere; and, secondly, it was plainly proportionate to the loss they suffered by non-fulfilment of the contract obligation.

"I am, therefore, of opinion, that what was stipulated by this clause was not a penalty; but that the clause is an obligation to pay a sum for every week during which the completion of the works was delayed beyond the time agreed on, and that that was a reasonable and appropriate stipulation; and that, therefore, it may be enforced *in terminis*, and without modification. ...

"The next question is, whether the defence on this clause of the contract can be made *ope exceptionis*, or whether it requires a separate action? ...

"The defence arises out of an obligation in a mutual contract, which is to be enforced at the same time as the stipulations in favour of the pursuer. Even that consideration might not be conclusive against the objection that a separate action should be raised to enforce this claim under the contract. But then we must take into consideration this other principle, that in a mutual contract, where one party seeks performance of the stipulations in his favour, he must show that he has given or tendered performance of his part of the contract. Every action on a mutual contract implies that the pursuer either has performed, or is willing to perform, his part of the contract; and it is, therefore, always open to the defender to say, that under the contract a right arises also to him to demand performance of the contract before the pursuer can insist in his action."

NOTE

On mutuality, see also *Graham & Co.* v. *The United Turkey Red Co. Ltd.* (p. 205, above), and *Dingwall* v. *Burnett*, below.

Liquidate damages or penalty: claim for damages not limited by penalty clause: mutuality

Dingwall v. Burnett

1912 S.C. 1097

In April 1911 B., proprietor of the St. George Hotel, Dunbar, entered into an agreement with D. for the lease of the hotel to D. from Martinmas 1911. The minute of agreement provided that D. was to take over the furniture and stock valued as at Martinmas 1911 and was meantime to deposit £200 in a bank to account of the valuation price.

In August 1911 D. intimated that he did not intend to fulfil his part of the agreement. He brought an action against B. for delivery of the deposit receipt.

B. lodged a counterclaim of damages for breach of contract.

Held that as D. had refused to perform his part of the contract, he was not entitled to call on B. to fulfil his obligation by delivery of the deposit receipt until B. had had an opportunity of constituting his claim of damages.

The minute of agreement between B. and D. further provided: "Both parties hereto bind and oblige themselves to implement their part of this agreement under the penalty of £50 to be paid by the party failing to the party performing or willing to perform over and above performance."

Held that the sum stipulated was not liquidate damages but a penalty and that accordingly B.'s claim for damages was not limited to that sum.

LORD SALVESEN (at p. 1102): "It is true that the principle of compensation or set-off is not applicable to such a claim. But there is another principle equally well recognised which was expressed by Lord Justice-Clerk Moncreiff in *Turnbull* v. *McLean* ((1874) 1 R. 730) as follows: 'I understand the law of Scotland, in regard to mutual contracts, to be quite clear—first, that the stipulations on either side are the counterparts and the consideration given for each other; second, that a failure to perform any material or substantial part of the contract on the part of one will prevent him from suing the other for performance; and third, that where one party has refused or failed to perform his part of the contract in any material respect, the other is entitled either to insist for implement, claiming damages for the breach, or to rescind the contract altogether—except so far as it has been performed.' The present case seems to me to fall within these rules. The pursuer has declined to perform his contract altogether, and he cannot therefore call upon the defender to fulfil his obligations until the latter has had an opportunity of constituting his claim of damages for the breach of the contract. As Lord Benholme said in *Turnbull's* case, 'In mutual contracts there is no ground for separating the parts of the contract into independent obligements, so that one party can refuse to perform his part of the contract, and yet insist upon the other performing his part. The unity of the contract must be respected.' ...

" ... I do not find anything in the penalty clause to suggest that the sum of £50 there mentioned was an agreed-on pre-estimate of the damage which either might sustain by the failure of the other to perform his part of the contract. In the first place, the word used is 'penalty' and not liquidate damages. I attach some importance to this, although the Courts have in special circumstances construed the word 'penalty' as equivalent to liquidate damages, and conversely. A more important point is, however, that the penalty is to be 'over and above performance.' Now, it is also true that these words will be implied where the Court is of opinion that the sum agreed on for breach of the agreement is so agreed on by way of penalty merely, and is not to be treated as liquidate damages; but I do not know of any case, and we were referred to none, where such words, when expressed, were held to be consistent with an intention of parties to fix the liquidate damages. An even more important consideration in determining whether the sum stipulated to be paid in the event of a breach of contract is liquidate damages or merely represents a penalty, is to ascertain whether the sum conditioned to be paid bears (in the words of Lord Justice-Clerk Inglis in *Craig* ((1863) 1 M. 1020)), 'a clear proportion to the amount of loss sustained by the party entitled to claim it'; and very similar language was used by some of the noble Lords who decided the case of *Elphinstone*. The Lord Chancellor (Lord Herschell), in holding that the stipulated sum in that case represented liquidate damage, said: 'The agreement does not provide for the payment of a lump sum upon the non-performance of any one of many obligations differing in importance. It has reference to a single obligation, and the sum to be paid bears a strict proportion to the extent to which that obligation is left unfulfilled.' In this case the very opposite holds good. The agreement imposes on the pursuer many obligations of an entirely different kind. There is first an undertaking that he shall duly lodge and follow forth an application for a transfer of the licence to himself. Then he is taken bound to take over at mutual valuation certain furniture, fittings, and stock. Further, he undertakes to act as the defender's manager, and account to him for the whole drawings of the hotel—also week by week to consign the surplus of drawings over expenses in bank in name of the defender, and to conduct the hotel on a proper businesslike footing, and do nothing likely to prejudice the licence. For a breach of any of these obligations—some of them of a kind which might not involve actual loss, and others a loss that could certainly not be material, as, for instance, the failure to consign in a single week the surplus drawings—the same penalty is prescribed. ... I do not think the clause with which I am dealing could have been more clearly expressed as a penalty clause or one which is less calculated to indicate an intention of the parties to treat the stipulated sum as liquidate damages, whether in respect of a partial or entire breach of the obligations undertaken by the pursuer."

Lord Salvesen then considered Scottish authorities which appeared to support the argument that B. could not recover more than the stipulated penalty. He also referred to English cases which had fixed the rule in the opposite way for England, and concluded (at p. 1107): "I have come, therefore, in the end to be very clearly of opinion that the laws of England and Scotland are the same as regards the matter; and that the defender is entitled to recover whatever loss he is able to qualify in respect of the pursuer's breach of contract."

NOTES

1. For the case of *Elphinstone*, see p. 239, above.

2. On mutuality, see also *Graham & Co.* v. *The United Turkey Red Co. Ltd.* (p. 205, above) and *Johnston* v. *Robertson* (p. 240, above).

3. For *Turnbull's* case, see NOTE 1 to *Graham & Co.* v. *The United Turkey Red Co. Ltd.* (p. 208, above).

Retention: claims arising out of the same contract

Gibson and Stewart v. Brown and Co.

(1876) 3 R. 328

Storekeepers received from a firm of merchants a quantity of corn to be stored.

After redelivering the greater part, the storekeepers presented a petition to the sheriff for warrant to sell the remainder and apply the proceeds towards payment of their charges, which the merchants refused to pay.

The merchants stated as a counterclaim damage to a greater amount done to the corn redelivered, owing to the neglect of the storekeepers. The merchants, by minute, restricted their counterclaim to the amount of the petitioners' claim.

Held that set off was competent, since both claims arose out of the same contract; the objection that this was an attempt to set off an illiquid against a liquid claim was repelled.

LORD PRESIDENT (INGLIS) (at p. 330): "If this were an action for payment, the pursuer would be put to prove his case, and, in the same way, if the merchant were to allege in such an action as he does here that the storekeeper has not done his part, but ill-treated the grain by omitting to turn it, and in other respects, that claim of damages arising out of the same mutual contract would constitute a good counter claim which could be pleaded by the defender.

"The peculiarity of this case is that it is a petition to enforce a lien or right of retention. The petitioners have retained a portion of the corn, and they ask that it should be sold, and the proceeds applied in extinction *pro tanto* of their claim. . . .

". . . Looking to the fact that the prayer of the petition, though it takes the form of asking for a warrant to sell, would operate, if granted, payment in money of their claim, I do not see sufficient ground for making a distinction between the question as it arises here, and in a proper petitory action. If I am right in that, and if it is clear that the two claims arise out of stipulations in the same mutual contract, the only question remaining in point of law is, whether the law applicable to cases of express contract is equally applicable where all the terms of the contract are ascertained by usage merely.

"On full consideration, I do not find any sufficient reason for drawing a distinction."

NOTE

Redpath Dorman Long Ltd. v. *Cummins Engine Co. Ltd.*, 1981 S.C. 370, was an action by contractors R. Ltd. against employers C. Ltd. under a building contract where the contract architects had certified sums as due to R. Ltd.

C. Ltd. claimed the right of retention on the ground that R. Ltd. were in breach of the contract in certain respects, as a result of which C. Ltd. had suffered loss and damage far exceeding the sums sued for. R. Ltd. contended that a clause in the contract relating to set-off had to be substituted for the common law right.

Held that the terms of that clause were not sufficient to show, in clear and unequivocal words, that the common law right of retention had been excluded.

Retention: claims not arising out of the same contract

Smart v. Wilkinson

1928 S.C. 383

S. sold his medical practice to W. for £500, payable in three instalments.

W. paid the first two instalments, but when sued for the balance of the price, viz., £200, he pleaded that he had been induced to enter into the contract by false and fraudulent misrepresentations made by S. regarding the practice, and he counterclaimed for £500, the figure at which he estimated the loss which he had suffered as a result of S.'s representations.

Held that as W.'s claim did not arise out of the contract it could not be pleaded by way of defence to S.'s claim and was not a competent counterclaim.

LORD ORMIDALE (at p. 389): "The present action concludes for payment of a liquid and clearly ascertained sum of money; and the only ground on which the defender claims that he is entitled to withhold payment of the debt due by him is that he has a claim for damages of a random and illiquid amount. I agree that the rule of liquid and illiquid will not avail a pursuer, if his claim and the defender's counter-claim arise out of the same contract, and if the defender's declinature to pay is based on a failure on the pursuer's part to implement the obligations incumbent on him under the very contract on which he sues. But that is not the position disclosed in this case. ... The contract is clear and express. What the pursuer agreed to sell and the defender agreed to buy ... was 'the benefit of' the 'practice and professional connexion' of the pursuer in and around Creetown 'on such terms and subject to such conditions as are hereinafter set forth for the price or sum of £500.' The pursuer does not purport to sell a practice of the value said to have been imputed to it prior to the formal agreement. The pursuer's claim arises *ex contractu*, and may be quite accurately described as liquid. The defender, on the other hand, is unable to point to any condition or obligation, imposed on the pursuer by the contract, on the non-fulfilment of which he rests his counter-claim. It arises solely *ex delicto*, and refers for its origin to something independent of, and antecedent to, the contract."

Special lien

Meikle & Wilson v. Pollard

(1880) 8 R. 69

In January 1880 S., a merchant in Kirkliston, consulted M. & W., "accountants and business agents," as to outstanding accounts which were due to him, and M. & W. accepted employment to recover these debts. For this purpose two books and relative documents belonging to S. were delivered to M. & W.

Shortly afterwards S. became insolvent, and the following month he signed a trust deed appointing P. trustee for behoof of his creditors.

P. applied to M. & W. for delivery of the books and papers, but M. & W. claimed that they were entitled to retain these until their account of £16 1s. 10d. for the work which they had done was paid.

Held that they were entitled to retain them in security of that amount.

LORD JUSTICE-CLERK (MONCREIFF) (at p. 70): "It certainly is not a question of law-agent's lien. The real question is whether, when documents or any other article are put into the hands of a professional man to enable him to do any particular piece of business, he is bound to part with those documents or other articles until he is paid for having done the work, and that in a question with the person who employed him. ... The question of property does not arise, the man was simply employed to do a piece of work, for which the possession of these documents was necessary, and we have to say whether, when he had done the work, he was bound to hand back those documents before he was paid for the work. These circumstances do not raise the general question of lien, but the general case of counter obligations under a contract, and on that consideration I am of opinion that there is no necessity for the man to give up the documents till the other party has performed his obligation under the contract."

LORD GIFFORD (at p. 71): "I concur with your Lordship on the special ground on which your Lordship's opinion is rested. If I thought that by this decision we were extending directly or indirectly the legal right of law-agents and others, or extending the number of the old liens, I should require more argument and further consideration before I took part in it. But I agree that this is not a case of lien. It is simply a case of the retention of a subject put into a person's hands for a special purpose, and resolves itself into a case of the relative duties of parties under a contract. The one party to it is bound to perform his part of the contract just as much as the other. The counterpart here of the duty of the one party to do the piece of business is that the other shall pay the price, and I think that until the latter is done the party employed need not hand over articles which were put into his hands to enable him to fulfil his part of the contract. The effect of this judgment is not to extend general lien."

LORD YOUNG (at p. 71): "There is certainly here no case of general lien. If it is a lien at all it is a special one. All liens arise primarily from contract, and the name is not an inconvenient one to express the right of certain parties to keep articles belonging to a person with whom they have contracted, until he has fulfilled his part of the contract.

". . . I am not disposed to speak sneeringly of accountants and business agents; they are carrying on a useful and legitimate business, and people may properly employ them, but then they must also pay them for what they do. A carrier or a stabler does not belong to any body of legal practitioners, but they are entitled to keep articles that have come into their hands under a contract until they are paid for their work—the stabler may keep a horse which he has been keeping until he is paid for its keep, or a coachbuilder may keep the carriage which he has stored until he is paid for storing it. All the people who carry on lawful businesses under which the property of others comes into their possession are not exceptionally privileged, but under the common law are entitled to retain possession of that property until the true proprietor performs his part of the contract. That is just the case here. These accountants were employed by a baker to do something which he thought would be useful to him. To that end his business books were handed over to them to enable them to collect the debts, and in the course of this employment the baker incurred debts to these accountants to the amount of £16, and the accountants got decree for that amount. On no exceptional rule, but on the ordinary rule of law, I think that these persons are not bound to part with these documents which came to them under a contract until their claim under the same contract is satisfied. There is a counterpart in every contract, and here it is that the man of business is not entitled to get his money until he gives up the books, and his employer is not entitled to get his books till he pays the money. These are obligations *hinc inde* prestable by both parties."

NOTES

1. In *Brown* v. *Sommerville* (1844) 6 D. 1267 a printer into whose hands stereotype plates had been put for the purpose of printing from them was held to have no right of lien or retention over them for his printing account. A distinction was drawn between detention of a manufactured product and detention of the machine.

Lord Justice-Clerk (Hope) (at p. 1274): "The meaning of a special lien is, that the footing on which possession was given authorizes retention for the particular claim in question, and that if that claim is satisfied, possession must be given up. It is surely of the very essence of a special lien that possession must be given up whenever the special claim which retention may enforce is satisfied."

Lord Moncreiff (dissenting) (at p. 1283): "The distinction between general and special lien is probably . . . new to the law of Scotland. . . . The doctrine of retention, in the law of Scotland, rests on broad principles of equity of very old establishment, sufficient, as I think, to sustain the claim in the present case, although it is not placed on work done for the improvement or alteration of the thing itself submitted to the printer."

2. In *Miller* v. *Hutcheson & Dixon* (1881) 8 R. 489 auctioneers were held to have a general lien where there had been a previous course of dealing.

Lord Young (at p. 492): "Lien is just a contract of pledge collateral to another contract of which it is an incident. If the principal contract be about a horse—that it is to be fed and kept by one man for another,—to that contract there is the incident called lien—that is, an agreement that the person to whom the possession of the horse is committed shall have right to retain the possession till his claim for the food and attention given to the horse shall be satisfied. That is a special lien, and it stands like general lien . . . upon contract, express or implied. The law always, in the absence of evidence of an agreement to the contrary, assumes that the owner of the horse shall not reclaim possession till he has satisfied the claim of the other party for what he has done under the contract.

"There is also general lien, which is this, that a factor possessing goods, having that possession as a lawful contract, may retain that possession until the general balance due to him by the owner of the goods is satisfied. Such a lien may in any case be constituted by contract. It stands on contract. That contract may be expressed, or it may be implied from the course of dealing of the parties, or from the usage of trade. . . . The law of general lien, which does not differ in England and Scotland to any material degree, is most accurately stated by Mr Bell (*Com.* ii., p. 87 of McLaren's ed.),—'General retention or lien is a right to withhold or detain the property of another in respect of any debt which happens to be due by the proprietor to the person who has the custody, or for a general balance of accounting arising on a particular term of employment. These rights are either founded on express agreement, or are raised by implication of law, which again may be from the understood and accustomed construction of particular contracts and connections, or from the usage of trade, or from the course of dealing between the parties.' "

3. There is no lien where such a right would be inconsistent with the terms under which possession has been obtained, as is illustrated by *Middlemas* v. *Gibson*, 1910 S.C. 577: a law-agent in whose hands a sum had been placed for the purpose of effecting a composition settlement with the depositor's creditors was held not entitled, after the proposed settlement had fallen through, to plead retention or compensation in respect of a business account due to him by the depositor.

Lord Kinnear (at p. 579): "It is well-settled law that specific appropriation is an absolute bar both to the plea of compensation and to the plea of retention, and here it is perfectly clear that the money was put into the pursuer's hands for a specific purpose, and that that purpose has failed. I am therefore of opinion that the obligation on the pursuer to return the money is absolute, and that his claim for a deduction cannot be allowed."

Lien: the need for possession as distinct from custody

Gladstone v. McCallum

(1896) 23 R. 783

G., who had been appointed liquidator of the Australian Land and Exploration Syndicate Ltd., presented a petition against McC., a chartered accountant who had been secretary of the company, for delivery of the company's minute-book.

McC. claimed that he was entitled to retain the minute-book until he was paid the £17 11s. due to him for his services as secretary.

Held that McC. had no lien over the minute-book.

LORD PRESIDENT (J. P. B. ROBERTSON) (at p. 784): "Now, has any law been shewn in support of the proposition that the secretary of a company, who has been employed to write up the minutes, has a right of lien over the minute-books? There are well-known and well-recognised liens applicable to a different relationship of the parties and to a different possession of the articles in dispute from what we find here; and we could not give judgment for the respondent unless we were to affirm—what has not as yet been decided—that every man who has been employed to write in the books in his master's office has a right of lien over the books until he has been paid for his services."

LORD MCLAREN (at p. 785): "I think there is no foundation in the facts as stated for any claim either of retention or of lien. Retention, as I understand it, is the right of an owner of property to withhold delivery of it under an unexecuted contract of sale or agreement of a similar nature, until the price due to him has been paid, or the counter obligation fulfilled. Lien, again, is the right of a person who is not the owner of property but is in possession of it on a lawful title, and whose right of lien, if it is not a general one—of which class of liens there are not many examples—is a right to retain the property until he has been compensated for something which he has done to it. In this case there is no right of retention, because the books belong to the company, and there is no right of lien, because they are not in the possession of the respondent but of the company. Accordingly this case is in a different category from that of a claim by a writer who is lawfully in possession of his client's papers under a contract of agency."

CHAPTER 7

TERMINATION OF CONTRACT

Performance: in general, exact performance required: non-material deviation in building contract

Ramsay & Son v. Brand

(1898) 25 R. 1212

R. & Son, builders, raised an action against B. for payment of £79 10s., the contract price of the mason work of a cottage.

B. argued that the work done was not conform to the contract.

Held that B. was bound to pay the contract price under a deduction of £41 4s., being the cost of bringing the building into conformity with the contract.

LORD PRESIDENT (J. P. B. ROBERTSON) (at p. 1213): "This house is certainly a very small affair; but although we are in the meantime only in the second of its lawsuits, its value already lies rather in the region of jurisprudence than in the regions of architecture or commerce. The present phase of the dispute involves principles of considerable importance.

"The contract . . . was for the execution of the mason-work of a cottage, according to plans and specifications, for the lump sum of £79 10s. Accordingly, the right of the builder was to payment of this lump sum upon his executing the work according to the plans and specification. . . . In several specified particulars the plans and specification have been departed from, and . . . the building is in those respects disconform to contract. The defender has moved that the action be dismissed, while the pursuer claims decree for the contract price, less, it may be, certain small deductions.

" . . . No man can claim the sum stipulated to be paid on the completion of certain specified work unless he has performed that work *modo et forma*, and this applies to building contracts just as much as to other contracts. The parties may if they please, and very often do, agree to vary the contract, but we have nothing of that kind here. The builder has no right either to disregard the specification altogether or to modify it as by supplying one material in place of another; and neither in the case of total departure nor in the case of partial deviation from the specification will it avail to prove that what has been done is as good as what was promised.

259

Accordingly the rule is, that if the builder chooses to depart from the contract he loses his right to sue for the contract price. But further, losing his right to sue for the contract price he does not acquire right to sue for *quantum meruit*, the other party never having agreed to pay according to its value for work which *ex hypothesi* he never ordered.

"In the application of this rule it suffers a modification which in no way invades the principle. A building contract by specification necessarily includes minute particulars, and the law is not so pedantic as to deny action for the contract price on account of any and every omission or deviation. It gives effect to the principle by deducting from the contract price whatever sum is required to complete the work in exact compliance with the contract.

"The question whether, in any given case, the deviations are of such materiality as to fall within the general rule, or are of such detail as to fall within the modification of the rule, is necessarily one of degree and circumstance. If the deviations are material and substantial, then the mere fact that the house is built would not prevent the proprietor of the ground from rejecting it and calling on the contractor to remove it, and he might do so if not barred by conduct from insisting in his right. If this right were so insisted in, then the contractor would of course have right to the materials, but he would have no right to payment. If, on the other hand, the proprietor made the best of it and let the house stay, the only claim which the contractor could have would be a claim of recompense; and this, be it observed, would be not for *quantum meruit* the builder, but for *quantum lucratus est* the proprietor. . . .

". . . This is a case of detail, and therefore one for deduction."

NOTE

See also *Speirs Ltd.* v. *Petersen*, below.

Performance: materiality in building contracts: instance of non-material breach

Speirs Ltd. v. Petersen

1924 S.C. 428

S. Ltd., structural engineers, entered into a contract with P. to erect a mansion house for P. upon the island of Eigg. The price of £16,400 was to be paid in five instalments.

The house was erected and was not rejected, but P., who had paid four instalments, refused to pay the fifth, on the ground that S. Ltd. had failed to take the usual and necessary precautions against damp.

Held that this failure amounted to a breach of contract, but that the breach was not so material as to disentitle S. Ltd. from recovering the balance of the price under deduction of the cost to P. of bringing the building into conformity with the contract.

LORD JUSTICE-CLERK (ALNESS) (at p. 433): "It is plain that the remedy for breach of contract varies, according as the contract is one for a lump sum or is a measure and value contract. The former type of contract falls to be performed in its entirety. In the latter the various parts of the contract are separable, with a different value attaching to each, and it would be inequitable, merely because some small slip has been made, to deny the contractor the right to sue upon his contract. In a lump sum contract it is plain that, if the deviation complained of is substantial, the contractor may not sue, but that, on the other hand, if the deviation is trivial, he may. I may add that, in the observations which I have made on this subject I am dealing in particular with building contracts, which, in the way of complexity and of control, often differ widely from other contracts which one can figure.

"In this case Mr Macmillan [K.C. for P.] maintained that the pursuers' deviation from their contract is so material that they are disabled from suing upon it. Having regard to the dimensions, the complexity, and the value of this contract, I am not prepared to sustain that contention. I am of opinion that the materiality of the breach of contract proved against the pursuers is not such as to yield that result. What then? If the breach is not so material as to disentitle the contractor to sue, he may recover the contract price less the sum required to bring his work into conformity with the conditions of the contract."

LORD ORMIDALE (at p. 434): "The pursuers having thus failed to implement the contract in its entirety, the defender maintains that they are not entitled to sue on the contract, and that he should be assoilzied. He claims, under reference to the cases of *Ramsay* v. *Brand, Steel* v. *Young* (1907 S.C. 360), and *Forrest* (1916 S.C.(H.L.) 28; 1915 S.C. 115), the right to retain the building without further payment in the present action, leaving the pursuers to raise another action, if so advised, in which to sue not for the contract price, or the balance of it, but for the value of the building to the defender. In ordinary circumstances, this being a lump sum contract, that might be an appropriate remedy. In the present case ... the failure of the pursuers to conform to the implied conditions of the contract with regard to the precautions against damp is not so material as to disentitle them to sue on it, and . . . the true and appropriate remedy for the defender is to deduct from the contract price such a sum as will be necessary to bring the work into compliance with the contract. The materiality of a deviation or omission must always depend largely on the amount of the sum required to rectify it relatively to the whole contract price. Applying that test here, I think the result is as I have indicated. The total value of the contract is round about £19,000. The required sum is £700."

LORD HUNTER (at p. 435): "The defender strenuously maintained to us that, if he established the additional defects of which he made complaint, he was entitled to say that the pursuers could recover nothing in the present action, but were left to sue an action against him in respect of any benefit which he might derive from the house which he now retains in his hand. For that proposition in law he founded upon the Scottish cases of *Ramsay* v. *Brand* and *Steel* v. *Young*. In the first of these cases, according to the rubric, where a building contractor fails to follow the plans agreed upon, the general rule is that he is not entitled to the contract price, and that the proprietor has the option of calling upon him to remove the materials from his ground, or of retaining them subject to the builder's claim against him *in quantum lucratus est*; but, when the deviations are not material, the proprietor may be ordained to pay the contract price under deduction of the cost of bringing the building into conformity with the plan. The Lord President, after pointing out the necessity of a building contractor performing his contract *modo et forma*, explained that the law was not so pedantic as to refuse him any recovery where the deviations from the contract were in immaterial particulars. His Lordship put his opinion thus (at p. 1214): 'If the deviations are material and substantial, then the mere fact that the house is built . . . [see passage quoted in *Ramsay & Son* v. *Brand* (p. 260, above)] . . . *quantum lucratus est* the proprietor.' In the case of *Steel* v. *Young* that doctrine was carried to an extent that would appear at all events somewhat extreme. In that case, the contract had provided for the use of cement mortar, and instead of the cement mortar lime had been used as a substitute. The substitution did not lead to any saving of expense beyond a few pounds; but the contractor, who sued for the balance of the price (£85), was deprived of his right to any payment. Lord Low, in giving the leading judgment in the case, said this: 'The general rule is that a building contract, like any other contract, must be performed *modo et forma*, and if the builder departs from the contract he loses his right to sue for the contract price.' If these two decisions stand in their entirety, there is a complete discrepancy between the law applicable to a building contract and the law applicable to a contract in general. It is quite well settled that, in the case of an ordinary contract, if a purchaser has been supplied with an article that is disconform to contract and chooses to retain that article, the seller is entitled to sue upon the contract for the contract price, but the purchaser, who is not getting an article conform to contract, is entitled either to maintain a separate action of damages in respect of the loss which he has sustained, or to plead by way of set-off against the contract price the extent of damage which he has sustained. . . . I am satisfied that the rule of *Ramsay*, given effect to in the case of *Steel*, does not apply in the present case at all."

LORD ANDERSON (at p. 438): "Difficulty is created by the decisions in *Ramsay* and *Steel*, when it is attempted to reconcile what was decided in these cases with such a general statement of the law as is found in the opinion of Lord McLaren in *Louttit's Trustees* ((1892) 19 R. 791 at p. 800). The decision of the House of Lords in *Forrest* is not helpful on this point, as the judgment in that case determined that there had been no breach of contract, and that the contractor was therefore entitled to the balance of price sued for. The view I take of the law is that, in a case like the present, the building owner, complaining of breach of contract, has a choice of two remedies: (1) He may reject the building as disconform to contract. If he does so, he may also sue the contractor for damages sustained by reason of the breach of contract. He is not bound to pay any balance of price due and may demand repetition of any instalments paid to account. On the other hand, the contractor is entitled to the materials used in the building, which he is bound to remove. If there is no time limit to the contract, the Court will, in general, give the contractor an opportunity of remedying the defects complained of and thus fulfilling the contract. (2) The other remedy of the building owner is to retain the building and counter-claim for damages. If the building is retained, it seems to me that the contract price must be paid, less the proved amount of damages in respect of breach of contract. Payment of the price is the counterpart of retention of the building. And it does not appear to me to be relevant to inquire whether or not the breach has been substantial or trifling; in neither case can the contractor be deprived of his right to sue for the price; in either case the only answer to a demand for the price is a counter-claim for damages."

NOTES

1. For *Ramsay & Son* v. *Brand*, see p. 259, above.

2. *Louttit's Trustees* v. *Highland Railway Co.* involved the question whether, where ground had been sold with absolute warrandice and was later discovered to be subject to building restrictions, the purchaser was entitled to retain possession and claim damages. Of the *actio quanti minoris* Lord McLaren said (at p. 800): "At one time it was doubted whether we had this form of action in relation to sales of moveable property, but it was never doubted that under the clause of warrandice such a right did belong to the purchaser of heritable estate, who discovered that some part of the subject of sale had not been conveyed to him. Now, however, it is quite settled, and has been explained in the valuable expositions of the law of sale given by the late Lord President [Inglis], that in such cases as sales of ships and fixed machinery, which cannot be returned after they have been in use, if it is discovered after they are in use that the extent or quality of the subjects sold is disconform to contract, the purchaser's remedy takes the shape of an *actio quanti minoris*. Under this form of action the pursuer may recover such sum as will enable him to put the subject in proper repair, or compensate him for loss of profit, where the subject is of less value than he originally bargained for."

See, however, David M. Walker, *Principles of Scottish Private Law* (4th ed.), Vol. III, p. 300: "If the seller produces a title which is not a valid and marketable title to the subjects sold the buyer is probably not entitled to take or retain the subjects purchased subject to an abatement from the price (the *actio quanti minoris*), but must rescind the entire contract and claim damages for loss of the bargain."

See also Sale of Goods Act 1979, s. 11 (5), and comments thereon.

Payment: ascription of payments

Cuthill v. Strachan

(1894) 21 R. 549

S., one of three cautioners for a cash-credit account with a bank, was sequestrated at a time when the balance against the principal debtor, George Cuthill, was £599.

The bank made no claim in S.'s sequestration, S. paid a composition of 7s. 6d. in the £ to his creditors and was discharged.

George Cuthill continued to operate on the cash-credit account until he granted a trust deed for creditors.

The bank then closed the account and called on William Cuthill, one of the other cautioners, to pay the balance of £615 then due on the account.

William Cuthill paid this amount and subsequently obtained relief from F., the third cautioner, to the extent of F.'s liability for himself and for S.

William Cuthill then brought an action against S. for payment of £37, which represented 7s. 6d. in the £ on one-half of S.'s third of £599.

S. maintained that he was not liable because between the date of his sequestration and the closing of the account sums had been paid into the account by the principal debtor which exceeded the amount for which S. had been liable at the date of his sequestration. The balance on the account had, however, never fallen below about £550.

Held that the rule applicable was that in an account-current where payments were made by a debtor and not appropriated by the parties to any particular debts the law appropriated them to the extinction of the items of debt in their order in the account, and that S.'s cautionary obligation had therefore been extinguished.

LORD YOUNG (at p. 550):"The rule of law stated in the case of *Lang* v. *Brown* ((1859) 22 D. 113) is conclusive, and it is stated as a principle held by the Court to be well settled, that to an account-current the principle is applicable that where payments are made by a debtor and are not appropriated by the parties, the law appropriates them to the extinction of the items of debit in their order in the account. Applying that principle to the facts of the present case, I think that the various entries by the principal debtor after the sequestration of the defender settles the debt just as clearly as if the first payment had been an entry by the principal debtor of £600, which admittedly would have extinguished the debit balance on the account. He had no doubt the intention of continuing to operate upon the account, and as circumstances arose he might thereafter continue to draw on his account, thereby making himself a debtor to the bank, or by paying in a larger sum make himself a creditor, but at the date of the sequestration the defender's cautionary obligation was extinguished for the future. What the condition of the cash-credit was when it came to an end does not signify."

Compensation: concursus debiti et crediti

Stuart v. Stuart

(1869) 7 M. 366

Colonel S. brought an action against his brother, Rev. A. S., for repayment of an alleged loan.

Rev. A. S. alleged that Colonel S. had received large advances from their father, and pleaded that, as executor of the father, he, Rev. A. S., had counterclaims against Colonel S. to an extent exceeding the sums sued for.

Held that Rev. A. S. could not plead the alleged counterclaims in compensation, there being no *concursus debiti et crediti.*

LORD KINLOCH (at p. 369): "As to the counter claims, it is an insuperable objection to them . . . that the defender makes them in his capacity of executor, and not in his individual character. There is in that view no *concursus debiti et crediti.*"

Compensation: both debts must be liquid

Scottish North-Eastern Railway Co. v. Napier

(1859) 21 D. 700

A railway company raised an action against N. to recover the amount of an account for carriage of goods.

N. answered that he believed the account to be correct but that he had a counterclaim of damages arising out of an earlier contract of carriage.

Held that N. had to be taken as having admitted the debt, and that he was not entitled in this action to prove his alleged claim of damages.

LORD JUSTICE-CLERK (INGLIS) (at p. 703): "It appears very distinctly that the counter claim was one of damages, arising from goods belonging to the defender being spoiled in the hands of the Railway Company; such goods, however, not being any part of those for the carriage of which the action was raised, but having been consigned for carriage at a period anterior to the date of any of the entries in the account sued on.

"The defence, therefore, was entirely based on the counter claim, and the pursuers replied by this plea, that the account libelled being admitted,

while the alleged counter claim, arising on a previous transaction between the parties, was matter of dispute, the defender could not plead the
latter as a set off against the pursuers' liquid ground of debt. I think this
plea is well founded. That the account libelled was admitted is instructed
by the record; and that the counter claim was illiquid is clear in point of
fact. . . .

"I will not say that a claim of damages can never be stated by way of
compensation. . . .

"All, however, that we decide here is, that in the case of an admitted
debt in the person of the pursuer, it is incompetent to sustain as a defence
an illiquid claim of damage."

LORD WOOD (at p. 705): "The question here is, whether there was a
plea of compensation . . . which ought to have been entertained. . . . Now I
cannot go along with the argument for the respondent, by which it was
contended that there never was any admission of the debt sued for by the
Railway Company. The pursuers' claim was met, not by a denial of its
being just in itself, but by a counter claim. In my opinion, therefore, there
was nothing at all in the action to be disposed of but the counter claim.
And thus the only question comes to be, whether the counter claim, which
resolved into a claim of damages, on account of alleged failure in duty on
the part of the pursuers in reference to the forwarding of goods entrusted
to them at a date prior to the commencement of the account sued for, and
consequently not even relating to any failure in regard to goods during the
currency of the account, and the carriage for which formed an item of that
account, ought to have been allowed to be investigated, so that it might be
liquidated in the original action, to meet the liquid claim of the pursuers?

". . . This is a case where there was no ground for entertaining the
defence upon the compensatory claim, which required investigation, . . .
and . . . , consequently, . . . the pursuers ought to have got immediate
decree for the admitted claim."

LORD COWAN (at p. 705): "The admitted claim of the pursuers was met
by a counter claim for damages, not arising out of any matters connected
with the account sued for, or in any way with the action as laid by the pursuers, but founded on an alleged transaction different from and prior to
that which formed the subject of the pursuers' claim. I never heard of such
a compensatory claim being sustained as a valid ground of defence
against an action for payment of a claim, the justice of which was admitted. It is neither liquid nor capable of being immediately liquidated."

NOTE
See also *Gibson and Stewart* v. *Brown and Co.* and *Smart* v. *Wilkinson* (pp. 251 and 253, above, respectively).

Supervening impossibility: constructive total destruction

Mackeson v. Boyd

1942 S.C. 56

B. granted to M. a 19-year lease commencing in 1926 of a furnished mansion house and its grounds.

In 1940 the mansion house and grounds were requisitioned by the military authorities, and M. brought an action against B. for declarator that the lease had ceased to be binding.

Held that, as the action of the military authorities had made it impossible during the period of the requisition for M. to occupy the subjects as a furnished mansion house, there was constructive total destruction of the subjects let, and that, accordingly, M. was entitled to abandon the lease.

LORD PRESIDENT (NORMAND) (at p. 61): "I am of opinion that the Lord Ordinary was right in holding that the present case is ruled by *Tay Salmon Fisheries Co.* v. *Speedie*, 1929 S.C. 593.

"In that case two grounds of judgment were put forward, eviction and *rei interitus*. I am bound to say, with respect to the learned judges who were parties to the decision, that I think that there was no eviction in the proper sense, for there was no breach of warrandice. ... But there is no guarantee against *damnum fatale* or inevitable loss arising from causes independent of the title. Moreover, warrandice is an express or implied term of the contract, and its breach gives rise to an action of damages. When, therefore, a tenant is excluded from possession by *vis major, damnum fatale*, or the action of Government under subsequent legislation, he has neither the remedy of an action of damages nor a right to terminate his lease on the ground of eviction. But it is now well settled in our law that, when the subjects let are wholly destroyed, the tenant has at once the right to claim cancellation of the lease, or, which is the same thing, to abandon it. I do not doubt that the landlord has a corresponding right, although in the usual case it is the tenant who has the interest to abandon.

"In the *Tay Salmon Fisheries* case there was no actual *rei interitus*, for the salmon fishings remained as they were before the danger zone was

created by the lawful action of the Air Council, but it had become impossible for the tenant or for anyone to exercise the right of salmon fishing. In
a practical sense the salmon fishings were, while the Air Council continued its by-laws, wholly destroyed. There was not actual destruction, but
there was what may be conveniently called constructive total destruction.
The effect of the decision is to extend the law applicable to physical or
actual *rei interitus* to constructive total destruction. ...

"... The subjects are, for the present, non-existent for practical purposes as a furnished house, just as the salmon fishings were in the *Tay Salmon Fisheries* case practically non-existent while the Air Council
by-laws were in force. ...

"A decision of the House of Lords in an English case (*Matthey* v. *Cur-
ling* ([1922] 2 A.C. 180) is referred to by the Lord Ordinary. No English
case was cited to us. In this, counsel exercised a wise discretion. In the
chapter of leases of heritage, and I think also in the chapter of *rei interitus*,
our law is by no means the same as the law of England, and, to quote Lord
Justice-Clerk Hope, if we were to attempt to apply that law in these cases,
we should run the greatest risk of spoiling our own by mistaking theirs."

LORD FLEMING (at p. 63): "I concur. I wish, however, to make it clear
that I am not committing myself to the opinion that in every case of a
requisition by the Crown of let subjects a right is necessarily given to the
landlord or to the tenant to bring the lease to an end."

LORD MONCRIEFF (at p. 63): "I am of the same opinion. Although our
earlier law as formulated by the Institutional writers would appear to have
been less determinate, it must be recognised as having been settled, in any
event since the decision in 1870 of the case of *Duff* v. *Fleming* (8 M. 769),
that any actual, although temporary, physical destruction of the leasehold
subjects is a *rei interitus* which entitles the tenant *ex debito justitiae* to
avoid the lease and not merely to claim an equitable abatement of rent. In
the case of a notional rather than an actual destruction of the subjects the
same doctrine was applied in 1929, in the case of *Tay Salmon Fisheries
Co.* v. *Speedie*, and was applied no less conclusively and to the same
effect, although certain of the learned Judges further thought that the *rei
interitus* upon which they proceeded had inferred against the landlord a
breach of warrandice."

LORD CARMONT (at p. 64): "The decision in the case of *Tay Salmon
Fisheries Co.* v. *Speedie* I also agree, shows it is not only in the branch of
law which deals with marine insurance that there can be constructive total

loss. By *Speedie's* decision this Court decided that the principle of the right to avoid a lease on *interitus rei* can be applied where the lessee is wholly, or almost wholly, deprived of his occupation, although the subjects let still exist. The present case seems to me to fall within the principle of *Speedie's* case, and, indeed, in some respects it is a stronger case than was *Speedie's*."

Supervening impossibility: commercial impossibility is not enough

The Hong-Kong and Whampoa Dock Co. Ltd. v. The Netherton Shipping Co. Ltd.

1909 S.C. 34

The owners of the s.s. *Netherton* which was lying damaged at Singapore contracted with a company at Hong-Kong to repair her. The owners undertook to deliver the ship at Hong-Kong and for that purpose to execute preliminary repairs, which the repairers were to allow for in so far as the work was permanent.

The port authorities at Singapore refused to allow the ship to leave unless she was repaired to an extent far beyond what the owners had anticipated. The owners therefore decided to sell the ship as a constructive total loss.

The repairers brought an action of damages for breach of contract, and the owners pled in defence that it had become no longer "commercially possible" for them to deliver the ship at Hong-Kong within a reasonable time.

Held that this defence was irrelevant, and that the owners were liable in damages for breach of contract.

LORD PEARSON (at p. 40): "It was known to both parties from the first that she was unseaworthy as she stood. All that happened was that the port authorities demanded more costly repairs than were anticipated before they would allow her to leave the port; and the owners, or the underwriters, made up their minds that the expense would be prohibitive, and resolved to sell the ship as she stood. The defenders now say that it was an implied condition of the contract that in such circumstances it was not to be enforced. The difficulty which meets the defenders is well illustrated by the language in which they state their case, namely, that they are not bound to what is commercially impossible. That is a very far-reaching doctrine, and its application would lead to startling results. This was not a contract of sale; but if the defenders' proposition is sound, I see no reason why a seller of goods should not be entitled to say to the purchaser, 'It was an implied condition of our contract that its fulfilment should be commercially possible; and really prices have risen so much that I must take advantage of the implied condition, and declare the bargain off.' "

LORD DUNDAS (at p. 41) adopted the statement of the Lord Ordinary (Mackenzie) including the sentence: "This only means they made a bad bargain, and that could in no view excuse performance of the contract."

Supervening impossibility: caused by the other party to the contract

T. & R. Duncanson v. The Scottish County Investment Co. Ltd.

1915 S.C. 1106

A firm of joiners contracted to perform work on four tenements which were to be erected, and undertook to complete the work by April 15, 1910.

The building owner, to the joiners' knowledge, entered into similar contracts with other tradesmen.

The building owner, however, neglected to have the plasterer sign his contract, with the result that the plasterer was not bound to complete his work within any specified time.

Owing to delay in the execution of the plaster work, it became impossible for the joiners to complete their work within the stipulated time, but they completed it with all reasonable dispatch after it became possible for them to proceed.

The building owner resisted payment to the joiners on the ground that the joiners, having failed to complete the work within the stipulated time, were in breach of their contract.

Held that the joiners were absolved from the obligation of the time limit, and decree for payment *granted*, on the ground that the impossibility of performance was caused by the act or omission of the building owner because of his failure to fix a time limit for the completion of the plasterer's contract.

LORD SALVESEN (at p. 1117): "There is admittedly in such a contract as that with which we are here dealing an implied term to the effect, as the Sheriff-substitute has expressed it, 'that where the failure of the contractor to complete the work by a specified date has been brought about by the act of the employer, he is exonerated from the performance of the contract by that date.' I would extend this statement of the law by including omission of the employer as well as his acts. Thus if the employer through some omission on his part does not give possession of the subjects within a reasonable period after the execution of the contract, the contractor is not bound by the original time limit fixed; nor is the contract time necessarily only extended by the period during which the employer's omission has continued. Again, if, as here, the employer through his agent has informed the contractor that one of the tradesmen on whom the performance of his contract is necessarily dependent has been taken bound to complete his work by a stipulated date, and he has in fact not been so bound and delay in consequence takes place, it appears to me to follow that the time limit is discharged and a reasonable time substituted. Now that is exactly what happened in the present case. The plasterer Mr McKinlay did not undertake to finish his part of the work by any given date; although in the contract which it was intended that he should sign, but which he in fact never signed, a time limit [30th March] was inserted ... McKinlay ... only finished the first of the four tenements by the 25th of March, the second on the 1st of April, the third on the 9th of April, and the fourth on the 25th. It became therefore impossible for the pursuers to have their work finished by the contract date. ... The chief cause of the delay in the completion of the building was due to the failure of the building owner to tie the plasterer down by a time limit. It is reasonable to suppose that if he had been so tied he would have conformed to his contract; and it is certain that but for the slow progress of his work the pursuers would have had a reasonable prospect of implementing their contract. Whatever else may be implied in a contract such as the one now under consideration I think there is at least an implied condition that the other contractors on the job shall be taken bound to finish their part of the work in sufficient time to make it possible for the last contractor to carry out his part. ... The usual method of avoiding such difficulties is to have one contract for the whole building; in which case the contractor is not exonerated by the failure or delay of the sub-contractors whom he may select to execute the several parts."

LORD GUTHRIE (at p. 1118): "The pursuers were informed of the contracts entered into with the other contractors for the tenements, each of which contained a time limit, although in the case of the plasterer the defenders neglected to have the contract signed. ...

"... [The pursuers] contracted with the defenders on the footing of the contracts with the mason, plasterer, and plumber, which they were informed had been entered into. But it now turns out that, through the defenders' negligence, the alleged contract with the plasterer was never executed, and it is proved that some at least of the pursuers' delay beyond the contract period was due to the plasterers exceeding the time to which, when the joint scheme was framed, it was intended by the defenders that they should be limited. In this view, even if the defenders' construction of the pursuers' obligation as unconditional, independent, and absolute were well founded, they would be barred from enforcing the pursuers' contractual time limit, because the pursuers would then be able to claim the benefit of the second case in which the pursuers, in the defenders' view, might be excused, namely, the fault of the employer."

NOTES

1. Lord Dundas reached the same conclusion, on the ground that it was a condition precedent of the contract that the pursuers should obtain timeous access to the subjects on which the work was to be performed, and that, if this was withheld from them by any cause, they were proportionally freed from the operation of the time limit. Lord Guthrie agreed to this ground as well as to the ground of impossibility caused by act or omission of the building owner.

2. In *John Milligan & Co. Ltd.* v. *Ayr Harbour Trustees*, 1915 S.C. 937, the question was left open whether persons on whom a duty is laid by a private Act of Parliament can plead impossibility of performance of that duty as relieving them of liability for non-performance.

Supervening illegality: legislation rendering contract less advantageous

McMaster & Co. v. Cox, McEuen & Co.

1921 S.C.(H.L.) 24

At the beginning of November 1917 McM. & Co., jute manufacturers in Dundee, agreed to supply jute goods to C. & Co., jute merchants there, in January and February 1918.

On November 23, 1917, the Jute (Export) Order was issued, prohibiting the manufacture and delivery of jute goods for export without a permit.

C. & Co. applied for but were refused a permit for the manufacture of the goods for export, and thereupon cancelled their contracts with McM. & Co.

McM. & Co. sued for £520 16s. 8d. as damages for breach of contract.

Held that, as the contracts contained no conditions relating to the markets in which the goods were to be disposed of by the purchasers, the fact that the Order prevented the purchasers from exporting the goods did not affect their obligation to accept the goods and pay the price; and that accordingly they were liable in damages for breach of contract.

LORD CHANCELLOR (BIRKENHEAD) (at p. 27): "This was a sale without any condition by a seller to a purchaser, and ... , on the terms of this agreement, the pursuers were entitled to treat themselves as completely disinterested in all questions affecting the purchaser alone, such as a consideration of the markets which might be open to that purchaser at the moment when he disposed of that which he bought."

VISCOUNT FINLAY (at p. 27): "The Jute Order concerned the purchasers. It may be that it rendered their contract a much less advantageous one for them than it otherwise would be, but it could not exonerate them from the performance of the contract as between themselves and the pursuers. As Lord Dundas said (1920 S.C. 566 at p. 578): 'For the rest, there were, in my judgment, simply agreements to sell goods at a stipulated price.' ... It appears to me quite impossible to find in the documents or in the surrounding circumstances any sufficient foundation for making it a term of the contract that liberty of export should exist at the time it was to be performed."

LORD DUNEDIN (at p. 28): "The whole doctrine of frustration of contracts goes to this, that there is something which a *vis major* (using that expression in the widest sense) has prevented the party from doing in the fulfilment of his contract. Now the duties of the respondents under this contract were only two, namely, to accept the goods and to pay the price; and nothing that the Government did with respect to preventing goods going abroad, or imposing conditions on their going abroad, interfered with either of those duties."

LORD ATKINSON (at p. 29): "It is quite clear to my mind that no contract was entered into between the parties here to sell these goods for export. The purchaser had a perfect right when he got them to export them, but that was a right which sprang from his ownership of them and not from any stipulation in the contract."

LORD SHAW OF DUNFERMLINE (at p. 30): "If the supervenient legislation declares the annulment, or forbids the execution of, contracts as between the parties, then, of course, these contracts fall; otherwise the presumption is all to enable the commercial business of the country to proceed without interruption."

NOTE

An instance of supervening legislation which made a contract impossible was *George Packman & Sons* v. *Dunbar's Trustees*, 1977 S.L.T. 140 (O.H.).

In 1964 D. agreed to sell land to builders, who undertook to pay a grassum of £340 per acre and that a feu-duty would be imposed in subsequent sales by them at £20 per acre. An advance of £3,000 towards the grassum was immediately paid, but no further steps were taken to implement the missives.

In 1973 the sellers wished to regard the agreement as void and returned the grassum with interest. The following year the Land Tenure Reform (Scotland) Act 1974 was passed, prohibiting the creation of new feu-duties. The builders raised an action for declarator that the missives were valid and subsisting.

Action *dismissed*.

Frustration

James B. Fraser & Co. Ltd. v. Denny, Mott & Dickson Ltd.

1944 S.C.(H.L.) 35; 1943 S.C. 293

F. Ltd. entered into an agreement with D. Ltd., under which F. Ltd. was to purchase all its requirements of red and white pine wood from D. Ltd., and F. Ltd.'s timber yard at Grangemouth was to be occupied by D. Ltd.

The agreement provided that it might be terminated by either party's giving notice of termination, and that D. Ltd. should in the event of such termination have an option to purchase the yard.

War-time regulations made it impossible and unlawful for D. Ltd. to supply F. Ltd. with the specified wood.

D. Ltd. purported to terminate the agreement by giving notice, and intimated its intention to exercise the option of purchase.

Held that the option had lapsed, since the agreement had been terminated by the impossibility of trading, and that the option was exercisable only if it was by notice that the agreement had been terminated.

LORD CHANCELLOR (VISCOUNT SIMON) (at p. 39) [After expressing approval of the course of reasoning of Lord Wark in the Court of Session]:

"The option of purchase conferred by clause 8 on the appellants only arises 'in the event of the foregoing trading agreement being terminated by either party as aforesaid' (*i.e.*, by notice under clause 5). If, therefore, the agreement had already been terminated by intervening events such as the war regulations ... , and its further performance had been frustrated by supervening illegality, the basis upon which the option might have been exercised by the appellants had ceased to exist."

LORD MACMILLAN (at p. 40): "The principle of contract law which has come to be known as the doctrine of frustration, and which has recently in England been accorded statutory recognition, is common to the jurisprudence alike of Scotland and of England, although the leading cases are to be found in the English law reports. It is a principle so inherently just as inevitably to find a place in any civilised system of law. The manner in which it has developed in order to meet the problems arising from the disturbances of business due to world wars is a tribute to the progressive adaptability of the common law. In the works of the Scottish institutional writers, the matter receives only rudimentary treatment. In Bell's *Principles of the Law of Scotland*, it is not until after the death of the original author that, in the editions which we owe to Sheriff Guthrie, the doctrine begins to assume its modern shape, and is well stated as follows: 'When by the nature of the contract its performance depends on the existence of a particular thing or state of things, the failure or destruction of that thing or state of things, without default on either side, liberates both parties' (10th ed., section 29). The earlier cases, both in England and in Scotland, are mostly concerned with the consequences of the perishing of the thing on whose continued existence the contract depended for its fulfilment, but many of the recent cases have arisen from the supervention of emergency legislation rendering the implement of the contract illegal. It is plain that a contract to do what it has become illegal to do cannot be legally enforceable. There cannot be default in not doing what the law forbids to be done.

"The present case belongs to the latter category. It seems to me a very clear one for the application of the principle I have just enunciated. Here is an agreement between two parties for carrying on dealings in imported timber. By emergency legislation the importation of timber has been rendered illegal. Neither party can be said to be in default. The further fulfilment of their mutual obligations has been brought to an abrupt stop by an irresistible extraneous cause for which neither party is responsible. ... The right to require ... a sale ... is conferred upon the appellants only as a consequence of one or other of the parties having voluntarily taken advantage of the right to terminate the agreement on notice. The operation of the agreement having been compulsorily terminated, neither party can thereafter terminate it voluntarily. You cannot slay the slain.

"I would only add that, in judging whether a contract has been frustrated, the contract must be looked at as a whole. The question is whether its purpose as gathered from its terms has been defeated. A contract whose purpose has been defeated may contain subsidiary stipulations which it would still be possible and lawful to fulfil, but to segregate and enforce such a stipulation would be to do something which the parties never intended. It cannot be suggested with any reason in the present case that the respondents would have conferred on the appellants an option to purchase or take on lease the respondents' timber yard independently of the trading arrangements into which they had agreed to enter. The consideration for the option was the fulfilment of those arrangements and there was no severable consideration. The House is not concerned in this appeal with any question as to the reliefs consequent on frustration as to which the law of Scotland may differ from the law of England."

LORD WRIGHT (at p. 42): "The rule [as to frustration of a contract] has sometimes been described as an exception to the general principle that parties must perform their obligations or pay damages for breach of contract. I should prefer to describe it as a substantive and particular rule which the common law has evolved. Where it applies there is no breach of contract. What happens is that the contract is held on its true construction not to apply at all from the time when the frustrating circumstances supervene. From that moment there is no longer any obligation as to future performance, though up to that moment obligations which have accrued remain in force. . . .

"It is now, I think, well settled that, where there is frustration, a dissolution of a contract occurs automatically. It does not depend, as does rescission of a contract on the ground of repudiation or breach, on the choice or election of either party. It depends on what actually has happened and its effect on the possibility of performing the contract. Where, as generally happens, and actually happened in the present case, one party claims that there has been frustration and the other party contests it, the Court decides the issue and decides it *ex post facto* on the actual circumstances of the case. . . . It is the Court which has to decide what is the true position between the parties. . . . The Court has formulated the doctrine by virtue of its inherent jurisdiction, just as it has developed the rules of liability for negligence, or for the restitution or repayment of money where otherwise there would be unjust enrichment. I find the theory of the basis of the rule in Lord Sumner's pregnant statement (*Hirji Mulji* v. *Cheong Yue Steamship Co. Ltd.* [1926] A.C. 497 at p. 510) that the doctrine of frustration is really a device by which the rules as to absolute contracts are reconciled with the special exceptions which justice demands. Though it has been constantly said by high authority, including Lord Sumner, that the explanation of the rule is to be found in the theory that it depends on an implied condition of the contract, that is really no explanation. It only pushes back the problem a single stage. It leaves the question what is the reason for implying a term. Nor can I reconcile that theory with the view that the result does not depend on what the parties might, or would as hard bargainers, have agreed. The doctrine is invented by the Court in order to supplement the defects of the actual contract. The parties did not anticipate fully and completely, if at all, or provide for what actually happened. It is not possible, to my mind, to say that, if they had thought of it, they would have said: 'Well, if that happens, all is over between us.' On the contrary, they would almost certainly on the one side or the other have sought to introduce reservations or qualifications or compensations. As to that, the Court cannot guess. What it can say is that the contract either binds or does not bind. ... To my mind, the theory of the implied condition is not really consistent with the true theory of frustration. It has never been acted on by the Court as a ground of decision, but is merely stated as a theoretical explanation. ... I must admit that the view I have stated is somewhat heretical, but the general nature of the doctrine of frustration has given rise to many irreconcilable explanations."

LORD JUSTICE CLERK (COOPER) (at 1943 S.C. p. 312): "The consequence of frustration must be termination of an agreement unless the parties have plainly evinced their intention that, on the occurrence of the event which destroys the foundation of the contract, some other consequence than frustration is then to ensue. They have not done so in this case."

The Lord Justice-Clerk treated the case as one of "frustration by delay."

(At p. 314): "The established effect of the operation of frustration is to terminate the contract automatically as regards future performance, leaving it alive only for the purpose of vindicating rights already accrued, and to do so without regard to the individuals concerned or to their supposed interests, intentions or opinions (*Hirji Mulji* v. *Cheong Yue Steamship*

Co.). There is, in my view, no room in this or any similar case for the enquiry suggested by the Lord Ordinary into what the parties would have agreed if they had expressly contemplated a frustration of the trading agreement. The law supplies the only answer—(the *Fibrosa* case ([1943] A.C. 32), *per* Lord Wright at p. 70). . . .

". . . The enquiry is directed, not to each of the detailed stipulations of a contract, but to its 'main basis' or 'foundation' or 'substratum' or 'commercial or practical purpose.' Moreover, it is tacitly assumed in most of these pronouncements that a commercial contract has only one such 'main basis' or 'foundation.'

". . . I have already given my reasons for regarding the present contract as having one foundation or substratum and not two, and for thinking that that single foundation or substratum has vanished."

LORD WARK (at 1943 S.C. p. 328): "If I am right in thinking that the object and basis of the contract was continuous trading, that basis has disappeared three years ago, and no one can prophesy when it will revive. If, therefore, the principle of the doctrine of frustration be that the parties contemplated a certain state of things which fell out otherwise, and that the foundation of the contract is therefore gone . . . , or that there has eventuated an interruption of the contract which has been or may be so great and long as to make it unreasonable to require the parties to go on . . . , I am of opinion that the circumstances here are such as to make the doctrine of frustration apply."

LORD JAMIESON (*diss.*) (at 1943 S.C. p. 337): "Where frustration of the purpose of a contract occurs, the law implies a term such as the contracting parties as reasonable men would have inserted bringing it to an end, if they had had the event in contemplation."

Supervening illegality: recovery of payments: condictio causa data causa non secuta

The Cantiere San Rocco S.A. v. The Clyde Shipbuilding and Engineering Co. Ltd.

1923 S.C.(H.L.) 105

In May 1914 an Austrian company entered into a contract with a Scottish company whereby the Scottish company was to build and supply to the Austrian company a set of marine engines. The price of £11,550 was to be paid by stated instalments, the first instalment being £2,310 paid on the signing of the contract in May 1914.

Some preliminary work was done, but the contract became impossible of fulfilment on the outbreak of war between Austria and Britain in August 1914.

After the war an action was brought for repetition of the instalment paid.

Held that as failure to deliver the engines was due to a cause for which neither of the parties was responsible, the Scottish company was bound to make restitution of the instalment on the principle of the *condictio causa data causa non secuta*.

Earl of Birkenhead (at p. 108): "The action was brought for a decree that a contract between the parties, dated 4th May, 1914, had been abrogated by the outbreak of war, and that the appellants were entitled to repayment of a sum of £2,310 paid by them to the respondents under the terms of that contract. On 7th July, 1921, Lord Hunter found in favour of the appellants, but on appeal the Lords of the First Division recalled the interlocutor and assoilzied the respondents from the conclusions of the action. ...

"Authorities have been cited in support of the proposition that, according to the law of England, the sum of £2,310 so paid is not recoverable; and it has been argued that the law of England is the same as the law of Scotland in that respect. I do not propose to refer to those authorities. The question is as to the law of Scotland. ...

"In my opinion the appellants are entitled to succeed. The payment was made in consideration of the supply of the set of engines contracted for. These engines were never made, and consequently never supplied, and the contract has been put an end to without the fault of either party. The result is that the appellant Company has got nothing in return for the payment of this money. ...

"In order to formulate the rule applicable to this case it is necessary to consider first the Roman law as a source of Scottish law, and secondly, the Scottish authorities, which show how far the Roman law applicable to this topic has been received and applied in the law of Scotland.

"First, as to the Roman law. This is treated in the Digest and other authoritative texts in connexion with the procedure known as *Condictio*. This process was available to recover money or things which had been parted with by the owner, at such a time as he became entitled to reclaim them.

... The underlying principle of the *Condictio* was that a person had received from another some property, and that, by reason of circumstances existing at the time or arising afterwards, it was or became contrary to honesty and fair dealing for the recipient to retain it. The particular case which is in point is the *Condictio causa data causa non secuta*. ... An exact translation is not easy. ... It is, however, sufficient for my present purposes to translate the expression by the words 'Action to recover something given for a consideration which has failed.' ... The *Condictio causa data* was competent where a person, who had given something for a future lawful purpose which had not been realised, sought to recover from the recipient what the latter had received. ...

"The rule may, I think, be fairly stated thus: A person who had given to another any money or other property for a purpose which had failed could recover what he had given, except where there had been no fault on the recipient's part, and he had not been enriched thereby. If the recipient had been enriched, then he would, if the purpose failed and he retained the property, be acting unjustly, and, consequently, he was under an obligation to return it. ... Such being the Roman law as embodied in the *Corpus Juris Civilis*, it now becomes necessary to examine the application of the rule in Scotland."

The Earl of Birkenhead then referred to passages in Stair, Bankton, Erskine and Bell, and continued: "I do not find it necessary to discuss the earlier cases which have been cited in argument, for in *Watson* v. *Shankland* ((1871) 10 M. 142), Lord President Inglis delivered a celebrated judgment which has since been regarded as an authoritative statement of the law. He said (at p. 152):—'The general principles of law applicable to the contract of affreightment are not essentially different from those applicable to other similar contracts, such as contracts of land carriage, or building contracts, or any others, in which one party agrees to pay a certain price as the return for materials furnished or work done, or services rendered by the other party. No doubt maritime contracts are *juris gentium*.,' and he then deals with special meanings placed upon words and phrases by mercantile custom; and continues:—'There is no rule of the civil law, as adopted into all modern municipal codes and systems, better understood than this—that if money is advanced by one party to a mutual contract, on the condition and stipulation that something shall be afterwards paid or performed by the other party, and the latter party fails in performing his part of the contract, the former is entitled to repayment of his advance, on the ground of failure of consideration. In the Roman system the demand for repayment took the form of a *condictio causa data causa non secuta* or a *condictio sine causa*, or a *condictio indebiti*, according to the particular circumstances. In our own practice these remedies are represented by the action of restitution and the action of repetition. And in all systems of jurisprudence there must be similar remedies, for the rule which they are intended to enforce is of universal application in mutual contracts. ... ' The judgment in that case was affirmed with variations (see (1873) 11 M.(H.L.) 51 ...). ...

"So far as I am able to form an opinion, neither the Roman law nor, before the recent war, the Scottish law had considered expressly how far the principles which I have examined apply to a contract which has been abrogated by the outbreak of war. In the present instance neither party was in fault, nor was there any object in existence in which the property could pass. The contract was not abrogated *ab initio*, and consequently there can be no question of restitution *in integrum*. The only alternatives are either that the parties are left in the position in which they were at the outbreak of war, or that the party who paid and has received no benefit is entitled to some measure of relief. The remedy now sought is not an action on the contract, but is independent of such an action. On principle I cannot see any reason for holding that the outbreak of war leads to any result different from that which follows ... from any other act or event beyond the control of the parties. ... There has been in fact a *causa non secuta*. ... To apply the general rule to the circumstances of this case is in my opinion in accordance with the true principles of Scots law, for any other result would leave the respondents with money paid to them for a purpose which has failed."

VISCOUNT FINLAY (at p. 115): "In my opinion, the result of the authorities is that the doctrine of English law on this subject as expounded in the judgments of the Court of Appeal in England is at variance with the law of Scotland. ... I cannot find that the English doctrine has ever been incorporated with the law of Scotland. It would be unfortunate that in matters of this kind, which may, as here, affect foreigners, the results should be different in the two parts of Great Britain. But we must apply the law of Scotland in a Scottish case, and, in my opinion, the conclusion arrived at by the Lord Ordinary and by Lord Mackenzie was in conformity with the law of Scotland."

LORD SHAW OF DUNFERMLINE, after referring to Roman law and to Stair, Bankton, Erskine and Bell, stated (at p. 120): "The law of Scotland may be said for over half a century to have stood expounded with un-questioned authority by Lord President Inglis in *Watson & Co.* v. *Shankland.* ...

"It is true that since that judgment was pronounced a good deal has hap-pened in England to make or to widen the breach between the English practice and that of Scotland and other nations. The particular instance of divergence in regard to this principle was as to advance of freight, on which subject the Lord President referred to the practice of 'all the nations of the trading world with the exception of England.' The divergence of law may be said to have culminated in what are known as the Coronation cases."

LORD DUNEDIN (at p. 123): "Lord Shaw has traced with great precision and accuracy ... the origin of the doctrine in the Roman law to which the appellants appeal. After all, however, the Roman law, though interesting, is only of service as showing the foundation on which the Scots law rests. The real question must always be what is the law of Scotland. ...

"... And that brings me to the very short point on which, in my view, the whole case turns. Was the £2,310 paid in respect of the signing of the contract? If it were, then it cannot be said that there was a *causa non sec-uta.* In other words, if the £2,310 had been conditioned to be paid *for* sign-ing the contract, my opinion would have been different. But it is not so. It is to be paid *on* signing the contract. It had, indeed, no separate existence. It is only an instalment of the total price, which is the consideration for the total engine. There is no splitting of the consideration."

NOTES

1. English law was altered by the Law Reform (Frustrated Contracts) Act 1943.

2. The Coronation cases founded on by the respondents were *Krell* v. *Henry* [1903] 2 K.B. 740 and *Chandler* v. *Webster* [1904] 1 K.B. 493.

Irritancies: conventional irritancy: not purgeable after action has been brought

McDouall's Trustees v. MacLeod

1949 S.C. 593

MacL. was the tenant of a farm under a lease which provided that in the event of the tenant's allowing one term's rent to remain unpaid for three months the proprietor was to be entitled to put an end to the lease and resume possession of the farm.

MacL. did not pay the rent due at Whitsunday 1948 within the following three months, and McD.'s trustees, who were then proprietors, brought an action on October 22, 1948, for declarator that MacL. had incurred an irritancy of the lease and for an order ordaining him to remove.

MacL. paid the arrears of rent on November 9 and then lodged defences to the action, contending that the irritancy had been purged by that payment.

Held that payment after the action had been brought did not purge the irritancy, and that the proprietors were entitled to decree.

Semble that a different decision might be given in a case where the landlord had made a misuse or an oppressive use of his powers under the lease, or where the stipulation in the lease was merely an echo of the common or statutory law.

LORD JUSTICE-CLERK (THOMSON) (at p. 598): "I could understand an argument that, if all that the lease did was in substance to incorporate into its provisions the irritancies which the law itself implies, then it should be assumed that the parties meant no more than to draw attention to the legal irritancy. It is on that basis that some of the authorities save the case of a conventional irritancy which is no more than a copy of a legal irritancy and indicate that, where the conventional irritancy is only a copy, its inclusion in the lease adds nothing to its force. However, it was not argued that this stipulation fell within this doctrine and I need say no more about it. . . .

". . . The argument for the defender amounts simply to this that, however expressed, a stipulation in a lease seeking to irritate the lease on the ground of non-payment of rent is merely an added compulsitor and therefore can always be purged before extract.

". . . I can see no ground on principle for holding that this argument is sound. I turn now to the authorities. The earlier ones have to be used with caution. There appears to have been a tendency to protect tenants who had found themselves in difficulties, a tendency understandable in a period when political conditions were unstable and when agriculture was still so primitive that periods of depression and scarcity were frequent. That tendency still operates in our law. It is open to a tenant to invoke the equitable jurisdiction of the Court and to plead that there has been a misuse or an oppressive use of the powers conferred on the landlord by the contract.

This aspect has no direct bearing on the present case, as the defender did not appeal to the Court's equitable jurisdiction but put his case purely on the question of law. . . .

". . . While the authorities indicate a tendency on the Court's part not to give, in all cases, full effect to conventional irritancies proceeding on non-payment of rent, they do not go the length of saying that such a stipulation is only an additional remedy and always purgeable. All that the authorities show is that for varying reasons the Courts have from time to time refused to give full effect to such a stipulation. . . .

". . . *Stewart* v. *Watson* ((1864) 2 M. 1414) states the law in its modern accepted form and is conclusive of the present case. . . . It establishes that, if the true construction of the lease shows that the parties intended to provide for irritance of the lease on non-payment of rent,—provided it be not a mere expression of a legal irritancy—the irritancy is not purgeable. Finally it reserves the right of the Court to interfere to prevent oppressive use or abuse of irritancies. . . .

"Accordingly, in my view, on a sound construction of this lease, it appears that the parties stipulated that non-payment of rent, in the circumstances set out, should operate not merely as an additional compulsitor but as an irritancy of the lease. I can find no ground for thinking that under our modern law the Court is entitled to refuse to give effect to such a stipulation, at any rate in the absence of any averments of oppressive use or abuse."

LORD MACKAY gave an extensive review of the authorities. He regarded *Stewart's* case as having firmly settled the law.

LORD JAMIESON (at p. 617): "The result of [the cases] is, I think, that while at one time the Court showed a tendency to allow conventional irritancies to be purgeable on equitable grounds in cases of hardship, a consideration which clearly does not arise in this case, effect will now be given to the terms of the contract agreed on by the parties and a conventional irritancy cannot be purged by payment, although in exceptional circumstances the Court might exercise an equitable jurisdiction and allow purgation."

NOTES

1. This case was followed in *Dorchester Studios (Glasgow) Ltd.* v. *Stone*, below.

2. The common law as to conventional irritancy clauses in certain

leases was modified by the Law Reform (Miscellaneous Provisions) (Scotland) Act 1985, ss. 4–6 (see Appendix A).

Irritancies: conventional irritancy: averments of oppression

Dorchester Studios (Glasgow) Ltd. v. Stone

1975 S.C.(H.L.) 56

Samuel and Jack Stone were tenants of a ground-floor shop in Glasgow under a sub-lease which included a clause of irritancy applicable in several events, one of which was the event of the sub-tenants allowing any part of the rent to remain unpaid for 21 days.

The principal tenants, D. Ltd., raised an action for declarator that the sub-tenants had incurred an irritancy in respect of the rent due at Martinmas 1972.

The sub-tenants pleaded that the irritancy had been purged by tender of payment on December 13, 1972, and that the purported exercise by D. Ltd. of the right to irritate the lease was oppressive.

Held that a conventional irritancy could not be purged and that the averments of oppression were irrelevant.

LORD KILBRANDON (at p. 66): "Whatever may be said of the policy, looked at from the standpoint of modern conditions, which seems to underlie the law of Scotland relating to purging an irritancy incurred from non-payment of rent, it is not possible to say that that law is now or has been for many years, in doubt. ... The law was firmly laid down, after some uncertainties, in *Stewart* v. *Watson* (1864) 2 M. 1414, to the effect that (*a*) such a provision in a lease is a conventional irritancy and not the mere expression of a legal irritancy which might have been purged before decree, (*b*) as such it is not purgeable, (*c*) it is a reasonable and lawful stipulation, (*d*) it is not to be compared with a stipulation in a feu contract, by which a right of property is conferred in a sense in which it is not conferred under a lease. Nearly a century later that decision was confirmed in the case of *McDouall's Trustees* v. *MacLeod*. ... As counsel for the appellants conceded, the appeal must fail if *McDouall's Trustees* was rightly decided. ... In my opinion it was. ...

"The cases make it plain that the law of Scotland in this matter stands on a different footing from that concerned with the relief from a forfeiture for non-payment of rent forming a condition in an English lease. ...

"... The distinction between the feu contract and the lease has become unsubstantial since the former took to its death-bed. Moreover, the old view that the lease, unlike the feu contract, does not convey a right of property, wears today an air of unreality. Statutes governing successively dwelling-houses, agricultural subjects and business premises, have gone far to confer on tenants interests more easily classified as proprietorial than ephemeral. And the long investment-lease has in recent years become a feature in Scottish cities. All these considerations point, in my opinion, to the need for the Scottish doctrine to be re-examined from the policy point of view, and for my part, I would recommend this service to the Scottish Law Commission. But I have no doubt as to what the law now is."

LORD FRASER OF TULLYBELTON (at p. 72): "In my opinion it is hopeless to suggest that the decision in *McDouall's Trustees* was not soundly based on authority, particularly having regard to *Stewart* v. *Watson* which has stood since 1864. ... The argument for the appellants was that there was something unfair or harsh in holding that a tenant who was late (perhaps only one day late) with his rent had forfeited his lease which might be of great value. Speaking for myself, I am not impressed by that argument. In the first place, if the tenant has agreed to a lease containing an irritancy I do not think it is in principle unfair to hold him to his bargain. In the second place, leases which are of great value are likely to be leases of commercial, rather than of residential, property and tenants of commercial property should be able to manage their affairs so as to avoid accidental late payment of rent. In the third place, if the late payment is not accidental, but is either deliberate or due to impecuniosity, I see nothing unreasonable in the landlord's relying on an irritancy to get rid of an unsatisfactory tenant. Finally, of course, the court always has the power to give relief to a tenant against oppressive use of the irritancy.

"... English authority on this matter is ... not relevant in Scotland.

"Mr Caplan [counsel for the appellants] referred to the change brought about by the Land Tenure Reform (Scotland) Act 1974, which prohibits the imposition of new feu duties. The result may be to discourage feuing and to increase the importance of leases, and therefore of provisions for their irritancy. It may be that for that reason the general question raised by this appeal is worthy of consideration by the Scottish Law Commission.

"Counsel submitted an alternative argument to the effect that, even if a conventional irritancy of this sort was not normally purgeable, yet in the circumstances of this case the irritancy was purgeable because it was being misused or used oppressively. ... I have no doubt that if the facts warranted such a conclusion the court would permit purgation by the tenant, but on the facts of the present case I am of opinion that the suggestion is wholly unwarranted. It was admitted by counsel for the appellants that the respondents gave them warning of the need to pay the rent on 11 November, 1972, by a demand note sent on 30 October. The appellants explain their failure to pay as being due simply to an oversight for which clearly the respondents cannot be blamed. The only suggestion of 'oppression' was that the respondents ought to have given them notice after 11 November that continued default would lead to irritancy, but, in my opinion, there was no obligation on the respondents to do so."

Opinion of the First Division (LORD PRESIDENT (EMSLIE), LORDS CAMERON AND JOHNSTON) (at p. 154): "In our opinion the sheriff and the sheriff principal were perfectly correct in holding that the irritancy with which this action is concerned is a conventional one, and that once it had been incurred it could not be purged, and the right of the pursuers to enforce it could not be diminished by the tender of payment which the pursuers were not bound to accept. Since the case of *McDouall's Trustees* v. *MacLeod* . . . at the latest, this must be regarded as settled law."

NOTE

See NOTE 2 to *McDouall's Trustees* v. *MacLeod*, p. 285, above.

STATUTORY MATERIAL

Unfair Contract Terms Act 1977

(1977 c. 50)

. . . . . .

PART II

AMENDMENT OF LAW FOR SCOTLAND

Scope of Part II

[1] **15.**—(1) This Part of this Act is subject to Part III of this Act and does not affect the validity of any discharge or indemnity given by a person in consideration of the receipt by him of compensation in settlement of any claim which he has.

(2) Subject to subsection (3) below, sections 16 to 18 of this Act apply to any contract only to the extent that the contract—

   (*a*) relates to the transfer of the ownership or possession of goods from one person to another (with or without work having been done on them);

   (*b*) constitutes a contract of service or apprenticeship;

NOTE

[1] As amended by the Law Reform (Miscellaneous Provisions) (Scotland) Act 1990, s. 68(2) and Sched. 9, in relation to liability for any loss or damage which is suffered on or after April 1, 1991 (*ibid.*, s. 68(6); S.I. 1991 No. 330).

(*c*) relates to services of whatever kind, including (without prejudice to the foregoing generality) carriage, deposit and pledge, care and custody, mandate, agency, loan and services relating to the use of land;

(*d*) relates to the liability of an occupier of land to persons entering upon or using that land;

(*e*) relates to a grant of any right or permission to enter upon or use land not amounting to an estate or interest in the land.

(3) Notwithstanding anything in subsection (2) above, sections 16 to 18—

(*a*) do not apply to any contract to the extent that the contract—

(i) is a contract of insurance (including a contract to pay an annuity on human life);

(ii) relates to the formation, constitution or dissolution of any body corporate or unincorporated association or partnership;

(*b*) apply to—

a contract of marine salvage or towage;

a charter party of a ship or hovercraft;

a contract for the carriage of goods by ship or hovercraft; or,

a contract to which subsection (4) below relates,

only to the extent that—

(i) both parties deal or hold themselves out as dealing in the course of a business (and then only in so far as the contract purports to exclude or restrict liability for breach of duty in respect of death or personal injury); or

(ii) the contract is a consumer contract (and then only in favour of the consumer).

(4) This subsection relates to a contract in pursuance of which goods are carried by ship or hovercraft and which either—

(*a*) specifies ship or hovercraft as the means of carriage over part of the journey to be covered; or

(*b*) makes no provision as to the means of carriage and does not exclude ship or hovercraft as that means.

in so far as the contract operates for and in relation to the carriage of the goods by that means.

Liability for breach of duty

[1] **16.**—(1) Subject to subsection (1A) below where a term of a contract or a provision of a notice given to persons generally or to particular persons purports to exclude or restrict liability for breach of duty arising in the course of any business or from the occupation of any premises used for business purposes of the occupier, that term or provision—

(*a*) shall be void in any case where such exclusion or restriction is in respect of death or personal injury;

(*b*) shall, in any other case, have no effect if it was not fair and reasonable to incorporate the term in the contract or, as the case may be, if it is not fair and reasonable to allow reliance on the provision.

(1A) Nothing in paragraph (*b*) of subsection (1) above shall be taken as implying that a provision of a notice has effect in circumstances where, apart from that paragraph, it would not have effect.

(2) Subsection (1)(*a*) above does not affect the validity of any discharge and indemnity given by a person, on or in connection with an award to him of compensation for pneumoconiosis attributable to employment in the coal industry, in respect of any further claim arising from his contracting that disease.

(3) Where under subsection (1) above a term of a contract or a provision of a notice is void or has no effect, the fact that a person agreed to, or was aware of, the term or provision shall not of itself be sufficient evidence that he knowingly and voluntarily assumed any risk.

Control of unreasonable exemptions in consumer or standard form contracts

17.—(1) Any term of a contract which is a consumer contract or a standard form contract shall have no effect for the purpose of enabling a party to the contract—

(*a*) who is in breach of a contractual obligation, to exclude or restrict any liability of his to the consumer or customer in respect of the breach;

(*b*) in respect of a contractual obligation, to render no performance, or to render a performance substantially different from that which the consumer or customer reasonably expected from the contract;

if it was not fair and reasonable to incorporate the term in the contract.

NOTE
[1] As amended by the Law Reform (Miscellaneous Provisions) (Scotland) Act 1990, s. 63(3)(*a*), (*b*) and (*c*), in relation to liability for any loss or damage which is suffered on or after April 1, 1991 (*ibid*., s. 68(6)).

(2) In this section "customer" means a party to a standard form contract who deals on the basis of written standard terms of business of the other party to the contract who himself deals in the course of a business.

Unreasonable indemnity clauses in consumer contracts

18.—(1) Any term of a contract which is a consumer contract shall have no effect for the purpose of making the consumer indemnify another person (whether a party to the contract or not) in respect of liability which that other person may incur as a result of breach of duty or breach of contract, if it was not fair and reasonable to incorporate the term in the contract.

(2) In this section "liability" means liability arising in the course of any business or from the occupation of any premises used for business purposes of the occupier.

Law Reform (Miscellaneous Provisions) (Scotland) Act 1985

(1985 c. 73)

Provisions relating to leases

. . . . . .

Irritancy clauses etc. relating to monetary breaches of lease

4.—(1) A landlord shall not, for the purpose of treating a lease as terminated or terminating it, be entitled to rely—

(*a*) on a provision in the lease which purports to terminate it, or to enable him to terminate it, in the event of a failure of the tenant to pay rent, or to make any other payment, on or before the due date therefor or such later date or within such period as may be provided for in the lease; or

(*b*) on the fact that such a failure is, or is deemed by a provision of the lease to be, a material breach of contract,

unless subsection (2) or (5) below applies.

(2) This subsection applies if—

(*a*) the landlord has, at any time after the payment of rent or other payment mentioned in subsection (1) above has become due, served a notice on the tenant—

(i) requiring the tenant to make payment of the sum which he has failed to pay together with any interest thereon in terms of the lease within the period specified in the notice; and

(ii) stating that, if the tenant does not comply with the requirement mentioned in sub–paragraph (i) above, the lease may be terminated; and

(*b*) the tenant has not complied with that requirement.

(3) The period to be specified in any such notice shall be not less than—

(*a*) a period of 14 days immediately following the service of the notice; or

(*b*) if any period remaining between the service of the notice and the expiry of any time provided for in the lease or otherwise for the late payment of the sum which the tenant has failed to pay is greater than 14 days, that greater period.

(4) Any notice served under subsection (2) above shall be sent by

recorded delivery and shall be sufficiently served if it is sent to the tenant's last business or residential address in the United Kingdom known to the landlord or to the last address in the United Kingdom provided to the landlord by the tenant for the purpose of such service.

(5) This subsection applies if the tenant does not have an address in the United Kingdom known to the landlord and has not provided an address in the United Kingdom to the landlord for the purpose of service.

Irritancy clauses etc. not relating to monetary breaches of leases

5.—(1) Subject to subsection (2) below, a landlord shall not, for the purpose of treating a lease as terminated or terminating it, be entitled to rely—

  (*a*) on a provision in the lease which purports to terminate it, or to enable the landlord to terminate it, in the event of an act or omission by the tenant (other than such a failure as is mentioned in section 4(1)(*a*) of this Act) or of a change in the tenant's circumstances; or

  (*b*) on the fact that such act or omission or change is, or is deemed by a provision of the lease to be, a material breach of contract,

if in all the circumstances of the case a fair and reasonable landlord would not seek so to rely.

(2) No provision of a lease shall of itself, irrespective of the particular circumstances of the case, be held to be unenforceable by virtue of subsection (1) above.

(3) In the consideration, for the purposes of subsection (1)(*a*) or (*b*) above, of the circumstances of a case where—

  (*a*) an act, omission or change is alleged to constitute a breach of a provision of the lease or a breach of contract; and

  (*b*) the breach is capable of being remedied in reasonable time, regard shall be had to whether a reasonable opportunity has been afforded to the tenant to enable the breach to be remedied.

Supplementary and transitional provisions relating to sections 4 and 5

6.—(1) The parties to a lease shall not be entitled to disapply any provision of section 4 or 5 of this Act from it.

(2) Where circumstances have occurred before the commencement of sections 4 and 5 of this Act which would have entitled a landlord to terminate a lease in reliance on a provision in the lease or on the ground that the circumstances constituted a material breach of contract, but the landlord has not before such commencement given written notice to the

tenant of his intention to terminate the lease in respect of those circumstances, he shall, after such commencement, be entitled to terminate the lease in respect of those circumstances only in accordance with the provisions of section 4 or 5 (as the case may be) of this Act.

(3) Nothing in section 4 or 5 of this Act shall apply in relation to any payment which has to be made, or any other condition which has to be fulfilled, before a tenant is entitled to entry under a lease.

Interpretation of sections 4 to 6

7.—(1) In sections 4 to 6 of this Act "lease" means a lease of land, whether entered into before or after the commencement of those sections, but does not include a lease of land—

(a) used wholly or mainly for residential purposes; or

(b) comprising an agricultural holding, a croft, the subject of a cottar or the holding of a landholder or a statutory small tenant.

[1] (2) In subsection (1) above—

"agricultural holding" has the same meaning as in the Agricultural Holdings (Scotland) Act 1991;

"cottar" has the same meaning as in section 28(4) of the Crofters (Scotland) Act 1955;

"croft" has the same meaning as in section 3 of the Crofters (Scotland) Act 1955; and

"holding" (in relation to a landholder or statutory small tenant).

"landholder" and "statutory small tenant" have the same meanings as in the Small Landholders (Scotland) Acts 1886 to 1931.

Provisions relating to other contracts and obligations

Rectification of defectively expressed documents

8.—(1) Subject to section 9 of this Act, where the court is satisfied, on an application made to it, that—

(a) a document intended to express or to give effect to an agreement fails to express accurately the common intention of the parties to the agreement at the date when it was made; or

(b) a document intended to create, transfer, vary or renounce a right, not being a document falling within paragraph (a) above, fails to

NOTE
[1] As amended by the Agricultural Holdings (Scotland) Act 1991, Sched. 11, para. 42.

> express accurately the intention of the grantor of the document at
> the date when it was executed,

it may order the document to be rectified in any manner that it may specify
in order to give effect to that intention.

(2) For the purposes of subsection (1) above, the court shall be entitled
to have regard to all relevant evidence, whether written or oral.

(3) Subject to section 9 of this Act, in ordering the rectification of a
document under subsection (1) above (in this subsection referred to as
"the original document"), the court may, at its own instance or on an
application made to it, order the rectification of any other document intended for any of the purposes mentioned in paragraph (*a*) or (*b*) of subsection (1) above which is defectively expressed by reason of the defect in
the original document.

(4) Subject to section 9(4) of this Act, a document ordered to be rectified under this section shall have effect as if it had always been so
rectified.

(5) Subject to section 9(5) of this Act, where a document recorded in
the Register of Sasines is ordered to be rectified under this section and the
order is likewise recorded, the document shall be treated as having been
always so recorded as rectified.

(6) Nothing in this section shall apply to a document of a testamentary
nature.

(7) It shall be competent to register in the Register of Inhibitions and
Adjudications a notice of an application under this section for the rectification of a deed relating to land, being an application in respect of which
authority for service or citation has been granted; and the land to which
the application relates shall be rendered litigious as from the date of registration of such a notice.

(8) A notice under subsection (7) above shall specify the names and
designations of the parties to the application and the date when authority
for service or citation was granted and contain a description of the land to
which the application relates.

(9) In this section and section 9 of this Act "the court" means the Court
of Session or the sheriff.

Provisions supplementary to section 8: protection of other interest

9.—(1) The court shall order a document to be rectified under section
8 of this Act only where it is satisfied—

(*a*) that the interests of a person to whom this section applies would not be adversely affected to a material extent by the rectification; or

(*b*) that that person has consented to the proposed rectification.

(2) Subject to subsection (3) below, this section applies to a person (other than a party to the agreement or the grantor of the document) who has acted or refrained from acting in reliance on the terms of the document or on the title sheet of an interest in land registered in the Land Register of Scotland being an interest to which the document relates, with the result that his position has been affected to a material extent.

(3) This section does not apply to a person—

(*a*) who, at the time when he acted or refrained from acting as mentioned in subsection (2) above, knew, or ought in the circumstances known to him at that time to have been aware, that the document or (as the case may be) the title sheet failed accurately to express the common intention of the parties to the agreement or, as the case may be, the intention of the grantor of the document; or

(*b*) whose reliance on the terms of the document or on the title sheet was otherwise unreasonable.

(4) Notwithstanding subsection (4) of section 8 of this Act and without prejudice to subsection (5) below, the court may, for the purpose of protecting the interests of a person to whom this section applies, order that the rectification of a document shall have effect as at such date as it may specify, being a date later than that as at which it would have effect by virtue of the said subsection (4).

(5) Notwithstanding subsection (5) of section 8 of this Act and without prejudice to subsection (4) above, the court may, for the purpose of protecting the interests of a person to whom this section applies, order that a document as rectified shall be treated as having been recorded as mentioned in the said subsection (5) at such date as it may specify, being a date later than that as at which it would be treated by virtue of that subsection as having been so recorded.

(6) For the purposes of subsection (1) above, the court may require the Keeper of the Registers of Scotland to produce such information as he has in his possession relating to any persons who have asked him to supply details with regard to a title sheet mentioned in subsection (2) above; and any expense incurred by the Keeper under this subsection shall be borne by the applicant for the order.

(7) Where a person to whom this section applies was unaware, before a document was ordered to be rectified under section 8 of this Act, that an application had been made under that section for the rectification of the

document, the Court of Session, on an application made by that person within the time specified in subsection (8) below, may—

(*a*) reduce the rectifying order; or

(*b*) order the applicant for the rectifying order to pay such compensation to that person as it thinks fit in respect of his reliance on the terms of the document or on the title sheet.

(8) The time referred to in subsection (7) above is whichever is the earlier of the following—

(*a*) the expiry of five years after the making of the rectifying order;

(*b*) the expiry of two years after the making of that order first came to the notice of the person referred to in that subsection.

Negligent misrepresentation

10.—(1) A party to a contract who has been induced to enter into it by negligent misrepresentation made by or on behalf of another party to the contract shall not be disentitled, by reason only that the misrepresentation is not fraudulent, from recovering damages from the other party in respect of any loss or damage he has suffered as a result of the misrepresentation; and any rule of law that such damages cannot be recovered unless fraud is proved shall cease to have effect.

(2) Subsection (1) applies to any proceedings commenced on or after the date on which it comes into force, whether or not the negligent misrepresentation was made before or after that date, but does not apply to any proceedings commenced before that date.

Age of Legal Capacity (Scotland) Act 1991

(1991 c. 50)

. . . . . .

Age of legal capacity

1.—(1) As from the commencement of this Act—

(*a*) a person under the age of 16 years shall, subject to section 2 below, have no legal capacity to enter into any transaction;

(*b*) a person of or over the age of 16 years shall have legal capacity to enter into any transaction.

(2) Subject to section 8 below, any reference in any enactment to a pupil (other than in the context of education or training) or to a person under legal disability or incapacity by reason of nonage shall, insofar as it relates to any time after the commencement of this Act, be construed as a reference to a person under the age of 16 years.

(3) Nothing in this Act shall—

(*a*) apply to any transaction entered into before the commencement of this Act;

(*b*) confer any legal capacity on any person who is under legal disability or incapacity other than by reason of nonage;

(*c*) affect the delictual or criminal responsibility of any person;

(*d*) affect any enactment which lays down an age limit expressed in years for any particular purpose;

(*e*) prevent any person under the age of 16 years from receiving or holding any right, title or interest;

(*f*) affect any existing rule of law or practice whereby—

(i) any civil proceedings may be brought or defended, or any step in civil proceedings may be taken, in the name of a person under the age of 16 years who has no guardian or whose guardian is unable (whether by reason of conflict of interest or otherwise) or refuses to bring or defend such proceedings or take such step;

(ii) the court may, in any civil proceedings, appoint a curator *ad litem* to a person under the age of 16 years;

(iii) the court may, in relation to the approval of an arrangement under section 1 of the Trusts (Scotland) Act 1961, appoint a curator *ad litem* to a person of or over the age of 16 years but under the age of 18 years;

(iv) the court may appoint a curator bonis to any person;

(*g*) prevent any person under the age of 16 years from—

(i) being appointed as guardian to any child of his, or

(ii) exercising parental rights in relation to any child of his.

(4) Any existing rule of law relating to the legal capacity of minors and pupils which is inconsistent with the provisions of this Act shall cease to have effect.

(5) Any existing rule of law relating to reduction of a transaction on the ground of minority and lesion shall cease to have effect.

Exceptions to general rule

2.—(1) A person under the age of 16 years shall have legal capacity to enter into a transaction—

(*a*) of a kind commonly entered into by persons of his age and circumstances, and

(*b*) on terms which are not unreasonable.

(2) A person of or over the age of 12 years shall have testamentary capacity, including legal capacity to exercise by testamentary writing any power of appointment.

(3) A person of or over the age of 12 years shall have legal capacity to consent to the making of an adoption order in relation to him.

(4) A person under the age of 16 years shall have legal capacity to consent on his own behalf to any surgical, medical or dental procedure or treatment where, in the opinion of a qualified medical practitioner attending him, he is capable of understanding the nature and possible consequences of the procedure or treatment.

(5) Any transaction—

(*a*) which a person under the age of 16 years purports to enter into after the commencement of this Act, and

(*b*) in relation to which that person does not have legal capacity by virtue of this section,

shall be void.

Setting aside of transactions

3.—(1) A person under the age of 21 years ("the applicant") may make application to the court to set aside a transaction which he entered into while he was of or over the age of 16 years but under the age of 18 years and which is a prejudicial transaction.

(2) In this section "prejudicial transaction" means a transaction which—

(*a*) an adult, exercising prudence, would not have entered into in the circumstances of the applicant at the time of entering into the transaction, and

(*b*) has caused or is likely to cause substantial prejudice to the applicant.

(3) Subsection (1) above shall not apply to—

(*a*) the exercise of testamentary capacity;

(*b*) the exercise by testamentary writing of any power of appointment;

(*c*) the giving of consent to the making of an adoption order;

(*d*) the bringing or defending of, or the taking of any step in, civil proceedings;

(*e*) the giving of consent to any surgical, medical or dental procedure or treatment;

(*f*) a transaction in the course of the applicant's trade, business or profession;

(*g*) a transaction into which any other party was induced to enter by virtue of any fraudulent misrepresentation by the applicant as to age or other material fact;

(*h*) a transaction ratified by the applicant after he attained the age of 18 years and in the knowledge that it could be the subject of an application to the court under this section to set it aside; or

(*j*) a transaction ratified by the court under section 4 below.

(4) Where an application to set aside a transaction can be made or could have been made under this section by the person referred to in subsection (1) above, such application may instead be made by that person's executor, trustee in bankruptcy, trustee acting under a trust deed for creditors or curator bonis at any time prior to the date on which that person attains or would have attained the age of 21 years.

(5) An application under this section to set aside a transaction may be made—

(*a*) by an action in the Court of Session or the sheriff court, or

(*b*) by an incidental application in other proceedings in such court,

and the court may make an order setting aside the transaction and such further order, if any, as seems appropriate to the court in order to give effect to the rights of the parties.

Ratification by court of proposed transaction

4.—(1) Where a person of or over the age of 16 years but under the age of 18 years proposes to enter into a transaction which, if completed, could be the subject of an application to the court under section 3 above to set aside, all parties to the proposed transaction may make a joint application to have it ratified by the court.

(2) The court shall not grant an application under this section if it appears to the court that an adult, exercising reasonable prudence and in the circumstances of the person referred to in subsection (1) above, would not enter into the transaction.

(3) An application under this section shall be made by means of a summary application—

(a) to the sheriff of the sheriffdom in which any of the parties to the proposed transaction resides, or

(b) where none of the said parties resides in Scotland, to the sheriff at Edinburgh,

and the decision of the sheriff on such application shall be final.

Guardians of persons under 16

5.—(1) Except insofar as otherwise provided in Schedule 1 to this Act, as from the commencement of this Act any reference in any rule of law, enactment or document to the tutor or tutory of a pupil child shall be construed as a reference to the guardian or, as the case may be, guardianship of a person under the age of 16 years; and accordingly the guardian of such a person shall have in relation to him and his estate the powers and duties which, immediately before such commencement, a tutor had in relation to his pupil.

(2) Subject to section 1(3)(f) above, as from the commencement of this Act no guardian of a person under the age of 16 years shall be appointed as such except under section 3 (orders as to parental rights) or section 4 (power of parent to appoint guardian) of the Law Reform (Parent and Child) (Scotland) Act 1986.

(3) As from the commencement of this Act, no person shall, by reason of age alone, be subject to the curatory of another person.

(4) As from the commencement of this Act, no person shall be appointed as factor *loco tutoris*.

Attainment of age

6.—(1) The time at which a person attains a particular age expressed in years shall be taken to be the beginning of the relevant anniversary of the date of his birth.

(2) Where a person has been born on 29th February in a leap year, the relevant anniversary in any year other than a leap year shall be taken to be 1st March.

(3) The provisions of this section shall apply only to a relevant anniversary which occurs after the commencement of this Act.

Acquisition of domicile

7. The time at which a person first becomes capable of having an independent domicile shall be the date at which he attains the age of 16 years.

Transitional provision

8. Where any person referred to in section 6(4)(*b*), 17(3), 18(3) or 18A (2) of the Prescription and Limitation (Scotland) Act 1973 as having been under legal disability by reason of nonage was of or over the age of 16 years but under the age of 18 years immediately before the commencement of this Act, any period prior to such commencement shall not be reckoned as, or as part of, the period of five years, or (as the case may be) three years, specified respectively in section 6, 17, 18 or 18A of that Act.

Interpretation

9. In this Act, unless the context otherwise requires—
"existing" means existing immediately before the commencement of this Act;
"parental rights" has the same meaning as in section 8 (interpretation) of the Law Reform (Parent and Child) (Scotland) Act 1986;
"transaction" means a transaction having legal effect, and includes—
(*a*) any unlitateral transaction;
(*b*) the exercise of testamentary capacity;
(*c*) the exercise of any power of appointment;
(*d*) the giving by a person of any consent having legal effect;
(*e*) the bringing or defending of, or the taking of any step in, civil proceedings;
(*f*) acting as arbiter or trustee;
(*g*) acting as an instrumentary witness.

. . . . . .

Short title, commencement and extent

11.—(1) This Act may be cited as the Age of Legal Capacity (Scotland) Act 1991.

[1] (2) This Act shall come into force at the end of the period of two months beginning with the date on which it is passed.

(3) This Act shall extend to Scotland only.

NOTE
[1] This Act received the Royal Assent on July 25, 1991.

APPENDIX B

GLOSSARY OF LATIN WORDS AND PHRASES USED IN THIS BOOK

ab ante: beforehand (p. 168).

ab initio: from the beginning (p. 282).

actio popularis: action of the people, *i.e.* an action brought by a member of the public as such (*e.g.* to assert a right of way belonging to all members of the public) (p. 216).

actio quanti minoris: literally, action of how much the less; an action in which a claim for damages is made, the damages to be measured by the extent to which performance has fallen short of the performance contracted for (pp. 114, 264).

ad factum praestandum: for the performance of an act; requiring specific performance (pp. 126, 189).

ad hunc effectum tantum: to this effect only (p. 148).

assignatus utitur jure auctoris: the assignee enjoys the right of the cedent (but no greater right) (p 203).

bona fide: good faith (Latin ablative case of *bona fides*, the ablative case being used in Latin after the preposition "*in*") (pp. 43, 227).

causa non secuta: consideration which has not followed; an absence of consideration; see *condictio causa data causa non secuta* (pp. 282, 283).

certamen de virtute: contest about merit; "contest of prowess or skill" (p. 16).

concursus debiti et crediti: concurrence of debit and credit, *i.e.* the parties must be debtor and creditor to one another at the same time and in the same capacity (p. 266)

condictio: action; form of legal process (pp. 87, 88, 280, 281).

condictio causa data: short for *condictio causa data causa non secuta* (*q.v.*) (p. 281).

condictio causa data causa non secuta: action applicable where consideration has been given (by one party) and consideration has not followed (from the other party); "action to recover something given for a consideration which has failed"; it justifies a claim, based on quasi-contract, for recovery of the consideration which has been given by the first party (pp. 279, 280, 281).

305

condictio indebiti: literally, action of a thing not due; action for the recovery of a payment which was not due; it justifies a claim, based on quasi-contract, for recovery of the amount not due (pp. 86, 87, 282).

condictio sine causa: action applicable in the absence of consideration—a form of Roman legal process, not used in Scots law, but similar to the *condictio causa data causa non secuta (q.v.)* and the *condictio indebiti (q.v.)*, which were adopted into Scots law from the same area of Roman law (p. 282).

consensus: agreement (pp. 10, 28, 55).

consensus in eundem contractum: agreement for the same contract (p. 27).

consensus in idem: agreement on the same terms; exact agreement (pp. 23, 24, 26, 27, 28, 29, 30, 32, 34, 54, 55, 63, 85, 92, 159).

consensus in idem placitum: agreement on the same intention; exact agreement as to the terms (pp. 10, 25, 91).

contra: against, to the contrary (p. 34).

contra bonos mores: contrary to good behaviour; immoral (p. 139).

contra proferentem: against the party putting (it) forward (pp. 174, 177, 178, 179, 183).

Corpus Juris Civilis: literally, body of civil law; the name given to the works of the Roman emperor Justinian on Roman private law, namely the *Institutes*, the *Digest*, the (new) *Code* and the *Novels* (later legislation), taken together (p. 281).

curator bonis: guardian for property, the term used of the guardian appointed to look after the property of an insane person (p. 71).

damnum fatale: fated loss; predestined loss; "act of God" (p. 268).

de die in diem: from day to day (p. 241).

de minimis: concerning the smallest things; concerning trifles; this refers to the principle more fully expressed as "*de minimis non curat lex*," the law does not concern itself with trifles (p. 213).

delectus personae: literally, choice of person; this is used to indicate that there is a reason for choosing a particular person, with the result that the substitution of a different person is not permissible (pp. 201, 202).

dicta: statements (plural of "*dictum*") (pp. 54, 66, 127).

dictum: statement (p. 128).

ejusdem generis: of the same kind (pp. 168, 169, 170, 171).

electio est debitoris: the choice belongs to the debtor; it is for the debtor to choose (p. 171).

error calculi: an error in calculation; an arithmetical error (p. 75).

essentialia: essentials (p. 59).

est jus quaesitum tertio: there is a right acquired by a third party (*i.e.* by a person who is not one of the two contracting parties) (p. 197).

ex contractu: out of contract (pp. 67, 253).

ex debito justitiae: as a matter of right (p. 269).

ex delicto: out of delict (pp. 67, 254).

ex facie: literally, on the face; as an express term (pp. 34, 102).

ex gratia: gratuitous; voluntary; made without consideration (p. 5).

ex hypothesi: literally, as a result of the hypothesis; according to the supposition which has been made (pp. 36, 57, 94, 260).

ex post facto: after the event has occurred (p. 277).

genus: kind; category (pp. 168, 170).

hinc inde: on the one side and on the other side (pp. 7, 256).

ibid.: abbreviation for "*ibidem*"—at the same place (pp. 55, 61, 101).

ignorantia iuris haud excusat: ignorance of the law does not excuse; ignorance of the law is no excuse (p. 88).

in bona fide: in good faith (pp. 123, 227).

in dubio: literally, in a doubtful thing; in the case of doubt; on a doubtful point; in the event of an ambiguity (pp. 173, 178).

in essentialibus: in the essentials (pp. 78, 79, 89).

in idem: in agreement; at one (p. 34).

in idem placitum: on the same intention (p. 10).

in idem placitum concursus et conventio: literally, a concurrence and a coming together on the same intention; a complete agreement (p. 41).

in integrum: to the original position (pp. 111, 282).

in intuitu: in contemplation (p. 164).

in mala fide: in bad faith (p. 227).

in modum probationis: by way of proof (p. 66).

in nudis finibus: literally, within bare boundaries; without consideration of outside matters (p. 51).

in quantum lucratus est: for the amount by which he has been enriched (p. 262).

in re mercatoria: on a commercial matter (pp. 63, 64, 65).

in solidum: for the whole; for the full amount (contrast with *pro rata*) (pp. 187, 188).

in statu quo ante: in the (same) position as before (p. 113).

in suo: on one's own property (p. 230).

in terminis: according to its terms; strictly (p. 248).

in terrorem: as a threat (pp. 244, 245, 246).

in toto: in full; completely; in every respect (pp. 131, 152).

in turpi causa melior est conditio possidentis: in an immoral situation, it is the possessor who is in the better position (p. 134).

incapax: incapable; lacking legal capacity (p. 125).

inter alia: amongst other things (p. 164).

inter vivos: between living persons; an *inter vivos* deed is contrasted with a testamentary deed (such as a will), the latter being one which operates on death (p. 128).

interitus rei: destruction of the subject-matter (p. 270).

juris gentium: literally, of the law of nations; part of the law common to all peoples ("*juris*" is the genitive case of "*jus*") (p. 281).

jus: right (p. 197).

jus quaesitum: right acquired; vested right (pp. 2, 194, 198, 199).

jus quaesitum tertio: right acquired by a third party, *i.e.* by a person who is not one of the two contracting parties (pp. 5, 189, 191, 192, 193, 195, 196, 197, 200).

jus tertii: literally, right of a third party, *i.e.* of someone other than the person who is claiming it; the phrase implies a negative—if it is said of a person, X, that a right is "*jus tertii*," this means that X is not entitled to the right, because it is a right which arises out of a contract between A and B, with the result that A or B is entitled to the right (p. 189).

jus tertio: abbreviation for "*jus quaesitum tertio*" (*q.v.*) (p. 199).

locatio operis: literally, hiring of work; contract for work (p. 23).

locus: place (p. 165).

locus poenitentiae: literally, room for repentance; freedom to withdraw; opportunity for change of mind (pp. 36, 51, 52, 53, 54, 60, 61, 62, 66).

lucratus: enriched (p. 206).

melior est conditio defendentis: literally, the position of the defender is better; it is the defender who is in the better position, *i.e.* the decision will be in favour of the defender (p. 138).

melior est conditio possidentis: literally, the position of the possessor is better; it is the possessor who is in the better position; the possessor's right will be given preference (p. 14).

modo et forma: literally, according to the method and the form; in the exact way agreed on; exactly (pp. 206, 207, 259, 262).

nudum pactum: literally, bare agreement; agreement without consideration (p. 20).

obiter: by the way; not essential for the decision of the case; not forming part of the *ratio decidendi* of the case (pp. 20, 87).

obiter dicta: things said by the way (plural of "*obiter dictum*" (*q.v.*) (p. 87).

obiter dictum: thing said by the way; remark not essential for the decision of the case; statement which is not part of the *ratio decidendi* (p. 114).

obligationes literis: contracts requiring writing for their constitution (pp. 21, 51, 52, 54, 58, 60, 67).

ope exceptionis: by way of defence (p. 248).

pacta illicita: illegal agreements (plural of "*pactum illicitum*") (pp. 133, 135, 138).

pactum illicitum: illegal agreement (pp. 13, 17, 136).

pendente lite nihil innovandum: while a litigation is pending, nothing new must be done; the meaning is that once a court action has been brought, nothing done by either party to the action will affect the outcome of the case (p. 217).

per: in the words of (pp. 160, 279).

per expressum: by means of an express term; expressly (p. 188).

per se: of itself; alone; by itself (pp. 15, 56, 79, 115, 227).

prima facie: at first sight; until the contrary is proved (opposite of "conclusive") (pp. 36, 77, 99, 186, 187, 193, 222, 246).

pro non scripto: as if not written; as non-existent (pp. 67, 147).

pro rata: according to a proportionate (share); proportionate (the word "*parte*" is to be understood as following "*rata*") (pp. 186, 187, 188).

pro tanto: for so much; to such extent (p. 252).

proferens: party putting (it) forward (pp. 175, 183).

prout de jure: by any evidence (*i.e.* writing is not required) (pp. 61, 67, 70, 151).

quadriennium utile: literally, the useful four-year period; the four years immediately after the age of majority (p. 71).

quaesitum: obtained; acquired (the word may be followed by "to," *e.g.* a right may be said to be "*quaesitum* to a *tertius*"; this is because the dative case, usually translated by "to," would follow "*quaesitum*" in Latin to indicate that the right has been obtained or acquired for the benefit of the third party) (p. 196).

quantum: amount (p. 207).

quantum lucrati: as much as (they have been) enriched (plural of "*quantum lucratus*") (p. 207).

quantum lucratus est: as much as he has been enriched (pp. 137, 260, 262).

quantum meruit: as much as he has earned; amount earned (pp. 106, 107, 137, 207, 260).

quoad: as regards (pp. 121, 126).

ratio decidendi: reason for deciding; the essential reasoning which leads to the decision in a particular case (contrast with *obiter dicta*) (p. 95).

rebus integris: literally, the matters being whole; the position being unaltered; things being as they originally were, *i.e.* no steps having been taken (in the performance of the contract) (p. 91).

rei interitus: destruction of the subject-matter (pp. 268, 269).

rei interventu: by "*rei interventus*" (ablative case of "*rei interventus*" (*q.v.*)) (pp. 52, 58).

rei interventus: subsequent actings; a form of personal bar (pp. 3, 37, 51, 52, 53, 54, 55, 56, 57, 58, 59, 60, 61, 62, 63, 64, 65, 67, 69, 151).

repugnantia: inconsistency (p. 84).

res judicata: literally, a matter decided; the phrase is used to indicate that the question has already been decided and cannot be reconsidered in a later action (p. 217).

res non sunt integrae: literally, matters are not whole; the situation is not as it originally was; there has been some alteration in the position of the parties (resulting from part-performance of the contract) (p. 91).

res noviter: short for "*res noviter veniens ad notitiam*," a matter newly coming to knowledge, *i.e.* a new matter not available for the earlier case (pp. 216, 218).

restitutio: restoration (p. 109).

restitutio in integrum; restoration to the original (position) (pp. 106, 107, 108, 109, 110, 113).

sponsio ludicra: sportive promise; undertaking made in jest (and therefore not worthy of serious consideration) (pp. 13, 14, 15, 16, 17, 18).
sponsiones ludicrae: sportive promises (plural of "*sponsio ludicra*" (*q.v.*)) (pp. 12, 14, 15, 17, 18).
status quo ante: position in which (they were) before; original position (p. 110).
sub modo: under a condition (p. 58).
sub voce: literally, under the word; under the heading (p. 126).

tertius: third party; person other than one of the two contracting parties (pp. 194, 196, 197, 198).
turpis causa: an immoral situation (p. 134).

uberrima fides: the utmost good faith (p. 131).
uberrimae fidei: of the utmost good faith (genitive case of "*uberrima fides*") (p. 100).
ultra vires: beyond the powers: unauthorised (p. 8).
uno flatu: literally, by one breath; by a single transaction; easily; simply; without a series of complicated transactions (p. 221).
unum quid: single entity (p. 206).

versans in illicito: involved in an illegal matter; in an illegality (p. 137).
vide: see (p. 65).
vis major: greater power; superior force which the parties to the contract are powerless to resist (pp. 268, 274).
vitium reale: basic fault; fundamental invalidity which cannot be cured (pp. 95, 96).